SIMULTANEITY IN SIGNED LANGUAGES

Volume 281

Myriam Vermeerbergen, Lorraine Leeson and Onno Crasborn (eds)

Simultaneity in Signed Languages
Form and Function

SIMULTANEITY IN SIGNED LANGUAGES

FORM AND FUNCTION

Edited by

MYRIAM VERMEERBERGEN
Research Foundation - Flanders & Vrije Universiteit Brussel

LORRAINE LEESON
University of Dublin

ONNO CRASBORN
Radboud University Nijmegen

JOHN BENJAMINS PUBLISHING COMPANY
AMSTERDAM/PHILADELPHIA

∞ ™ The paper used in this publication meets the minimum requirements of American National Standard for Information Sciences — Permanence of Paper for Printed Library Materials, ANSI Z39.48-1984.

Library of Congress Cataloging-in-Publication Data

Simultaneity in signed languages : form and function / edited by Myriam Vermeerbergen, Lorraine Leeson and Onno Crasborn.

    p.   cm. -- (Amsterdam studies in the theory and history of linguistic science. Series IV, Current issues in linguistic theory, ISSN 0304-0763 ; v. 281)

Includes bibliographical references and index.

1. Sign language.

P117 .S56 2007

419--dc22   2006047945

ISBN 978 90 272 4796 4 (Hb; alk. paper)

John Benjamins Publishing Co. • P.O.Box 36224 • 1020 ME Amsterdam • The Netherlands

John Benjamins North America • P.O.Box 27519 • Philadelphia PA 19118-0519 • USA

Dedicated to Mary Brennan (1944–2005)

Contents

Simultaneity in signed languages

A string of sequentially organised issues

Myriam Vermeerbergen, Lorraine Leeson and Onno Crasborn
Research Foundation Flanders & Vrije Universiteit Brussel / University of
Dublin, Trinity College / Radboud University Nijmegen

1. Introduction

Signed language users can draw on a range of articulators when expressing linguistic messages, including the hands, torso, eye gaze, mouth, and, as many studies have shown, other facial actions (e.g. Liddell 1980; Baker-Shenk 1983; Sutton-Spence & Woll 1999; Sandler & Lillo-Martin 2006, and also Boyes Braem & Sutton-Spence 2001 for the use of mouth actions across a range of signed languages). Sometimes these articulators work in tandem to produce one lexical item while in other instances, they operate to convey different types of information.

This can include simultaneously using the two hands as parallel autonomous channels, where one hand encodes signs distinct from those on the other hand. The signs articulated on the two hands can be complete signs (Miller 1994a, b); or one hand can hold the end-state of a sign *in situ* while the other hand continues to sign – a structure that has been described as 'perseveration' (Miller 1994a), 'scaffolding' (Leeson & Saeed 2003), and 'buoys' (Liddell 2003; Liddell, Vogt-Svendsen & Bergman, this volume; Vogt-Svendsen & Bergman, this volume). Simultaneity can also include the mouthing of lexical items that are lexically, semantically and syntactically distinct from the sign(s) they accompany (Boyes Braem & Sutton-Spence 2001). These are just some of the possible forms where we can observe simultaneity in signed languages.

In the rest of this paper, we start by outlining the range of simultaneous constructions covered in this volume (Sections 2 and 3). Section 4 discusses the extent to which simultaneity has been a factor in the linguistic analysis of spoken languages, while Section 5 contains a discussion of simultaneity in signed languages. Finally, Section 6 introduces the main themes addressed by the authors contributing to this volume.

2.   Simultaneous structures discussed in this book

This book presents a collection of papers dealing with different forms of simultaneity in signed languages. These forms can be roughly grouped under three headings: (1) manual simultaneity, (2) manual-oral simultaneity, and (3) simultaneous use of other (manual or non-manual) articulators. Here we discuss each in turn.

1. *Manual simultaneity* occurs when each hand conveys different information. This may take the form of 'full simultaneity', which we define as the simultaneous production of two different lexical items. Alternatively, one hand may hold a sign in a stationary configuration while the other hand continues signing. For example, one hand can articulate the perseveration of a topic while the other hand continues with the realisation of the comment. Examples of manual simultaneity also include simultaneous constructions involving 'classifiers'.[1] This can take the form of expressing the relative location of actors in a motion event (each actor being represented by a distinct 'classifier') on either hand, etc.

2. *Manual-oral simultaneity*: this category refers to the simultaneous use of the oral channel and the manual channel, and may take different forms. One form is the simultaneous articulation of lexical items from a spoken language (so-called 'mouthings'). For example, as Sutton-Spence (this volume) notes, the British Sign Language (BSL) sign meaning 'roll over in bed' can be combined with the silent articulation of the English word 'bed'.

   In some instances, a mouthing is combined with a sign that is morphologically and lexically unrelated. For example, the French words *quoi* (what) and *après* (after), by virtue of their use without any lexically related sign, appear to have been introduced into Quebec Sign Language (LSQ) as oral loan words (Chris Miller, personal communication). In Flemish Sign Language (VGT), we note that the mouthing *op* (on) can be combined with verb signs such as SIT, resulting in a combined meaning 'sit on'.

   Another form is the simultaneous production of mouth gestures with manual signs. Sutton-Spence (this volume) follows Raino's (2001) definition of mouth gestures as idiomatic gestures produced by the mouth, which cannot be traced back to spoken language. An example from VGT is a signer using her mouth to

---

1.   In the signed linguistic literature the notion 'classifier' is understood to refer to a handshape or a combination of a handshape and a specific orientation of the hand used to represent a certain referent; often aspects of the form or dimensions of the referent play an important part in the choice of a certain (classifier) handshape. However, a number of authors have argued against the appropriateness of this notion and have proposed alternatives (see Schembri 2003), which are touched upon later in this paper.

imitate the sound of a truck while signing TRUCK (Vermeerbergen & Demey, this volume).

These subcategories all cover non-manual items that exist separately from simultaneously produced manual signs – in contrast with non-manual features that combine with manual activity to create a sign.

3. *Simultaneous use of other (manual or non-manual) articulators*: this category extends to non-manual articulators other than the mouth, which can combine with each other or with manual and oral action. Examples that feature in several of the papers in this volume include the eye gaze channel and body leans. This type of simultaneity is often discussed in relation to the simultaneous expression of different points of view , which is in itself an example of simultaneity at a semantic level (see for example the papers in this volume by Perniss; Leeson & Saeed; Risler; and Sallandre). Another example is that of the simultaneous articulation of manual signs with certain non-manual lexical items such as the American Sign Language (ASL) and LSQ 'nose-squinch WHO' (Chris Miller, personal communication).

3. What this book is not about

As will be clear from the categorisation above, the volume does *not* focus on the simultaneous presence of phonological parameters within a sign. The traditional phonological parameters handshape, location, orientation and movement are present in any manual lexical item at the same time. In fact, Stokoe's (1960) first analysis labelled this a central difference between signed languages and spoken languages. In phonological analyses of spoken languages at that time, there was a strong focus on the sequential ordering of 'phonemes' or 'phonological segments', languages differing in both the set of phonemes they allow and also in the linear combinations of phonemes within syllables (Anderson 1985). Stokoe (1960) considered the parameters that constitute a sign to be the 'phonemes' of signed languages, a change in a single phoneme potentially leading to a change in meaning; he coined the term 'chereme' for these parameters.

Later research on both types of languages made this contrast between the sequential ordering of phonemes in a word and the simultaneous presence of cheremes in a sign appear less black and white. The advent of distinctive features which together make up a phoneme (Chomsky & Halle 1968), and later the development of autosegmental phonology which stressed the possibility for these distinctive features to spread across multiple segments (Goldsmith 1976; Clements 1985), both indicated that in the phonology of spoken languages too, it is relevant to look at simultaneous properties of sounds. Conversely, in the phonological analysis of signed languages, several researchers have argued that it is necessary to describe signs partly in terms of sequentially ordered location and movement segments (Liddell 1984; Liddell & Johnson 1986, 1989; Sandler 1989; Perlmutter 1990). While there is ongoing debate on the question how exactly these segments should be represented, whether and how segments are grouped into syllables (e.g. Wilbur 1985; Perlmutter 1992, 1993; Corina 1996), and especially whether it is necessary to include movement segments or not (Hayes 1993; van der Hulst 1993), there is wide agreement on the idea that indeed there is a need for sequentially ordered segments to describe changes of properties of signs over time.

The papers in the present volume do not investigate the simultaneous presence of phonological (and therefore meaningless) aspects of the form of lexical items, but instead they focus on cases where different articulators are employed to express different information, whether at a semantic, pragmatic, or discourse level.

4.   Simultaneity in spoken languages

The general view in linguistics has been that spoken languages show relatively little simultaneity in their structure, from phonology to discourse (for example, see Sandler & Lillo-Martin 2006).[2] Spoken languages are characterised by the many *sequential* phenomena that occur, from the sequencing of segments in a syllable to the concatenation of sentences at discourse level (Bloomfield 1933; Levelt 1989). The extent to which this generalisation is valid is dependent on which aspects of spoken language interaction are taken into consideration. In many earlier studies, spoken language researchers in fact concentrated on written language, thereby ignoring phonetic and phonological information that is not represented in the writing system of the language at hand (e.g. Lüdtke 1969; Aronoff 1992). For this reason, it was not until the middle of the twentieth century that intonation became a common object of study (see for example Harris 1944; Pike 1945; Lieberman 1967). More recently, an increasing number of researchers have started to look at gesture and non-verbal behaviour more generally, as an integrated part of face-to-face spoken language communication (McNeill 1992; Goldin-Meadow 2003; Kendon 2004; Gullberg 1998). Both intonation and gesture will be briefly discussed in the remainder of this section. They lead to the recognition that the amount of simultaneous structuring in spoken language depends on which aspects of spoken language communication one considers to be part of language. Consequentially, it is not possible to draw a simple contrast between highly simultaneous signed languages and highly sequential spoken languages.

---

2.   In the spoken language literature, the terms 'simultaneity' and 'sequentiality' have not always been used to explicitly describe the contrast that is the focus of this volume; for that reason, it may be hard to find discussion on this theme in the literature.

4.1 Prosody

Research on prosody began in the mid 20th century and has since revealed a complex system of suprasegmental features comprising duration, pitch, and stress (Gussenhoven 1983, 2001, 2004; Bolinger 1986, 1989; Ladd 1996). Pitch has particularly been shown to play an important role as the primary phonetic correlate of the phonological categories tone and intonation (Gussenhoven 2001). Sentences in languages like English can be articulated in different ways: the words and their ordering remains unchanged, while the intonation with which these words are produced can lead to different interpretations. A sentence like 'John plays badminton' can, as a result, be understood as a statement, but also as a (surprised) question. Gussenhoven states that "the tonal structure can be thought of as a string of tones arranged in parallel to the segmental structure provided by the string of consonants and vowels, that is, as an *autosegmental* representational tier" (2001:15, 296 italics in original). In so-called 'tone languages', these tones are specified at the level of the lexicon, while in other languages, they serve as the phonological representation of intonation at the sentence level. In both cases, tones clearly form separate simultaneous channels, whether in their abstract phonological representation or in their concrete phonetic manifestation (Gussenhoven 2004). Similar observations can be made with respect to other aspects of prosody, such as duration: lengthening is a phonetic cue that marks sentence boundaries (e.g. Nespor & Vogel 1986; Edwards, Beckman & Fletcher 1991), but no languages have been found that are phonologically dependent on the nature of the segments that are lengthened.

In addition to these linguistic functions, pitch also expresses universal messages. For example, common emotional states such as surprise are universally expressed by high pitch (Ohala 1984; Chen 2005). These paralinguistic signals also occur simultaneously with the rest of the linguistic signal. As the term 'paralinguistic' indicates, they are generally not considered to be part of the linguistic structure characterising a particular language, but occur in the same channel, and thus can be said to be parasitic on the speech stream. Depending on which aspects of spoken language interaction are investigated, such paralinguistic signals may also contribute to a view of spoken language as containing several simultaneous channels.

4.2 Nonverbal communication

When speakers talk, they almost always gesture at the same time: they use their hands to point at things, places or people, to beat the rhythm of speech, or to exploit visual imagery in order to stress or complement the content of the spoken signal (McNeill 1992; Goldin-Meadow 2003). Traditionally, these movements are considered to form a non-linguistic system, i.e. they are seen as extra-linguistic features of face-to-face communication, independent of the speech channel. There is, however, also research that shows that gesture is integral to language itself (e.g. McNeill 1992; Kendon 1997; Gullberg 1998; Goldin-Meadow 2003). From this point of view, meaning is expressed by speech, the more categorical, arbitrary and conventionalised system of representation, while gesture is "created on the fly to capture the meaning of the moment" (Goldin-Meadow 2003: 193) to show a more global representation.

Gestures may be used without speech, e.g. when a speaker says 'Does someone have a...', stops speaking and subsequently produces an iconic gesture referring to a bottle opener, but most of the gestures that speakers produce occur simultaneously with the speech signal. Kendon (1988) has categorised different kinds of gesture use on the basis of the relationship to speech, the degree of conventionalisation and on the basis of how language-like they are. He proposes a gradual transition across gesture categories, which has become known as 'Kendon's continuum' (McNeill 1992; see also Vermeerbergen & Demey, this volume). Signed languages are placed at the '+convention; -speech' end of the continuum, whereas at the other end we find what Kendon (1988) calls 'gesticulation', or what McNeill (1992) refers to as 'speech-associated gestures'. These non-conventional gestures are "created spontaneously by the speaker during the act of speaking and adhere to no standards of form" (McNeill 1998: 12).

Four types of such spontaneous, speech-associated gestures are recognised: iconics, metaphorics, deictics and beats (McNeill 1992). Iconic gestures show a form that is in close relation to the semantic content of speech. These gestures usually represent body movements, movements of people and objects in space and shapes of referents. Often speech and the co-speech iconic gesture both refer to the same event, but each presents a somewhat different aspect of it, e.g. the gesture revealing the path of the movement expressed in the spoken signal. Metaphoric gestures are also pictorial, but "the pictorial content present[s] an abstract idea rather than a concrete object or event" (McNeill 1992: 14). When producing a beat, a speaker moves her hand along with the rhythm of the spoken signal. According to McNeill, beats are much more important than they appear, for they mark a word or phrase as being significant for their discourse-pragmatic function. Deictic gestures may be used to point at present objects and people, but speakers may also point at abstract concepts located in space.

Other authors have also proposed a scheme for categorising co-speech gestures. Most of these classification systems are based on a combination of an analysis of form and a semantic-semiotic analysis. A discussion of such taxonomies falls outside the scope of this introduction. We refer readers to Gullberg (1998: 47–51) for an outline and comparison of a number of the most influential classifications.

While all gesture researchers stress the importance of gesture in human inter-action, the precise function of gesture is still the topic of much debate. Gesture is considered to fulfil many functions, such as conveying information to the addressee, facilitating lexical retrieval, functioning as a link to speech hesitations and repair, facilitating speech production and/or shaping thoughts of the speaker, re-flecting speakers' thoughts and/or saving cognitive effort, etc. (cf. Emmorey 1999 and Goldin-Meadow 2003 for overviews). As such, the hands play an important role in communication, not only for signers but also for speakers. It has even been argued that when signers' and speakers' communication is being compared, it is speech in combination with co-speech gesture – and not speech by itself – that constitutes the appropriate level for cross-linguistic analysis (e.g. Taub, Pinar & Galvan 2002; Enfield 2004).

While many researchers have focused on the gesturing behaviour of the hands, the role of eye gaze, head movements, body postures, and displacement of the whole body are widely recognised as other aspects of nonverbal behaviour that are relevant in face-to-face communication (e.g. Ekman & Friesen 1969).

The possible parallels between simultaneous constructions in signed lan-guages and concurrent speech and gesture in spoken languages are explored by Vermeerbergen & Demey (this volume). Due to our limited understanding of the role(s) that simultaneity plays in signed languages themselves, we see a clear need to begin exploring this issue by documenting the range of forms and functions taken by simultaneity that arise in related and unrelated signed languages. From there, there is a need to conduct cross-linguistic work on phenomena related to simultaneity, and positing possible theoretical accounts for them. Some of the au-thors in this volume have begun this work, and we suggest that on the basis of such accounts, more in-depth comparisons between simultaneity in spoken languages and signed languages can be carried out.

5. Simultaneity in signed languages: An overview of work to date

5.1 Research focusing on simultaneous constructions in signed languages

In 1994, no fewer than four papers on the issue of simultaneity in signed lan-guages appeared (Engberg-Pedersen 1994; Pinsonneault & Lelièvre 1994; Miller 1994a, b). Because these were the first papers specifically devoted to simultaneous constructions, we consider them to be seminal in this area of description. How-ever, as Miller (1994a) points out, even at that point in time the signed language literature contained several references to constructions involving the simultaneous production of distinct elements (for example, see Friedman 1975; Klima & Bellugi 1979; Frishberg 1985).

Miller's (1994a) literature review makes reference to the earliest known published work on simultaneity (Friedman 1975) which looked at the syntax and discourse structure of American Sign Language and discusses a number of different simultaneous constructions. Given that in the 1970s and 1980s ASL was the most extensively studied signed language, it is not surprising that the majority of references in Miller's literature review relate to ASL, although reference is also made to early work on simultaneity in other signed languages (e.g. Moody 1983 for French Sign Language (LSF); Kyle & Woll 1985 for British Sign Language (BSL); Engberg-Pedersen 1991 for Danish Sign Language).

Miller then presents examples from Quebec Sign Language, selected from a corpus consisting of over 200 examples of simultaneous constructions found in videotaped informal conversations between LSQ users. The variety of simultaneity discussed here includes the following constructions:

- The articulation of an index sign (or 'pointing sign') simultaneous with a sign or signs on the other hand;
- Perseveration of one sign on one hand while the second hand articulates a series of other signs;
- Placing a sign articulated on the dominant hand on or in relation to an enumeration morpheme, which is expressed by the non-dominant hand;
- Two hands producing two different lexical items simultaneously.

Miller also briefly discusses the simultaneous mouthing of spoken language words that are distinct in content from the signs that they accompany. This, along with other examples of simultaneity involving the use of the mouth, is focussed on by Sutton-Spence (this volume).

Miller suggests that one important function of manual simultaneity is the encoding of the distinction between foregrounded and backgrounded information, where the normal division of labour between the two hands results in the dominant hand acting as carrier of the foregrounded or otherwise primary information, an idea that has been explored by linguists looking at other signed languages (e.g. Engberg-Pedersen 1994; Leeson & Saeed 2004; this volume).

With 'foregrounded' Miller means that this information is central to the current discourse, whereas background information is peripheral. As such the non-dominant hand can be seen to produce signs "whose function is the management of the discourse situation rather than the communication of propositional content" (Miller 1994a: 103) or to articulate signs that modify information presented on the dominant hand. An example of this is where the non-dominant hand *holds* the sign FLASH-ON-AND-OFF which modifies the sign LIGHT produced by the dominant hand (Miller 1994a: 99, example (17)). Other functions include establishing contrast and the expression of a direct conditional relationship between two propositions. Miller's example (25) is an illustration of this latter function:

CL. I (person: approaches)   Cl. I (person: moves away)
KNOWLEDGE-INCREASE KNOWLEDGE-DIMINISH
Translation: "When I'm around them (i.e. ASL signers), (my ability) increases
and when I'm not around them, it decreases."

Miller (1994a, b) also raises the issue of the ambiguous status of (some of) the
elements in simultaneous constructions. Miller (1994b) particularly focuses on
this issue, and here he also presents an overview of the different types of manual simultaneity in signed languages, concentrating on how we should analyse
complex signs whose meaningful components can interact independent of other
signs. In one of the LSQ-examples (1994b: 136–137, example (13)), the signer first
introduces the idea of a piece of paper, which is articulated using a B-classifier
handshape. This classifier is held across two sentences and is involved in the production of the sign WRITE, a sign for which a B-classifier handshape is part of
the citation form. However, the same handshape is also used as the complement
of a deictic pronoun. According to Miller, this directing an index at the B-classifier
does not imply reference to the sign WRITE but rather to the piece of paper. This
means that the handshape is itself referential and autonomous with regard to the
syntax of the sentence. The classifier is an integral part of the sign WRITE, but it is
also accessible to the syntactic structure and to the discourse structure (because it
is also the topic of this part of the discourse). This is why Miller finds it important
to think about the status of this handshape and to ask how the constructions the
classifier appears in should be characterised.

He suggests a distinction between (1) morphologically complex signs whose
component parts do not play any role at the level of syntax (i.e. they are single
syntactic units), and (2) complex signs that are also simultaneous syntactic constructions. The sign WRITE is an example of the latter category. Such complexes
accessible to syntax pose a problem for theories that draw a sharp distinction between morphology and syntax. Miller further explores how these structures relate
to the ongoing "tug of war over the proper place of word formation in grammar"
(Miller 1994b: 138) and to the interaction between syntax and morphology in linguistic theory. He suggests that the structural ambiguity between morphology and
syntax in complex signs can be treated within the framework of Borer (1998). Beginning by noting that the interaction between syntax and word formation has
been a battle ground in many linguistic wars, Borer argues that since the 1980s,
research on the lexicon has led to important insights about the nature of word
formation, which has strengthened the view of morphology as an autonomous
module on a par with the syntax and phonology modules. At the same time, she
notes that work carried out over the same period on syntax led to the emergence
of syntactic systems that were "capable of handling word formation operations
in a more restricted way, thereby avoiding many of the pitfalls encountered by

earlier less constrained such work" (1998:151). She explores the issue of whether morphology can be considered a stand-alone module or if it should be subsumed under syntax and argues that empirical evidence is essential in addressing the issues raised. Borer proposes that morphology and syntax act in parallel, where words formed in the morphology can be inserted into the syntax at any level where there is a syntactic structure that is compatible with their morphological structure. Miller discusses the consequences of this for linguistic theory.

One of the LSQ simultaneous construction types briefly discussed by Miller (1994a, b) is the subject of a separate paper by Pinsonneault & Lelièvre (1994). These authors present and discuss many examples of enumeration and the anaphoric use of fingertip loci found in the same LSQ corpus that Miller drew on. The issue of enumeration has been explored also for ASL (Liddell 2003). In this volume, this structure is discussed for several other signed languages (Liddell et al.; Hendriks; Vermeerbergen & Demey).

Presenting on simultaneous constructions in Danish Sign Language, Engberg-Pedersen (1994) focuses on a 'central type' where two polymorphemic verbs (i.e. verbs of motion and location including a stem expressed by a 'classifier handshape') are articulated simultaneously and express the locative relation between two or more referents. We note here that while Engberg-Pedersen has referred to these structures as 'polymorphemic', other terms abound for such structures in the signed linguistics literature. Schembri (2003) outlines these, noting that

> [i]n Australia, they are generally known as *classifier signs* or simply *classifiers* (Bernal 1997, Branson et al. 1995), whereas elsewhere they have variously been referred to as *classifier verbs* or *verbs of motion and location* (Supalla 1986, 1990), *classifier predicates* (Corazza 1990, Schick 1987, 1990, Smith 1990, Valli & Lucas 1995), *spatial-locative predicates* (Liddell & Johnson 1987), *polymorphemic predicates* (Collins-Ahlgren 1990, Wallin 1990), *polysynthethic signs* (Takkinen 1996, Wallin 1996, 1998), *productive signs* (Brennan 1992, Wallin 1998), *polycomponential signs* (Slobin et al. 2001) and *polymorphemic verbs* (Engberg-Pedersen 1993).
>
> (Schembri 2003:4, emphasis in original)[3]

Schembri himself follows Slobin, Hoiting, Anthony, Biederman, Kuntze, Lindert, Pyers, Thumann & Weinberg (2000) in using the term 'polycomponential verb', given that the question of whether the forms in question include classifier morphemes has not been resolved and the analysis of such forms as multimorphemic is problematic (Cogill 1999). We refer the reader to Schembri (2003) for an in-depth discussion of 'classifiers' in signed languages.

---

3.   Please note that the Slobin et al. (2001) reference should read Slobin et al. (2003). The full reference for this 2003 publication has been included in our list of references.

Returning to Engberg-Pedersen's analysis of simultaneous structures in Danish Sign Language, we should note that she queries whether these constructions should be analysed as compounds, i.e. as one polymorphemic verb with two (simultaneously articulated) stems. Like Miller, Engberg-Pedersen considers 'backgrounding' as one of the factors involved in simultaneous constructions, though only in relation to polymorphemic verbs. She notes that keeping one of the hands motionless results in information being backgrounded, at least when the foregrounded information is simultaneously presented by the other (moving) hand.

Engberg-Pedersen also briefly discusses 'non-central types' of simultaneity:

1. A combination of the passive hand holding the stem of a polymorphemic verb or the handshape of a sign modified for a locus while the active hand articulates one or more other signs that are not of the polymorphemic type. Such constructions do not describe a locative relation between referents. Engberg-Pedersen discusses a description of a ferry collision which includes a non-central type of simultaneity. It involves the less active hand producing a polymorphemic verb with a handshape referring to a boat and the active hand explaining how many people were onboard the ferry. This relates to the topic-comment type of simultaneous constructions discussed by Miller (1994a, b).

2. Constructions representing a special kind of modification for distribution where one hand, held motionless, shows the stem of the polymorphemic verb and the other hand moves in relation to this less active hand. Engberg-Pedersen (1994:82) gives the example of a signer description of a row of cars where the signer "holds one hand motionless and moves the other hand with the same handshape in a line away from the motionless hand". She analyses such examples as simultaneous at the morphological level.

3. Signs modified for distribution by means of a simultaneously produced pointing sign. The sign DEAF in Danish Sign Language cannot take a modification expressed in space, which means that it cannot be modified to show 'multiple'. However, the sign can be accompanied by a simultaneously produced pointing sign made with a linear movement, as such taking over part of the form of the multiple modification. This too is analysed as an example of simultaneity at the morphological level.

Like Miller, Engberg-Pedersen believes that how we understand simultaneity can shed more light on the boundaries between morphology and syntax in signed languages. She also raises questions that still have relevance today, including: (1) given that signed languages have the possibility to express information consecutively or simultaneously, what sort of information is expressed simultaneously?, and (2) when do simultaneous constructions have obligatory status?

While recent work on simultaneity has begun to explore this first question in more depth (e.g. Leeson & Saeed 2004, this volume; Perniss, this volume; Risler, this volume), the second question remains unaddressed. Clearly this is an area for further consideration.

5.2 Dominance reversals

Frishberg (1985) discusses how the ability to use both hands independently of one another to articulate different signs allows for simultaneous constructions and makes it possible for a signer to alternate between the two manual articulators. These alternations are known as 'dominance reversals' and occur when the expected use of the active and passive hand in signed languages are reversed. Frishberg distinguishes between two distinct types of dominance reversal: (1) at a syntactic or semantic level and (2) those triggered by lexical or formational structure.

Regarding (1), Frishberg claims that dominance reversals (DR) at the syntactic level mark strong contrast, e.g. the contrast between "two arguments, two times (narrative time and speech time), two forms of gestural behaviour" (1985: 85) but also says that dominance reversals may serve a cohesive or discourse function.

Type (2) refers to signs that are consistently produced with a reversal of what would be expected in a signed language discourse (e.g. a right handed signer signing a one handed sign with the left hand) and are "instances in which a signer switches the expected dominance relations between the hands for a stretch of one or more signs" (1985: 81), while the same signs are elsewhere performed with expected dominance relations.

Frishberg concludes with a list of observations concerning dominance reversals, including the fact that there is a great deal of individual variation in ASL, that left-handed signers are more likely to show dominance reversals than right-handed signers, and that dominance reversals do not seem to be obligatory in any specific context given that signers can draw on a range of options to express the same information in another way. Similar observations have been made for other signed languages, for example Flemish Sign Language (Vermeerbergen 1996), Jordanian Sign Language (Hendriks, this volume) and Irish Sign Language (ISL) (Leeson & Saeed 2004; this volume).

5.3 The French tradition

While the role of iconicity has been downplayed in much of the mainstream international signed linguistics literature, a French tradition, spearheaded by Christian Cuxac (e.g. 1985, 2000) has emerged that considers iconicity to be the central organising and structuring principle in signed languages.

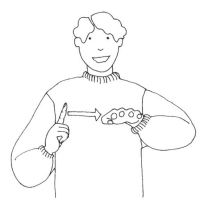

Figure 1. An example of a VGT construction representing a person approaching a car

Cuxac proposes a semiogenetic model that assumes that all signed languages emerge from the same cognitive-communicational process. This process is anchored in (a) the practical-perceptual world, (b) visual cognition, (c) the semiotic intentionality of communication proper to human beings and (d) face-to-face discourse interactions (cf. Fusellier-Souza 2006).

Within the framework of this semiogenetic model, Cuxac differentiates between two aspects of signed language use: (1) *'la branche à visée iconicisatrice'* or *'dire en montrant'* (saying by showing) and (2) *'la branche hors visée iconicisatrice'* or *'dire sans montrer'* (saying without showing). Here (2) is roughly equivalent to the use of the established lexicon while (1) implies that a signer makes visible her real life or imaginary experiences and observations through the use of what is called *'des structures de grande iconicité'* (or *'transfers'*). These are not lexical signs but complex structures, which Cuxac (1985, 2000) categorises in a three-way system of transfers:

1. *'Transferts de taille et/ou de forme'* ('transfers of size and/or form'), allow for the representation of the size and/or form, in part or whole, of places, objects and persons. An example from Flemish Sign Language is where a signer traces the form of the hearts present on the wall of the *peperkoekenhuisje* (gingerbreadhouse) by means of her two index fingers (Demey 2005:428).

2. *'Transferts situationnels'* ('transfers of situation') iconically 'reproduce' a scene which demonstrates the spatial relationship between a character and a stable locative point of reference, typically the movement of a character in relation to a fixed location; the scene is presented as seen from a distance. The example from Flemish Sign Language in Figure 1 refers to a person approaching a car (Vermeerbergen 1996:52).

3. *'Transferts personnels'* ('transfers of person') occur when the signer uses her body to 'represent' the actions or poses of a protagonist in the discourse; the signer 'becomes' the entity or character discussed. An example of such a transfer from VGT shows a signer 'impersonating' a witch by means of her body posture (bending forward and leaning on a walking stick) and facial expression (looking very disturbed) (Demey 2005: 430).

The *'transfers'* include structures that have also been discussed outside the French tradition, where instances of transfers are described: for example instances of *'transferts personnels'* are referred to as 'role shift' or 'perspective shift' (see for example Janzen 2005) and examples of the *'transferts situationnels'* as 'classifier constructions' (Emmorey 2003). Given that these transfer constructions often involve the use of different articulators, they necessarily involve instances of simultaneity.

While Cuxac (1985) is one of the first to explicitly mention these and other simultaneous aspects in both the lexicon and beyond, Cuxac (2000) provides a more comprehensive discussion of *'multilinéarité'*, the notion the author prefers over the more traditional term 'simultaneity'. (See Sallandre (this volume) for reviews of both these publications.) A final point that we would like to raise regarding Cuxac's work and simultaneity relates to his claim that the possibility to say different things in parallel is not unique to signed languages like LSF. He argues that, albeit it to a minor extent, spoken languages also allow for such structures. What he believes to be an important difference between signed languages and spoken languages in this respect is the semantic specialisation of the signer's different body parts. He attributes the following specialisations to body parts as follows:

> [...] au regard, incombe la rection de l'interaction et l'inscription (identification) des énoncés dans des genres; à la mimique faciale, pour l'essentiel, les valeurs modales; aux signes, le contenu de l'énoncé (l'information); aux hochements du visage, le contact phatique avec le récepteur et la garantie que les propos tenus sont placés sous la responsabilité du point de vue du sujet énonciateur; enfin, aux mouvement corporels, la rythmique qui permetta de démarquer les changements de thématique et les frontières de syntagmes.   (Cuxac 2000: 256)

> English: [...] the gaze directs the interaction and identifies the utterance genre; facial expression generally reflects modality; signs represent the information content while nodding the head ensures the communicative contact with the receiver and reflects point of view. Finally, movements of the body produce the rhythmic structure which indicates changes in theme and sentence boundaries (our translation).

The author states that these specialisations seem to be present in every signed language studied so far.

5.4 Beyond the seminal works on simultaneity

Since Miller's (1994a, b) work on Quebec Sign language (LSQ), there has been a growing interest in the description of similar structures across a broad range of signed languages as well as attempts to account for simultaneity from a number of theoretical perspectives. However, comprehensive treatments of simultaneity are scarce: they typically arise within extended discussions of broader issues for signed languages (for example, Vermeerbergen 1996, 1997 for Flemish Sign Language; Sutton-Spence & Woll 1999 for British Sign Language; Leeson 2001 for Irish Sign Language; Liddell 2003 for American Sign Language). To date there has not been a single focused volume that solely addresses the issues of simultaneity. This volume fills that gap. It offers consideration of a range of aspects of simultaneity across several related and unrelated signed languages. It includes both descriptive and cross-linguistic treatments of data from a variety of theoretical frameworks.

6. Outline of the volume

The first part of this book considers simultaneity within the broad framework of cognitive linguistics (Perniss; Leeson & Saeed; Sallandre and Risler). Pamela Perniss investigates the use of simultaneous constructions in German Sign Language narratives, considering the competing pressures of articulatory constraints on referent and information type representation, and discourse structure constraints of efficiency and informativeness of expression. Focusing on constructions that involve the simultaneous depiction of elements associated with both observer and character perspectives using both manual and non-manual articulators – constructions which she terms simultaneous perspective constructions – Perniss explains their occurrence in narrative discourse with respect to the encoding of locative information about referent location, motion, and action in complex events.

Lorraine Leeson and John Saeed consider how simultaneous constructions in Irish Sign Language are used to foreground and background attention. Drawing on Fauconnier's Mental Space theory and the work of Paul Dudis and Scott Liddell, they offer an account of grounded blends in ISL, arguing that such blends are made possible because of the potential to partition space effectively and elegantly using the body of the signer and the major articulators. They note that simultaneity operates at several cognitive and linguistic levels, reporting specifically on the ways in which simultaneity is used to mark information structure and discourse prominence relations including listing, topic and focus partitioning and narrative dynamism. They also discuss how simultaneity is essential to the creation of grounded blends in ISL discourse.

Annie Risler looks at the composition of simultaneous constructions that encode processes in French Sign Language. She specifically considers the expression of cognitive representations by means of the following parameters: hand configuration, location and movement of the hands, the role of the torso, 'mimicry' and eye gaze. Risler discusses how these parameters allow for the construction of both simple and complex structures, (1) where the hand may refer to the hand itself; (2) where it may act in relation to (or independent from) the body of the signer; or (3) where it may constitute an anaphoric reference of some sort. She develops the notion that signing space is constructed in an iconic mode and that the parameters that operate here are not and cannot be interpreted independently.

Marie-Anne Sallandre first introduces Christian Cuxac's model for the analysis of signed languages. She particularly discusses the function of highly iconic structures in French Sign Language and presents Cuxac's three-way classification of '*transfers*'. Drawing on Cuxac's work on simultaneity, Sallandre explores simultaneity in LSF discourse and discusses constructions involving signs with illustrative intent (i.e. those described as being highly iconic structures) and signs without illustrative intent (i.e. lexical items). Based on this discussion and other observations on LSF discourse, Sallandre suggests that we consider referring to 'multilinearity' rather than seeing an opposition between sequentiality and simultaneity.

Victoria Nyst presents work on Adamorobe Sign Language (AdaSL), a signed language found in a village in Ghana, which has an unusually high Deaf population. She analyses examples of both manual simultaneity and of oral-manual simultaneity and observes that unlike many Western signed languages, AdaSL does not make extensive use of manual simultaneity. She also outlines how AdaSL instead makes use of another type of simultaneous construction, where mouthings influenced by Twi, the local spoken language, co-occur with lexical signs.

Rachel Sutton-Spence develops this theme of oral-manual simultaneity by focusing on mouthings in British Sign Language, paying specific attention to 'mismatches'. These are mouthings that do not correspond exactly with the meaning of the manual sign that is produced at the same time. One example that Sutton-Spence discusses occurs where a signer signs ARMY BOAT, and mouths 'army'; she may extend or stretch the mouthing of 'army' so that it continues while she signs BOAT. While there has been work on mismatches for other signed languages (cf. Boyes Braem 2001 for Swiss German Sign Language and Ebbinghaus & Heßmann 1996 for German Sign Language), this is the first detailed exploration of mismatches in British Sign Language. Sutton-Spence finds that they are surprisingly common in the data considered and reports that these mouthings function lexically, grammatically, prosodically and for discourse and stylistic reasons.

Anna-Lena Nilsson describes the range of ways in which the non-dominant hand is used when it does not participate in the production of a two-handed sign.

Having listed all instances of one-handed signs in a whole Swedish Sign Language discourse, an approximately ten minutes long monologue, she then analyses and categorises the production of these signs. Nilsson proposes a continuum, ranging from those where the non-dominant hand is least active and adds least to the content of the discourse, and gradually moving towards more active participation and contribution to content. Simultaneity turns out to be a key concept and several factors contributing to a markedly two-handed impression of this signed discourse are discussed.

Next are two cross-linguistic papers on 'buoys'. Buoys are weak hand signs that are held in a stationary configuration while the strong hand continues producing signs (Liddell 2003). Scott Liddell, Marit Vogt-Svendsen and Brita Bergman examine the use of list buoys, THEME buoys, fragment buoys and the POINTER buoy in American, Norwegian and Swedish Sign Language. They find evidence for each type of buoy in each of the three languages and raise the question of why these buoys should be so similar in both form and function across unrelated signed languages.

Marit Vogt-Svendsen and Brita Bergman show that, in addition to the range of buoys identified in the previous paper, both Norwegian and Swedish Sign Language demonstrate another category of buoys which the authors refer to as 'point buoys'. In contrast to other types of buoys, point buoys do not represent or point at a prominent discourse entity. Instead, they serve as a prop (Grimes 1975) in relation to which the strong hand acts, and through their physical presence, they help visualise temporal and spatial relationships between entities. Drawing on videotaped dialogues for Norwegian Sign Language and monologues for Swedish Sign Language, the authors argue that point buoys, while sharing some properties with other types of buoys, constitute a category of their own.

Bernadet Hendriks then presents an overview of manual simultaneity in narrative discourse in Jordanian Sign Language, arguing that a phonological rule restricts the range of options available to signers of this signed language. As a result, full simultaneity where both hands move at the same time is possible only when one of the signs produced does not have an inherent movement. Hendriks notes that this situation aside, all other examples of simultaneity that she has recorded entail perseveration. She claims that there does not seem to be evidence to support a claim for a special category of buoys in Jordanian Sign Language. Instead, she sees these constructions as well-formed instances of simultaneity that are closely paralleled by structures that contain elements that would not be considered buoys.

Myriam Vermeerbergen and Eline Demey present different forms of simultaneity in Flemish Sign Language (VGT) and also take us on a brief excursion into the field of gesture studies. Within that field, it is often claimed that for spoken languages, speech and gesture form a single system. In signed languages, 'speech' moves from the mouth to the hands. In theory, four possibilities arise from this:

(1) gesture disappears, (2) gesture and 'speech' trade places, resulting in the manual articulators producing the linguistic component and the mouth producing the gestural component of a message, (3) gesture and sign become integrated, (4) gesture and sign co-exist in the manual modality. The authors report that in Flemish Sign Language, possibilities (2) to (4) are realised. Most of the paper is devoted to the discussion of (4). Vermeerbergen and Demey explore whether these examples of manual simultaneity in VGT can be analysed as combinations of a linguistic (sign) component and a gestural component, and whether these can be equated with speech-with-gesture as produced by speakers of oral languages.

The next two papers offer some insights into some applied aspects of simultaneity. Gladys Tang, Felix Sze and Scholastica Lam introduce us to issues relating to the acquisition of simultaneous constructions in Hong Kong Sign Language, while Martha Tyrone introduces us to the potential impact of brain disorder on the use of simultaneous articulators.

Tang, Sze and Lam discuss the acquisition of simultaneous constructions involving classifiers in Hong Kong Sign Language (HKSL) by a group of deaf children aged 6–13, with particular reference to (1) the developmental sequence of simultaneous construction; (2) the non-dominant hand, and (3) the role of semantic classifiers as triggers for language acquisition. They report that simultaneous classifier predicates, despite their iconic base, are not usually fully acquired before the age of 8–9 and explore the developmental sequence for acquisition of these structures in HKSL along with the error patterns that arise. Further, they look at the role of the non-dominant hand in the acquisition of simultaneous constructions. They report on the important role played by semantic classifiers in HKSL in triggering grammatical re-analysis of handshapes, which, they argue, lead children to begin to incorporate the non-dominant hand in classifier predicates as well as in other simultaneous constructions.

While focusing on simultaneity within the sign is not the express aim of this volume, Martha Tyrone's contribution does consider this, in large part due to the fact that the impact of brain disorders on simultaneity in its broader context has not yet been explored for atypical signers. Here, Tyrone explores how simultaneity in signed language use is preserved or lost in a range of groups of atypical signers. She begins by introducing the physical structure and neural basis of signed languages. She then goes on to discuss specific neural pathologies and hypothesises how they may impact on simultaneity. Finally, Tyrone considers what disruptions to simultaneity can reveal about the structure of signed languages.

The final paper, by Bencie Woll, begins by briefly reviewing 18th, 19th and 20th century approaches to simultaneity and linearity, before turning to emphasise the presence of both linearity and simultaneity in signed languages. Drawing on the earlier papers in this volume, Woll notes that while this volume offers the most comprehensive collection on the issue of simultaneity in signed languages to date, marking an important step towards understanding the interplay between linearity and simultaneity in both spoken and signed language, there is still a long way to go before we can truly claim to understand the role of simultaneity in signed languages. Thus Woll identifies possible pathways for future research stemming from this work, most notably the as yet unanswered questions of (1) when do simultaneous constructions have obligatory status? and (2) to what extent does the simultaneity-linearity opposition arise from a linguistic base and to what extent from a psychological base?

7. Some notes on terminology and formatting

7.1 'Sign language' versus 'signed language'

In this volume, authors use the phrase 'signed language' as opposed to 'sign language'. We follow Janzen (2005) who notes that there are at least two reasons for doing this:

> First, grammatically, the adjective form 'signed' aligns with the adjective 'spoken'. In other words, we are discussing languages that are signed and those that are spoken. Second, it is common for people to talk about 'sign language' as the language they know and use, meaning ASL or another specific signed language, but 'sign language' is not itself the name of any language... (2005:19)

We would like to point out, however, that some authors usually prefer to use 'sign languages' instead of 'signed languages'. Such a preference may be related to the terminology in the author's native language. In French, for example, the notion 'langue signée' is used more often to refer to 'signed French' and not (or not generally) to French Sign Language. This seems to be why for some French authors/readers using the English term 'signed languages' to refer to 'langues des signes' feels strange. The Dutch notion 'gebarentaal' literally means 'language of signs' and the notion 'sign language' may feel like a more accurate rendering than the term 'signed language' for which there is not really a Dutch alternative (a spoken language is a 'gesproken taal' but it is not possible to translate 'signed language' as 'gebaarde taal').

7.2 Referring to individual signed languages

Throughout this volume, authors use the name of the signed language/s that they specifically wish to refer to (e.g. Danish Sign Language, Irish Sign Language, VGT, etc.) and use the term 'signed languages' to refer to signed languages in general.

The exception to this is when they wish to contrast or distinguish between spoken language and signed language, where the singular terms are then used.

7.3 The hands

The functioning of the hands has been referred to in many different yet sometimes overlapping ways in the signed language literature. Human beings typically have a preferred hand for many one-handed tasks such as writing, opening a door, and holding a knife (Warren 1980; MacNeilage, Studdert-Kennedy & Lindblom 1997).

Signed language users typically have a preferred hand for signing; the hand used for one-handed signs and acting as the active hand in asymmetric constructions. Left-handed and right-handed signers have no problem interacting with each other: a difference in preferred hand has not been known to lead to increased difficulty in perception by native signers. Signers also easily switch their use of handedness for linguistic or non-linguistic reasons (e.g. Frishberg 1985).

Several sets of terms have been proposed to describe the interaction (and, indeed the non-interaction) of two hands. Perhaps most frequently, researchers refer to 'dominant' and 'non-dominant' hands, though 'weak hand' and 'strong hand' is also sometimes used, most often by phonologists. We should note that at morpho-syntactic level and discourse level, both sets of terminology can be found. This is reflected in the papers in this volume. In addition, Hendriks uses the terms 'preference' and 'non-preference hand'.

7.4 Presentation of examples

Finally, given the variety of traditions represented here, we have left decisions about the presentation of examples to the discretion of authors. Individual authors outline the transcription conventions that they use in their papers.

References

Anderson, Stephen. 1985. *Phonology in the twentieth century*. Cambridge: Cambridge University Press.

Aronoff, Mark. 1992. "Segmentalism in linguistics", *The Linguistics of Literacy* ed. by Pamela A. Downing, Susan D. Lima & Michael Noonan, 71–82. Amsterdam: John Benjamins.

Baker-Shenk, Carol. 1983. *A Microanalysis of the Non-manual Components of Questions in American Sign Language*. Doctoral dissertation, University of California, Berkeley.

Bernal, Brian. 1997. *Teaching Classifiers in Australian Sign Language*. Unpublished master's research essay, La Trobe University.

Bloomfield, Leonard. 1933. *Language*. New York: Henry Holt and Co.

Bolinger, Dwight. 1986. *Intonation and its Parts: Melody in Spoken English*. Stanford: Stanford University Press.

——. 1989. *Intonation and its Uses: Melody in Grammar and Discourse*. Stanford: Stanford University Press.

Borer, Hagit. 1998. "The Morphology-Syntax Interface". *The Handbook of Morphology* ed. by Andrew Spencer & Arnold Zwicky, 151–190. London: Blackwell.

Boyes Braem, Penny. 2001. "Functions of Mouthings in the Signing of Deaf Early and Late Learners of Swiss German Sign Language (DSGS)". *The Hands are the Head of the Mouth: The Mouth as Articulator in Sign Languages* ed. by Penny Boyes Braem & Rachel Sutton-Spence, 99–132. Hamburg: Signum Press.

—— & Rachel Sutton-Spence, eds. 2001. *The Hands are the Head of the Mouth: The Mouth as Articulator in Sign Languages*. Hamburg: Signum Press.

Branson, Jan, Don Miller, Jennifer Toms, Brian Bernal & Robert Adam. 1995. *Understanding Classifiers in Auslan*. Melbourne: La Trobe University.

Brennan, Mary. 1992. "The Visual World of BSL: An Introduction". *Dictionary of British Sign Language/English* ed. by David Brien, 1–133. London: Faber and Faber.

Chen, Aoju. 2005. *Universal and Language-Specific Perception of Paralinguistic Intonational Meaning*. Utrecht: LOT / Doctoral dissertation, Radboud University Nijmegen.

Chomsky, Noam & Morris Halle. 1968. *The Sound Pattern of English*. Cambridge, Mass.: MIT Press.

Clements, Nick. 1985. "The Geometry of Phonological Features". *Phonology Yearbook* 2.225–252.

Cogill, Dorothea. 1999. "Classifier Predicates: Linguistic Structures or Templated Visual Analogy?" Unpublished manuscript, University of New England.

Collins-Ahlgren, Marianne. 1990. "Spatial-locative Predicates in Thai Sign Language". *Sign Language Research: Theoretical Issues* ed. by Ceil Lucas, 103–117. Washington, D.C.: Gallaudet University Press.

Corazza, Serena. 1990. "The Morphology of Classifier Handshapes in Italian Sign Language (LIS)". *Sign Language Research: Theoretical Issues* ed. by Ceil Lucas, 71–82. Washington, D.C.: Gallaudet University Press.

Corina, David. 1996. "ASL Syllables and Prosodic Constraints". *Lingua* 98.73–102.

Cuxac, Christian. 1985. "Esquisse d'une Typologie des Langues des Signes". *Autour de la Langue des Signes* ed. by Christian Cuxac, 35–60. Paris: Académie de Paris.

——. 2000. *La Langue des Signes Française (LSF). Les Voies de l'Iconicite*. Paris: Ophrys.

Demey, Eline. 2005. *Fonologie van de Vlaamse Gebarentaal. Distinctiviteit & Iconiciteit*. Doctoral dissertation, Ghent University, Ghent.

Ebbinghaus Horst & Jens Heßmann. 1996. "Signs and Words: Accounting for spoken language elements in German Sign Language". *International Review of Sign Linguistics. Vol. 1* ed. by William H. Edmondson & Ronnie B. Wilbur, 23–56. Mahwah, N.J.: Lawrence Erlbaum Associates.

Edwards, Jan, Mary E. Beckman & Janet Fletcher. 1991. "The Articulatory Kinematics of Final Lengthening". *Journal of the Acoustic Society of America* 89.369–382.

Ekman, Paul & Wallace V. Friesen. 1969. "The Repertoire of Nonverbal Behavior: Categories, Origins, Usage, and Coding". *Semiotica* 1:1.49–98.

Emmorey, Karen. 1999. "Do Signers Gesture?". *Gesture, Speech, and Sign* ed. by Lynn S. Messing & Ruth Campbell, 133–159. Oxford: Oxford University Press.

——, ed. 2003. *Perspectives on Classifier Constructions in Sign Languages*. Mahwah, N. J./London: Lawrence Erlbaum Associates.

Enfield, Nick J. 2004. "On Linear Segmentation and Combinatorics in Co-speech Gesture: A Symmetry-dominance Construction in Lao Fish Trap Descriptions". *Semiotica* 149:1.57–124.

Engberg-Pedersen, Elisabeth. 1991. "Some Simultaneous Constructions in Danish Sign Language". Paper presented at the Word Order Issues in Sign Languages Workshop, Durham, England. (Published 1994).

——. 1993. *Space in Danish Sign Language: The Semantics and Morphosyntax of the Use of Space in a Visual Language*. Hamburg: Signum Press.

——. 1994. "Some Simultaneous Constructions in Danish Sign Language." *Word-order Issues in Sign Language. Working Papers* ed. by Mary Brennan & Graham H. Turner, 73–88. Durham: International Sign Linguistics Association.

Friedman, Lynn. 1975. "Time, Space and Person Reference in American Sign Language". *Language* 51.940–961.

Frishberg, Nancy. 1985. "Dominance Relations and Discourse Structures". *Proceedings of the III International Symposium on Sign Language Research, Rome 22–26 June 1983* ed. by William C. Stokoe & Virginia Volterra, 79–90. Rome: CNR.

Fusellier-Souza, Ivani. 2006. "Emergence and Development of Signed Languages: From Diachronic Ontogenesis to Diachronic Phylogenesis". To appear in *Sign Language Studies* 7:1 (Fall 2006).

Goldin-Meadow, Susan. 2003. *Hearing Gesture: How Our Hands Help Us Think*. Cambridge, Mass.: Harvard University Press.

Goldsmith, John. 1976. *Autosegmental Phonology*. Doctoral dissertation, MIT.

Grimes, Joseph E. 1975. *The Thread of Discourse*. The Hague: Mouton.

Gullberg, Marianne. 1998. *Gesture as a Communication Strategy in Second Language Discourse. A Study of Learners of French and Swedish*. Lund: Lund University Press.

Gussenhoven, Carlos. 1983. *On the Grammar and Semantics of Sentence Accents*. Dordrecht: Foris.

——. 2001. "Suprasegmentals". *International Encyclopedia of the Social and Behavioural Sciences* ed. by Neil J. Smelser & Paul B. Baltes, 15,294–15,298. Oxford: Pergamon.

——. 2004. *The Phonology of Tone and Intonation*. Cambridge: Cambridge University Press.

Harris, Zellig. 1944. "Simultaneous Components in Phonology". *Language* 20.181–205.

Hayes, Bruce. 1993. "Against Movement: Comments on Liddell's Article". *Phonetics and Phonology, Volume 3: Issues in ASL Phonology* ed. by Geoffrey Coulter, 213–226. San Diego, Calif.: Academic Press.

Hulst, Harry van der. 1993. "Units in the Analysis of Signs". *Phonology* 10.209–241.

Janzen, Terry. 2005. *Perspective Shift Reflected in the Signer's Use of Space*. CDS/CLCS Monograph Number 1. Centre for Deaf Studies. University of Dublin, Trinity College.

Kendon, Adam. 1988. "How Gestures Can Become Like Words". *Cross-Cultural Perspectives in Nonverbal Communication* ed. by Fernando Poyatos, 131–141. Toronto: Hogrefe.

——. 1997. "Gesture". *Annual Review of Anthropology* 26.109–128.

——. 2004. *Gesture: Visible Action as Utterance*. Cambridge: Cambridge University Press.

Klima, Edward & Ursula Bellugi. 1979. *The Signs of Language*. Cambridge, Mass.: Harvard University Press.

Kyle, Jim & Bencie Woll. 1985. *Sign Language. The Study of Deaf People and Their Language*. Cambridge: Cambridge University Press.

Ladd, D. Robert. 1996. *Intonational Phonology*. Cambridge: Cambridge University Press.

Leeson, Lorraine. 2001. *Aspects of Verbal Valency in Irish Sign Language*. Doctoral dissertation, University of Dublin, Trinity College.

—— & John I. Saeed. 2003. "Exploring the Cognitive Underpinning in the Construal of Passive Events in Irish Sign Language (ISL)". Paper presented at the 8th International Cognitive Linguistics Association Conference, Spain, July 2003.

—— & John I. Saeed. 2004. "Windowing of Attention in Simultaneous Constructions in Irish Sign Language". *Proceedings of the Fifth High Desert Linguistics Conference, 1–2 November 2002, Albuquerque, University of New Mexico*, ed. by Terry Cameron, Christopher Shank & Keri Holley, 1–18. University of New Mexico.

Levelt, Willem J.M. 1989. *Speaking. From Intent to Articulation*. Cambridge, Mass.: MIT Press.

Liddell, Scott. 1980. *American Sign Language Syntax*. The Hague: Mouton.

——. 1984. "THINK and BELIEVE: Sequentiality in American Sign Language". *Language* 60.372–399.

——. 2003. *Grammar, Gesture and Meaning in American Sign Language*. Cambridge: Cambridge University Press.

—— & Robert E. Johnson. 1986. "American Sign Language Compound Formation Processes, Lexicalization and Phonological Remnants". *Natural Language & Linguistic Theory* 4.445–513.

—— & Robert E. Johnson. 1987. "An Analysis of Spatial-locative Predicates in American Sign Language". Paper presented at the Fourth International Symposium on Sign Language Research, Lappeenranta, Finland.

—— & Robert E. Johnson. 1989. "American Sign Language: The Phonological Base". *Sign Language Studies* 64.195–278.

Lieberman, Philip. 1967. *Intonation, Perception, and Language*. Cambridge, Mass.: The MIT Press.

Lüdtke, Helmut. 1969. "Die Alphabetschrift und das Problem der Lautsegmentierung". *Phonetica* 20.147–176.

MacNeilage, Peter, Michael Studdert-Kennedy & Björn Lindblom. 1987. "Primate Handedness Reconsidered". *Behavioral and Brain Sciences* 10.247–303.

McNeill, David. 1992. *Hand and Mind. What Gestures Reveal about Thought*. Chicago & London: The University of Chicago Press.

——. 1998. "Speech and Gesture Integration". *The Nature and Functions of Gesture in Children's Communication (New Directions for Child Development, No. 79)* ed. by Jana M. Iverson & Susan Goldin-Meadow, 11–27. San Francisco: Jossey-Bass.

Miller, Christopher. 1994a. "Simultaneous Constructions in Quebec Sign Language". *Word-order Issues in Sign Language. Working Papers* ed. by Mary Brennan & Graham H. Turner, 89–112. Durham: International Sign Linguistics Association.

——. 1994b. "Simultaneous Constructions and Complex Signs in Quebec Sign Language". *Perspectives on Sign Language Structure. Papers from the Fifth International Symposium on Sign Language Research* ed. by Inger Ahlgren, Brita Bergman & Mary Brennan, 131–148. Durham: International Sign Linguistics Association.

Moody, Bill. 1983. *La Langue des Signes. Tomes 1, 2, and 3*. Vincennes: International Visual Theatre.

Nespor, Marina & Irene Vogel. 1986. *Prosodic Phonology*. Dordrecht: Foris.

Ohala, John J. 1984. "An Ethological Perspective on Common Cross-language Utilization of F0 in Voice". *Phonetica* 41.1–16.

Perlmutter, David. 1990. "On the Segmental Representation of Transitional and Bidirectional Movements in ASL Phonology". *Theoretical Issues in Sign Language Research, Volume 1: Linguistics* ed. by Susan Fischer & Patricia Siple, 67–80. Chicago: University of Chicago Press.

——. 1992. "Sonority and Syllable Structure in American Sign Language". *Linguistic Inquiry* 23.407–442.

——. 1993. "Sonority and Syllable Structure in American Sign Language". *Phonetics and Phonology, Volume 3: Current Issues in ASL Phonology* ed. by Geoffrey Coulter, 227–261. San Diego, Calif.: Academic Press.

Pike, Kenneth L. 1945. *The Intonation of American English*. Ann Arbor, Mich.: University of Michigan.

Pinsonneault, Dominique & Linda Lelièvre. 1994. "Enumeration in LSQ (Québec Sign Langage): The Use of Fingertip Loci". *Perspectives on Sign Language Structure. Papers from the Fifth International Symposium on Sign Language Research. Volume 1* ed. by Inger Ahlgren, Brita Bergman & Mary Brennan, 159–172. Durham: International Sign Linguistics Association.

Raino, Päivi. 2001. "Mouthings and Mouth Gestures in Finnish Sign Language (FinSL)". *The Hands are the Head of the Mouth: The Mouth as Articulator in Sign Languages* ed. by Penny Boyes Braem & Rachel Sutton-Spence, 41–50. Hamburg: Signum Press.

Sandler, Wendy. 1989. *Phonological Representation of the Sign. Linearity and Nonlinearity in American Sign Language*. Dordrecht: Foris.

—— & Diane Lillo-Martin. 2006. *Sign Language and Linguistic Universals*. Cambridge: Cambridge University Press.

Schembri, Adam. 2003. "Rethinking 'Classifiers' in Signed Languages". *Perspectives on Classifier Constructions in Sign Languages* ed. by Karen Emmorey. 3–34. Mahwah, N.J./London: Lawrence Erlbaum Associates.

Schick, Brenda. S. 1987. *The Acquisition of Classifier Predicates in American Sign Language*. Doctoral dissertation, Purdue University.

——. 1990. "Classifier Predicates in American Sign Language". *International Journal of Sign Linguistics* 1:1.15–40.

Slobin, Dan.I., Nini Hoiting, Michelle Anthony, Yael Biederman, Marlon Kuntze, Reyna Lindert, Jennie Pyers., Helen Thumann & Amy Weinberg. 2000. "The Meaningful Use of Handshapes by Child and Adult Learners: A Cognitive/Functional Perspective on the Acquisition of 'Classifiers'". Paper presented at the Classifier Constructions in Sign Languages workshop, La Jolla, California.

——, Nini Hoiting, Marlon Kuntze, Reyna Lindert, Amy Weinberg, Jennie Pyers, Michelle Anthony, Yael Biederman & Helen Thumann. 2003. "A Cognitive/Functional Perspective on the Acquisition of 'Classifiers' ". *Perspectives on Classifier Constructions in Sign Languages* ed. by Karen Emmorey. 271–296. Mahwah, N. J./London: Lawrence Erlbaum Associates.

Smith, Wayne H. 1990. "Evidence of Auxiliaries in Taiwanese Sign Language". *Theoretical Issues in Sign Language Research, Linguistics* ed. by Susan Fischer & Patricia Siple, 211–228. Chicago: Chicago University Press.

Stokoe, William C. 1960. *Sign Language Structure. An Outline of the Visual Communication Systems of the American Deaf*. Buffalo, N.Y.: University of Buffalo.

Supalla, Ted 1986. "The Classifier System in American Sign Language". *Noun Classification and Categorisation* ed. by Colette Craig, 181–214. Philadelphia: John Benjamins.

——. 1990. "Serial Verbs of Motion in ASL". *Theoretical Issues in Sign Language Research, Linguistics* ed. by Susan Fischer & Patricia Siple, 129–152. Chicago: Chicago University Press.

Sutton-Spence, Rachel & Bencie Woll. 1999. *The Linguistics of British Sign Language: An Introduction*. Cambridge: Cambridge University Press.

Takkinen, Ritva. 1996. "Classifiers in a Sign Language Dictionary". Paper presented at the Fifth International Conference on Theoretical Issues in Sign Linguistics, Montreal, Canada.

Taub, Sarah, Pilar Pinar & Dennis Galvan. 2002. "Comparing Spatial Information in Speech/Gesture and Signed Language". Manuscript. Paper presented at the "Gesture: The Living Medium" conference, Austin, 5–8 June 2002.

Valli, Clayton & Ceil Lucas. 1995. *Linguistics of American Sign Language. A Resource Text for ASL Users*. 2nd ed. Washington D.C.: Gallaudet University Press.

Vermeerbergen, Myriam. 1996. *ROOD KOOL TIEN PERSOON IN: Morfo-syntactische Aspecten van Gebarentaal*. Doctoral dissertation, Vrije Universiteit Brussel.

——. 1997. *Grammaticale Aspecten van Vlaams-Belgische Gebarentaal*. Gentbrugge: Cultuur voor Doven.

Warren, J.M. 1980. "Handedness and Laterality in Humans and Other Animals". *Physiological Psychology* 8.351–359.

Wallin, Lars. 1996 *Polysynthetic Signs in Swedish Sign Language*. (English ed.) Stockholm: University of Stockholm.

——. 1998. "Reflections on Productive Signs in Swedish Sign Language". Paper presented at the Sixth International Congress on Theoretical Issues in Sign Language Research, Washington D.C.

——. 1990. "Polymorphemic Predicates in Swedish Sign Language". *Sign Language Research: Theoretical Issues* ed. by Ceil Lucas, 133–148. Washington D.C.: Gallaudet University Press.

Wilbur, Ronnie B. 1985. "Towards a Theory of 'Syllable' in Signed Languages: Evidence from the Numbers of Italian Sign Language". *Proceedings of the III International Symposium on Sign Language Research, Rome 22–26 June 1983* ed. by William C. Stokoe & Virginia Volterra, 160–174. Silver Spring, Md.: Linstok Press.

Locative functions of simultaneous perspective constructions in German Sign Language narratives

Pamela M. Perniss

Max Planck Institute for Psycholinguistics, Nijmegen

1. Introduction

Signed and spoken languages differ most obviously in the modalities in which they are produced and perceived. Spoken languages rely on the oral production and aural perception of sequentially ordered elements. Though there are exceptions, e.g. tone, the sequentialization of phonemes determines a primarily linear organization of morphosyntactic structure. Signed languages, on the other hand, are produced and perceived in the visual-spatial modality, and rely on the manipulation of articulators within three dimensional space. The use of space for linguistic expression affords the notion of simultaneity a special status in signed language, and indeed simultaneous patterning and marking characterizes signed language at all levels of linguistic analysis, including phonology, morphology, and syntax. Moreover, the availability of multiple independent articulators makes possible the simultaneous representation of independent meaningful elements. These 'simultaneous constructions' are defined as representations that are produced in more than one articulatory channel, whereby each channel bears distinct and independent meaning units, which stand in some relationship to each other (Miller 1994; Engberg-Pedersen 1994; Leeson & Saeed 2002; Vermeerbergen 2001).

Although this general definition of simultaneous constructions makes no commitment to the involvement of specific articulators, examples of simultaneous constructions within existing typologies in the literature typically involve the two manual articulators. Researchers of different sign languages have identified numerous types of bimanual simultaneous constructions based on formal and functional properties (Miller 1994 for Quebec Sign Language; Engberg-Pedersen 1993, 1994 for Danish Sign Language; Leeson & Saeed 2002 for Irish Sign Language; Vermeerbergen 2001 for Flemish Sign Language; Liddell 2003 for American Sign Language; cf. also the review of literature on American Sign Language presented in Miller 1994, including Friedman 1975; Klima & Bellugi 1979; and Gee & Kegl 1983; Section 2 elaborates on previous research on simultaneous constructions). Formally, two independent signs can be produced simultaneously (two one-handed signs produced at the same time) or sequentially (one sign is produced first and holds during the production of one or more other signs). The functions that have been described for simultaneous constructions are primarily locative or discursive in nature, and include:

1. referent representation on both hands to express locative information (in the depiction of the spatial relationship between two referents);
2. referent representation on both hands to express the temporal and locative simultaneity of events (in the depiction of action or interaction between referents);
3. the expression of temporal simultaneity of events or states (aspectual information);
4. the hold of a topic on one hand while the other hand signs related information (topic – comment structure);
5. the hold of an enumeration morpheme on one hand while the other hand signs one or more related signs;
6. the hold of an index sign on one hand while the other hand signs one or more related signs.

In this paper, I expand the existing typologies of simultaneous constructions in two interrelated ways. Firstly, I include the simultaneous use of articulators other than the hands. In addition to the hands, the body, face, eyes, and mouth are taken to function as independent articulators. Secondly, I include the simultaneous use of different perspectives. The representation of event space in sign space determines the two signing perspectives that are relevant in this paper. In one case, signers are external to the event and represent the event space in the area of space in front of the body from an *observer perspective*. In the other case, signers become part of the event by assuming the role of an animate referent and the event space is represented as life-sized from a *character perspective*. The use of character perspective entails the use of articulators other than the hands, since assuming the role of an animate referent entails mapping the referent onto the body. Signing perspective is discussed in detail in Section 3.

    This paper presents a discourse-based analysis of the use of simultaneous constructions that involve the production of meaningful elements associated with both character and observer perspectives on both manual and non-manual articulators in German Sign Language (Deutsche Gebärdensprache, DGS) event narratives. Specifically, I focus on how signers use simultaneity to encode locative information in discourse, and present two different main functions of the use of simultaneous constructions of this type (as introduced in Section 6). In the first function, a simultaneously articulated observer perspective form serves to fully semantically specify a character perspective form by disambiguating it or by supplementing additional spatial information (Section 7). In the second function, simultaneously articulated observer and character perspective forms create a mapping between meaningful locations in the event spaces of both perspectives (Section 8). Moreover, these constructions are characterized by expressing the *same* event in different ways, i.e. with elements associated with observer and character perspective.

The analysis of the special confluence of form and function in the German Sign Language examples presented here is novel compared to previous analyses in the literature. With respect to function, previous analyses describe the use of simultaneous constructions to express locative information as involving the representation of two referents on the two hands in an observer perspective event space projection. In addition, in representations that include a temporal component, it is typically not the same event that is simultaneously depicted in different ways, but rather the simultaneity of two different events or elements of an event that is represented. With respect to form, the simultaneous use of different perspectives has been described by a handful of researchers (Liddell 1998, 2000; Dudis 2004; Engberg-Pedersen 1993; Aarons & Morgan 2003; Morgan 2002; see Section 4 for detailed descriptions). These analyses focus on the development of conceptual frameworks to explain what elements of an event can get expressed simultaneously and what properties of the modality make this possible.

The simultaneous constructions presented in this paper are analyzed as a strategy for encoding locative information under the pressures of discourse constraints of clarity, efficiency, and informativeness of expression (Section 5). I argue that the motivation for encoding the same event in different ways has to do with the interplay of, on the one hand, articulatory constraints on the type of information that can be represented through certain forms, and, on the other hand, discourse-structure constraints on the way that space is structured for representation. On the one hand, articulatory constraints affect the type of information that can get represented in a particular perspective. On the other hand, discourse constraints affect signers' readiness to switch between signing perspectives in the course of a narrative. To ensure the explicit encoding of relevant locative information under these constraints, signers rely on constructions in which an event or components of an event are simultaneously represented on independent articulators in different perspectives.

2.   Previous research on simultaneous constructions

Previous research on simultaneous constructions has focused on the use of the two manual articulators to express locative information or to contribute to discourse structure. Though it is possible for both hands to appear in sign space simultaneously, in most cases the hands appear sequentially, such that a one-handed sign or one hand of a two-handed sign holds or perseveres during the production of one or more other signs. Sequentially produced simultaneous constructions contain what Engberg-Pedersen (1993, 1994) analyzes as a *hold*-morpheme. The *hold*-morpheme typically appears on the non-dominant hand, and remains in place while something is predicated of it or brought into a certain relationship with it by signs on the dominant hand. It functions to keep a discourse referent visually accessible, e.g. as backgrounded information, while the dominant hand signs related information that is foregrounded or focused. Moreover, the *hold*-morpheme is analyzed as neutral with respect to the semantic distinction between location and motion. This means that when the locative and temporal interaction between two moving referents is depicted in sign space, only the foregrounded referent is associated with a movement morpheme.

For example, to depict the interaction of two basketball players, where both players are running and one is overtaken by the other, the hand depicting the overtaken player remains stationary, while the hand depicting the player doing the overtaking moves in space (Engberg-Pedersen 1993). The action of overtaking is foregrounded, and thus the movement of the player doing the overtaking is represented by the movement of the hand in space. The player being overtaken is represented as a backgrounded predicate with a *hold*-morpheme on the non-dominant hand. The backgrounded player's motion is not actually represented by movement of the hand in space, but rather must be inferred from the context.

In simultaneous constructions that express only locative information, i.e. that encode the spatial relationship between two stationary referent objects, the *hold*-morpheme typically represents the ground referent. The ground object is identified and located in space and then held in place until the figure object is located appropriately in relation to it. In expressing the temporal simultaneity or temporal overlap of two non-locative events, the *hold*-morpheme backgrounds one event while the co-occurring event is depicted on the other hand. For example, to express drinking coffee while reading a newspaper, a signer can sign a sequence in which she first depicts reading the newspaper (i.e. holding a newspaper open in front of her with both hands), and then maintains the newspaper on her non-dominant hand with a *hold*-morpheme while she depicts drinking coffee with the dominant hand (cf. Mathur 2002, for American Sign Language, who refers not to the use of a *hold*-morpheme, however, but rather to a HOLD).

Similarly, in simultaneous constructions that express topic-comment structures, information about a discourse referent is provided on one hand, while it is held in place as a topic on the other hand. For example, Miller (1994) gives an example in which one hand signs SUN while the other hand signs a sentential clause (consisting of four signs) that predicates something about the held discourse topic. Engberg-Pedersen (1993) describes a narrative about two ferries colliding, where the signer holds the sign representing one of the ferries in place while signing attributive information about the ferry with the other hand, e.g. the name of the ferry. In this type of construction, the depiction of an entity on one hand typically perseveres while the other hand describes a property of that entity.

Other discourse-structural relationships that are expressed with simultaneous constructions include the simultaneous appearance of an enumeration morpheme or an index sign on one hand together with one or a series of other signs on the other hand. For these constructions, in contrast to those that express primarily locative and/or temporal relationships, it is not uncommon for the signs on the two hands to get produced simultaneously. For example, to identify the chairperson at a meeting, one hand may point at the person in question while the other hand simultaneously signs CHAIRPERSON (Vermeerbergen 2001). Enumeration morphemes may be used, for example, in the production of a list of colours. A signer may use the enumeration morphemes corresponding to the numerals ONE, TWO, and THREE on one hand, while simultaneously signing the colours RED, WHITE, and YELLOW on the other hand (Vermeerbergen 2001).

Although he does not use the term 'simultaneous construction', Liddell (2003) discusses similar constructions containing signs he calls 'buoys' that are produced on the non-dominant hand and held in place while the dominant hand continues signing. Semantically, their presence in sign space helps guide the procession of discourse. Liddell identifies four different types of buoys, two of which have counterparts in existing typologies of simultaneous constructions, examples of which have been described above. 'List buoys' and 'pointer buoys' correspond essentially to simultaneous constructions with index and enumeration signs, respectively. A 'THEME buoy' takes the form of a raised, vertical index finger on the non-dominant hand and signifies the discussion of an important discourse theme. Finally, a 'fragment buoy' is an articulatory trace of a two-handed sign during a subsequent one-handed sign. Similar to what Mathur (2002) calls RESIDUE, it does not serve a semantic or syntactic function. Thus, they are not true simultaneous constructions as Miller (1994) defines them, where the use of the term 'construction' is emphasized because the elements that are simultaneously expressed must stand in some relationship to each other, be it syntactic, discursive, or iconic.

3. Signing perspective

In event narratives, signing perspectives are differentiated by the way in which event space is projected onto sign space. The place that the signer occupies conceptually with respect to the represented event is an important diagnostic feature and motivates the terminology used in this paper. In 'character perspective', the signer is within the event conceptually and has the vantage point of a character in the event. In the character's role, the signer "constructs" the actions, thoughts, and emotions attributed to it (cf. Metzger 1995, on the notion of constructed action). The projected event space is life-sized, encompassing and extending around the signer. In 'observer perspective', the signer is outside of the event conceptually, and views the scene from the vantage point of an external observer. The event space is projected onto the area of space in front of the signer.

For what I call character perspective and observer perspective, Liddell (2003) distinguishes between 'surrogate space' and 'depictive space',[1] while Dudis (2004) distinguishes between a 'participant viewpoint' and a 'global viewpoint', and Morgan (2002) uses the terms 'shifted referential space' and 'fixed referential space'.[2] Slobin, Hoiting, Kuntze, Lindert, Weinberg, Pyers, Anthony, Biederman & Thumann (2003) also use the term 'perspective', but distinguish between a 'protagonist perspective' and a 'narrator perspective'. The terms 'character' and 'observer', as used here, stem from McNeill's (1992) distinction between a 'character viewpoint' and an 'observer viewpoint' in gestures accompanying speech.

3.1 Prototypical manifestations of signing perspective

The perspective from which an event space is mapped onto sign space is determined to a large extent by articulatory constraints on the type of information that can be expressed by different classifier forms used for referent representation. In classifier predicates, referents are mapped onto the signer's hands at different levels of representation by reflecting certain salient geometric properties in the handshape. The representation of intransitive event types of motion and location entails the mapping of whole referents onto the signer's hands with entity classifiers. Referent location, orientation, and motion is depicted by the position, orientation, and movement of the hands in sign space. The signer is external to the event and projects event space onto sign space from an observer perspective. To represent transitive event types of handling and manipulating objects, however, the active

---

1.   Liddell (1994, 1995) distinguishes between surrogate and token space.

2.   Morgan (1999) uses the terms 'shifted referential framework' and 'fixed referential framework'.

referent is mapped onto the signer's body, and the hands represent the referent's hands. Handling classifiers depict the referent's handling of objects through the appropriate position and configuration of the hands. The signer's role as a character within the event means that the event space is projected as life-sized from that character's perspective.

These relationships between referent representation, information type representation, and event space projection determine what I take to be the prototypical manifestations of observer perspective and character perspective signing. In addition, the vantage point from which an event is represented – either from the perspective of an external observer or from the perspective of an event protagonist – influences the localization of referents in sign space. Canonically, two animate referents are represented in sign space as located across from each other. The spatial locations in which these referents appear differ depending on the perspective from which the event space is depicted. In observer perspective, where the signer is not a part of the event, the canonical locations of two animate referents are opposite each other to the left and the right of the signer's body. In character perspective, however, where one of the referents is mapped onto the signer's body, the other referent is located opposite the signer's body. Thus, the direction of movement of signs depicting interaction between the two referents is along the lateral (left-right) axis for observer perspective and along the sagittal (front-back) axis for character perspective representations.

Summing up, the prototypical manifestations of the two signing perspectives can be characterized in terms of the signer's vantage point on the event, the size of the event space, the type of classifiers used for referent representation, and the canonical direction of movement of signs depicting interaction between two referents (see Figure 1). A schematic-pictorial representation of the prototypical manifestations of character and observer perspectives is given in Figure 2.

	Character perspective	Observer perspective
Vantage point	Signer part of event	Signer outside of event
Event space projection	Life-sized	Model-sized
	(space surrounding signer)	(space in front of signer)
Classifiers	Handling	Entity
Direction	Sagittal axis	Lateral axis

Figure 1. Prototypical manifestations of signing perspective

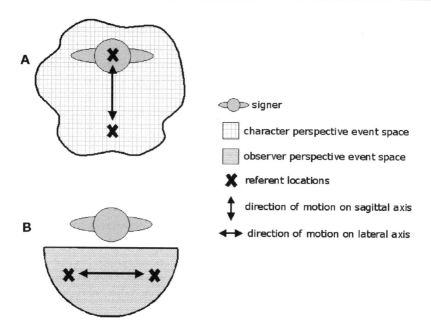

Figure 2. Schematic-pictorial representation of (A) prototypical character perspective and (B) prototypical observer perspective signing

3.2 Non-prototypical manifestations of signing perspective

The relationship between type of information and referent representation determines different conceptual locations of the signer with respect to the event, and forms the basis for distinguishing between event space representation from observer or character perspective. In the section above, I presented four interdependent criteria that define the manifestation of signing perspective: (1) the signer's vantage point on the event, (2) the size of the projected event space, (3) the type of classifiers that occur, and (4) the main direction of movement of the interaction-depicting sign. The alignment of these criteria as they appear in Figure 1 represents the prototypical manifestations of character and observer perspective. Different alignments are characterized by a combination of elements associated with both perspectives, and display what I call non-prototypical manifestations of signing perspective.

An example of a non-prototypical alignment of the features that determine perspective is the use of an entity classifier to depict referent motion along the sagittal axis in an otherwise (contextually-determined) life-sized projection of event space which contains the signer as a referent (as evidenced, for example, by the facial expression). This example shows that the information type, here encoding an intransitive event of motion, determines the use of an entity classifier, which is prototypically aligned with observer perspective. The other criteria that contribute to signing perspective, however, are prototypically aligned with character perspective. Taken together, the manifestation of the criteria that determine signing perspective display a non-prototypical alignment.

Importantly, non-prototypical manifestations of perspective contain elements prototypically associated with both observer and character perspective. In terms of referent representation, this entails the involvement of two or more articulators to encode event information. Thus, formally, non-prototypical alignments can be subsumed under simultaneous constructions, according to the criteria of the general definition given by Miller (1994). They involve the production of distinct, but related meaning units on independent articulators, representing referents on different scales of representation. The next section gives an overview of previous research on this type of simultaneous construction that expresses information in both perspectives.

4.   Previous research on the simultaneous use of different perspectives

The simultaneous representation of referents on both observer and character event space scales has not been widely discussed in the literature, but is recognized as a frequent phenomenon in narratives by the researchers who have studied it (Liddell 1998, 2000, 2003; Liddell & Metzger 1998; Fridman-Mintz & Liddell 1998; Dudis 2002, 2004; Engberg-Pedersen 1993; Aarons & Morgan 2003; Morgan 2002). Liddell and Dudis use mental spaces and conceptual blending theories (cf. Fauconnier 1997; Fauconnier & Turner 1996) to describe the production of 'simultaneous blends', where elements from two conceptual event spaces (one corresponding to an observer perspective view on the event, the other to a character perspective view) are mapped onto different articulators and/or locations in space. The availability of different 'partitionable zones' of the body, including the hands, face, mouth and body, makes possible the simultaneous representation of elements from conceptual spaces with different scale properties (i.e. the scale of an observer perspective vs. a character perspective event space) (Dudis 2004).

Liddell (2000) and Dudis (2004) give examples from American Sign Language of simultaneous blends involving the representation of a vehicle on one hand using an entity classifier and the simultaneous representation of the vehicle's driver on the body. A 'zoomed out', or observer perspective, view of the scene is portrayed through the use of an entity classifier to depict, in Liddell's example, a car stopped at an intersection, and in Dudis' example, a motorcycle going up a hill. By mapping the drivers of the vehicles onto the body, the signer can simultaneously depict their facial expressions and behaviours (e.g. the driver of the car looking both ways before crossing the intersection) through a 'zoomed in' or character perspective view of the scene. Aarons & Morgan (2003) describe similar constructions from South African Sign Language in what they call the creation of multiple perspectives. For example, to simultaneously depict different event components of an intransitive motion event, a signer simultaneously maps a moving animate referent (i.e. a parachutist floating through the air) onto his hand and onto his body.

In addition, Aarons & Morgan (2003) and Engberg-Pedersen (1993), for Danish Sign Language, describe the encoding of transitive relationships between two referents through the simultaneous representation of one referent on the body and the other referent on the hand. For Engberg-Pedersen, the backgrounded referent is represented on the body as the patient or spectator of the event. The motion and location of the agent is represented with an entity classifier from the patient's vantage point. For example, the interaction between two basketball players can be depicted by mapping one player onto the body and representing the motion of the other player relative to the body with an entity classifier on the hand. The referent mapped onto the body is backgrounded with respect to the referent mapped onto the hand (cf. the mapping of the backgrounded player onto the non-dominant hand with a *hold*-morpheme discussed in Section 2). Finally, Morgan (2002) discusses the use of overlapping reference spaces (i.e. perspectives) to represent either the same referent or two different referents in encoding the temporal simultaneity of events in British Sign Language narratives.

5.   Signing perspective and discourse structure constraints

All of the examples discussed in the previous section exhibit what I call non-prototypical alignments of signing perspective. Their use and occurrence is analyzed within conceptual frameworks that explain the specific combination of elements they exhibit, including assumptions about the role of agentivity and point of view marking in encoding events. In this paper, I explain the occurrence of non-prototypical alignments in narratives in terms of discourse structure constraints and semantic-pragmatic conventions for representing events. Different event types entail referent representation on different scales, i.e. corresponding to both observer and character perspective, yet the use of prototypical manifestations of perspective to encode these event types is relatively rare in discourse. Instead, event narratives exhibit a high degree of non-prototypical alignments, representing elements from both perspectives. I argue that the use of non-prototypically aligned forms can be motivated by discourse constraints of efficiency and informativeness, in conjunction with a pragmatically-determined preference to focus on the interaction between characters (Leeson & Saeed 2002) and to represent events from an egocentric point of view (Engberg-Pedersen 1993).

The explication of efficiency and informativeness principles in discourse dates back to Grice's (1975) conversational maxims. Grice's two principles of quantity are formulated as 'make your contribution as informative as required' (Q1) and 'do not make your contribution more informative than is required' (Q2). In later research on pragmatic theory, the essence of these maxims was reformulated as the 'Q-principle' ('Principle of Quantity') and the 'I-principle' ('Principle of Informativeness'), respectively (Horn 1984; Atlas & Levinson 1981; Levinson 2000).[3] In a discourse context, the two principles pull in opposite directions, minimizing the speaker's effort on the one hand (i.e. maximizing the speaker's efficiency via the 'I-principle'), and minimizing the addressee's effort on the other hand (i.e. maximizing the hearer's input via the 'Q-principle').

In this paper, efficiency and informativeness are examined with respect to the expression of locative information in narratives. Specifically, the focus of analysis is on the representation of referent location, motion, and action in event spaces projected from character and/or observer perspectives. Efficiency and informativeness are measured as the amount of separate, i.e. sequential, constructions used by a signer in order to express these types of locative information.

The projection of two event spaces, or the use of both observer and character perspective event spaces, in a narrative has the consequence that referents in the event get associated with different locations in sign space. For example, a signer may locate two animate referents opposite each other on the lateral axis in an event space determined by observer perspective (see Figure 2 (B)). However, to construct the actions of a referent, the signer must switch to character perspective and map the referent onto the body. In doing so, because the relative spatial relationships between referents in the event space remain the same, the referent-location associations in sign space change. Thus, the referents that were located across from each other to the right and left on the lateral axis in observer perspective are now located at the signer's location and opposite the signer on the sagittal axis in character perspective (see Figure 2 (A)).

Given these changes in referent-location associations and thus changes in the way sign space is inscribed, narratives in which signers use both perspectives, i.e. both observer and character event space projections, are potentially neither very efficient in terms of the signer's effort nor very clear in terms of the amount of information integration that the addressee is faced with. I argue that simultaneous constructions that *simultaneously* depict information from both observer and character perspective help to clarify and make explicit the relationship between the two event spaces. In this way, non-prototypical manifestations of signing perspective are a response to discourse constraints on efficiency and informa-

---

3.   Horn uses the label 'R-principle' for what Levinson calls the 'I-principle'.

tiveness. Their function is especially important with respect to referent-location associations and the encoding of spatial information.

Alternatively, a signer may project event space from only one perspective in the course of a narrative. Both Engberg-Pedersen (1993) and Leeson & Saeed (2002) note a semantic-pragmatic convention or preference for encoding events, especially transitives, from the point of view of an agentive referent. In terms of signing perspective, this means that signers prefer to map an animate referent onto the body and project a life-sized event space from that character's perspective. The efficiency of using only one event space projection is potentially high in terms of both the signer's and the addressee's effort. In prototypical character perspective, however, the information the addressee receives, especially concerning spatial relationships, may remain underspecified. As argued, the expression of different types of information, specifically, transitive and intransitive event types, is tied to referent representation at different levels, i.e. with handling and entity classifiers, respectively. Through the use of simultaneous constructions characterized by non-prototypical perspective alignments, signers can represent both types of information within a character perspective event space projection. Thus, here too, non-prototypical manifestations of perspective serve both informativeness (or clarity) and efficiency of expression in discourse.

6.   Locative functions of non-prototypically aligned simultaneous constructions

This paper looks at the use of non-prototypical manifestations of signing perspective in event narratives to make locative information about referent location, action, and motion in transitive and intransitive event types explicit. These non-prototypically aligned forms are subsumed under the general definition of simultaneous constructions, because they involve the use of independent articulators to encode distinct meaning units. They differ from the locative simultaneous constructions usually presented in the literature in two crucial respects: (1) they are not simultaneous *classifier* constructions, that is, they involve the use of articulators other than the hands; and (2) they involve the expression of elements from different perspectives, i.e. observer and character perspective, at the same time.

In German Sign Language event narratives, the use of such simultaneous constructions is common. I argue in this paper that their occurrence can be linked to the pressures of discourse structure constraints, in particular with respect to encoding spatial relationships. On the one hand, there is pressure to be as informative and precise as possible in encoding referent location, action, and motion within event space. On the other hand, there is pressure to be as efficient and clear as possible in presenting this information.

As noted in the previous section, signers may use both observer and character event space projections or project event space only from a character perspective. In dependence of the event space projections used by signers in the course of a narrative, I present two different types of non-prototypical forms that demonstrate two main functions with respect to making spatial information explicit. In one case, non-prototypical manifestations of signing perspective function to provide a full semantic specification of an encoded event. These forms primarily occur when signers narrate an event from character perspective, projecting a life-sized event space and keeping an animate referent mapped onto the body throughout. In the other case, when signers use both an observer and a character perspective event space projection, simultaneous constructions that utilize both event spaces function to create a mapping between meaningful locations in the two representations.

I present an analysis of the use of such simultaneous constructions in German Sign Language event narratives. Narratives were elicited from German signers on the basis of short cartoon stimulus clips featuring animate referents engaged in activity in a fixed event space. Pairs of signers were videotaped during data collection sessions. One signer watched the stimulus film and narrated the story to the second signer, who then retold the story to the first signer without having seen the video clip. The narratives were transcribed and coded using ELAN.[4] Coding was for classifier forms, signing perspective, simultaneous constructions, locative constructions, and location-referent associations. The narratives chosen for analysis in this paper are of a single cartoon[5] and are taken from a larger corpus of German Sign Language data.[6] The constructions presented in the following sections are exemplary of occurrences in the data corpus as a whole.

---

4.   ELAN is the European Distributed Corpora Linguistic ANnotator (ELAN), a multimedia annotation tool developed at the Max Planck Institute for Psycholinguistics.

5.   See the Appendix for a content description and stills of the stimulus film.

6.   The whole corpus consists of video recordings of elicited event narratives, spatial descriptions of object configurations, and route descriptions. Additionally, recordings of natural conversation supplement the elicited material. In total, narratives were elicited from seven pairs of different signers for eighteen cartoon stimulus clips, comprising five hours of recorded material. Of these stimulus clips, six were chosen for detailed analysis and coding. Data was collected from seven pairs of signers for five of these six stimulus films, and from six pairs for one stimulus film. A total of fourteen signers participated in the narrative task.

7.   Simultaneous constructions in character perspective narratives

In signed language, decisions about narrative structure, that is, about which aspects of an event to represent and how, are directly reflected in the choice of signing perspective. As discussed in Section 5 above, Engberg-Pedersen (1993) notes that narrators are inclined to represent events from an egocentric point of view, which entails mapping an animate referent onto the body in signing (see also Leeson & Saeed 2002). In addition, a preference for signing from character perspective seems to be supported by certain factors inherent in the event structure. For example, if there is only one animate referent, or a referent that is identified as the primary protagonist, signers tend to adopt this referent's perspective as the dominant point of view from which to narrate an event (cf. Engberg-Pedersen's (1993) empathy convention for referent mapping). This is strengthened further if the protagonist engages in manual activity, which the signer must necessarily represent in character perspective. In addition, a fixed vantage point from which the event is viewed also seems to influence the choice to represent the event from one dominant perspective. This is especially relevant for event narratives elicited from stimulus films where there can be an effect of a fixed versus a variable camera angle. The stimulus film used to elicit the narratives presented here has a fixed camera angle and features a primary protagonist engaged in manual activity (see stimulus description in Appendix). The features that characterize it may thus encourage signing from the main protagonist's point of view.

Sections 7.1 and 7.2 below present examples of simultaneous constructions that occur in narratives told in character perspective. The signers depict the event from the perspective of the primary protagonist (i.e. the mouse), who is kept mapped onto the body, and construct the referent's actions and emotions through the use of the head, body, and handling classifiers mapped onto the hands. The simultaneous constructions, i.e. non-prototypically aligned forms, occur to represent information that is not felicitously or unambiguously represented in prototypical character perspective signing – in particular, referent change of location and/or orientation. They provide a full semantic specification of events either by supplementing an event component that cannot be depicted by a character perspective-aligned form (Section 7.1) or by disambiguating such a form (Section 7.2).

7.1   Full semantic specification through supplementation

The type of simultaneous construction presented in this section is characterized by the simultaneous depiction of different event components of the same event on different articulators. The encoding of both components is necessary to fully specify the totality of semantic content of the event. In the stimulus film, the mouse

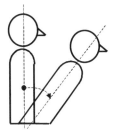

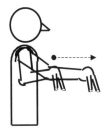

Figure 3. Mouse's change of posture encoded by moving torso from **posture₁** to **posture₂**

Figure 4. Mouse's change of location encoded by moving hand from **location₁** to **location₂**

moves forward in an exaggerated lunge attempting to catch a pancake in a pan that it holds in its hand (see stills 3 and 4 in the Appendix). The mouse's movement consists of two separate event components: (1) a change of location, i.e. the mouse runs forward, and (2) a change of posture, i.e. the mouse leans forward. Of these two components, only the change of posture can be represented with a form prototypically aligned with character perspective, i.e. by leaning the torso forward (see Figure 3). Representing the mouse's change of location with a character perspective form would entail an infelicitous movement of the whole body, and thus must be encoded instead with an entity classifier, a form prototypically aligned with observer perspective (see Figure 4).

In the example presented here, the signer encodes both the change of posture and change of location event components simultaneously by combining the representations in Figures 3 and 4. The resulting simultaneous construction is a non-prototypically aligned form that involves the use of the body as a character perspective articulator and the hand as an observer perspective articulator.[7] This is schematically represented in Figure 5 (a–b), and shown in video stills from the signer's narrative in Figure 6.[8] Both articulators encode distinct pieces of information that are necessary to achieve full semantic specification of the event. Moreover, each articulator is associated with a particular perspective and

7. Note that Figure 4 represents a non-prototypically-aligned form in and of itself, because the hand moves along the sagittal axis. In prototypical observer perspective, the entity classifier would move along the lateral axis. For the sake of simplicity and clarity, the change of location information is depicted in Figure 4 as the signer actually encodes it.

8. The following abbreviations are used in the transcriptions of the sign language examples: RH: right hand; LH: left hand; CL: classifier predicate; LocR: entity located on the right of observer perspective sign space; LocL: entity located on the left of observer perspective sign space.

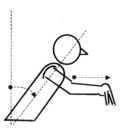

Figure 5a. The hand and the torso are at location₁/posture₁

Figure 5b. The hand and the torso are at location₂/posture₂

Figure 6. Move from location₁/posture₁ to location₂/posture₂: mouse(signer)-hold-pan (LH: handlingCL)-lean-forward + mouse(RH: entityCL)-run-forward; at location₂/posture₂: pancake(RH: entity CL)-land-on-forehead

encodes information that is felicitously represented only in that perspective. The meaning contributed by the entity classifier supplements the otherwise character perspective-determined representation.

With respect to encoding locative information, the use of this simultaneous construction is both very efficient and informative. Different components of the event that are prototypically aligned with different perspectives and necessarily have to be depicted on different articulators, can be represented simultaneously. The efficiency of the single construction with the non-prototypical manifestation of perspective allows the signer to remain in a character perspective event space, with the animate referent mapped onto the body. In addition, it is maximally informative to the addressee because it fully specifies the mouse's movement. All of the relevant spatial information is simultaneously encoded in a complex form involving two independent articulators and elements from both perspectives.

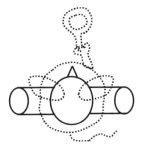

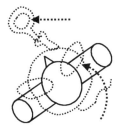

Figure 7a. Signer faces forward = mouse faces stove

Figure 7b. Signer turns torso ≠ mouse turned from stove

7.2 Full semantic specification through disambiguation

Instead of encoding different components of the same event, it is also possible that the two active articulators in a simultaneous construction encode the same information. In narratives signed predominantly from character perspective, with the primary protagonist mapped onto the body, the use of the body as an independent articulator is limited to movements that do not involve actual changes of body location. Possible meaningful movements include turns of the torso from side to side and leans forward and backward (as in the example in the previous section). However, the meaning of these movements may be ambiguous. In the stimulus film, the mouse moves repeatedly back and forth between two distinct orientations that differ by 90° (see still 1 (facing stove) and still 2 (turned from stove) in the Appendix). To represent the mouse's change of orientation in character perspective, a corresponding 90° turn of the torso and shoulders is not felicitous. Instead, signers can felicitously turn only about 45° from the middle, as shown in the schematic representation in Figure 7 (a–b).

As it is, however, this form is ambiguous, and could be interpreted in several different ways in this context [9]

1. as a small turn of the body (i.e. a gradient interpretation of about 45°);
2. as a large, substantial turn of the body (i.e. ≥ 90°);
3. as a lateral displacement of the pan (i.e. to the left).

In my data, the majority of signers used a torso turn to encode this event, and simultaneously articulated an oral component that has the form of the German preposition *um* ('about, at'). In German Sign Language, *um* is used in both the

---

9. A turn of the torso and shoulders is also associated with the phenomenon of role shift (cf. Padden 1990). Because there is only one animate referent involved in this specific event, however, the phenomenon is not relevant here.

concrete and abstract domains to mean 'turn around, turn over' or to signify a change of state. The semantic contribution of *um* fully specifies the character perspective form by disambiguating it. It signifies to the addressee that the turn of the body is to be interpreted as a substantial change in referent orientation (i.e. interpretation (2) above).[10]

The simultaneous construction used here thus involves the use of the torso and the mouth as independent articulators. Although both articulators encode the same event component, the information is not redundant. The use of the torso alone to encode the referent's change of orientation (in prototypical character perspective signing) cannot convey the intended information unambiguously. The specific semantic contribution of the oral component clarifies the meaning of the other form. In addition to its efficiency, the simultaneity of expression provides the addressee with explicit information about the nature of the spatial relationship.

This example departs somewhat in form from the type of non-prototypically aligned simultaneous constructions discussed in this paper. Oral components, articulated on the mouth, are not as such associated with a particular signing perspective. In the case of *um*, the form appears simultaneously with signs that depict or denote the turning of a concrete or abstract entity. Thus, semantically, it encodes information whose expression in sign space is associated with an observer perspective event space projection. In this example, an entity classifier form depicting the mouse's change in orientation could additionally have accompanied the torso turn and the mouthed element *um*.

8.   Simultaneous constructions in observer and character perspective narratives

Speakers make choices about what aspects of an event to focus on and which forms to choose for linguistic packaging. No two narratives of the same event will be exactly alike in terms of hierarchical structure, foregrounding and backgrounding, or choice of perspective. When signers inscribe sign space from both an observer and a character perspective event space projection in the course of a narrative, however, the relationship between the two spaces with respect to referent-location associations has to be clear. One way of doing this is through the use of simultaneous

---

10.   One signer turned his torso to depict the mouse's change of orientation without a simultaneously accompanying form (or any other related spatial information). The signer to whom the narrative was told, who retold the event, misinterpreted the intended meaning of the torso turn as a lateral displacement of the pan subsequently (i.e. interpretation (3) above). In a repeat of the narrative by the original signer to clarify the misunderstanding, the oral component *um* did accompany the torso turn.

perspective constructions. The simultaneous representation of an event from both observer and character perspectives, i.e. in both event space projections, is able to explicitly establish a mapping between corresponding meaningful locations in the two event spaces.

The next two sections illustrate examples of such simultaneous constructions in event narratives in which signers use both observer and character perspective event spaces. With these constructions, signers explicitly encode the same locative information about referent location and orientation in both spaces at the same time. In both examples given, the simultaneous construction contributes to discourse coherence with respect to the expression of spatial information by increasing efficiency while being maximally informative. In the first case, the signer simultaneously represents a referent's change of orientation with forms accessing both character and observer perspective space, thereby establishing a distinctive link between the corresponding locations in the two spaces (Section 8.1). In the second case, the signer uses a simultaneous construction to identify the goal location of a transitive motion event in both observer and character perspective event spaces at the same time (Section 8.2).

8.1 Mapping between perspectives for efficiency and explicitness of expression

I have emphasized the role of articulatory constraints in determining the relationship between referent and information type representation, and have aligned signing perspective with certain ways of structuring space. Here, as in the example in Section 7.2, the relevant spatial relationships are the two orientations of the main protagonist, i.e. the mouse, with respect to the stove. The mouse either faces the stove or is turned 90° to the left of the stove (see stills 1 and 2 in the Appendix). At the beginning of the narrative in this example, narrative structure is determined by a linear sequence of prototypical manifestations of observer and character perspectives. The signer first uses entity classifier forms in a 'traditional' observer perspective simultaneous construction to depict the spatial relationship between the mouse and the stove, and then represents the mouse's manual activity in this orientation (facing the stove) in character perspective. The signer returns to an entity classifier observer perspective representation to depict the mouse's change of orientation, and again follows it with character perspective signing to construct the mouse's activity in the new orientation.

Having established both orientations in an observer perspective event space, the signer employs a simultaneous perspective construction to map them onto two distinct orientations of the torso in character perspective event space. The construction itself consists of a lateral turn of the hands, shoulders, and torso from left to right (see Figure 8). The beginning location indexes the mouse in

Figure 8. Mouse(signer)-hold-pan(RH:handlingCL)-turn-right(to stove) + BACK/
RETURN-TO(LH: loc$_2$-to-loc$_1$)

the orientation turned away from the stove; the end location indexes the mouse facing the stove. Character perspective is manifested through the presence of a handling classifier on the signer's dominant (right) hand and the turn of the torso and shoulders representing the mouse's body turning. Simultaneously, the spatial orientations specified in observer perspective event space are accessed by a spatially modifiable lexical predicate meaning BACK/RETURN-TO, executed by the non-dominant (left) hand. This sign is not a typical observer perspective form, i.e. not an entity classifier. However, the spatial modification of the sign is understood with conceptual recourse to the spatial information previously specified in observer perspective using entity classifiers to represent the mouse.

Through the simultaneous construction, the slightly left orientation of the torso and shoulders is distinctively linked to the orientation of the mouse turned 90° from the stove, and the slightly right orientation is linked to the orientation of the mouse facing the stove. As illustrated by the example presented in Section 7.2 above, the body cannot be used as the sole articulator to unambiguously depict a significant change of orientation of an animate referent mapped onto the signer's body. Additional locative information has to be supplied in order to correctly interpret the meaning of a torso turn. In this example, the simultaneous perspective construction supplies this additional information by utilizing the meaningful locations already established in an observer perspective event space. After the simultaneous construction, moving between the two orientations of the body in character perspective explicitly and unambiguously encodes the mouse's movement between the two orientations with respect to the stove. The signer's efficiency in discourse is increased through the use of the simultaneous perspective construction, because it allows him to remain in character perspective while maintaining maximal precision in the encoding of spatial information regarding the mouse's location and orientation. A schematic representation of the signer's narrative is given in Figure 9.

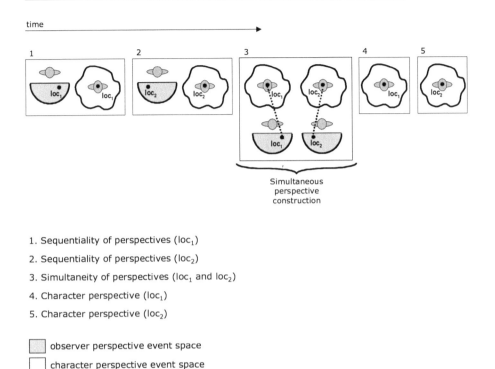

1. Sequentiality of perspectives (loc_1)
2. Sequentiality of perspectives (loc_2)
3. Simultaneity of perspectives (loc_1 and loc_2)
4. Character perspective (loc_1)
5. Character perspective (loc_2)

☐ observer perspective event space

☐ character perspective event space

Loc_1: referent orientation = facing stove
Loc_2: referent orientation = turned from stove

Figure 9. Schematization of the use of sequentiality and simultaneity of perspectives in discourse

8.2 Mapping between spaces to shift event component focus

Transitive motion events are often characterized by the transfer of an inanimate referent between two animate referents. The localization of referents and the representation of the path of motion in space is influenced by which aspects of the event a signer chooses to focus on in narration, and can be aligned either with character or with observer perspective. On the one hand, a signer who focuses on the interaction between animate referents and the manner of object transfer is more likely to represent the event from character perspective. Thus, the location and motion of referents in space would correspond to the depiction in Figure 2 (A) in Section 3.1 above, with the path of motion represented along the sagittal axis from a referent mapped onto the signer's body to a referent conceptually located across from the signer (see also Figure 10). On the other hand, depiction of the path of motion is more likely to be along the lateral axis (between two referents

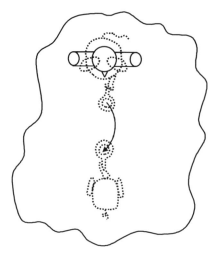

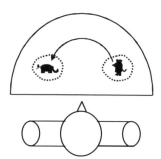

Figure 10. Locations of mouse and elephant in character perspective event space

Figure 11. Locations of mouse and elephant in observer perspective event space

located to the right and left of the signer, as in Figure 2 (B) in Section 3.1) when the narrative focus is on the path component itself (see also Figure 11).

In the example presented here, the signer focuses on the interactional and manner components, as well as on the path component of the relevant transitive event by representing the former in character perspective and the latter in observer perspective. The relationship between the two event spaces with respect to referent locations is created through the use of a simultaneous construction with which the signer changes from one representation to the other. In the stimulus film, two animate referents (i.e. the mouse and the elephant) stand across from each other, each holding a pan, flipping a pancake between them (see still 5 in the Appendix). This is represented schematically in a character perspective event space in Figure 10 and in an observer perspective event space in Figure 11 (cf. Fridman-Mintz & Liddell 1998 for the use of the wavy line and semi-circle to symbolize character and observer event spaces, respectively).

The signer begins in character perspective with the mouse mapped onto the body, encoding the manner in which the pancake is caused to move through the air with a handling classifier (i.e. by flipping the pancake out of the pan). The signer's eyes follow the path of the pancake upward out of the pan, but do not follow it back down to the conceptual location of the elephant opposite the signer's body. Instead, the eyes follow the path of the pancake to a goal location located to the left of the signer's body. Thus, at the apex of the pancake's path, the eyes separate out as an independent articulator from the character perspective representation, completing the trajectory at a location determined by an observer

Figure 12. Mouse(signer)-hold-pan(RH: handlingCL)-flip-pancake(eyes: path sagittal)-to-elephant(opposite signer) + pancake(eyes: path lateral)-to-elephant(locL)

Figure 13. Pancake(RH: entity CL)-flip-between-elephant(locL)-and-mouse(locR)

perspective event space representation. This simultaneous construction, involving the body and dominant hand as articulators in character perspective and the eyes as articulators in observer perspective, explicitly identifies the pancake's goal location simultaneously on the sagittal and lateral axes. The handling classifier form on the dominant hand remains in place, keeping the character perspective space simultaneously active until the transitive event is completely encoded, i.e. until the transferred object reaches its goal location, the elephant. The simultaneous construction is shown in Figure 12. The signer's subsequent focus on the path component of the event is shown in Figure 13.

Through the simultaneous construction, the signer links corresponding referent locations in observer and character perspective representations. The signer uses the left side of space for the elephant's location in previous observer perspective representations in the narrative, and thus the simultaneous construction does not newly establish the elephant's observer perspective location. However, the construction is a unique example of the simultaneous use of different articulators and different perspectives to encode the same event in different ways. In terms of discourse structure, it is extremely efficient and informative in explicitly and distinctly mapping referent locations between event spaces. Other means, e.g.

sequentiality of perspectives in conjunction with lexical identification of referents at specific locations, could achieve such explicit marking, but certainly at the cost of efficiency and clarity. Moreover, the switch from character to observer perspective marks a shift in focus from the manner to the path component of the motion event.

9. Summary and discussion

This paper investigated the use of simultaneous constructions in German Sign Language narratives under the pressures of articulatory constraints on referent and information type representation, on the one hand, and discourse structure constraints of efficiency and informativeness of expression, on the other hand. The focus was on constructions that involved the simultaneous depiction of elements associated with observer and character perspectives using manual and non-manual articulators. These constructions were characterized as non-prototypical manifestations of signing perspectives, and differ in both form and function from similar constructions discussed in the previous literature. The explicit encoding of locative information is generally discussed within typologies of bimanual simultaneous constructions, where referents are represented by entity classifiers on the hands. The simultaneous representation of elements from different perspectives, i.e. both observer and character perspective, has not been extensively investigated with an eye to specific functions within discourse.

I presented two main functions related to the encoding of spatial relationships that the use of non-prototypically aligned forms perform in discourse. In one function, non-prototypically aligned forms appear in narratives encoded predominantly or exclusively in character perspective. Event information that cannot get represented in character perspective is simultaneously encoded on an articulator that accesses an observer perspective representation. In this way, the simultaneous construction functions to provide a full semantic specification of the character perspective form by disambiguating it or by supplementing it with additional locative information. In the other function, non-prototypically aligned forms appear in narratives that use both observer and character perspective event space projections. Here, the use of simultaneous perspective constructions serves to create a mapping between the two event spaces by simultaneously encoding the same information in both spaces. The use of simultaneous constructions of both types allows signers to be very precise in encoding locative information about referent location, motion, and action, while maintaining clarity and efficiency of presentation.

The representations illustrated in this paper hinge both on the simultaneity of expressed elements and on the close relationship between them, and are truly *si-*

multaneous constructions in this sense. To emphasize the importance of this point, it is necessary to elaborate on the example of the simultaneous blend described by Dudis (2004), in which a signer depicts a motorcyclist ascending a hill (see Section 4). Dudis notes that the representation of the motorcyclist alone, i.e. in a character perspective representation with the motorcyclist mapped onto the body, would suffice to convey the information that the top of the hill had been reached, without showing any path movement of the motorcycle using an entity classifier. For example, Dudis lists the following cues on the face and body from which the completion of the ascent of the hill could be inferred: the eye gaze changes from being directed upward to horizontal; the facial expression changes from tense to relaxed; the torso and hands (gripping the handlebars) move slightly forward. However, the existence of partitionable zones of the body, i.e. the availability of different independent articulators for information representation, presents the signer with the possibility of simultaneously representing the motorcycle's advance up the hill through the use of an entity classifier. Again, it is important to note here that, as Dudis states, the cues available in one perspective (for example, the character perspective cues listed above) would suffice for the specification of the motorcycle's having reached the top of the hill. The partitionable zones of the body allow the signer to depict additional distinct visible elements to give a richer, more detailed representation of the event.

In contrast to this, the type of simultaneous constructions that I have presented in this paper do more than give a richer, more detailed representation. The information encoded in one perspective cannot be inferred from what is encoded in the other perspective. The full semantic specification of the mouse's movement in the example discussed in Section 7.1, for example, necessarily involves the encoding of both the mouse's change of location and its change of posture. Thus, the totality of the event cannot be encoded without both the representation associated with observer perspective (i.e. to encode the change of location with an entity classifier) and the representation associated with character perspective (i.e. to encode the change of posture with the torso). The possibility of encoding both event components simultaneously makes use of a unique affordance of the visual-spatial modality and allows precise encoding of locative information that is both elegant in form and efficient in expression.

Further research on German Sign Language will determine how frequently the types of simultaneous constructions identified in this paper occur within different types of discourse, and whether different populations of signers exhibit similar uses. In addition, comparisons with corpora from other signed languages will reveal whether and how frequently such simultaneous constructions occur, and whether similar discourse functions may be ascribed to them. Differences between signed languages may appear as a result of different linguistic or discourse constraints on the use of space.

References

Aarons, Deborah & Ruth Morgan. 2003. "Classifier Predicates and the Creation of Multiple Perspectives in South African Sign Language". *Sign Language Studies* 3:2.125–156.

Atlas, Jay D. & Stephen C. Levinson. 1981. "IT-clefts, Informativeness, and Logical Form". *Radical Pragmatics* ed. by Peter Cole, 1–62. New York: Academic Press.

Dudis, Paul. 2002. "Grounded Blend Maintenance as a Discourse Strategy". *Turn-taking, Fingerspelling, and Contact in Signed Languages (Sociolinguistics in Deaf Communities 8)* ed. by Ceil Lucas, 53–72. Washington, D.C.: Gallaudet University Press.

——. 2004. "Body Partitioning and Real-Space Blends". *Cognitive Linguistics* 15:2.223–238.

Engberg-Pedersen, Elisabeth. 1993. *Space in Danish Sign Language: The Semantics and Morphosyntax of the Use of Space in a Visual Language*. Hamburg: Signum Press.

——. 1994. "Some Simultaneous Constructions in Danish Sign Language". *Word-order Issues in Sign Language. Working Papers* ed. by Mary Brennan & Graham H. Turner, 73–87. Durham: International Sign Linguistics Association.

Fauconnier, Gilles. 1997. *Mappings in Thought and Language*. Cambridge: Cambridge University Press.

—— & Mark Turner. 1996. "Blending as a Central Process of Grammar". *Conceptual Structure, Discourse and Language* ed. by Adele E. Goldberg, 113–129. Stanford, Calif.: CSLI.

Fridman-Mintz, Boris & Scott K. Liddell. 1998. "Sequencing Mental Spaces in an ASL Narrative". *Discourse and Cognition: Bridging the Gap* ed. by Jean-Pierre Koenig, 255–268. Cambridge: Cambridge University Press.

Friedman, Lynn A. 1975. "Space, Time, and Person Reference in American Sign Language". *Language* 51.940–961.

Gee, James P. & Judy A. Kegl. 1983. "Narrative/Story Structure, Pausing, and American Sign Language". *Discourse Processes* 6:3.243–258.

Grice, H. Paul. 1975. "Logic and Conversation". *Speech Acts* ed. by Peter Cole & Jerry L. Morgan, 41–58. New York: Academic Press.

Horn, Laurence R. 1984. "Toward a New Taxonomy for Pragmatic Inference". *Meaning, Form, and Use in Context* ed. by Deborah Schiffrin, 11–42. Washington, D.C.: Georgetown University Press.

Klima, Edward S. & Ursula Bellugi. 1979. *The Signs of Language*. Cambridge, Mass.: Harvard University Press.

Leeson, Lorraine & John Saeed. 2002. "Windowing of Attention in Simultaneous Constructions in Irish Sign Language (ISL)". Paper presented at HDSL 5, University of New Mexico, Albuquerque, November, 2002.

Levinson, Stephen C. 2000. *Presumptive Meanings*. Cambridge, Mass.: MIT Press.

Liddell, Scott K. 1994. "Tokens and Surrogates". *Perspectives on Sign Language Usage: Papers from the Fifth International Symposium on Sign Language Research* ed. by Inger Ahlgren, Brita Bergman & Mary Brennan, 105–120. Durham: International Sign Linguistics Association.

——. 1995. "Real, Surrogate, and Token Space: Grammatical Consequences in ASL". *Language, Gesture, and Space* ed. by Karen Emmorey, 19–41. Hillsdale, N.J.: Lawrence Erlbaum Associates.

——. 1998. "Grounded Blends, Gestures, and Conceptual Shifts". *Cognitive Linguistics* 9–3.283–314.

——. 2000. "Blended Spaces and Deixis in Sign Language Discourse". *Language and Gesture* ed. by David McNeill, 331–357. Cambridge: Cambridge University Press.

——. 2003. *Grammar, Gesture, and Meaning in American Sign Language*. Cambridge: Cambridge University Press.

—— & Melanie Metzger. 1998. "Gesture in Sign Language Discourse". *Journal of Pragmatics* 30.657–697.

Mathur, Gaurav. 2002. "On the Syntax-Phonology Interface in ASL: The Case of HOLD". Paper presented at the LSA Annual Meeting, 2002.

McNeill, David. 1992. *Hand and Mind: What Gestures Reveal about the Mind*. Chicago: University of Chicago Press.

Metzger, Melanie. 1995. "Constructed Dialogue and Constructed Action in American Sign Language". *Sociolinguistics in Deaf Communities* ed. by Ceil Lucas, 255–271. Washington, D.C.: Gallaudet University Press.

Miller, Chris. 1994. "Simultaneous constructions in Quebec Sign Language". *Word-Order Issues in Sign Language. Working Papers* ed. by Mary Brennan & Graham H. Turner, 89–112. Durham: International Sign Linguistics Association.

Morgan, Gary. 1999. "Event Packaging in British Sign Language Discourse". *Story Telling and Conversation: Discourse in Deaf Communities* ed. by Elizabeth Winston, 27–58. Washington, D.C.: Gallaudet University Press.

——. 2002. "Children's Encoding of Simultaneity in BSL Narratives". *Sign Language & Linguistics* 5:2.131–165.

Padden, Carol A. 1990. "The Relation between Space and Grammar in ASL Verb Morphology". *Sign Language Research: Theoretical Issues* ed. by Ceil Lucas, 118–132. Washington, D.C.: Gallaudet University Press.

Slobin, Dan I., Nini Hoiting, Marlon Kuntze, Reyna Lindert, Amy Weinberg, Jennie Pyers, Michelle Anthony, Yael Biederman & Helen Thumann. 2003. "A Cognitive/Functional Perspective on the Acquisition of 'Classifiers'". *Perspectives on Classifier Constructions in Sign Languages* ed. by Karen Emmorey, 271–298. Mahwah, N.J./London: Lawrence Erlbaum Associates.

Vermeerbergen, Myriam. 2001. "Simultane Constructies in de Vlaamse Gebarentaal". *Handelingen LIV (2000)* ed. by Rita Beyers, 69–81. Brussel: Koninklijke Zuid- Nederlandse Maatschappij voor Taal- en Letterkunde en Geschiedenis.

Appendix: Description of stimulus film

The stimulus film features a personified mouse, engaged in the activity of preparing a pancake. The mouse is seen from the back, facing a stove, with its arms and shoulders moving (still 1). The mouse then turns from the stove to face left, such that the viewer can see that it is holding a pan in which it has prepared the pancake (still 2). The mouse makes numerous attempts at flipping the pancake into the air to catch it in the pan that fail because the pancake lands on the floor some distance in front of the mouse instead. Each time, the mouse picks up the pancake and turns right to face the stove again to prepare a new pancake. In a last attempt, the mouse flips the pancake into the air (still 3) and then lunges forward to catch the pancake at the location it has landed previously, but the pancake lands on its head instead (still 4). Finally, the mouse calls its friend, the elephant, gives it a pan, and they flip the pancake back and forth between them (still 5). This sequence repeats three times.

Still 1   Still 2   Still 3   Still 4   Still 5

Still 1: mouse faces stove
Still 2: mouse turns 90° to left, holds pan with pancake in it
Still 3: mouse moves pan upward to flip pancake into air
Still 4: mouse lunges forward to catch pancake, pancake lands on head
Still 5: mouse and elephant flip pancake back and forth

Conceptual blending and the windowing of attention in simultaneous constructions in Irish Sign Language

Lorraine Leeson and John I. Saeed
School of Linguistic, Speech, and Communication Sciences, University of Dublin, Trinity College

1. Introduction

Simultaneity in signed languages has been described at the lexical, sub-lexical and syntactic level (see for example, Frishberg 1985; Miller 1994; Dudis 2002; Liddell 2003; Leeson & Saeed 2004; Janzen 2005). Recent work in a cognitive linguistic framework notes how simultaneity functions to maintain what have been called 'grounded blends' in Mental Space Theory (Fauconnier 1997). This theory seeks to show how linguistic structures lead speakers to set up mental referential models to represent entities and relations between them. Blends are spaces where speakers integrate elements from distinct cognitive models ('input spaces') to develop novel conceptualisations, often to create vividness and communicative force. Grounded blends, in particular, are blends of two or more mental spaces, where one of the spaces is 'Real Space', a person's representation of his or her actual surroundings; the 'here and now' of the communication. Although this too is of course a mental model, it is 'grounded' in the actual discourse by being perceptually accessible (Liddell 1995; Dudis 2002 for American Sign Language (ASL)). We shall discuss examples of grounded blends in Irish Sign Language (ISL) below.

Dudis (2002, 2004a) shows how ASL signers use simultaneous constructions involving the signer's hands and body (including eye-gaze) to create and maintain grounded blends. He reports that a signer's narrative goals interact with the physiological limits associated with articulation of a manually articulated language in affecting the construction and flow of a signed language narrative. He posits that in order to overcome such constraints, signers frequently establish simultaneous blends by assigning different body parts to separate blends, leading to a range of narrative strategies that signers can draw on. In this paper, we draw on Fauconnier's Mental Space Theory and the work on American Sign Language in this domain (Van Hoek 1996; Dudis 2002, 2004a; Liddell 2003) in considering how such blends are established and maintained in ISL narratives. We also draw on Leeson & Saeed (2004), who discuss how ISL signers window attention through the use of simultaneous constructions.

We note too the role that iconicity plays in establishing and maintaining blends. For example, certain spatial verbs in ASL can be modulated to represent iconically the signer's perspective of height relations in the real world (Lucas & Valli 1990; Dudis 2004b), while Janzen (2005) demonstrates that signers modulate discourse in order to convince their interlocutors to see the world from their point of view.

2.   The data

All examples in this paper are taken from two monologues. The first is a narrative delivered by a Deaf woman who is very active in the Irish Deaf Community, and who is aged 60+ years. In her monologue, she outlines her educational experiences from primary school, through to the experience of becoming a Fulbright Student; and talks about her career history in draftsmanship and television, and her voluntary work in the Irish Deaf Community.[1] For ease of reference, we call this the *My Educational and Career Experience* footage.

The second monologue was delivered by a Deaf man in his thirties. He is also a very active member of the Irish Deaf Community, and like the female signer, he has experience of presenting on Irish television in ISL. This piece was prepared as a current affairs narrative for an interpreting examination in 2003. It discusses the lead up to the war in Iraq and the strategic invasion by the 'coalition of the willing'. We refer to this as the *War in Iraq* footage.

The two narratives are very different in content and in the nature of simultaneous constructions that arise. The *War in Iraq* footage is typified by the extensive use of simultaneous constructions marking locative relations mapped onto topographical space, while *My Educational and Career Experiences* makes greater use of simultaneous constructions for listing purposes, or to mark reciprocal interactions (where the relative locations of participants are established).

---

1.   This video footage was collected by Michele Clapp, a Fulbright Student in the Centre for Deaf Studies, University of Dublin, Trinity College in 2004. This footage forms part of a Fulbright corpus of ISL and English language materials.

3.   Simultaneous constructions in ISL

The broad range of simultaneous constructions noted by Miller for Quebec Sign Language (LSQ) (1994) (and outlined earlier in this volume) have been identified as occurring in Irish Sign Language (Leeson 2001; Leeson & Saeed 2004). Other simultaneous structures such as 'buoys' discussed by Liddell (2003) for American Sign Language, and described for a range of other signed languages in this volume also occur in ISL. Example (1) shows a list buoy in ISL, which Liddell (ibid.: 223) reports are used to mark associations with a range of one to five entities.

(1)   INDEX+sl WEST WORLD
      dh: AMERICA ENGLAND u.k. LIST ALL-OF-THEM+sl
      nd: CL.5 (list)^2 -
      "The Western world, namely America, England – the UK. ….."

In example (1) from *War in Iraq*, the signer raises an open CL.5 handshape on his non-dominant hand, which seems to be in anticipation of the sign LIST, articulated on the dominant hand. For this sign, the index finger on the dominant hand interacts with the already established non-dominant CL.5 handshape. The non-dominant hand then remains active, seemingly an act of perseveration while the signer continues to sign ALL-OF-THEM+sl, which establishes a locus for the 'coalition of the willing' at side left of the signer's signing space. Thus, we can say that the signer has used simultaneity here in his discourse planning and further, that after the LIST sign has served its purpose, it perseveres for the remainder of this utterance. We can also say that this is an instance of an unordered set of entities (Liddell 2003: 224) insofar as the signer does not follow the numerical ordering (first, second, third, etc.) that is also possible to establish in ISL (Leeson 2001; Leeson & Saeed 2004).

   In the data that we report on here, fragment buoys, such as those described by Liddell (2003) for ASL, seem very common. Liddell describes fragment buoys as follows:

> When a one-handed sign follows a two-handed sign, it is common for the weak hand to maintain its configuration from the preceding two-handed sign as the strong hand produces the following one-handed sign. When this occurs, the weak hand is said to perseverate into the succeeding one-handed sign.   (ibid.: 248)

---

2.   In this paper, our glosses attempt to maintain consistency with respect to how signs have been glossed in the 'Signs of Ireland' corpus of ISL project. Here, we made the decision to list handshapes that are typically listed as 'classifier handshapes' in ISL, following McDonnell (1996: 91–109), even though the function of the handshape in this instance is to list items rather than classify them. Another reason is that there is a two-handed lexical sign for LIST in ISL and in glossing, we did not wish to confuse that lexicalized item with the form used here.

He goes on to note that while fragments do not normally appear to serve any semantic function, Dudis (2000), also describing these features in ASL, has distinguished between perseveration and situations where the signer does assign meaning to the fragment, creating a blend, a point that we return to again below. Example (2) shows another example of perseveration in ISL:

(2)   dh: BEFORE-THAT-POINT THAT c.s. DISABLED PEOPLE
       nd: BEFORE (CL.B.) -
       "Before then, disabled people. . ."

In example (2), from *My Educational and Career Experience*, the female signer signs BEFORE, a two handed sign where both the dominant and non-dominant hand take a 'B' handshape. She holds the non-dominant hand in space for the duration of this utterance, perhaps because (subconsciously) she knew that she was about to sign DISABLED, another two handed sign, where the non-dominant hand takes a CL.B handshape and is located at the same point in neutral space as for BEFORE. Thus, this non-dominant activity functions as a fragment buoy – it maintains the non-dominant handshape of the sign for BEFORE-THIS-POINT (cf. Liddell 2003), and at the same time, it also serves an anticipatory function, which, as we shall see, can also play a role at discourse level in terms of maintaining aspects of grounded blends in narratives (Dudis 2002). Before we turn our attention to blends, we need to consider briefly another cognitive linguistic concept, that of 'windowing of attention'.

4.   Windowing of attention

Talmy (1996) considers how a speaker focuses or 'windows' attention onto a certain portion of an event. He describes windowing as:

> the inclusion in a sentence of explicit material referring to the portion or portions of the total scene that are to be foregrounded, and the omission of material that would refer to the portion or portions of the scene intended for backgrounding.
> (1996: 236–237)

Talmy suggests that in any given speech act, only a certain portion of an event that is encoded is focused upon (i.e. only certain participants will be encoded and referred to). Depending on the lexicalisation patterns of the language, certain elements of a motion event are likely to be encoded (e.g. Figure and Ground, Motion and Manner, etc.) and the interlocutor will infer the totality of the event on the basis of what is windowed in the discourse. Talmy regards the 'windowed' portions of discourse as attentionally foregrounded and argues that a single scene can be windowed in many different ways. For example, he suggests that while one scene exists, a number of templates for viewing the event can be exploited by a speaker. In this way, windowing can be 'initial', 'medial' or 'final'. A scene may also have a section that is not windowed. Talmy refers to this as 'gapping', which can be described as data that has to be inferred from context or on the basis of prior knowledge. As a listener reconstructs the gapped path (i.e. the gapped data), she conceptualises what would be a complete path. Both windowing and gapping can be 'initial', 'medial' or 'final'.

Windowing differentiates between two types of material that is missing from a sentence:

– where the referent needs to be understood as belonging to the represented scene;
– where the referent is peripheral or incidental.

Writing from a related perspective, Shibitani (1985) has written that similar attentional strategies are used within the material present in the sentence, in decisions about which elements are foregrounded and backgrounded, in what is often called focus structure:

> All entities which correspond to the elements of a semantic frame or valence can be considered as focused to some extent. That is, they are singled out as essential elements, requiring the listener's attention in decoding the message: they are highlighted against the background of all other entities which may be in the consciousness of the speech-act participants, but are not semantically coded. These semantically coded entities are correlated with different degrees of importance; certain elements are more prominent than others, since they are most salient in the speaker's mind, and call for more attention on the part of the listener. (1985:832)

Leeson & Saeed (2004) note that simultaneous constructions play an important role in windowing and focusing in ISL, in particular in the representation of locative relations, where they focus attention on the activities of one entity with respect to another. Following Talmy (1996), they tentatively outline the characteristics of prototypical simultaneous constructions in ISL, suggesting that the features foregrounded, animacy and activity typically map into articulation on the dominant hand while the features backgrounded, inanimacy, and inactivity map into articulation on the non-dominant hand. They further note that prototypical windowing and focusing choices are subject to discourse processes. This is in line with Frishberg's (1985) suggestion that signers can manipulate dominance reversals (i.e. use the opposite hand than expected to produce a signed utterance) across narratives in order to create semantic connections or contrasts between elements within a narrative. She notes that what can appear in such contexts

(i) varies from utterance to utterance, (ii) is not dependent on the lexical identity of the signs, nor (iii) on some rigid assignment of dominance relations at the beginning of the narrative. (1985:83)

An example of where pragmatic or other discourse-related factors influence the assignment of the most active element to the non-dominant hand can be seen in example (3) below:

(3)   CL.B.-vehicle IN p.**r.³ STREET
    dh: **CAR** *CL.B. "vehicle"+be-located+sr* - - - - - - - -
    nd: **GIRL MAN**
    dh: *CL.B. "vehicle"+be-located+sr* -
    nd: *CL.Legs+trace-arc+sl+move-to+c.*
    "A car was coming up P*** Street when a person walked out (onto the street)." (Informant: female aged 45–55 years, deaf sibling/s and spouse: *Horizon* footage, Leeson 2001). (Example 12, Leeson & Saeed 2004:10).

Leeson & Saeed (ibid.) note that in this example, the signer introduces both of the constituents CAR and GIRL MAN ("person") before assigning them to loci in signing space that expresses their relative location to one another. We should note that the signer self corrects in this utterance: she first signs GIRL, then corrects by adding MAN, the intended item. Thus, she is clearly referring to an adult male who walks into the road – not two people as might otherwise be inferred from the gloss.

    What is most interesting in example (3) is the fact that the non-dominant hand represents the activities of the most animate element, the person who is knocked down, while the less animate entity, the car, is articulated on the dominant hand. On the face of it, this seems to contradict the general principles posited by Leeson & Saeed (2004) for simultaneous constructions, which see the semantic roles of Actor and Figure associated with the dominant hand and the roles of Undergoer and Ground with the non-dominant hand. However, they note that in the extended discourse, higher-level pragmatic principles such as topic identification and maintenance may overrule the default principles. In the wider context of this example it becomes clear that the driver of the car in this example is the narrator's husband and his journey in the car is the topic of the narrative.

    We also note that real world locations are mapped onto signing space in this example: in Ireland, people drive on the left hand side of the road. Here the signer establishes the car in a location that is isomorphically commensurate with the location a vehicle would be in from the perspective of a bystander on the pavement nearest the car: that is, the signer perspective at this point in the discourse seems to

---

3.   Fingerspelling in this clip is not clear. '*' represents items that are not discernible on the VHS tape.

be that of a bystander on the pavement where the vehicles closest to the signer are those travelling in the left hand lane. Furthest away from the signer is the location that would be commensurate with vehicles travelling in the right hand lane. The car in example (3) is moving leftwards. The location of the phone box is on the same plane as the signer perspective, but further along the mapped road, still on the left hand side. Thus, we have an instance of topographical mapping (for example, see Sutton-Spence & Woll 1999 for a discussion of topographical and syntactic space in British Sign Language), which as we shall see in later examples, is frequent in establishing blends in ISL.

However, generally speaking, the principle of most animate, more foregrounded data occurring on the dominant hand holds for ISL signers, as we will see later. In the next sections we examine the role of simultaneity in the construction of conceptual blends, before returning briefly in Section 7 to this question of the relationship between dominant and non-dominant hands in simultaneous constructions.

5.   Mapping thought and language: Mental spaces

Fauconnier's (1997) Mental Spaces Theory is a cognitive semantic theory that began by describing the complexity of referential strategies (indirect reference, shifts of reference, referential opacity etc.) that occur in ordinary spontaneous communication. The theory does this in terms of mental models, or spaces, that communicators mutually create and manipulate. These spaces contain representations of entities and relations currently under discussion. New spaces are created, for example, when speakers talk about hypothetical scenarios or events in the past. Such spaces have their internal coherence, but are also linked to other spaces, including a link to the present utterance space, by various linguistic devices. Although the referential strategies are triggered by language, Fauconnier identifies a range of cognitive processes that are used to 'flesh out' the under-represented meaning that the language input provides. The theory has been extended to describe a wide range of behaviour in spoken and signed languages. As the theory has developed, a number of cognitive processes have been identified in the use of such spaces, including: partitioning, analogy, schema induction, structure projection, and conceptual blending.

All of these processes take place within the general processes of meaning construction. Fauconnier argues that 'language expressions' (E) possess a 'meaning potential'. As discourse unfolds, complex cognitive processes are called into play. An expression thus generates meaning:

> when the grammatical information E contains is applied to an existing cognitive configuration, several new configurations will be possible in principle (i.e. comparable with the grammatical clues). One of them will be produced, yielding a new step in the construction underlying the discourse.   (1997:38)

Fauconnier sees this as a process in which unfolding discourse is a "succession of cognitive configurations" (1997:38). He argues that each successive cognitive configuration gives rise to the next under pressure from grammar and context: that is, both grammar and the unfolding context affect the interpretation of a linguistic event. Pragmatic factors may also affect the establishment of a new configuration. He argues that as discourse unfolds, the discourse participants metaphorically move through the 'space lattice', that is, the series of connected spaces that are established to represent the base viewpoint, conditional/ hypothetical events, temporal variations, etc., referred to in discourse. Discourse participants' viewpoints and focus shift as they move through the space lattice while the base space remains accessible as a starting point for another construction. To allow discourse participants to find their way through this 'maze of mental spaces', and to use the partitioning of the spaces to draw appropriate inferences, Fauconnier argues that three dynamic notions are crucial: Base. Viewpoint and Focus:

> At any point in the construction, one space is distinguished as Viewpoint, the space from which others are accessed and structured or set up; one space is distinguished as Focus, the space currently being structured internally, – the space, so to speak, upon which attention is currently focused; and one space is distinguished as the Base – a starting point for the construction of which it is always possible to return. Base, Viewpoint and Focus need not be distinct: more often than not, we find the same space serving as Viewpoint and Focus, or Base and Focus, or Base and Viewpoint, or all three: Base, Viewpoint and Focus.   (1997:49)

While he uses a slightly different vocabulary, Fauconnier's ideas are clearly compatible with those of Talmy and Shibitani as discussed above. All consider focus and viewpoint as crucial in the encoding of linguistic events, and previous work on simultaneity in ISL has demonstrated that simultaneous constructions embed the windowing of attention in ISL narratives (Leeson & Saeed 2004).

Dudis (2002) discusses a range of grounded blends in ASL where, across a discourse, interlocutors have access to a base space that has been established by the signer. One example relates to a hunter's encounter with a deer, where the hunter and the deer are two elements that compose the base space, while use of the plain verb HUNT adds a hunting frame to the mental space. Dudis describes in detail how the signer creates a grounded blend when, without need to explain to his audience what he is doing:

> the base-space element **h** *hunter* is mapped onto the signer, resulting in a visible blended element, the |hunter|. The audience understands the head tilt, eye gaze

and hand configurations to be the |hunter|'s. The blended element |hunter| exists only in the blend. It is distinct from the signer in Real Space and from the element **h** *hunte*r in the base space.   (2002:59)[4]

Dudis goes on to describe how the audience, without any explicit mention of it by the signer, understands that a weapon is involved in the blend on the basis of the information given by the signer, coupled with their understanding of the hunting frame.

So mappings can occur between base spaces and Real Space, mapped onto the physical world or onto the signer's body, encoded partially or inferred via the interlocutor's access to a base frame that suggests the range of likely or possible actions associated with that frame (e.g. the hunting frame entails use of a weapon, a hunter and something that is hunted).

A key aspect of retrievability in such narratives is that of accessibility. Van Hoek (1996) looks at the relationship that exists between mental spaces and referential loci in ASL. She argues that the most salient referents are accessed even where other loci have previously been used for pronominal reference for the same referent. Van Hoek assumes that:

> loci may vary in their imagistic content; in one discourse (or at one moment in a particular discourse) a locus may be conceived as a detailed, highly specific mental image of the referent, and in another discourse (or at another point in time) may be a highly schematised, non-specific image – which includes the possibility that the image may consist of an association between the referent and the point in space, with no other visual-imagistic content.   (1996:234)

She goes on to develop her concept of the relationship between referents and loci by arguing that:

> these quasi-imagistic associations between referents and loci may involve much more than simply the establishment of the referent, as an isolated notion, with a particular point in space. Referential loci are frequently associated with the larger 'scenes' or spatial settings which the referent occupies.   (1996:234)

Van Hoek notes that this viewpoint is 'roughly equivalent' to Liddell's observations (1990; 1995). Liddell notes that, in ASL, instead of a locus being associated with a referent, it represents the referent's conceived location. This, claims Van Hoek, is relevant for the application of Mental Spaces Theory (Fauconnier 1985), as briefly outlined above. Indeed, Fauconnier (1997) makes reference to Liddell's work, noting that his findings support the cognitive validity of Mental Spaces as a theory.

---

4.   In the representation used here vertical line brackets enclose entities in a blended space.

Van Hoek's work aims to establish that there is a relationship between mental spaces and referential loci. She provides evidence which supports the view that the most salient referents in a discourse event are accessed even where other loci have previously been used for the same pronominal referent. She suggests that the principles of locus selection in ASL seem congruent with the general principles of accessibility that have been developed by Givón (1989) and Ariel (1988, 1990). She says that:

> Accessibility Theory holds that a particular nominal form is selected for reference in a given context to reflect the degree of accessibility (roughly 'retrievability') of the referent in that context. Cross-linguistically, full nominals (names and descriptive phrases) are markers of relatively low accessibility, used where the referent is not highly active in the addressee's awareness. Pronouns are markers of relatively high accessibility and null anaphora (i.e. no phonological marking of co-reference) marks still higher accessibility.   (1996: 337)

It is possible that this last point plays some role in the fact that fluent signers can distinguish between c. locus as first person and c. locus as non-specified agent in discourse (see Leeson & Saeed 2003 for discussion of passives in ISL). Similarly, as noted by Van Hoek, in passive constructions the patient is the most highly activated referent in both the signer's and the addressee's awareness, licensing the signer's use of constructions with little or no attention focused on the agent. As such, we can agree with Van Hoek's claim that:

> Accessibility is essentially a matter of how 'active' a referent is in a conceptualiser's awareness. It is influenced by salience, both perceptual and conceptual.
>
> (1996: 338)

In the following section, we look at how conceptual blends are created using simultaneous constructions in ISL.

6. Conceptual blends in ISL

The *War in Iraq* narrative was prepared as a current affairs narrative. In this piece the signer establishes the discourse topic at the outset and establishes the historical context to this war, clearly establishing, in example (4) a base space for Iraq, which he then locates in neutral signing space. From here on in, he is going to relate different sections of the country to security operations. He discusses how the northern sector of Iraq was deemed a no-fly zone. He establishes this in the bolded utterances below. Here he uses a baby-C handshape to mark the relative part of Iraq where planes are not allowed to fly. This baby-C is superimposed on the non-dominant CL.B. handshape which serves to represent the entire country of Iraq. In addition to being a structure that illustrates relative location, there is an iconic

relation: the baby-C handshape is mapping out the real-world geographical terri-
tory that was designated a no-fly zone by the UN, and creates a grounded blend,
drawing on the previously established referential locus assigned to Iraq (CL.B.).
There is the added specificity of the information about where the no-fly zone is in
relation to Iraq's geographical spread. So, we can say that in this case, the simultaneous construction does not serve to mark the relative location of two elements
but instead, allows for a backgrounding-foregrounding contrast between the areas
in Iraq which could be accessed by aircraft.

(4)
dh: INDEX+f i.r.a.q.
nd: CL.5+c
dh: CL.B 'THAT-AREA'
nd: CL.B.- - - - - - - - -
dh: HAVE u.n. u.n.i.t.e.d. n.a.t.i.o.n.s. INDEX+sl DECIDE TAKE k.u.w.a.i.t.
nd: CL.B.- - - - - - - - - - - -
dh: CL.B.- - - - - - - - - - - - - - - - -
nd: CL.B + AREA-TO-NORTH i.r.a.q.
dh: CL.B. 'FURTHER-NORTH' NORTH INDEX+trace-arc-over'Iraq'
nd: CL.B- -
dh: NOT-ALLOW FLY-AIRPLANE INDEX+f NAME QUOTE[5] NO FLY
nd: CL.B- -
dh: **z.o.n.e.** CL.B+touch-n.d.hand NOT-ALLOW AIRPLANE FLY-OVER WOF[6]
nd: CL.B.- -
                                     hs
dh: INDEX+f sl+PLANE-FLY+sr
nd: CL.B

                                                    _____ hs
dh: ONLY CL.Baby-C.+be-located-at-centre-of (nd)   c+PLANE-FLY+sl
nd: CL.B.- -
dh: sl+PLANE-FLY+sr
nd: CL.B.- - - - - - - -
     "The United Nations (UN) decided to take Kuwait. The area to the north of
     Iraq was designated a no fly zone, meaning that it was forbidden for aircraft
     to enter into the specified region"

---

5. QUOTE is a two-handed sign. Thus, the signer here drops the perseveration to engage in
articulating this sign.

6. WOF is typically used by female signers (Leeson & Grehan 2004) and is typically used to
modify a noun. It means that something is forbidden or that it would be crazy to do a certain
thing. It is interesting that this male signer in his 30s is using WOF in the same sense, (and we
note anecdotally, others in their 30s and early 40s), suggesting that some female signs may be
entering more general ISL usage.

Example (5) is another instance of the signer using a simultaneous construction to create a grounded blend, very similar in nature to that in example (4) above. Here, the signer makes use of what has been called topographical space (Sutton-Spence & Woll 1999): the relative locations of Iraq and Kuwait are mapped onto signing space. The non-dominant hand marks the geographical area that represents Iraq's locative position, while the dominant hand indicates the relative positioning of Kuwait vis-à-vis Iraq.

(5) dh: i.r.a.q. Cl.B+touch-n.d.-hand
     nd: CL.C - - - - - - - - - - - - - - -
     dh. Cl.B+ CIRCLE (small)-ON-MAP-AT-SOUTH-OF-LOC
     nd: CL.C -
     dh: INDEX+ at-bottom-of-Cl.C.(knuckle of thumb)
     nd: CL.C -
     dh: k.u.w.a.i.t. INDEX+f
     nd: CL.C   CL.C+f
     dh: 'GRABBED' NOW TAKE-OVER
     "Kuwait is located to the south of Iraq. Iraq took Kuwait. . ."

The next two examples also demonstrate simultaneity being used to establish relative location. The first part of example (6) sets the scene, locating again the geographical location of Kuwait relative to the location for Iraq, which is represented here on the non-dominant hand by the CL.C. handshape, holding Iraq's location firm. The signer explains that the invading forces wished to move on Iraq from the south (i.e. troops would march northwards, from Kuwait, into Iraq). The signer goes on to note that the invading forces also wished to move simultaneously, from the north, through Turkey, moving southwards into Iraq. The bolded segments indicate the relevant areas of text establishing these notions.

Here, several things are happening:

1. The signer establishes locative relationships (where Turkey and Kuwait are positioned relative to Iraq).

2. The signer builds on the fact that the location of Iraq is active for interlocutors when it comes to expressing the proposed simultaneous invasion of Iraq from the north and south. Thus, the non-dominant hand does not even need to maintain an explicit reference to Iraq. While we can say that Iraq is currently gapped insofar as it is not explicitly referenced, pragmatically it is active as a discourse topic.

3. In this example, the simultaneous nature of the invasion is expressed simultaneously in ISL. The signer maps the invading forces onto the loci previously established for Turkey and Kuwait, again using topographical space to locate the relative locations of these countries. The facing of the fingertips in the CL5+open classifier demonstrates a movement away from Turkey/Kuwait, to-

wards a central locus, that of Iraq. The movement of this classifier ends at the locus for Iraq.

4. There is iconicity encoded in the relative locations of Turkey, Iraq and Kuwait. The signer maps real world relative locations onto signing space, creating a conceptually complex representation.

5. There is a blending of spaces involving locations and entities in the real world, a projected map of these, and elements of the signer's real space. The signer uses parts of his body to represent entities moving around the war zone, while his eye gaze is directed towards the projected map, representing the viewpoint of the signer himself as narrator/viewer of the events.

(6) dh: SO PLAN FIRM WAR SHRUG
     dh: u.n. INSPECTOR EXAMINE ++
     dh: INDEX+various-locations+sr FOR WEAPONS EXAMINE SHRUG
     dh: HAVE-TO LEAVE   sr.+FLY-OUT-OF+sl   OUT-OF i.r.a.q.
     nd: CL.B - - - - - - - - - -
     dh: SAME TIME BEFORE-THAT-TIME AMERICA PLAN WANT WAR
     dh: INDEX+sr
     dh: INDEX+trace-circular-path-at-c.
     nd: INDEX+f
     dh: AREA AROUND k.u.w.a.i.t. 2/h CL.5+OPEN 'MANY-MOVE-NORTH'
     nd: CL.B - - - - - - - -
     dh: ALSO WANT TURKEY
     dh: t.u.r.k.e.y. CL.B+MOVE-FROM-NORTH-TOWARDS-SOUTH
     nd: CL.B+MOVE-FROM-SOUTH-TOWARDS-NORTH
     dh:
     nd: CL.B-BENT sl+'MOVE-IN-FROM'+c
     dh: c+ASK+sl TURKEY PERMISSION ASK 2/h c+ASK+sl

     "And so the war was planned. The UN inspectors who were in Iraq to search for weapons (of mass destruction) had to leave Iraq. At the same time, America was planning what they wanted in terms of a war plan. Specifically, they intended to move north from Kuwait and, at the same time, move south from Turkey, but in order to do this, they needed to get permission from the Turks."

In the next example, the signer continues to draw on the locative relations that he has established. He re-activates Kuwait, foregrounding the location for further discussion (in an instance of topicalisation) and again, represents the simultaneous invasion of Iraq (still considered active at the central locus) from north and south by many invaders (MANY-MOVE-FROM-POINT-IN-SOUTH-TOWARDS-NORTH).

(7)   dh: ASK PERMISSION TURKEY   INDEX+sl
      nd: CL.Baby-C
      dh: TURKEY SHRUG EXTRA
      nd: INDEX+sr
      dh: IF LET ACCESS u.k.
      dh: i.r.a.q.   Baby-C+c TURKEY
      nd: CL.C.+c - - - - - - - -
      dh: CL.S. 'BORDER'-at-north-of-nd hand INDEX+north-of-nd-hand
      nd: CL.C.+c -
      dh: k.u.w.a.i.t. (articulated-at-south-of-nd-hand) TIDY
      nd: CL.C -
      dh: MANY-MOVE-FROM-POINT-IN-NORTH-TOWARDS-SOUTH
      nd: MANY-MOVE-FROM-POINT-IN-SOUTH-TOWARDS-NORTH
      dh: INDEX+sl TURKEY SHRUG c+ASK+f PERMISSION GOVERNMENT
      dh: PARLIAMENT/ASSEMBLY
      "Turkey was asked for permission to let the UK access (Iraq) via their borders.
      If they gave this access, the invasion would be a very tidy affair, allowing for
      simultaneous invasion from the north and south (of Iraq) (via Turkey to the
      north and Kuwait to the south). And so the Turkish government's permission
      was sought."

7.   The role of the non-dominant hand in simultaneous constructions in ISL

Earlier we noted that Leeson & Saeed (2004) suggested a general principle that
items articulated on the non-dominant hand are typically less animate and are
more backgrounded while the dominant hand articulates more animate and more
foregrounded items. At present it is not possible to state with accuracy exactly how
frequently these exceptions operate in ISL narratives. However, we are currently in
the process of transcribing a corpus of ISL using ELAN, which will allow us to
systematically review the frequency of such structures. However, while the general
principle posited broadly holds, we can summarize circumstances where this does
not seem to be the case:

1.   Where the signer's decisions reflect discourse dynamism (as in example (3)
     earlier).
2.   Where real world location is mapped onto signing space (example (3) also
     illustrates this phenomena).
3.   Where the topic is articulated on the dominant hand and the comment is
     articulated on the non-dominant hand (as in example (8) below).
4.   In situations where the motion events are reciprocal and/or simultaneous in
     nature.

(8) KNOW THAT NOW TYPE COMPUTER DIFFERENT
     THAT TIME

                    ‘a’ ‘b’ ‘c’ ‘d’

dh: TYPE
nd: a.b.c.d.
dh: CL.5 -
nd: TOUCH-TIP-OF-FINGERS-ON-d.h RED

                                  ee
_____
2/h Baby-O-touching-at-fingertips

In the above example from *My Educational and Career Experience*, the signer is discussing learning to type. She makes a point of comparison between the physical pressure of typing on an 'old fashioned' typewriter as opposed to a modern computer. On the dominant hand she signs TYPE, while on the non-dominant hand she specifies what was being typed – in this case, the letters of the alphabet. Interestingly, her mouthing links in with the articulation of the non-dominant hand rather than mouthing 'type', which we might expect, as TYPE is articulated on the dominant hand. This suggests that this is an instance of dominance reversal rather than an instance of the signer mouthing in conjunction with the articulations on the non-dominant hand. Evidence to support this view includes the fact that the fine motor movements needed to fingerspell items is typical of dominant hand activity rather than non-dominant hand activity, suggesting that phonological articulatory constraints may play a role in constraining what can or cannot occur on dominant/ non-dominant hands in simultaneous constructions.[7]

In the next example we see the female signer discussing how her bosses solved the problem of her not being able to use the telephone in her first job:

(9) . . . f+PICK+c ME THUMBS-UP

     dh: BUT   SAY HAVE ONE PROBLEM WITH TELEPHONE
     nd: INDEX
     BUT NOT WORRY
     SEE NEW YOUNG BOY TRAIN INDEX +sl
     dh: JOB IS ANSWER MY TELEPHONE
     nd: INDEX+sl - - - - - - - - - - - - - - - -
     dh: PUT-TELEPHONE-IN-CRADLE sl+GIVE+c ME   MESSAGE
     nd: INDEX+sl -
     dh: THEN C+TELL+sl
     nd: INDEX +sl

_____

7. Many thanks to Rachel Sutton-Spence for her comments on this example.

dh: WHAT c+TELL+f sl+INDEX-TO+sr
nd: INDEX+sl - - - - - - - - - - - -
dh: sr+INDEX-TO+sl
nd: INDEX+sl

"... They chose me, which was great. But I said that I'd have just one problem – that of using the telephone. They said not to worry about that as they would assign a young boy whose job it would be to answer my phone. So if someone called, he gave me the message and then I'd tell him what to say to the callers..."

We see that the signer allocates a locus (side left) to the young boy, then, with her non-dominant hand, she maintains reference to his presence throughout the subsequent description of how the telephone calls were managed. His role is backgrounded by the fact that he is not explicitly referred to again, but more importantly, because his role contrasts with that of the signer's: she is the woman who is doing the job while he is her assistant. She is the primary actor, and here this is reinforced by her actions being associated with c. locus, while his actions are secondary. If the signer had wished to foreground his role further, she had the option of reference shifting towards his locus in order to 'become' him and enact how he facilitated the telephone conversations, but she chose not to do so here. Instead, she reinforces the fact that her role is foregrounded while his role is backgrounded through the simultaneous discourse structures that she chooses.

8. Summary

We have drawn on examples of simultaneous constructions from two ISL signers, which reinforce the claim made in Leeson & Saeed (2004) that the windowing of attention is mediated by dominant and non-dominant hand functionality in ISL. We have noted that simultaneous constructions operate at several linguistic and cognitive levels. Firstly we have noted the existence of buoys, which may be considered a phonetic feature of the communication; secondly, we have seen that simultaneity is used to mark information structure and discourse prominence relations, including: listing, topic and focus partitioning, and narrative dynamism. Thirdly, we have seen that simultaneity is essential to the creation of grounded blends. In the *War in Iraq* narrative, for example, the signer's hands simultaneously represent armies moving from different directions across a projected map, while his gaze and bodily orientation reflect the signer/narrator's viewpoint as he packages or 'windows' events for his audience. With these functions, simultaneity is revealed to be essential to the signer's construction of ISL discourse.

References

Ariel, Mira. 1988. "Referring and Accessibility". *Journal of Linguistics* 24.65–87.
——. 1990. *Accessing Noun-Phrase Antecedents.* London: Routledge.
Dudis, Paul. 2000. "Tokens as Abstract Visible Elements". Paper presented at the Conceptual Structures in Discourse and Language 5 Conference. University of California, Santa Barbara. May 11–14, 2000.
——. 2002. "Grounded Blend Maintenance as a Discourse Strategy". *Turntaking, Fingerspelling, and Contact in Signed Languages: Sociolinguistics in Deaf Communities Volume 7* ed. by Ceil Lucas, 53–72. Washington, D.C.: Gallaudet University Press.
——. 2004a. "Body Partitioning and Real-Space Blends". *Cognitive Linguistics* 15:2.223–38.
——. 2004b. "Signer Perspective in American Sign Language". *Deaf Worlds* 20:3.217–227.
Fauconnier, Gilles. 1985. *Mental Spaces.* Cambridge, Mass.: MIT Press.
——. 1997. *Mappings in Thought and Language.* Cambridge: Cambridge University Press.
Frishberg, Nancy. 1985. "Dominance Relations and Discourse Structures". *Proceedings of the IIIrd International Symposium on Sign Language Research. Rome, June 22–26, 1983* ed. by William C. Stokoe & Volterra, 79–90. Silver Spring, Maryland: Linstok Press and Rome: Istituto di Psicologia CNR.
Givón, Talmy. 1989. *Mind, Code and Context.* London: Lawrence Erlbaum Associates.
Janzen, Terry. 2005. *Perspective Shift Reflected in the Signer's Use of Space. CDS/CLCS Monograph Number 1.* Dublin: Centre for Deaf Studies, University of Dublin, Trinity College.
Leeson, Lorraine. 2001. *Aspects of Verbal Valency in Irish Sign Language.* Doctoral dissertation. Centre for Language and Communication Studies, University of Dublin, Trinity College.
—— & Carmel Grehan. 2004. "To the Lexicon and Beyond: The Effect of Gender on Variation in Irish Sign Language" *To the Lexicon and Beyond: Sociolinguistics in European Deaf Communities* ed. by Mieke Van Herreweghe and Myriam Vermeerbergen, 39–73. Washington D.C.: Gallaudet University Press.
—— & John I. Saeed. 2003. "Exploring the Cognitive Underpinning in the Construal of Passive Events in Irish Sign Language (ISL)". Paper presented at the 8th International Cognitive Linguistics Association Conference, Spain, July 2003.
—— & John I. Saeed. 2004. "Windowing of Attention in Simultaneous Constructions in Irish Sign Language". *Proceedings of the Fifth High Desert Linguistics Conference, 1–2 November 2002, Albuquerque, University of New Mexico,* ed. by Terry Cameron, Christopher Shank & Keri Holley, 1–18. University of New Mexico.
Liddell, Scott K. 1995. "Real, Surrogate, and Token Space: Grammatical Consequences in ASL". *Language Gesture and Space* ed. by Karen Emmorey & Judy Reilly, 19–41. Hillsdale, N.J.: Lawrence Erlbraum Associates.
——. 2003. *Grammar, Gesture, and Meaning in American Sign Language.* Cambridge: Cambridge University Press.
Lucas, Ceil & Clayton Valli. 1990. "Predicates of Perceived Motion in ASL". *Theoretical Issues in Sign Language Research, Volume 1: Linguistics* ed. by Susan Fischer & Patricia Siple, 153–166. Chicago: The University of Chicago Press.
McDonnell, Patrick. 1996. *Verb Categories in Irish Sign Language.* Doctoral dissertation. Centre for Language and Communication Studies, University of Dublin, Trinity College.
Miller, Chris. 1994. "Simultaneous Constructions in Quebec Sign Language". *Word Order Issues in Sign Language. Working Papers* ed. by Mary Brennan & Graham H. Turner, 89–112. Durham: International Sign Linguistics Association.

Shibitani, Masayoshi. 1985. "Passives and Related Constructions: A Prototype Analysis". *Language* 61:4.821–848.

Sutton-Spence, Rachel & Bencie Woll. 1999. *The Linguistics of British Sign Language: An Introduction*. Cambridge: Cambridge University Press.

Talmy, Leonard. 1996. "The Windowing of Attention in Language". *Grammatical Constructions. Their Form and Meaning* ed. by Masayoshi Shibitani & Sandra A. Thompson, 235–287. Oxford: Clarendon Press.

Van Hoek, K. 1996: Conceptual Locations for Reference in American Sign Language. *Spaces, Worlds and Grammar* ed. by Gilles Fauconnier & Eve Sweetser, 334–351. Chicago & London: The University of Chicago Press.

A cognitive linguistic view of simultaneity in process signs in French Sign Language

Annie Risler

UMR 8163 du CNRS "Savoirs, textes, Langage" – Université Lille 3

1. Approach to simultaneity

French Sign Language (LSF) is expressed in space, with signs arranged in a non-linear way in signing space and across time. LSF's morphosyntactic markers are based on both the spatial arrangement of the elements and on their sequencing. From this point of view, the signs that express processes (events and actions) constitute a type of fundamental unit in the construction of the signing space. Both the spatial relations and the movements of signs evoke the events described. As such, these signs are iconic because the space is constructed relative to the organisation of elements in the universe of reference (Peirce 1978). Cuxac (1996, 2000), who was the first to describe these signs in LSF, called them 'structures de grande iconicité' (SGI, highly iconic signs); e.g. 'transfert personnel' (personal transfer), 'transfert situationnel' (situational transfer), 'transfert de forme' (transfer of form), 'double transfer', 'semi-transfer', etc. (see also Sallandre, this volume).

These highly iconic signs (SGI) allow the speaker to 'say by showing' and they stand in opposition to standard signs (sometimes called established signs), which 'say without showing'. The speaker chooses the type of sign she employs as a function of her message. Such an approach makes the iconicity of the language the central focus of any analysis. In this approach, Sallandre (2003 and this volume) identifies 24 different categories of highly iconic signs. Each SGI is considered a global, multiparametric unit, because not only the hands, but the entire upper body is involved: arms, shoulders, chest, head, eyes, and mimicry.

My own work finds considerable support for the central role played by iconicity and by the simultaneity of different parameters. However, I propose a more functional approach here, which takes the special relations constructed by process signs and the space surrounding them as a point of departure, and attempt to define the link between the various constituents of the verbal sign and the syntactic relations expressed. In so doing, I undertake to identify the morphological components of the sign.

If we consider the process sign as a single unit, its meaning results from the simultaneous combination of variables relevant from physical shape, type of movement and spatial relations. Spatial relations are expressed as much by the movement of the hands, the torso, the head, shoulders and eye-gaze.

Readers should note that in the examples listed in this paper, the phrase in single quotation marks is an approximate translation of the meaning expressed by the process sign.

(1)   'He (a horse) gallops.'

The example in (1) is a process sign, where we see, in terms of morphology, the following aspects.

–   A physical shape: a handshape depicting the horse's legs and the ground. In other words we see an anaphoric representation of the entity expressed by a partial representation of its shape, as well as an anaphoric representation of the place of movement through the formal representation of its surface.
–   A trajectory from the dominant hand, indicating movement along a surface.
–   An internal movement of the fingers from the dominant hand.
–   A type of movement: repetitive double movement of the dominant hand along the non-dominant forearm, marking durational aspect.
–   Spatial relations between the two handshapes and the body, identifying the moving entity and the landmark.
–   Spatial location: the hands are raised very high on the signer's right side. In other words, the action is situated at a significant subspace, or locus, which refers to the horse's meadow. This locus can be looked at and referred to by indexing, and handshapes can be placed at the locus to express anaphoric reference to the horse.

In short, this sign expresses an entity's movement (path and manner) along a base in a defined space (the horse gallops in his field).

Each iconic parameter has a morphological value based on the shape of the different articulators: the hands, the torso, eye-gaze, and facial expression. For example, a particular handshape involved in a sign as a phonemic parameter can have an anaphoric value when the signer looks at it. The combination of different morphological parameters leads to a spatial representation of a specific meaning related to the process predicate. As a result, any change in the form of the process sign leads to corresponding semantic variation.

I distinguish the following levels:

– An articulatory level: hands, torso, head, eye-gaze;
– A morphemic level: shape, type of movement, location, spatial relations, etc.;
– A syntactico-semantic level: the combination of iconic morphemic variables.

We absolutely cannot attribute a semantic value to any one articulatory or morphological parameter in isolation. Each process sign corresponds to a certain syntactic structure with respect to its component parts. The morphemic arrangement is in a diagrammatic iconic link with the corresponding semantic representation.

The systematic decomposition of all the processes in a narrative text reveals the existence of two types of syntactic constructions. First, there are single predicates (cf. example (1)) where the simultaneity brings to light a complex composition linked to a single predicate. Such structures are often called 'classifier constructions' (see Emmorey (2003) for a recent collection of papers on these constructions). Second, there are complex syntactic structures in which several simultaneous predicates can be found, as in the next example, illustrated in (2).

(2) 'With surprise (the bird) watches the horse moving away.'

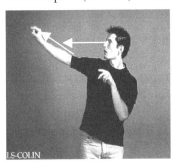

Two movements can be identified: (1) the trajectory of the right hand, moving away to the right of the signer; and (2) the movement of the head with accompanying mimicry (growing surprise) along with the signer's eye-gaze, which follows his right hand.

These two movements correspond to two processes expressed simultaneously. The first process (*the horse moving away from the bird*) is expressed by the right hand (at the locus for the horse's field) moving away from the chest, and by the left hand remaining in place, representing the bird. The second process (*the bird watches him with surprise*) is expressed by the facial activity and the eye-gaze of the signer, which follows his right hand.

There are two types of simultaneity. First, there is morphemic simultaneity, in which all process signs are the result of simultaneously combining the parameters of shape, movement and spatial relations. The second type is syntactic simultaneity: syntactic decomposition sometimes gives rise to two simultaneous movements, identifiable as two simultaneous predicative signs. These may be two process signs, or a process sign and an expression of 'enunciative modality' (cf. the '*théorie de l'énonciation*' of Culioli 1990).

In the first instance, I consider process signs and then explain how I break down process signs, showing that the iconicity of the sign allows me to uncover an archetypal formalisation related to meaning and cognition. I will attempt to describe a network of interdependence among the different parameters comprising such signs.

Secondly, I focus on the roles played by syntactic simultaneity, and demonstrate how simultaneity and sequentiality, the two components of syntax, combine to form complex syntactic structures.

2.   The corpus

The corpus consists of texts taken from a French Sign Language corpus called LS-Colin (see also Sallandre, this volume). This corpus is the result of interdisciplinary research (linguistic, IT and image processing) carried out from 2000 to 2002 and financed by the Ministry of Research as part of the '*Cognitique 2000; Langage et Cognition*' project. The corpus is a collection of texts from 12 signers. The texts come from several types of spontaneous discourse tasks: retelling of a story based on pictures, relating one's life story, discussion of current affairs, and explanation of a recipe. After a short preparation period, the signers were filmed with 3 cameras (shot with a medium shot, with a close-up on the face, and shot from above). They were addressing a deaf interlocutor located next to one of the cameras.

For the purposes of this study I chose one of the narrative texts, ANT-CHEV1, signed by a male native signer aged 20–30.[1] A brief summary of the story is as follows. 'A horse is bored in its meadow. It decides to jump the fence to join a cow in the next field. Unfortunately, when jumping the fence, the horse hurts its leg.

---

1.   The photos in this paper are taken from the LS-Colin corpus. The complete story can be viewed on the CD-Rom accompanying this volume.

A bird, who saw what happened, goes to get a first-aid kit, and gives it to the cow. The cow then attends to the leg of the poor horse.'

This recording was transcribed by myself and was then evaluated and approved by the signer involved.

3.   Structure of process signs

3.1 Signs which construct syntactic space

From the data we can isolate two very different types of signs: (1) nominal signs (i.e. signs expressing nouns) and (2) relator signs.[2] Nominal signs can be seen as producing a frozen image. Their function is to create reference and they are produced in citation form. Their component parts are motivated but do not have any morphemic value. In contrast, the function of relators is to establish syntactic relationships in space. A relational or syntactic relationship results from their movements and positions in space. For relator signs, certain component parts endow the status of anaphoric morpheme.

Eye-gaze is very important for determining the status of a sign: the signer looks at her interlocutor during the articulation of a nominal sign, but she glances at the signing space at least once during the production of a relator sign. In the latter, the eye-gaze reinforces or anticipates a spatial construction. For example, the lexical sign [SUN][3] is usually described as the movement of the hand with respect to the body (this is iconically motivated as *'spherical light above one's head'*). If [SUN] has nominal sign status, the body is not seen as representing the body of a specific individual, but rather it highlights a particular feature. However, the sign may be accorded relator status. Now, the signer represents a character in the story (indicated by altering the position of her head-and-shoulders [editors note: in a manner described as 'role shift' or 'reference shift' in other traditions] and looking at her moving hand or at the signing space). [sun] is signed slowly and in an exaggerated way, emphasising the action being carried out. In this way, a relationship is established between the signer's body as the body of a specific character and the location of the entity. Following from this, the sign is no longer articulated in citation form; instead, it is integrated into a spatial-temporal reference framework, simultaneously indicating a relationship based on location and a change of state

---

2.   Risler (1998, 2003) offers a comparative study of the iconic origin of signs and the ontologic distinction of nouns and verbs based on Langacker (1987).

3.   In this chapter nominal signs are written in small capitals while lower case is used for relation signs.

over the duration of the sign. As such it is a relator sign, constructing a relational space where the different points in space participate in a syntactic construction.

French Sign Language involves movement of various physical components including the hands, the chest and the face. As a result, any relational movement made outside the neutral signing space[4] suggests a relator sign, regardless of whether the movement concerns one or both hands or the upper body, or whether the eye-gaze is directed at a particular point in space. The category of relator signs essentially involves process signs and pointing signs.

Our basic hypothesis (discussed in Risler & Lejeune 2004) is that process signs carry the trace of the linguistic representations they support. There is a diagrammatic iconic rapport between the movement and the form of the process signs and the predicative schemes they encode. The iconic relation is situated in the traced path of the relator signs and the underlying predicative archetype. This does not imply a gestural representation of a scene but rather a gestural encoding of spatio-temporal components of a linguistic representation and thus, a spatial gestural syntax.

It is possible to link the syntactic schema (which is spatially constructed by the movement of the process sign) with the meaning of the utterance so that the schema is formalised by representations at the cognitive level. This indicates that there is a direct relationship between the formal and the semantic level, leading us to analyse French Sign Language units using terminology derived from cognitive prototypes by linking each form with a diagrammatic value.

3.2   Applicative and cognitive grammar

Any modification to the form of the relator sign corresponds to a variation in meaning. This is why I have considered a typology of processes derived from the spatial components of the cognitive-semantic prototypes: spatial operators and relators as described in Applicative and Cognitive Grammar (A&CG, a model developed by Desclés (1990)). I also attempt to relate the formalisations of predicative prototypes proposed under A&CG to the diagrammatic path of process signs in LSF. This is a three-tiered model which extends from the cognitive to the linguistic level, as illustrated in Figure 1.

This structure is based on the idea that each language creates its own semantico-cognitive representations. Depending on both the context and perspective, a single situation gives rise to a large number of utterances (Level I), the form of which depends on the semantico-cognitive representations applicable to the sit-

---

4.   I define 'neutral space' as the unmarked space in front of the signer at chest level, the space where isolated signs are realised.

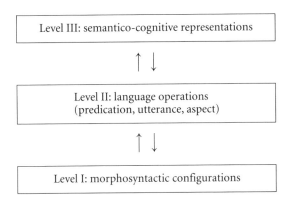

Figure 1. Structure of the A&CG (Desclés 1990)

uation (Level III) and the choice of utterance and predicate (Level II). At Level III the primitives of landmarks, mapping, spatial movement, change and control all come into play. It is at this level that we find a connection to signed languages, as the gestural modality prioritises movement, change, landmarks and control. Spatial concepts, such as the orientation of the predicative relationship, and the position of the signer relative to what is being signed also operate at Level II. These concepts are essential to analysing the place of the signer in the signing space.

Semantico-cognitive representations describe verbal meanings from a cognitive perspective, where language, perception and action all interact. They are arrangements of spatial and non-spatial primitives, which in A&CG can be interpreted as relators or operators. In order to construct a situation, entities of different types are employed as arguments.[5] For example, *someone pouring water into a saucepan* can be paraphrased in a range of different ways depending on the point of view taken and the choice of representation (predicative and enunciative), including *there is water in the saucepan; the water flows into the saucepan; the saucepan is full of water; Paul pours water into the saucepan; Paul fills the saucepan with water.*

Such semantico-cognitive representations give rise to static, cinematic and dynamic relators, as illustrated in Figure 2.

'Static relators' are applied to two arguments in order to construct a static situation. They are ordered on the basis of an indexing proto-relator (*REP*), which is specified in different mapping operators.

---

5.   The main types of entities are individual, mass, collective, placement and action, and are determined by cultural perception and custom. However, these categories are not fixed. In an utterance an entity can undergo a change of classification, for example, to an index in a situation conveying a spatial location.

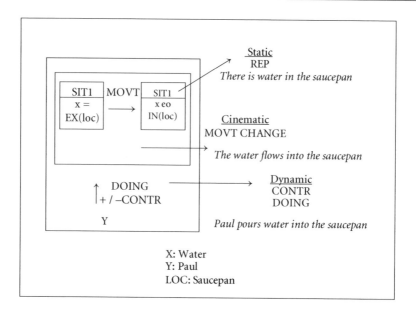

Figure 2. Semantico-cognitive representations with static, cinematic and dynamic relators

Consequently, spatial location is established by indexing an object in relation to a place, or a place in relation to another place. A place may be located according to different factors: it can be related to the interior of an entity (e.g. *there is water in the saucepan*), its extension (e.g. *there is water next to the saucepan*) and trace-outline (e.g. *there is water on the rim of the saucepan*) by combining indexing relators with mapping operators.

'Cinematic relators' are applied when moving from a static situation to another static situation. Cinematic relators express spatio-temporal modifications: a change of location (*MOVE*), or an internal movement or a change in a property (*CHANGE*). These relators construct a situation known as a cinematic situation. For example, *the water flows into the saucepan* expresses the movement of the water from outside the saucepan to the inside of the pan. Or *the saucepan is burned* expresses a change in the saucepan's properties.

'Dynamic relators' relate to agentive characteristics and are applied in cinematic situations to construct so-called 'dynamic situations'. These relators are essentially non-spatial primitives, such as:

– A primitive *DOING*, expressing the capacity to carry out an action
– A primitive *CONTR*, expressing the capacity to control an action; for example, *I pour water into the saucepan.*

Other primitives concerning intentionality link an agent entity and an end state. The primitive *TELEO* corresponds to an agent's capacity to aim at a final situation, e.g. *Paul is filling the saucepan with water*.

Therefore, a semantico-cognitive representation is a structured arrangement of different types of primitives, the aim of which is to represent the meaning of a linguistic predicate. Spatial primitives include *REP, CHANGE, MOVE*; while non-spatial primitives include *CONTR, DOING, TELEO*.

3.3 Iconic references in morphology: the link between the hands and the head and torso

A verb expressed at level I by the components of movement, space and hand-shape is a direct reference to the Level III schemata proposed in A&CG, as is outlined in Table 1.

The inclusion of the path of the relator sign in signing space depends on Level II operations. Thus, Level II operations are pragmatic choices that determine the position taken by the signer (that is, either the upper body has anaphoric value or expresses the speaker's point of view) and the orientation in the direction of movement of the predicate. Therefore, to break down process signs it is essential to identify the anaphoric referential value of the hands, head and torso, verifying whether there is a link between them or whether they each have their own independent value. To illustrate this we will consider the following examples.

Table 1. Correspondences between Level I and Level III

Level I	correspondences	Level III
Pointing	corresponds to	the indexing proto-relators (*REP*)
Movement of the process sign	creates an association between the sign and one of the two major types of relators:	it is either an external movement or path (*MOVE*) or an internal movement (*CHANGE*).
The movement's physical component in the form of anaphoric manual and corporal forms, as well as the spatial arrangement of the hands and certain locations or loci	correspond to	mapping operators
For example, a movement made relative to a type of extension entity (signed on a stationary hand) and a movement made relative to a place which is defined as a locus only (not by a manual form)	correspond to different syntactic structures because they involve	different semantico-cognitive formalisations

(3) 'He gallops': movement of the dominant hand in relation to the non-dominant hand.

In example (3), the hands assume anaphoric configurations representing the participants in the action: the horse and the ground. The movement made by the active hand represents the movement of a horse's legs when galloping. The hands are not in front of the signer (neutral space), but instead are placed to the side in a very high position. This location is significant in itself (the horse's meadow), and even more so as the eye-gaze of the signer is directed towards it.

(4) 'He gallops': movement of the whole upper body, with a downward movement of first one arm and then the other.

In (4), the hands represent the horse's legs. In this example we can see the parameter involving the head and torso because, unlike in example (3), where the movement is expressed with the hands only, in (4) the chest and arms move together, such that the entire upper body refers anaphorically to the protagonist in action.

(5) 'He approaches the fence': sharp movement of the hands in the direction of the body.

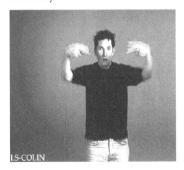

In (5), the head and torso also represent the protagonist of the action. The hands, however, represent the fence. The movement of the horse towards the fence is shown by the hand movement, while the eye-gaze is directed towards the space beyond the hands.

(6) 'He keeps galloping': movement of the right hand in space.

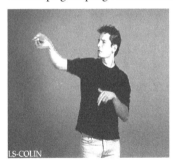

In (6), the head and torso are not significantly engaged in the movement. However, they represent the body of the horse, (with left hand and mimicry). At the same time the right hand also refers to the horse, but not to a specific part of the horse's body. Thus, the same agent is expressed twice, represented simultaneously by the head and torso along with one hand, and in another form by the dominant hand as it moves through a defined space.

(7) 'It looks at the horse': the hands are positioned one on top of the other; the face and the dominant hand are oriented towards a subspace.

In (7), the head and torso represent the bird as it looks in a particular direction. The hands represent the bird perched on the fence facing the same direction. Thus, in this example the bird is also presented in two different independent forms.

(8) 'The horse, on one side of the fence, looks at the cow on the other side of the fence': eye-gaze directed towards a point in space, hands remain in a fixed position.

In (8), the head and torso are those of the horse; the right hand represents the form of the fence and its position with respect to the horse. This is in contrast to the left hand which is signing with a conventional handshape (the sign [LOOK]), but which is directed toward the locus of the cow, on the other side of the fence.

(9) 'She soothes the horse by bandaging his leg.'

In (9), the head and torso and the right hand are those of the horse. The left hand moves around the right forearm, in the position of someone holding something. This refers anaphorically to the cow bandaging the horse's leg.

3.4 Network of the components of a verb sign

The different semantic values of the different parameters may be summarised as follows.

3.4.1 *Formal parameters*

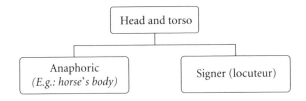

Figure 3. Semantic values of the head and torso

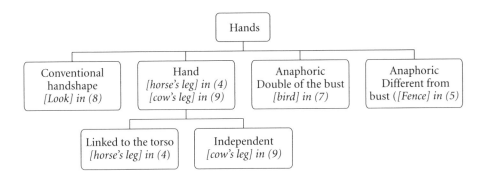

Figure 4. Semantic values of hands

It is possible that each hand holds its own value, independent of the other. As a result, the number of possible combinations is multiplied and, therefore, so is the potential complexity of the relationships expressed by the process. Eye-gaze and facial expression provide complementary information, which allows us to determine a value for these two essential parameters. As such, eye-gaze may have several values in process signs (as illustrated in Figure 5).

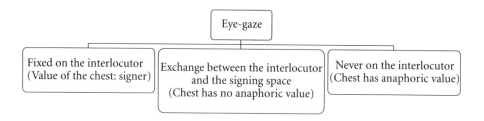

Figure 5. Eye-gaze types

3.4.2 *Movement parameters*

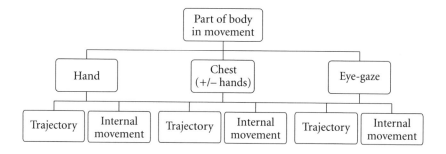

Figure 6. Movement types with respect to part of body

3.4.3 *Spatial parameters*

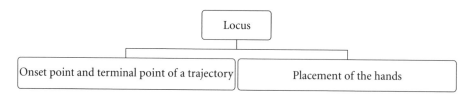

Figure 7. Relations between locus and movement

3.5 Anaphoric references

The examples I have analysed so far show that anaphoric forms constitute the basis of the semantic and syntactic values of process signs. An entity may be the subject of an anaphoric reference in two main ways: physical shape (manual or corporal) or location via the location towards which eye-gaze is directed, the location indexed towards or the location where a handshape is articulated. I will refer to formal references as 'proforms'[6] (Engberg-Pedersen 1989) and to spatial references as 'loci'[7] (Bras, Millet & Risler 2004). Accordingly, the same referent can be referred to with different proforms or loci, according to the type of entity featuring in the representation as classified according to the cognitive prototype: extension, place, index, individual, etc. and not the type inherent to the referent.

Here, we can also consider two kinds of proforms: 'manual proforms' and 'corporal proforms'. 'Manual proforms' are anaphoric configurations that refer to the abstract formalisation applied to an entity in the cognitive schema: an individual, a boundary, etc. Manual proforms can be further subdivided as follows: proforms that refer to the whole entity, to part of the entity, to a boundary; and double proforms (when handling an object). As such, in example (3) there is a moving manual proform representing a part of the horse (here, its legs) through the use of three fingers, and a reference to a boundary (i.e. the fence) with the forearm.

'Corporal proforms' are also anaphoric reference. They can involve the entire upper body: chest, shoulders, head and hands. These proforms can also be partial references in that they may be limited to the chest, to the head and shoulders, or to the head and shoulders with one or both hands, etc.

A corporal proform is used in example (4), where the signer refers to the horse with his entire upper-body. In this case the handshapes refer to a part of the body of the horse, which is not the same case as in example (3). In example (4), each hand represents a leg (index and middle fingers are extended), but in conjunction with the chest and the movement of the head and shoulders. Consequently, I do not consider these anaphoric manual configurations as manual proforms, but rather as part of a corporal proform.

Since corporal proforms are to a greater or lesser extent partial representations, there is room for possible relationships linking an increasing number of elements:

---

6.   Note that the term 'proform' ('*une proforme*' in French) is borrowed from Engberg-Pedersen (Engberg-Pedersen 1989) and is chosen because of its reference to the pronominal function taken on by these morphological units: they are expressed via a manual or corporal shape ('*une forme*' in French) which explains why the term is feminine in French. Cuxac and Sallandre also use the term 'proforme' in French (but as a masculine noun: '*un proforme*') to refer to highly iconic structures and more explicitly to transfers of shape, which do not always have an anaphoric value. Their approach is descriptive, rather than functional.

7.   The 'locus' is the area in space the eye-gaze is directed towards, or that is pointed at or where a manual form is placed, thereby attributing a referential value on the space. Loci are incorporated into the path of the process sign with an anaphoric value as either initial, final or intermediate points of a trajectory, or as the place of an action.

- Corporal proform of the head and torso only, associated with two manual proforms independent of the head and torso. For example, in (5) the head and torso is a proform of the horse, while the hands are a proform of the fence. The movement of the head and torso represents the movement of the horse, and the gradual movement of the hands towards the head-and-shoulders represents the approaching fence. In example (8) we see a corporal proform of the horse's head and upper body, a manual proform of the fence and a conventional sign.
- Corporal proform of the head and torso and a single hand, associated with a manual proform. For example, in (6) we see a manual proform articulated with the right hand and a simultaneous corporal proform involving the head and torso and left hand. The manual proform expresses movement with respect to the corporal proform, while the corporal proform itself indicates a prolonged state.
- Corporal proform of the head and torso and a single hand, associated with a double manual proform: in example (9) we see a corporal proform of the head and torso with a simultaneous proform of the dominant hand, which expresses a state and a change of state, as well as a double manual proform moving with respect to the corporal proform.

3.6 Cognitive-semantic interpretation and morpho-syntax in process signs

In order to investigate the values of the different parameters implicated in process signs, I will consider each of the following questions:

- Where is eye-gaze directed?
- Is there a corporal proform?
- Is each hand used as a hand (as part of a corporal proform), as a manual proform or as a conventional handshape?
- Which part of the body is moving?
- Is the part of the body that is moving following a trajectory or representing an internal movement?
- What subspaces are implicated?

Thus, rather than discussing syntactic constructions in LSF in terms of an action schema referring to the protagonists, I propose to link the types of processes to predicative prototypes. Modification of the different parameters of the relator sign refers directly to differences in representations at Levels II and III. We can assume that the signs which express the highest number of referents simultaneously reflect a complex syntactic structure.

Let us start with the question of how we should analyse the signs presented above.

(10) 'He gallops.'

[X = (MOVE + CHANGE) REP in support] REP locus

In example (1), repeated here in (10), there is a stative manual proform representing a boundary and a moving manual proform formally representing the horse. Eye-gaze is directed towards the hands, which are placed at a specific locus. There is no expression of a particular point of view. The moving proform progresses along a trajectory associated with an internal movement, relative to a spatial marker. Therefore, this process sign expresses both change of state and change of location, as a prolonged action carried out relative to a landmark in a specific place.

Movement can be represented in many ways: in relation to a landmark or a location, that is, relative to the boundary of a location; or in relation to a place. Examples of this nature can be found in our corpus as well.

(11) 'He gallops in his meadow.'

[X = (MOVE + CHANGE)] REP in locus

(12) '(The bird sees that) the horse is galloping.'

[*X* = (*MOV* + *CHANGE*) *in locus*] *REP next to Y*

Although the anaphoric configuration of the moving hand is the same, in (10) there is a change of location relative to a landmark; in (11) there is movement within a place signified by circular motion at a locus; and in (12) there is movement within this place, but relative to a landmark established by the body. The different uses of these processes are complementary; they indicate a construction of meaning that is slightly different each time.

(13) 'He gallops'

X = *CHANGE*

In example (4), repeated here in (13), we have a full corporal proform of the horse incorporating the chest, face and hands. The eye-gaze is vague and never directed at the interlocutor. The upper-body carries out an internal movement, which expresses a corporal action, namely galloping.

(14) 'He approaches the fence.'

$(B = MOV)$ *to* $(X = REP)$

In example (5), repeated here in (14), we see a corporal proform of the horse. This proform is limited to the head and torso. The hands are employed in a manual pro-form that represents a boundary. Eye-gaze is directed towards the space between the hands. The hands are moving progressively along a trajectory in the direction of the signer's body. This process expresses a movement relative to a landmark.

(15) 'He keeps galloping.'

$[X = (MOV + CHANGE)$ *in locus*$]$

In example (6), repeated here in (15), we see a manual proform signed on the right hand as a partial representation of the horse, with internal movement (wiggling of the fingers) and a circular trajectory within a locus. There is also a corporal proform representing the horse using the head and torso and the left hand, with the face and eye-gaze directed towards the moving right hand; the shoulders sway up and down. This is a complex sign composed of a trajectory within a locus and the establishment of a relationship to a landmark by means of eye-gaze.

(16) 'It watches the horse from its perch.'

[*X = REP on B*] *REP in relation to the locus*

The example in (7), repeated here in (16), can be seen as a partial corporal proform with the head and torso only. There are also manual proforms: the right hand acts as a supporting boundary proform, the left hand as a proform partially representing the bird and resting on the boundary proform. Both the left hand, as a proform of the bird, and the signer's head, are turned towards the horse's locus. Eye-gaze is clearly directed towards this locus (i.e. that of the horse).

In this sign the same spatial relation – between the bird and the horse – is presented twice: the first time by means of the signer's body and eye-gaze; the second time by the signer's hands, which express both the orientation towards the locus and their spatial relationship to one another. This is a complex sign composed of a location relative to a landmark (the bird on his perch) and the direction of eye-gaze towards a locus (i.e. that of the horse).

(17) 'The horse (on one side of the fence) looks at the cow (on the other side of the fence).'

X = (REP before B) + (MOV towards a locus)

In example (8), repeated here in (17), we see a partial corporal proform representing the horse (the arms are not used here). The manual boundary proform signed on the right hand represents the position of the fence in relation to the horse. The signer's eye-gaze is directed toward the locus where a handshape reference has previously indicated the location of the cow. The left hand assumes a conventional handshape, oriented towards the locus that the signer's gaze is also directed towards. In this sign we can see the location of the horse in relation to the fence, and the signer directing his gaze towards a location, showing an interactive relationship between the characters.

The left hand does not refer to any of the characters and it is not anaphoric. It expresses a conventional configuration, that is, the lexical sign [LOOK], with the fingers in a V shape directed towards the locus. The signer's eye-gaze accompanies the movement of the left hand, which remains in the V configuration, thereby establishing a spatial and relational connection between the horse and the cow, which are positioned on either side of the hand representing a fixed landmark.

These last two examples show that by examining the interplay of eye-gaze and the movement of the hands and head and torso as well as their configuration, it is possible to shed light on the processes resulting from the simultaneous combination of morphological elements and the simultaneous combinations resulting from several processes.

4.   Syntactic simultaneity

4.1 Components of syntactic simultaneity

A certain amount of time – the time used to complete the movement – is required to express a sign. Simultaneity consists of more than signing two things at the same time. Indeed, while it would be possible to only talk about simultaneity in cases where the movements of the two signs start and end at exactly the same moment, such situations are quite unusual. More commonly, the signer begins a sign and then begins a second sign before the completion of the first sign. The result is that at a particular point in time, the two signs are co-articulated. When the position of the body or the hands is maintained, this is significant. If the position is not maintained, the handshape is abandoned or relaxed considerably (see also the discussions of buoys in Liddell, Vogt-Svendsen & Bergman and Vogt-Svendsen & Bergman, this volume). This is the case in example (11), where the left hand no longer has a syntactic function and therefore gradually falls.

In the example in (6) (repeated in (15)), the corporal proform of the head and torso and left hand could be seen as the vestiges of a previous sign (this was the process sign in (4)) and these parameters could be considered separate from the sign currently being produced. I propose, however, that this sign be considered as comprising two processes: the expression of the movement of the horse in space (right hand), and the expression of the corporal action of the horse through the movement of the head and torso and the left hand.

As we will see below, the simultaneous expression of two process signs constitutes one means (among others) of linguistically expressing simultaneous processes.

4.1.1 *Two simultaneous processes*

In order to discuss two simultaneous process signs, I will focus on two movements (or two processes): state or event; quality or action. The two processes may relate to the same protagonist. Therefore, it is more frequent for an action to be combined with a state, property or location.

The two processes may also relate to two different characters. In this situation, the agreement or the dissociation between the referential value of the head and torso and hands is at work. More specifically, if the corporal proform and the moving manual proform both refer to the same character, the representation of the entity is repeated and two simultaneous points of view are expressed. The simultaneity introduces a double point of view on an event through the use of the cinematic relators *MOVE* and *CHANGE*. As such, in (6) (repeated in (15)), both refer to the horse, with the process sign simultaneously referring to movement and a prolonged action. In example (7) (repeated in (16)) the body and the manual proform signed on the left hand both refer to the bird. The verb simultaneously expresses a spatial relationship between the bird and the horse by means of the trajectory of the eye-gaze towards a locus (*the bird watches at the horse*), and the localisation of the bird by means of two manual proforms (*the bird is perched on the fence*).

Another complex simultaneous construction results when the simultaneous manual and corporal proforms, each expressing a process, do not refer to the same character, as in (2), repeated here in (18).

(18)   'The bird sees the horse moving away.'

[*X = MOVE*] *REP away from Y*
Y = LOOK at X (moving)

The moving manual proform (right hand) expresses the action of moving away relative to the manual proform positioned with respect to a landmark (left hand).

The trajectory of the eye-gaze towards a locus, along with a facial expression of doubt, is represented through the corporal proform (head and torso). Furthermore, in this case, as in example (7) (repeated in (16)), the position of the bird is shown twice simultaneously through (i) the corporal proform and (ii) a fixed manual proform (left hand). Therefore, there are two processes in this sign; two actions involving two different characters: the movement of the horse relative to the bird (*the horse moves away*), and the movement of the bird's gaze following the movement of the horse (*the bird watches the horse*).

This complex structure can also be seen in the sign in (9), repeated here in (19).

(19)   '(The cow) soothes the horse by bandaging (his leg).'

The corporal proform for the horse incorporates the chest, the head and the right hand in a fixed position, while the left hand, expressing a double manual proform, moves around the right hand.[8] Both facial expression and tension gradually relax during the extended movement. Consequently, this formation simultaneously expresses a modified state (relating to the horse) and the action of the cow along a trajectory relative to an index (the horse's leg). Each process relates to a different character: the active hand relates to the cow, the expressive body to the horse.

4.1.2 *A process and an enunciative modality*
Process signs both establish the relationships between all the elements in an utterance and also carry enunciative markers. That is, they indicate the position of the signer relative to what is being signed. This position is established by the referential value of the body, which allows a range of possibilities including: (i) a character in

---

8.   The signer's hand refers explicitly to the 'cow's hand'. So, the signer himself should be considered as part of the corporal proform. But as the signer's body refers to the horse, the handshape must be taken to refer to himself, as a manual proform. I call this a 'double manual proform', because the anaphoric component includes both the agent and the instrument of the action.

the process being discussed, or (ii) the signer referring to herself or using her own body to represent someone else (reported discourse).

The use of the signer's body to mark for narrator, the signer as herself, and the signer reporting the actions of another participant in an event is significant here. When functioning as signer-narrator, the signer's body, eye-gaze and facial activity all have enunciative value, while her hands have predicative value.

The gaze of the narrator is significant because it alternates between the signing space and the interlocutor, while a character's gaze never meets that of the interlocutor. This is illustrated in (11), repeated here in (20).

(20)   'He gallops in his meadow.'

[X = MOVE in locus] !!!

In this process sign, the signer's eye-gaze is directed towards the hands. The brow is furrowed, and the signer's facial expression denotes a prolonged action, marking durative modality. At the end of the trajectory the signer looks at his interlocutor, marking enunciative modality.

Is an enunciative marker a relator sign? Yes, in the sense that an enunciative marker introduces an intersubjective relationship, but this is a modality that is added to the sign. An enunciative marker does not establish a predicative relationship, but adds to it. The chest of the signer does not act as a corporal proform of a character in the action, independent of whether the signer is signing about herself or someone else. In this sense, the viewpoint on what the signer is expressing is literally addressed to the interlocutor. The relationship established by eye-gaze is situated in the enunciative space, not in syntactic space.

4.2 Function of syntactic simultaneity

4.2.1 Simultaneity of two perspectives on the same event

The sequentiality of processes plays an important role in narrative texts. This is most commonly associated with the expression of the sequence of actions. However, sequentiality also allows for the simultaneity of two points of view to be expressed. In fact, it is very common for the signer to switch between process signs of internal movement and of movement along a trajectory using corporal and then manual proforms.

Accordingly, in this corpus, sequentiality is used for more than just the chronological development of actions. At a key point in the story the signer switches between a corporal proform expressing action or change of state, and manual proforms along a trajectory relative to a location or index. Examples of process sequentiality in the corpus are as in (21).

(21)   Sequence: 'the horse as it jumps over the fence.'

These signs in sequence constitute alternatively two points of view and two statements about the same event. A corporal proform expresses prolonged action with respect to a position, the internal movement of the horse, and movement relative to a referent. This is initially expressed with a corporal proform and subsequently with manual proforms.

The same kind of sequentiality is used to express the fact that the bird takes flight, goes away and then comes back. In fact, the manual values allow for this series of sequential shifts, as the head and torso maintain this anaphoric value. This alternation enables the signer to express durative aspect as well as the fact that these two complementary processes are occurring at the same point in time. This is comparable to simultaneity involving a manual proform and a corporal proform to refer to the same protagonist. However, simultaneity permits two points of view to be synchronised.

4.2.2 *Complex syntactic constructions*

At this point I should note that simultaneity involving two different characters serves a different function: it allows for expression of a complex situation: the schema of the causative structure makes this possible as X causes [Y (*MOVE*) or (*CHANGE*)]. These process signs reproduce the schema of the dynamic situation (described by Desclés 1990) in signing space (see Figure 2). This is particularly evident in the example (9), repeated here in (22).

(22)   'She (the cow) soothes the horse by bandaging (his leg): the cow (right hand) makes the horse (chest, head and left hand) feel better.'

A very similar schema is seen with direct perception verbs: X sees [Y (*MOVE*)]. This construction is supported by the trajectory of eye-gaze towards a locus or towards a moving handshape, such as in example (2): *The bird* (chest and gesture) *sees the horse* (right hand) *going away*. This type of simultaneous construction is frequently used in narratives. The following examples are taken from another signer from the same LS-Colin corpus, NIC-11sep.

(23)   'I saw a television around which all the people were gathered.'

In (23) we see a corporal proform (head and torso) representing the signer himself at another point in time. His gaze is directed toward a locus at which he had previously located a television (*I saw a television*). He articulates a manual proform representing the people standing in front of him with their backs to him facing the locus where the television is situated.

(24)   'On the TV I saw an airplane crash into a building.'

In (24) the signer explains that he was looking at a television screen: we see a corporal proform (head and torso) corresponding to '*myself on that day*,' with the gaze directed toward the locus where he had previously located the television (*I was looking at the TV*). His gaze is directed toward a locus, the end point of a trajectory. This locus constitutes a location, or an event that is considered to occur at a location.

In neutral space, he simultaneously performs the signs for '*airplane crash into*' and maintains his gaze toward the locus with an expression of increasing shock. These signs are performed in neutral space, because they correspond to what he sees, and not the object that he is looking at.

These examples evoke discussion of modality because this verb of direct perception can also be used as a modal verb when the signer's body is in an enunciative position, and not representing a corporal proform. Looking attentively at a locus or looking at the interlocutor during an exchange can add weight to the assertion '*I see that…*', '*You see that…*'. In signed languages the role of the directionality of eye-gaze in syntactic structures, such as in these spatial statements, requires more in-depth analysis.[9]

In sum, the simultaneous construction with two characters constitutes a complex syntactic structure. It remains to be seen whether this type of structure is in fact acquired at a later stage by signed language users. In any case, this type of construction in a narrative demonstrates an advanced level of control of the possibilities offered by iconicity in LSF.

---

9.   There is a need for a comparative study of the use of verbs of perception or similar phenomena in signed and spoken languages. However, this subject is beyond the scope of the current paper.

5.   Conclusion

Because it is both visual and gestural, LSF can use space to convey syntactic meaning. In the same way, at the morphological level, we find traces of semantic spatial primitives, for example those that express movement or location.

For this reason, the breakdown of process signs into spatial or agentive relators and mapping operators provides a rich framework for the study of syntax. It requires us to distinguish different levels (semantic, syntactic, morphological), allowing us to abstract away from the visual effect produced by the linguistic form to then tease apart morphosyntactic units and their combination in syntactic structures. The same process may be implicated in different syntactic structures (cf. gallop, examples (10), (11) and (12)) depending on the number of arguments in the combination.

This work shows that two processes, or a process and a modality can be expressed simultaneously, a phenomenon called syntactic simultaneity, since the combination produces a syntactically complex sentence. I have also shown that there are several types of complex syntactic structures, depending on whether the two processes share a single agent or two distinct agents.

The sequential repetition of process signs and the simultaneous expression of two different process signs are revealed as two procedures accompanying a complex syntactic construction employed by experienced signers. In future studies, it would be interesting to study the emergence of such structures during acquisition.

References

Bras, Gilles, Agnès Millet & Annie Risler. 2004. "Anaphore et Deixis en LSF, Tentative d'Inventaire des Procédés". *Silexicales* 4.37–64.

Culioli, Antoine. 1990. *Pour une Linguistique de l'Énonciation. Opérations et Représentations. Tome 1*. Paris: Ophrys.

Cuxac, Christian. 1996. *Fonctions et Structures de l'Iconicité des Langues des Signes. Analyse Descriptive d'un Idiolecte Parisien de la LSF*. Doctoral dissertation, Université Paris 5.

——. 2000. *La LSF, les Voies de l'Iconicité (Faits de Langue n° 15–16)*. Paris: Ophrys.

Desclés, Jean-Pierre. 1990. *Langages Applicatifs, Langues Naturelles et Cognition*. Paris: Hermes.

Emmorey, Karen, ed. 2003. *Perspectives on Classifier Constructions in Sign Languages*. Mahwah, N.J./London: Lawrence Erlbaum Associates.

Engberg-Pedersen, Elisabeth. 1989. "Proformes en Morphologie, Syntaxe et Discours". *Etudes Européennes en Langues des Signes* ed. by Sophie Quertinmont & Filip Loncke, 35–52. Bruxelles: EDIRSA.

Langacker, Ron. 1987. *Foundations of Cognitive Grammar. Theoretical Prerequisites*. Stanford: Stanford University Press.

Peirce, Charles S. 1978. *Ecrits sur le Signe*. Paris: Seuil.

Risler, Annie. 1998. "L'Iconicité en Langue des Signes et les Procédés d'Imagerie à la Base de la Définition Notionnelle des Catégories Grammaticales de Nom et Verbe". *Cahiers du CISL* 13.121–135.

——. 2003. "Point de Vue Cognitiviste sur les Espaces Crées en Langue de Signes: Espace Lexical, Espace Syntaxique". *LIDIL* 26.45–61.

—— & Fanch Lejeune. 2004. "Trace des Représentations Cognitives et des Opérations Langagières dans la Forme Verbale en Langue des Signes Française". *Silexicales* 4.213–230.

Sallandre, Marie-Anne 2003. *Les Unités du Discours en Langue des Signes Française, Tentative de Catégorisation dans le Cadre d'une Grammaire de l'Iconicité.* Doctoral dissertation, Université Paris 8.

Simultaneity in French Sign Language discourse

Marie-Anne Sallandre
University of Paris 8, UMR 7023-CNRS

1. Introduction

1.1 The problem

Depending on the author and the linguistic trend, simultaneity in signed languages can have a phonological, morphological, syntactic or semantic explanation (Miller 1994; Emmorey 2002; Sandler 1999; Wilbur 2000; Cuxac 2000). In this paper I propose an analysis that is both morphological and semantic, in terms of semiotic intentionality. Depending on what the signer wants to express and how she wants to do it, she will use a more or less illustrative intent[1] and always reserve the possibility of going from one intent to another.

I follow the model proposed by Cuxac (2000) for the analysis of signed languages, in particular for French Sign Language (LSF). The model gives a great deal of importance to iconic phenomena in signed languages. To justify the vast amount of iconicity present in signed languages, in contrast to the phenomena observed in spoken languages, Cuxac proposes a cognitive linguistic explanation: there tends to be less iconicity in frozen signs[2] for reasons of linguistic economy (Frishberg 1975), on the contrary, iconicity is fully maintained for Highly Iconic Structures[3] (HIS).

---

1. See explanations of 'illustrative intent' in Section 2.1.

2. By 'frozen sign' ('*signe standard*' in French) I mean a lexicalized and standardized sign that could be found in LSF/French dictionaries, such as the IVT Dictionary (Girod 1997). By convention, LSF semantic units are written in capital letters (frozen signs) and in lower case (Highly Iconic Structures).

3. See the definition in Section 2.

To begin this paper, I present the articulators[4] I take into account in LSF, i.e. the parts of the body considered significant for sign formation. There is eye gaze, the two hands, facial expression, mouth movements (mouthing of the spoken word or mouth gestures accompanying HIS) and possibly body posture. In this type of analysis of a signed language, the relative hierarchy between the articulators should be noted, with the pre-eminence of eye gaze. It is in fact eye gaze that governs interaction, creates space, time and person reference and ultimately helps distinguish whether a given sign is uttered with the intent of showing (i.e. HIS) or not (frozen sign), according to Cuxac (2000) and Sallandre & Cuxac (2002). Taking all body articulators into account means that no particular emphasis is given to the hands.

For the definition of simultaneous constructions, I follow Miller (1994) and discuss his work in the light of Cuxac's model. For Miller (1994: 133),

> a simultaneous construction is a grouping of signs in which: (a) distinct lexical elements are produced independently and simultaneously in autonomous channels, and (b) these elements are bound together in some kind of syntactic relationship.

He continues, noting that:

> Within simultaneous constructions, two major types can be distinguished. The first involves the fully simultaneous production of distinct signs. The second type involves holding a handshape forming part of one sign while the other hand simultaneously produces different signs.

According to Miller (1994: 133), the term 'construction' with reference to simultaneous structures in signed language is important, since the different meaningful elements of these structures can be independent, but are always related (never existing at random).

1.2 Iconicity in signed languages

Iconicity is a theoretical notion in both spoken and signed languages. The most common form of iconicity in signed language is imagistic but can be completed by diagrammatic iconicity (Haiman 1985). Imagistic iconicity is a natural resemblance between the sign and the object it refers to in the world (Fischer & Nänny 2001). Diagrammatic iconicity is a type of syntactic iconicity and is present in signed languages in the creation of space, time and person references as well as in the order of signs in the utterance. Most signed language specialists focus on the

---

4. By 'articulators', I mean the different parts of the body that enter into constructing meaning in signed languages and by 'parameters', the four manual components (handshape, location, orientation and movement) used while constituting a manual sign, for each of the two hands.

imagistic iconicity of these languages (for example, Cuxac (1985, 1996, 2000) and Jouison (1995) for LSF; Klima & Bellugi (1979), Wilcox (2000) and Taub (2001) for American Sign Language; Pizzuto & Volterra (2000) for Italian Sign Language; and other signed languages). However, some researchers have also looked at diagrammatic iconicity (for example, Engberg-Pedersen (1993) for Danish Sign Language, Risler (2000), Cuxac (2003), Sallandre (2003) for LSF; Pietrandrea & Russo (2004) for Italian Sign Language).

1.3 The data

The examples in this paper are taken from two corpora. First, I used the database of the LS-COLIN project[5] that includes ninety LSF monologues by thirteen Deaf adult signers in several genres: narratives, explanations (*cooking recipes*), discussions of current events (*The switch from the franc to the euro in 2002; September 11th, 2001*), and linguistics. The examples studied here are selected from all these genres except the last one. The two simple narratives produced from an elicitation task using picture sequences, *The Horse Story* and *The Cat Story* (Hickmann 2003) have been extensively commented on in language acquisition research and, more recently, recorded in some signed languages.[6] The first story is about a horse that wants to jump over a fence to join a cow on the other side and falls. The second story is about a cat that climbs a tree to devour little birds in their nest. The second video corpus – Temporality[7] – involves one Deaf signer and was created to allow the study of some aspects of the LSF temporal system.

1.4 Outline in three parts

In the first part of this paper, I briefly present Cuxac's model for LSF and the three main categories of transfers he developed: 'transfers of form and size' (showing and describing the form or size of an object, without any process involved); 'situational transfers' (showing a situation as if one saw the scene from a distance) and 'transfers of person' (with processes and roles). Among transfers of person, 'double transfers' will be my core examples of HIS because by definition, these constructions combine two transfers simultaneously. In the second and third parts, I

---

5.   Cognitique Project, with grant LACO39 from the French Ministry of Research, 2002. This project involved Paris 8 University (Linguistics of LSF group), LIMSI/CNRS Laboratory and IRIT Laboratory (computer sciences and image processing).

6.   LSF (LS-COLIN Corpus and former data), LIBRAS (Brazilian Sign Language), Primary Signed Languages (signed languages used by isolated Deaf adults, Fusellier-Souza 2004).

7.   This corpus was set up in 2003 and studied in collaboration with Fusellier-Souza.

analyze LSF video examples of simultaneous constructions with both illustrative and non-illustrative intents.

2.   Cuxac's model

2.1   Brief presentation of Cuxac's model of intent

Before dealing with simultaneity, I briefly present Cuxac's model. Christian Cuxac is currently the most established LSF linguist. He has had a great influence on the research conducted on LSF in France since the end of the 70's and has published a large number of papers, chapters, and proceedings as well as two books in the field of cognitive grammar, with a functionalist and enunciative approach (Thom 1970; Martinet 1970; Culioli 1990).

For twenty-five years Cuxac has been developing a semiogenetic model whose guiding principle is the iconic nature of signed languages. Cuxac (2000) hypothesizes that there are two ways of signifying in LSF: by showing or not showing, which can be seen in two different intents – illustrative and non-illustrative. A signer can always choose to sign by adopting one strategy or the other, depending on her intent. For example, 'horse', signed by using either the frozen LSF sign [HORSE] or a transfer of form (by describing with hands the forms of ears, muzzle and tail).

The primary process of increasing iconicity is divided into two sub-branches, depending on whether or not the iconisation process serves the express aim of representing experience iconically. Cuxac terms this 'iconic intent'. This iconisation process represents the perceptual world, owing to the strong iconic resemblance between the forms and what they represent.[8] On the one hand, the formation of frozen signs 'without iconic intent' permits meaning which is attributed a general value and the iconicity established in discrete signs is preserved, but could become degenerated. On the other hand, iconic intent, characterized by meaning which is given a specific value, allows a range of meaningful choices in the larger iconic structure activated by the transfer operations. These constructions are called 'Highly Iconic Structures'.

Figure 1 illustrates these two sub-branches resulting from the process of iconisation and suggests a model for an iconic grammar of signed languages.

---

8.   Mandel (1977) deals also with iconisation process but for lexical units.

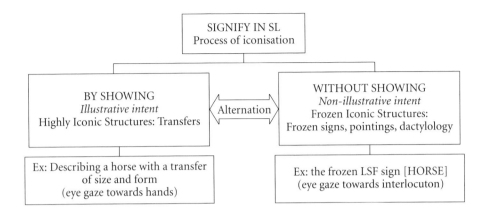

Figure 1. Overview of Cuxac's (2000) model

2.2 Highly Iconic Structures and transfer operations

Highly Iconic Structures are not discrete signs but whole structures. In HIS, the signer gives an imagistic reconstitution of experience. The demonstrative dimension can be activated at any moment through showing and imitating (as if one were the person one is speaking about, whatever her actions might be).

Transfer operations include the entire range of Highly Iconic Structures. They are mental operations which aim to identify forms and roles of discourse. The three main transfers (Cuxac 1985; Sallandre & Cuxac 2002) are defined below:

1. 'Transfers of form and size' (TF) describe the objects or persons according to their size or form (no process or role involved) and the object is described by means of proforms. Gaze is oriented towards the hands, and facial expression specifies the form.

2. 'Situational transfers' (ST) involve the movement of an object or character (the agent, by the dominant hand) relative to a stable locative point of reference[9] (by the non-dominant hand). The situation is shown as if the scene were observed from a distance; the signer keeps her distance relative to what she is conveying. Gaze is oriented towards the dominant hand and facial expression specifies the agent. (See Figure 2)

3. 'Transfers of person' (TP) involve a role (agent or patient) and a process; the signer 'becomes' the entity she is referring to. There is a phenomenon of in-

---

9. '*Locatif stable*' in French, and 'buoys' for Liddell (2003), in most of the cases. For Liddell (2003:223), "buoys are weak hand signs that are held in a stationary configuration as the strong hand continues producing signs." See also Liddell et al. (this volume) and Vogt-Svendson & Bergman (this volume) for further discussion of buoys.

corporation with the signer's entire body playing the role. (See examples in Sections 3 and 4).

These transfers are the visible traces of cognitive operations, which consist of transferring the signer's conceptualization of the real world into the four-dimensional world of signed discourse (the three dimensions of space plus the dimension of time).

2.3 Transfers of person

In transfers of person, as mentioned before, the signer 'disappears' and 'becomes' a protagonist in the discourse (any entity: human, animal or thing). Her gestures correspond to the gestures made by the character she is referring to and whose place she has taken. As such, the signer can embody a little boy, a horse, a tree and so on. These types of extremely iconic structures can be divided into different transfers of person arranged along a continuum, starting from a high to a low degree of embodiment: 'personal transfer' (PT) is a complete role playing; 'double transfer' (DT) combines simultaneously a personal transfer for acting and a situational transfer for locative information or for a second character; and 'semi personal transfer' is partial role playing, accompanied by brief frozen signs. There are in fact around twenty different transfers of person (Sallandre 2003) but these three categories are the most common in LSF discourse.

'Transfers of person' are the most complex constructions of Highly Iconic Structures, compared with 'transfers of form and size', which express no process, and 'transfers of situation', which can express only motion and locative processes. This is why I decided to analyze them in previous studies (Sallandre 2001, 2003) and to focus on them in this paper.

In international signed language literature, transfers of person are often considered as 'role playing'; they allow different 'points of view' to be expressed (Poulin & Miller 1995). Engberg-Pedersen (1995) analyzes some phenomena in Danish Sign Language that can be used to express a specific point of view. She talks about 'shifts' and 'perspectives', using the term 'role shifting', which has been used to describe how signers take on a referent's identity in certain types of signing. However in this case the term 'shifts' refers only to reported speech (direct and indirect discourse) and focuses on the pronominal system. In my description of LSF narratives (Sallandre 2003), I found a sub-group of categories that covers this and called it 'personal transfers with reported speech' (PT rs). This means that the signer has assumed the role of a character and that this character is speaking to one or more other characters. To do this, she can use frozen signs, cultural gestures, pointings or even transfers. In other words, the signer can once again draw on the whole range of LSF categories with or without an illustrative intent.[10] In fact, not all categories of transfers of person are reported speech, but the reverse seems to hold true: reported speech can be produced only with transfers. Lastly, the terms 'blend' and 'surrogate' used by Liddell (1998, 2003) would be very appropriate in dealing with cognitive operations like transfers of person.

2.4 Proforms, transfers and property markers, rather than classifiers

Miller (1994) notes that in the signed language literature, the notion of simultaneity often appears in relation to constructions with classifiers. Since the notion of classifier is close to that of iconicity (at least in terms of motivation), simultaneity should have pride of place in Cuxac's model. But Cuxac (2000, 2003) doesn't use the notion of classifier because he thinks that this concept does not sufficiently account for the iconicity of LSF.

Briefly stated, the common characteristic of the different types of classifiers identified in spoken languages is that they differentiate between entities on the basis of semantically defined classes (Craig 1986).[11] These so-called classifiers in signed languages do have a classifying function in that they indicate a relevant property of an entity (Emmorey 2003). As Slobin, Hoiting, Kuntze, Lindert, Weinberg, Pyers, Anthony, Biederman & Thumann (2003) point out however, this property does not mark the entity as belonging to a specific semantic class existing in the language, but rather serves to designate the entity in a specific context. The same object can be designated by using different handshapes, i.e. by selecting different properties of the object to represent it, depending on what the focus is on or what is considered relevant to discourse. Thus Slobin et al. (2003) propose the term 'property marker' instead of the widely used term 'classifier'.

Furthermore, Slobin et al. (2003: 273) emphasize the communicative function of property markers; in their words:

> Rather than emphasize classification as the central feature of 'classifier' handshapes in polycomponential signs, it seems more useful to treat them as marking a relevant property of a referent. The major function of such a handshape is to evoke a relevant referent in discourse, indexing a particular referent according to properties that are appropriate for the current discourse.

---

10. In fact, this is a second level of 'telling' in dialogues, so it is normal to find all the language categories that are available for the first level of 'telling'.

11. For a further discussion of classifiers and illustrated examples of proforms, see Sallandre (2006) (Section 1).

This means that Slobin et al. argue that a property marker does not classify, but serves a function within a polycomponential verb – namely, the function of indicating a referent.

In Cuxac's recent typology, property markers are proforms. Cuxac (2003) uses the term 'proform'[12] specifically for the manually configured parameter (hand-shape) used in HIS. Proforms are both highly iconic handshapes and generic forms (for example: 'flat', 'thick', 'vertical'). Thus a proform is included in a transfer (the whole structure) as handshape parameter, together with the other manual parameters (orientation, movement and location) and non-manual articulators (eye gaze, facial expression, body position).

Then Cuxac (2003) integrates proforms into a comprehensive model of iconicity while limiting them to Highly Iconic Structures, whereas Slobin et al. (2003) deal with entities that have already been mentioned (Cuxac's frozen signs).

2.5   Cuxac's discussion of simultaneity

Cuxac discussed simultaneity for the first time in a paper in 1985, but his major contribution is in his seminal book, published in 2000. The 1985 paper is really his first on LSF linguistics: in this paper, he defined the foundations of what later became his model: the importance of iconicity, form and size transfer, situational transfer, personal transfer, etc. At that time, he followed Martinet's (1970) concept of 'double articulation' of language (as did Stokoe (1960)). Later, Cuxac (2000) explicitly deals with simultaneity, identifying two 'intents': simultaneity with or without illustrative intent, i.e., in Highly Iconic Structures, as opposed to its presence in frozen signs. I develop these two directions in this paper and show examples in LSF. This quotation from Cuxac (2000:241) summarizes his view on multilinear inter-frozen signs, that is, with non-illustrative intent:

> On traitera ici des cas où les deux mains fournissent ensemble des informations hétérogènes. La plupart de ces relations n'ont en fait rien de simultané, puisqu'il s'agit du maintien d'un signe arrêté dans son mouvement pendant que l'autre main (en général la main dominante) réalise des signes standards. Mais la main arrêtée joue là le rôle d'un indice de permanence thématique ou syntagmatique et le récepteur du message ne peut faire autrement qu'appréhender visuellement cet indice en même temps que les signes standards émis par l'autre main se succèdent, conférant à ceux-ci un indiscutable étiquetage structural simultané.

---

12.   'Proform' is a term which was used by several signed language authors before Cuxac and with a different meaning: first by Friedman (1975) to refer to pointing signs and pronouns in American Sign Language, then by Engberg-Pedersen (1993) for Danish Sign Language and Sutton-Spence & Woll (1999) for British Sign Language.

> English: I will discuss here cases where the two hands together provide het-
> erogeneous information. Most of these connections do not in any way involve
> simultaneity, since one sign has been stopped in its movement and is held station-
> ary, while the other hand (generally the dominant hand) performs frozen signs.
> However, the holding hand serves to indicate thematic or syntagmatic duration
> and the person on the receiving end of the message can not help but perceive
> this indication visually at the same time as the frozen signs produced by the
> other hand follow one another. The interlocutor perceives these frozen signs as
> unquestionably simultaneous in structure.   (my translation)

According to Cuxac, many constructions that are often called 'simultaneous constructions' are not strictly simultaneous from an articulatory point of view, because the two hands don't move exactly at the same time; but they are perceived as
simultaneous by the interlocutor. Moreover, the crucial point in Cuxac's discussion
is that he emphasizes that these constructions are simultaneous from a semantic
point of view and provides different contexts in which simultaneous constructions
are likely to appear:

> Le principe est général: quand cela est possible, une des deux mains maintient en
> permanence soit un indice de frontière syntagmatique ou propositionnelle, soit
> un signe standard noyau, tandis que l'autre main réalise soit les signes standards
> (il faut pour cela que ceux-ci ne se réalisent qu'au moyen d'une seule main) ap-
> partenant au syntagme ou à la proposition, soit les satellites déterminant le signe
> noyau.   (Cuxac 2000: 241–242)

> English: The principle is a general one: when possible, one of the two hands con-
> stantly holds either an indication of syntagmatic or clausal border, or a core frozen
> sign, while the other hand performs either frozen signs (for this to be true, the
> frozen signs must be performed by only one hand) belonging to the phrase or
> clause, or satellites determining the core sign.   (my translation)

The clausal border can be indicated in different ways (Cuxac 2000: 242):

– The non-dominant hand is a numeral adjective (1, 2, etc. up to 5).
– The non-dominant hand performs the sign meaning there.
– The non-dominant hand is in a highly iconic configuration, i.e. a proform.
  The non-dominant hand is held stationary, while the dominant hand pro-
  duces the frozen sign(s) (core sign of the clause).

3.   Simultaneity in Highly Iconic Structures (illustrative intent)

Following this theoretical summary, I explore simultaneity in LSF discourse drawing on Cuxac's two types of intent and offering several LSF examples. Examples
are taken from the two corpora described in the introduction and analyzed via

simultaneity of articulators. The following examples are all simultaneous constructions of varying type: with wholly illustrative intent (Sections 3.1 and 3.2), with wholly non-illustrative intent (Sections 4.1 and 4.2) and with the two intents simultaneously articulated (Section 4.3). Each video example is briefly presented in the context of discourse. I present a photograph to illustrate the example, along with a table describing the example in detail, on an articulator by articulator basis. A categorization is provided, along with an English language translation that contextualized the example.

3.1   Simple transfers

'Simple transfers' are constructions that do not combine several transfers (Section 3.2) nor do they combine the two intents simultaneously (Section 4.4). As such, transfers of size and shape, and situational and personal transfers are termed 'simple'. Two examples are presented in this section (Figures 2 and 3).

The first example (Figure 2) shows a situational transfer of a cat climbing a tree. It is an excerpt from the *Cat Story*, from the LS-COLIN Corpus. In this situational transfer, the two hands convey a different meaning and serve a different grammatical function: (a) the dominant hand is the agent of the scene (a cat, with proforms 'X' following action of climbing); (b) the non-dominant hand is a stable locative place (a tree); (c) the eye gaze follows the dominant hand, and (d) the facial expression is that of the agent involved in this process.

Figure 2. Ois_Jul 00'27, simultaneity in a situational transfer

Table 1. Description of Figure 2

Discourse	LS-COLIN Corpus, *The Cat Story*: Ois_Jul
Timer	00'27
Articulators	– *Eye gaze*: towards non-dominant hand (the tree)
	– *Facial expression & mouth gesture*: of the cat (aggressive)
	– *Dominant hand*: the cat ('X' proform) = <u>ST agent</u>
	– *Non-dominant hand (and the arm)*: the tree ('5' proform)
	= <u>ST locative</u>
	– *Body posture*: of the signer (towards the non-dominant hand).
Summary: LSF category	Situational Transfer (ST)
Translation in English	"The cat climbs the tree aggressively."

The second example (Figure 3) shows a personal transfer of pie dough that has previously been rolled-out with a cook's rolling pin. As shown in Table 2, all the articulators are used, allowing the signer to embody the dough. Another part of the body that needs to be added here is the torso acting as an articulator. The torso represents part of the 'dough' entity and is therefore a meaningful articulator. It is the pertinent use of the torso that creates the meaning 'rolled out dough', implying rolled out over its whole surface, its whole 'being' and creates a comical effect.

It is relatively common for the torso to have semantic value in personal transfers, which are constructions that involve the signer's whole body. Generally speaking, all the upper parts of the body can become articulators and, as a result, they then take on a morphological and semantic value.

Figure 3. Cuis_Nas 03'01, simultaneity in a personal transfer

Table 2. Description of Figure 3

Discourse	LS-COLIN Corpus: Cuis_Nas
Timer	03'01
Articulators	– *Eye gaze*: of the pie dough (eyebrows: astounded)
	– *Facial expression & mouth gesture*: of the dough (astounded)
	= <u>PT agent</u>
	– *Dominant and non-dominant hand*: of the dough
	– *Body posture*: of the dough
Summary:	Personal transfer (PT)
LSF category	
Translation in English	"I really am pie dough now!"

3.2 In combined transfers: Double transfers

I would like to point out that certain Highly Iconic Structures can be combined. For example, a double transfer is made up of a personal transfer plus a situational transfer. This results in more complexity from the standpoint of form (semanticization of the body is even more stratified) and of function (these minimal structures are authentic utterances with multiple participant roles).

The first example (Figure 4) shows a complex double transfer in *The Horse Story*. The most striking feature of this example is the number of agents that the signer shows simultaneously. The signer shows not just one agent, as is usually the case in double transfers, but two agents performing different actions in the same setting. The first agent is marked by the set of articulators [eye gaze + facial expression + mouth gestures + body posture] and represents a horse in a personal transfer. The second agent is marked only by the dominant hand and represents

Figure 4. Chev1_Jul 00'29, simultaneity in a double transfer

Table 3. Description of Figure 4

Discourse	LS-COLIN Corpus: Chev1_Jul
Timer	00'29
Articulators	– *Eye gaze*: of the horse, beyond the fence
	– *Facial expression*: of the horse (determined)
	– *Mouth gesture*: of the horse (determined)
	= <u>PT agent</u>
	– *Dominant hand*: the bird's head ('duck beak' proform) = <u>ST agent</u>
	– *Non-dominant hand*: the fence held ('W' proform)
	= <u>ST locative</u>
	– *Body posture*: of the horse, beyond the fence
Summary:	PT + complete ST
LSF category	= Complex Double Transfer
Translation in English	"Here is the bird watching the horse getting ready to jump over the fence."

the bird (looking at the horse) in a situational transfer. A fence is the scene that the two agents act in relation to, and this (the fence) is expressed by the non-dominant hand in a situational transfer locative. As a result, this structure offers a complete situational transfer (locative + expressed agent), whereas ordinarily in a conventional double transfer the situational transfer is not complete (only one locative), with the agent expressed by personal transfer. This is why the example is termed a 'complex double transfer'. This type of example with a very high level of body and semantic division is fairly uncommon in LSF and demonstrates an excellent command of the language on the part of the signer.

In the second example (Figure 5), a description of the recipe for making apple pie, the signer simultaneously embodies the apple and the cook who cuts the apple up. The signer is again using a double transfer, but it is structured differently than in the previous example. His head, facial expression, eye gaze and the rest of his body represent the patient, the 'apple', with a personal transfer. His dominant hand acts as the agentive 'cook' who is cutting the apple with a knife. His non-dominant hand does not fulfill any function. The particularly interesting feature of this example is the two functions performed by the signer's head: it is both patient in a personal transfer (conventional function) and the locative of the situational transfer (original function, possible thanks to the similarity of the signer's oval head and the shape of the apple).[13] His head also functions as the locus that the cook acts on. Accordingly, this can be termed double simultaneity: simultaneity between articulators and simultaneity of the 'head' articulator occupying two semantic functions.

---

13.   This is a special case of iconicity that can be considered as isomorphy (similarity of shape) applied to signed language.

Figure 5. Cuis_Nas-04'21, simultaneity in a double transfer

Table 4. Description of Figure 5

Discourse	LS-COLIN Corpus: Cuis_Nas
Timer	04'21
Articulators	– *Eye gaze*: of the apple (patient)
	– *Facial expression*: of the apple = <u>PT patient</u>
	– *Mouth gesture*: –
	– *Head*: of the apple = <u>ST locative</u>
	– *Dominant hand*: of the cook (cutting the apple, with 'B' proform)
	= <u>ST agent</u>
	– *Non-dominant hand* : (nothing)
	– *Body posture*: of the apple
Summary:	PT + complete ST
LSF category	= Complex Double Transfer
Translation in English	"Ouch! I (the apple) am getting cut up into pieces by the cook."

3.3 Synthesis

As shown above, transfer structures are made up of internal morphemic elements, based on a very intense multilinear and paradigmatic semaniticization of the body: the paradigm includes eye gaze, facial expressions, movements of the face and manual gestures. The manual gestures are in turn composed of morphemic elements[14] that can not be performed in isolation: paradigms of hand configurations, their orientation in space, their location (on the body or in space), and paradigms of the movement(s) they make.

---

14.   For the signified value of these elements, see Cuxac (1996, 2000).

4. Simultaneity in frozen signs, pointing and mouthing (non-illustrative intent)

4.1 Two simultaneous frozen signs

I would now like to discuss constructions without illustrative intent using two ex-amples (Figures 6 and 7). The first example (Figure 6) shows two simultaneous frozen signs, with the first sign held. The signer, who is at the beginning of ex-plaining his recipe, warns the audience that he really is not a great cook. To do this, he first produces the sign CHEF with his dominant hand. He performs this sign emphatically (smile, negative mouth gesture and raised eyebrows) and pauses for a while after the sign, which allows him to introduce the theme. Then, at the same time as he maintains the location and configuration of the first sign, his non-dominant hand performs the sign NO, which allows him to make a comment on the first sign. This type of construction, also found in LSQ (Miller 1994), allows the signer to comment on a theme economically (without having to repeat the first sign or to say explicitly that he is going to comment on something). This is possible only with one handed signs.

The second example (Figure 7) is an excerpt from the LS-COLIN corpus on the euro. The sequence appears as follows: (a) BANKNOTE 'franc' mouthed and held, (b) FRANC 'franc' mouthed, (c) SORRY not mouthed. This construc-tion comes within a complex sequence, with the use of two channels (vocal and visual) and in the encoding of identical ('franc'/FRANC) or heterogeneous (FRANC/SORRY) information.

Figure 6. Cuis_Nas 00'09, simultaneity in a compound frozen sign

Table 5. Description of Figure 6

Discourse	LS-COLIN Corpus: Cuis_Nas
Timer	00'09
Articulators	– *Eye gaze*: of the signer, towards interlocutor
	– *Facial expression*: of the signer (smiling and negative)
	– *Mouth gesture*: of the signer (negative)
	– *Dominant hand*: holding the <u>frozen sign</u> CHEF ('V' proform)
	– *Non-dominant hand*: <u>frozen sign</u> NO ('index' proform)
	– *Body posture*: of the signer (face on)
Summary:	Two frozen signs, with one held
LSF category	= Compound frozen sign
Translation in English	"No, I'm not a chef!"

Figure 7. Euro_Jos 02'28-02'29, BANKNOTE held FRANC/SORRY, simultaneity in a compound frozen sign with mouthing

Table 6. Description of Figure 7, first picture

Discourse	LS-COLIN Corpus: Euro_Jos
Timer	02'28
Articulators	– *Eye gaze*: of the signer, towards interlocutor
	– *Facial expression*: of the signer (sad)
	– *Mouthing*: "franc"
	– *Dominant hand*: <u>frozen sign</u> FRANC mouthed ('F' proform)
	– *Non-dominant hand*: <u>frozen sign</u>
	BANKNOTE held ('C' proform)
	– *Body posture*: of the signer (face on)
Summary:	Two frozen mouthed signs, with one held
LSFcategory	= Compound frozen sign
Translation in English	"Some people are sorry that (banknote) francs have disappeared."

This example illustrates the possibility of using oral components in addition to the body as a linguistic channel, as also discussed by Miller (1994) for LSQ, where first, both channels encode the same lexical information, and then they go on to encode two items of lexical information independently.

In this connection, Emmorey (2002: 39) gives a clear definition of the 'mouth patterns' which are produced simultaneously with manual signs in several signed languages:

> *Mouth gestures* refer to mouth activity that is unrelated to spoken words, whereas *mouthing* refers to the production of a spoken word (or a part of a word), usually without voice, while simultaneously producing a corresponding manual sign or signs.

In LSF, mouth gestures are produced in HIS (for example to describe the size of an object), but mouthing is only observed with frozen signs (never with HIS, except in personal transfers with reported speech). This is an additional argument in favor of the existence of two completely distinct intents in LSF: illustrative (say by showing) and less illustrative (say without showing). With mouthed frozen signs, the signer really produces a double act of saying, without showing: she says with the manual sign (which may have a low, synchronically degraded degree of iconicity) and with the mouthing.

Emmorey (2002: 40) notes that "mouthing in European sign languages occurs much more often with nouns than with verbs, possibly because verbs occur with mouth gestures (e.g. facial adverbials)." This is exactly the case in our example where the two noun signs [BANKNOTE] and [FRANC] are mouthed with 'franc', whereas the verb 'to be sorry' is not. However, I would like to propose an explanation in terms of the signer's intent rather than of a verb/noun opposition. Emmorey (2002) also suggests the presence of mouth gestures by 'echo phonology' (the mouth articulation parallels the manual movement) and 'enactment'[15] (imitates the real action in a stylized way). The reader is referred to her work for discussion of a proposed phonological explanation for the different levels of articulation possible in signed languages, and includes summary overviews of the work of Sandler (1999) for Israeli Sign Language and Wilbur (2000) for American Sign Language.

4.2 An 'unfrozen' sign

For some LSF frozen signs where both hands normally have the same function, signers could choose to separate each hand. The example below (Figure 8) is taken from the Temporality Corpus. This example involves a frozen sign with two hands

---

15. Transfers of person, in my framework.

(left) Temp_Nas 10'19, pointing gestures in two places
(right) Temp_Nas 10'49, final sign TEACH in two referential spaces

Figure 8. Simultaneity in a 'unfrozen' sign

Table 7. Description of Figure 8, second picture: the 'unfrozen' sign TEACH

Discourse	Temporality Corpus: Temp_Nas
Timer	10'49
Articulators	– *Eye gaze*: of the signer, toward interlocutor
	– *Facial expression*: of the signer (smiling)
	– *Mouthing*: 'cours' ('course' in English)
	– *Dominant hand*: "unfrozen" sign TEACH spatialized on the right
	– *Non-dominant hand*: "unfrozen" sign TEACH spatialized on the left
	– *Body posture*: of the signer (face on)
Summary:	"Unfrozen" sign
LSF category	
Translation in English	"I teach LSF on Monday afternoons at the University and Friday mornings at the Museum".

in two distinct spaces. It shows a spatial construction in LSF where space is conceived of as a diagram. I asked the signer to explain his weekly timetable to us. He began by constructing a 'grid' in space, which is based on an upper range with a horizontal arrow (Monday to Friday) and continued from top to bottom with a vertical arrow (morning, noon, evening). I then excerpted a long sequence of 45 seconds close to the end of the performance where the signer realized that he had forgotten to mention an activity that he did every week, teaching LSF (first return to an earlier point), so he had to go back to mention it.

In this sequence, the elements *teach, Monday mornings, Friday afternoons, university* and *museum* are spatialized in their frozen form in relation to the grid of the timetable that he constructed at the beginning of the sequence. He began by speaking of *Friday* then continued with *Monday* (second return to an earlier point). The 'unfrozen' sign [TEACH] can be divided into: (a) 'space: Monday afternoon' with dominant hand (for university in real life); (b) 'space: Friday morning' with non-dominant hand (for museum in real life). The signer uses a linguistic strategy, made possible by the simultaneity of his hands.

4.3 Simultaneity combining both intents

The last example in this paper (Figure 9) shows a simultaneous construction with two intents expressed together. The illustrative intent is characterized by a double transfer made up of the non-dominant hand representing the fence in a situational transfer and the grouping of [eye gaze + facial expression + mouth gesture + body posture] representing the horse in a personal transfer. At the same time, the non-illustrative intent is present in the form of the frozen sign LOOK AT performed by the dominant hand. The signer chooses to use a frozen sign while he is in the role of an animal in order to underscore the action that this character is performing, thereby creating a semi double transfer.[16]

Figure 9. Chev1_Ant 01'08, simultaneity in a semi double transfer

---

16. It should be noted that the actions alone (often verbs of perception: see, hear, perceive) are signed with frozen signs in personal transfers, thereby producing semi personal transfers or semi double transfers.

Table 8. Description of Figure 9

Discourse	LS-COLIN Corpus: Chev1_Ant
	(left-handed signer)
Timer	01'08
Articulators	– *Eye gaze*: of the horse, to the right
	– *Facial expression*: of the horse (thoughtful)
	– *Mouth gesture*: of the horse = PT agent
	– *Dominant hand*: frozen sign WATCH (to the right), ('V' proform)
	– *Non-dominant hand*: the fence held ('V' proform) = ST locative
	– *Body posture*: of the horse (face on)
Summary:	Double Transfer + frozen sign
LSF category	= Semi Double Transfer
Translation in English	"The horse looks thoughtfully at the fence."

5.   Conclusion

In this paper I have attempted to show how the simultaneity of articulators is exercised in numerous constructions in LSF. Whether the transfer is simple, combined, or simultaneously expressing two intents, or whether two lexical signs are produced together, morphological and semantic simultaneity does exist. The first group of examples demonstrated illustrative intent, which mostly draws on imagistic iconic resources. In contrast, the second group of examples demonstrate non-illustrative intent and uses both imagistic and diagrammatic iconic resources. For example in Figure 8, the signer uses the signing space to refer to an actual space (the schedule on paper, i.e. imagistic iconicity) that he uses in turn to create two distinct sets of references: space (the museum and the university) and time (Monday and Friday), (i.e. diagrammatic iconicity). As such, these two types of iconicity merged together allow articulator simultaneity in LSF. More specifically, the small amount of imagistic iconicity characteristic of oral languages possibly explains the small amount of articulator simultaneity usually observed in them. Accordingly, it can be stated that iconicity and structure are compatible, in particular for the analysis of signed languages. In signed languages, signers resort to simultaneity of articulators for reasons of linguistic economy. Lastly, based on these observations of LSF discourse, I suggest referring to the concept of multilinearity of articulators rather than seeing an opposition between simultaneity and sequentiality.

Acknowledgments

I would like to thank the three editors of this book who have given me an opportunity to make my research available to a wider, non-French speaking readership. My gratitude also goes to the Deaf signers involved in the two corpora, and especially to Nasreddine Chab, Juliette Dalle, Josette Bouchauveau and Anthony Guyon, whose photographs have been used to illustrate this paper. Lastly, I extend my thanks to Barbara Balvet for the English translation and for being on call 24/7 as well as to Christian Cuxac for his precious comments, but all errors remain my own responsibility.

References

Craig, Colette, ed. 1986. *Noun Classes and Categorization*. Amsterdam/Philadelphia: John Benjamins.

Culioli, Antoine. 1990. *Pour une Linguistique de l'Énonciation. Opérations et Représentations.* Tome 1. Paris: Ophrys.

Cuxac, Christian. 1985. "Esquisse d'une Typologie des Langues des Signes". *Autour de la Langue des Signes. Proceedings of the Tenth Journée d'étude*s, *Paris, 4 June 1983* ed. by Christian Cuxac, 35–60. René Descartes University.

——. 1996. *Fonctions et Structures de l'Iconicité des Langues des Signes*. Thèse d'État, University of Paris V.

——. 2000. *La Langue des Signes Française; les Voies de l'Iconicité*. Paris : Ophrys.

——. 2003. "Une Langue Moins Marquée comme Analyseur Langagier : l'Exemple de la LSF". *Nouvelle Revue de l'AIS* 23.19–30.

Emmorey, Karen. 2002. *Language, Cognition, and the Brain: Insights from Sign Language Research*. Mahwah, N.J./London: Lawrence Erlbaum Associates.

——, ed. 2003. *Perspective on Classifier Constructions in Sign Languages*. Mahwah, N.J./London: Lawrence Erlbaum.

Engberg-Pedersen, Elisabeth. 1993. *Space in Danish Sign Language: The Semantics and Morphosyntax of the Use of Space in a Visual Language*. Hamburg: Signum Press.

——. 1995. "Point of View Expressed Through Shifters". *Language, Gesture, and Space* ed. by Karen Emmorey & Judy Reilly, 133–154. Mahwah, N.J./London: Lawrence Erlbaum Associates.

Friedman, Lynn. 1975. "Space, Time, and Person Reference in American Sign Language." *Language* 51.940–961.

Frishberg, Nancy. 1975. "Arbitrariness and Iconicity in the American Sign Language". *Language* 51.696–719.

Fischer, Olga & Max Nänny, eds. 2001. *The Motivated Sign. Iconicity in Language and Literature*, vol.2. Amsterdam/Philadelphia: John Benjamins.

Fusellier-Souza, Ivani. 2004. *Sémiogenèse des Langues des Signes. Primitives Conceptuelles et Linguistiques des Langues des Signes Primaires (LSP). Étude Descriptive et Comparative de Trois LSP Pratiquées par des Personnes Sourdes Vivant Exclusivement en Entourage Entendant.* Doctoral dissertation, University of Paris 8.

Girod, Michel, ed. 1997. *La Langue des Signes. Dictionnaire Bilingue LSF/français*. Paris: Editions IVT.

Haiman, John, ed. 1985. *Iconicity in Syntax*. Amsterdam/Philadelphia: John Benjamins.

Hickmann, Maya. 2003. *Children's Discourse: Person, Space and Time Across Languages*. Cambridge: Cambridge University Press.

Jouison, Paul. 1995. *Ecrits sur la LSF*. ed. by Brigitte Garcia. L'Harmattan: Paris.

Klima, Edward & Ursula Bellugi, eds. 1979. *The Signs of Language*. Cambridge, Mass.: Harvard University Press.

Liddell, Scott K. 1998. "Grounded Blends, Gestures, and Conceptual Shifts". *Cognitive Linguistics* 9:3.283–314.

———. 2003. *Grammar, Gesture, and Meaning in American Sign Language*. Cambridge: Cambridge University Press.

Mandel, Mark. 1977. "Iconic Devices in American Sign Language". *On the Other Hand* ed. by Lynn Friedman, 57–107. New York, London: Academic Press.

Martinet, André. 1970. *Eléments de Linguistique Générale*. Paris: Armand Colin.

Miller, Christopher. 1994. "Simultaneous Constructions in Quebec Sign Language". *Word-Order Issues in Sign Language*. Working Papers ed. by Mary Brennan & Graham H. Turner, 89–112. Durham: International Sign Linguistics Association..

Pietrandrea, Paola & Tommaso Russo. 2004. "Diagrammatic and Imagic Hypoicons in Signed and Verbal Languages". Paper presented at the conference on Verbal and Signed Languages, Rome, October 2004.

Pizzuto, Elena & Virginia Volterra. 2000. "Iconicity and Transparency in Sign Languages. A Cross-Linguistic Cross-Cultural View." *The Signs of Language Revisited. An Anthology in Honor of Ursula Bellugi and Edward Klima* ed. by Karen Emmorey & Harlan Lane, 261–286. Mahwah, N.J./London: Lawrence Erlbaum Associates.

Poulin, Christine & Christopher Miller. 1995. "On Narrative Discourse and Point of View in Quebec Sign Language". *Language, Gesture, and Space* ed. by Karen Emmorey & Judy Reilly, 117–131. Mahwah, N.J./London: Lawrence Erlbaum Associates.

Risler, Annie. 2000. *La Langue des Signes Française, Langue Iconique*. Doctoral dissertation, University of Toulouse Le Mirail.

Sandler, Wendy. 1999. "Prosody in Two Natural Language Modalities". *Language and Speech* 42:2–3:127–142.

Sallandre, Marie-Anne. 2001. "Va-et-vient de l'Iconicité en Langue des Signes Française". *Acquisition et Interaction en Langue Etrangère* 15.37–59.

———. 2003. *Les Unités du Discours en Langue des Signes Française. Tentative de Catégorisation dans le Cadre d'une Grammaire de l'Iconicité*. Doctoral dissertation, University of Paris 8.[17]

———. 2006. "Iconicity and Space in French Sign Language". *Space in Languages. Linguistic Systems and Cognitive Categories (Typological Studies in Language 66)* ed. by Maya Hickmann and Stéphane Robert, 239–255. Amsterdam/Philadelphia: John Benjamins.

——— & Christian Cuxac. 2002. "Iconicity in Sign Language: a Theoretical and Methodological Point of View". *Gesture and Sign Language in Human-Computer Interaction* ed. by Ipke Wachsmuth & Timo Sowa, 171–180. Berlin: Springer.

Slobin, Dan I., Nini Hoiting, Marlon Kuntze, Reyna Lindert, Amy Weinberg, Jennie Pyers, Michelle Anthony, Yael Biederman & Helen Thumann. 2003. "A Cognitive/Functional Perspective on the Acquisition of 'Classifiers'". *Perspective on Classifier Constructions in Sign Languages* ed. by Karen Emmorey, 271–296. Mahwah, N.J./London: Lawrence Erlbaum Associates.

Stokoe, William C. 1960. *Sign Language Structure (Studies in Linguistics. Occasional Papers 8)*. Buffalo, N.Y.: University of Buffalo Press.

Sutton-Spence, Rachel & Bencie Woll. 1999. *The Linguistics of British Sign Language. An Introduction*. Cambridge: Cambridge University Press.

---

17.   Available on: http://umr7023.free.fr/Downloads/Sallandre_these_tabmat.html

Taub, Sarah. 2001. *Language from the Body. Iconicity and Metaphor in American Sign Language.* Cambridge: Cambridge University Press.

Thom, René. 1972. *Stabilité Structurelle et Morphogenèse.* Paris: Ediscience.

Wilbur, Ronnie B. 2000. "Phonological and Prosodic Layering of Non-Manuals in American Sign Language". *The Signs of Language Revisited : An Anthology in Honor of Ursula Bellugi and Edward Klima* ed. by Karen Emmorey & Harlan Lane, 215–243. Mahwah, N.J./London: Lawrence Erlbaum Associates.

Wilcox, Phyllis. 2000. *Metaphor in American Sign Language.* Washington D.C.: Gallaudet University Press.

Simultaneous constructions in Adamorobe Sign Language (Ghana)

Victoria Nyst
ACLC, Universiteit van Amsterdam

1. Introduction

The papers in this book show that simultaneous constructions are a pervasive feature of signed languages of large Deaf[1] communities and have many similarities. This paper discusses simultaneous constructions in Adamorobe Sign Language (AdaSL). Investigating simultaneous constructions in an old signed language like AdaSL, unrelated as it is to any signed language of a large Deaf community, and having developed under unusual social circumstances, will add to our insight in the universality of these constructions. AdaSL uses simultaneous constructions consisting of a manual and an oral element. In its use of bimanual simultaneous constructions, AdaSL differs from Quebec Sign Language (LSQ) and probably most signed languages studied so far. In this first section, Miller's typology of simultaneous constructions is presented, and the village of Adamorobe and its languages are introduced. The second section presents the database. In the third section, two types of manual-oral simultaneous constructions are identified. In the fourth section, the occurrence of bimanual simultaneous constructions in AdaSL is investigated. The fifth and final section contains the conclusion.

The following transcription conventions are used. Glosses of signs are printed in capitals, e.g. ADAMOROBE. Akan words are rendered in italics. English translations are given between single quotes. Where information from the linguistic or situational context is needed for a correct interpretation, this information is added on the translation line in parenthesis, e.g. '(The child) refuses'. Mouthings and mouth gestures are represented between square brackets and superimposed

---

1.   In this paper, I follow the convention to use a capital to refer to deafness as a cultural identity label. As the presence of a deaf cultural identity can be debated in Adamorobe, I will refer to the deaf people in Adamorobe as deaf (Nyst 2007).

on the gloss they coexist with, whereby the underlining indicates the spread of the mouth activity. Descriptions of gestured or mimed forms in a signed utterance are rendered in normal font. In the glossed utterances containing manual simultaneous constructions, the first line, preceded by a capital R, shows the signs articulated by the right hand and the second line, preceded by a capital L, shows the left hand. An interrupted line following a gloss indicates the hold of a sign.

1.1 Simultaneous constructions in signed languages

Miller (1994) defines simultaneous constructions as the simultaneous production of distinct signs in two separate channels at the syntactic level. He investigates descriptions of such constructions in the signed language literature and notes their occurrence in many signed languages, including American Sign Language (ASL), British Sign Language (BSL), Danish Sign Language, and Sign Language of the Netherlands (Nederlandse Gebarentaal, NGT). Since then, they have been attested in German Sign Language (Deutsche Gebärdensprache, DGS), Flemish Sign Language (Vlaamse Gebarentaal, VGT), Irish Sign Language (ISL), and, as becomes clear from the collection of papers in this volume, many more signed languages.

Miller (1994, 2000) distinguishes five types of simultaneous constructions in his LSQ database:

1. Locative constructions, usually by means of classifiers (including constructions with a more abstract meaning that use classifiers in an 'abstract' space);
2. Holds of verbs or predicative adjectives with one or more proposition(s) on the other hand;
3. Holds of nouns on the non-dominant hand with (a) proposition(s) on the other hand;
4. Simultaneous pronouns and determiners on the non-dominant hand, closely related grammatically to information on the dominant hand;
5. 'Oppositive/synthetic' constructions. The defining properties of this type of construction are not clearly specified.

In this paper, the occurrence and types of simultaneous constructions in Adamorobe Sign Language are investigated. The village of Adamorobe and its signed language are introduced below.

1.2 Adamorobe

Adamorobe is a village in Ghana with an unusually high incidence of deafness. Of a total population of about 1,400, more than 30 persons are deaf. This represents 2% of the village population, compared to the estimated 0,4% for Africa in general (WHO/CBM 1998). Locally, several explanations are given for the high prevalence of deafness in the village: first, breaking the taboo on certain days by taking water from the stream between Adamorobe and the town of Aburi is believed to cause deafness. A further three historical explanations exist, two of them concerning war times. For example, during the war at Katamanso in 1826, Adamorobe warriors used a special concoction that made them fierce in battle, but which, when they returned, appeared to have left them deaf. Another explanation talks about how Adamorobe was short of warriors during wartime: the deaf god Adamorobe Kiti called animals from the bush and turned them into anthropomorphic soldiers; they looked like humans but could not speak. Finally, the deafness is sometimes ascribed to a tall and hard-working deaf man, who, according to the former chief Nana Kwaakwa Asiampong II, lived among the settlers of the village around the end of the 18th century (Frishberg 1987). This last explanation comes closest to scientific explanation, which attributes the deafness in Adamorobe to the mutation of the connexin 26 gene. This mutation must have arisen at least sixty generations ago (Brobby, Müller-Myhsok & Horstmann 1998). Both local and scientific sources thus indicate the considerable longitudinal presence of deafness in the village, possibly present for as long as 1,000 years. The rate of deafness has declined significantly in recent times, with a decrease from 10% in 1971 to around 2% today (David, Edoo, Mustaffah & Hinchcliffe 1971; Amedofu, Brobby & Ocansey 1997). However, in past decades, the actual number of deaf people has remained more or less stable at about 35.

1.3   Languages in Adamorobe

A local signed language has evolved in Adamorobe, which Frishberg (1987) named 'Adamorobe Sign Language' or AdaSL. Locally, the language is called *mumu kasa*, literally 'deaf language'. It is the primary means of communication for adult deaf inhabitants. Though most hearing villagers communicate relatively easily with deaf people, proficiency in the signed language depends on the degree of contact and ties with the deaf inhabitants. Since deafness appears to have a long history in Adamorobe, it is not unreasonable to assume that AdaSL has a history of about two centuries. Thus, AdaSL is certainly not a young language. The language is used by all deaf villagers (except one deaf immigrant who continues to use Ghanaian Sign Language) and by some of the hearing villagers in their communication with the deaf villagers. AdaSL is historically unrelated to Ghanaian Sign Language (GSL), which is used in Ghana's schools for the Deaf. GSL is in fact related to ASL. It is the 'offspring' of Signed English introduced with deaf education in Ghana in 1957 by the legendary Deaf missionary, Andrew Foster, who is considered to be Africa's Gallaudet (Oteng 1988; GNAD n.d.). Most deaf people in Adamorobe know some GSL and AdaSL contains a number of GSL loan signs. Adamorobe's deaf children attend the boarding school for the deaf in Mampong-Akuapim where Ghanaian

Sign Language is used, and as a consequence, GSL seems to be their primary language. The increasing use of GSL constitutes a serious threat to the future of AdaSL. Deaf pupils are taught to read and write in English, this being the official language in Ghana. Virtually all deaf adults are illiterate in Adamorobe.

Akuapim Twi, a dialect of Akan (belonging to the Kwa group of languages, it-self a branch of the Niger-Congo languages), is the primary spoken language of the community, although most hearing adults also know the neighbouring language Gã (Gã-Adangme, Kwa, Niger-Congo).

A community with a similar high incidence of deafness was found on the island of Martha's Vineyard (Groce 1985), although its signed language had dis-appeared before it could be described. Nowadays, the signed languages of similar communities, scattered around the globe, are starting to be studied: Kata Kolok in Bali (Branson, Miller, Gede Marsaja & Wayan Negara 1996; Zeshan 2004), Providence Island Sign Language (Washabaugh 1986) and Al-Sayyid Bedouin Sign Language in Israel (Kisch 2001; Sandler, Meir, Padden & Aronoff 2005).

2. Data

The present study is part of a large-scale study of AdaSL, aiming towards a descrip-tive analysis of the language. The data for this project were collected during three periods of fieldwork totalling ten months between January 2000 and May 2004. Approximately forty hours of signing material was collected on digital video-tape, featuring most of the adult deaf signers and some of the deaf children. The data consist of spontaneous signing of monologues that recount personal narratives, mythical stories and bible stories, as well as a number of church services in GSL, which are simultaneously interpreted into AdaSL. In addition to this spontaneous material, slightly more controlled data were elicited in the form of retellings of four 'Tweety and Sylvester' cartoons (Kita 1995) by three young AdaSL signers (11, 11, and 13 years old). All of these young signers have deaf parents. Their age, as well as the fact that they have had less exposure to AdaSL because of their education at a boarding school for the deaf, makes them less suitable as informants. However, collecting data through picture or video stimuli, like the 'Frog, where are you' story and the 'Tweety' cartoons, appeared to be a tedious task for adult signers, because of the non-local cultural specificity of these materials.

The description of the simultaneous manual-oral combinations presented here is based on the spontaneous texts. The analysis of bimanual simultaneous constructions is based in part on observations made during my fieldwork and the subsequent transcription of the spontaneous texts. It also relates in part to the more detailed transcription of a subset of about one hour of AdaSL data, consisting of spontaneous data and cartoon retellings (see Section 4.1).

3.   Simultaneous manual-oral combinations

While Miller (1994, 2000) does not extensively discuss simultaneous constructions consisting of a manual and a non-manual sign in his typology of simultaneous constructions in LSQ, it is this type of simultaneous construction that appears to be most common in AdaSL. Whereas the use of bimanual simultaneous constructions seems to be restricted in AdaSL, we do find extensive use of simultaneity in manual-oral constructions, especially in the semantic fields of size and shape and colour. Below, combinations of size and shape and combinations with colour mouthings are discussed.

3.1   Simultaneous combinations of a mouthing and a manual sign of size and shape

AdaSL uses several systems to indicate the size and shape of objects. One group of fixed signs present a relative judgement on the size of an object. The mouthing from these 'relative size signs' may also combine with the manual part of signs of absolute size and shape. The closed group of 'relative size signs' are BIG (Figure 1), SMALL (Figure 2), TALL, and SHORT. These come with fixed mouthings, as presented in Table 1. Mouthings are articulations of the mouth that are based on a word in a spoken language. They are distinct from mouth gestures, which are not based on a spoken word (see also Sutton-Spence, this volume).

The mouthing for BIG, [abo], comes from *agbo*, the word for 'big' in the neighbouring spoken language, Gā. This word is sometimes used by speakers of Akan as well. Semantically, these signs give a subjective, relative judgment about the size of entities. They are fixed and do not change according to the entity they modify.

Another prominent strategy to indicate size and shape is the use of 'measure stick signs'. In these signs, one hand shows the size of an entity on the other hand/arm by using it like a measuring stick. The other hand may or may not take a particular handshape to express a particular shape, e.g. a fist to express a lump. In some signs, a finger is used as a 'measuring stick' instead of an arm. Here, one of the fingers on the dominant hand acts on one of the fingers on the non-dominant

Table 1. The relative size signs in AdaSL and their mouthings

Sign	Mouthing	Spoken source
BIG	[abo + puffed cheeks]	from Gā *agbo*
SMALL	[spread lips, teeth closed + ttt]	from Akan *keteketekete*
TALL	[spread lips, teeth closed]	from Akan *tententen*
SHORT	[spread lips, teeth closed]	from Akan *tia*

Figure 1. BIG   **Figure 2.** SMALL

Figure 3. SIZE-OF-
THUMBTIP

Figure 4. SIZE-OF-
HAND

Figure 5. SIZE-OF-
ARM

hand, as for example in the sign SIZE-OF-THUMB-TIP (see Figure 3). In this way, a rather objective, absolute size is indicated.

Both 'measure stick signs' and 'relative size signs' follow the noun they modify, as illustrated in examples (1) and (2). The sign SIZE-OF-HAND in example (1) is shown in Figure 4.

(1)   BANANA SIZE-OF-HAND
       'A banana of about the size of a hand'

(2)   BANANA BIG
       'A big banana'

Both types of signs are often found to modify one and the same noun, resulting in forms that give information about both the absolute and the relative size of the entity. The combination of a 'measure stick sign' and a 'relative size sign' may take a sequential structure as in example (3).

Figure 6. SIZE-OF-HAND + the mouthing of BIG [abo]

(3)   [abo]
        BANANA SIZE-OF-HAND BIG

It may also take the form of a simultaneous structure as in example (4). The simultaneous structure is shown in Figure 6.

(4)   [abo-*repeated*]---
        BANANA SIZE-OF-HAND
        'A relatively big banana of about the size of a hand'

Whereas a banana that is the size of a hand is considered big by the signer, a bottle of the same size is considered small, as becomes clear from example (5) below. The mouthing accompanying the sign SIZE-OF-HAND is the mouthing of SMALL. This simultaneous structure is illustrated in Figure 4 (above).

(5)   [spread lips, teeth closed + ttt]
        BOTTLE SIZE-OF-HAND - - - - - - - - -
        'A relatively small bottle of about the size of a hand'

The sign SIZE-OF-THUMB-TIP may combine with the mouthing of SMALL (this combination is illustrated in Figure 3), or it may combine with the mouthing of BIG. The sign combined with the mouthing for SMALL may mean 'stock cube', when following SOUP and SWEET. The sign with the mouthing for BIG may mean 'sugar cube' when following SWEET/SUGAR, as illustrated in Figure 7.

(6)   [abo-*repeated*] - - - - - -
        SUGAR SIZE-OF-THUMB-TIP
        'A sugar cube'

The manual sign can also be located on the body, adding to the semantic weight of the combination: the SIZE-OF-THUMB-TIP sign moving and contacting a path halfway around the neck plus the mouthing of the sign BIG was used to mean

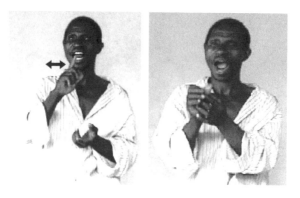

Figure 7. 'A sugar cube'

Figure 8. '(the person with the) big belly-button'

necklace. Another example is found in Figure 8, where the SIZE-OF-FIST sign is located on the belly accompanied by the mouthing of the sign BIG. This sign was used to refer to a person with a big belly button.

'Measure stick signs' and 'relative size signs' may co-occur in sequence or simultaneously. The simultaneous construction containing a mouthing of a relative size and a manual sign that expresses an absolute size may contain even more simultaneous information when the manual component is meaningfully located.

3.2 Simultaneous combinations of a colour mouthing and a manual sign

The systematic use of mouthings in combination with a manual sign is also found in the semantic field of colour terms. Three colours, 'white' (Figure 9), 'red' (Figure

Table 2. The mouthings of WHITE, RED and BLACK

Sign	Mouthing	Spoken Akan source
WHITE	[ftftft]	*fita*
RED	[ɔ:]	*kɔkɔ*
BLACK	Pursed lips	*tuntum*

10), and 'black' (Figure 11) have the same manual sign and are distinguished by mouthings.[2]

The same manual component of the sign with a wrinkled nose means 'bad smell'. Combined with a wiggling tongue, it means 'sweet', or 'sugar' (see Figure 7, first picture).

The manual sign thus seems to be a general quality sign that needs to be specified by a mouthing, a mouth gesture or a facial expression.

These 'colour mouthings' are not only used in colour signs: they are also found in combination with (1) a size and shape specifying fist and (2) a sign glossed as SURFACE. Together with a meaningful location and/or orientation, the mouthings add to or specify the meaning of these semantically light manual components of signs. Most of the examples involving colours have lexicalised meanings. Thus, a size and shape specifying fist, wiggling in front of the mouth, means 'garden egg' (a white, round aubergine species) when combined with the mouthing for 'white', but means 'tomato' when combined with the mouthing for 'red' (see Figure 12).

Examples of colour mouthings in combination with SURFACE (a B hand making a striking motion) are found in the signs POLICE, AMA-KOKO (name sign), OLD-PERSON, and FOREIGNER/ACCRA.

Figure 9. WHITE   **Figure 10.** RED   **Figure 11.** BLACK

---

2.   Neatly in line with the colour hierarchy of Berlin & Kay (1969), other colours are indicated by signs like LEAVES for 'green', CHICKEN FAT for 'yellow', etcetera.

Figure 12. TOMATO

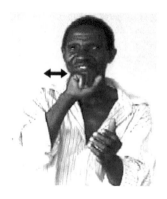

Figure 13. GARDEN EGG
(white aubergine species)

Figure 14. DARK-BODY

Figure 15. FOREIGNER/ACCRA

The sign POLICE is a compound of STRIPES-ALONG-LEGS + DARK-BODY. The latter sign is a simultaneous combination of a B hand tracing the surface of the body of the signer and the mouthing for 'black' (see Figure 14). The sign refers to the black uniform of the Ghanaian police. The simultaneous combination DARK-BODY may also refer to the dark complexion of a person. Similarly, the name sign AMA-KOKO is a compound of DEAF + LIGHT-COMPLEXION. The latter sign consists of a B hand tracing the surface of the body of the signer plus the mouthing for 'red'. Similarly, in Akan, the word for 'red' is used to refer to a light complexion of the skin or hair. The sign OLD-PERSON is a simultaneous combination of an indicative sign, striking the side of the head and the mouthing for 'white'. Another sign referring to hair colour is the sign for 'foreigner' or 'Accra', the capital of Ghana. This sign consists of a B hand tracing the surface of the top of the head plus the mouthing for 'red', referring to the light hair associated with Europeans (Figure 15).

The size and shape combinations and the colour combinations show that mouthings operate in a relatively independent way and that they are thoroughly integrated in the linguistic system.

4.   Bimanual simultaneous constructions

Observations from the fieldwork and the transcription of the larger body of data gave the impression of a restricted use of bimanual simultaneous constructions. As this kind of simultaneous constructions is a pervasive feature of signed languages, as illustrated by the contributions in this volume, the restricted use of simultaneous constructions in AdaSL is surprising. A sub-study was thus designed to investigate and quantify the types and occurrence of bimanual simultaneous constructions in AdaSL. The findings are compared with Miller's typology of simultaneous constructions in LSQ (1994, 2000).

4.1   Data

For the sub-study, a subset of the larger body of data was used, consisting of twenty short spontaneous AdaSL narratives, slightly more than half an hour in total. These narratives are signed by five different adults, although the majority are signed by two adult signers, KA (male) and AK (female). All are native users of AdaSL. The re-tellings of cartoon stories were also used: this includes renditions by three signers.

The selected data, consisting of the twenty spontaneous narratives and the three retellings of four cartoons, were checked for the occurrence of bimanual simultaneous constructions as described by Miller (1994, 2000). In order to collect as many potential simultaneous constructions as possible, our selection criteria were very loose: any instance of two hands active at the same time, expressing what was not known to be a lexical sign was to be collected. This probably resulted in a larger set of constructions than is usually discussed under the heading of simultaneous constructions. However, our guiding principle was that if simultaneous constructions still turned out to be rare, we could be sure we had not missed any of them because of the application of too narrow criteria regarding what constitutes a simultaneous construction.

4.2   Results

The impression of restricted use of bimanual constructions was confirmed by the semi-spontaneous data, being the retellings of the Tweety cartoons by three young signers. In fact, simultaneous constructions were entirely absent in these retellings.

All instances of two handed signing concerned lexical bimanual signs or one-handed signs that were phonetically doubled by adding an identical non-dominant hand. These 'doubled' one-handed signs did not give rise to a semantic interpretation of duality or plurality. For that reason, they can be considered 'phonetic' rather than phonological: they are not used for morphological purposes.

In the spontaneous data, examples of the independent use of two hands were only found in the signing of two signers, KA and AK. Together, they produced seven such examples in six utterances. No examples were found in the signing of the three other adult signers.

Signer KA shows a strong preference for one-handed signing with the right hand. In the examples where the left hand becomes active, this generally concerns lexical signs, both symmetric and asymmetric. Only two instances showed the left hand acting independently of the right hand. These are represented in (7) and in (10) below.

Signer AK uses her non-dominant hand much more than does KA, but this still mostly concerns bimanual signs or one-handed signs which are doubled, i.e. where the non-dominant hand is added, mirroring the dominant hand. In AK's signing, five examples were found in which the non-dominant hand is used independently of, but simultaneously with the dominant hand. Three of the five utterances are rendered in (8), (9) and (11). The totalling seven examples of relatively independent usage of the two hands in the signing of AK and KA, are grouped in three subtypes that are discussed in the Sections 4.3, 4.4, and 4.5 respectively.

4.3 Ground incorporation

Two examples of simultaneous and independent use of the two hands concerned signs that are normally one-handed or symmetric two-handed. In these examples an asymmetric non-dominant hand was added which had little meaning in itself other than providing the Ground[3] for the activity performed by the dominant hand.

The first of these cases was produced by KA in his rendering of the bible story of Abraham and Sarah (see example (7) below). A non-dominant B hand is added to the normally one-handed sign ENTER (see Figure 16). The same non-dominant hand is used in the homophonous sign BAG. The addition of the B hand seems to add an extra sense of 'insideness'.

---

3.   I use the term Ground as in Talmy (1985) to mean the reference point with respect to which an entities motion or location is specified.

Figure 16. The simultaneous construction in (7): ENTER + GROUND

(7)   R: LONG-TIME GOD ENTER   IND-Sarah PREGNANT BIRTH
      L: LONG-TIME   ENTER-ground   BIRTH
      'After a long time, God put (something) inside Sarah and she got pregnant
      and gave birth.'

The second example of this type (not illustrated) is produced by AK. In this
example the right bent B hand performs a scraping action on the left B hand representing 'taking out fufu (pounded yam or cassava) from the mortar'. This structure
is not known to be a lexical sign and was therefore included in this study.

In the two examples above, the timing of both hands is exactly the same. The
combinations look very much like asymmetric two-handed signs. They were included, however, as they were one of the few cases of two-handed signing that
were not readily identified as two-handed lexical signs, but it is possible, however,
that these two examples are merely free variants of lexical signs. No corresponding
type was found in Miller's typology. Productive combinations of this type may be
so common in other signed languages that they have not been counted as simultaneous constructions. In AdaSL however, such productive combinations appear
to be so rare that we felt they needed to be included in order to be complete. Irrespective of their status as simultaneous constructions, the marginality in AdaSL
of productive and synchronous combinations of one hand representing an action
and another hand representing the Ground remains striking.

4.4 A manual sign with a whole body sign expressing simultaneous events

In three examples, all signed by AK, the non-dominant hand of the signer represents the hand of a referent. The action of this hand is in fact part of a larger
role shift, showing the behaviour and emotion of the referent. These cases are thus

Figure 17. The simultaneous construction in (8): NO INSULT + NO-2 NO

examples of the simultaneous use of a whole body sign and a manual sign, rather than of two manual signs. In (8) the agreeing verb INSULT on the right hand coincides with a pacifying gesture directed to a projected interlocutor on the left hand (see Figure 17).

(8)   y/n
    R: INSULT INDEX-1 pacify INSULT NO INSULT-2 NO
    L: pacify - - - - - NO pacify - - - NO
    'Are you insulting me?' 'No, I did not insult you'

In this utterance, two separate aspects of one event are thus expressed: the pacifying gesture of a referent and the quoted speech of the same referent. Another example of two separate aspects of one event expressed by two independent hands is represented in (9).

(9) R: LIFT-shirt STRETCH-ACROSS-table BEAT-back
    L: IND-table LIFT-shirt STRETCH-ACROSS-table - - - - - - -
    'You lay down on a table and you are beaten'

This example contains a role shift. The sign LIFT-shirt and STRETCH-ACCROS-table both refer to the person that is beaten, the sign BEAT-back, articulated by the right hand, represents (the stick of) the beater. The simultaneous construction thus represents an action of the beater and the beaten. The last example of this type, which is not illustrated, was found in the same piece of discourse as the examples in (8) and (9). In this example, the right hand, index selected, beats the palm of the left B hand. As in (9), both the hand of the beater and the beaten are represented in one simultaneous construction. The three examples in this section can all be considered as instance of Miller's type two: 'Holds of verbs or predicative adjectives with one or more proposition(s) on the other hand'. Interestingly, the verbs that are held are all whole body signs.

4.5 Discourse marking hold

In two cases, the non-dominant hand is held while the dominant hand produces one or more other signs. The hold can be interpreted as having a discourse function, indicating the topic of the utterance. In (10), KA is talking about his two daughter's name signs; he signs that he and his daughter KW have the same name sign – a K hand touching the non-dominant palm:

(10)   R: ELDER KW(name) PERSON-short KW(name) IND-1
       L: ELDER KW (name) -
       R: SAME(GSL), IND-1 KW-school KW-here(rep) INDEX-1
       L: -
       R: KA(old name) IND-school
       L: KA
       R: KW CHANGE(GSL) KW SAME(GSL) SAME
       L: KW CHANGE(GSL) KW SAME(GSL)
       'The eldest is called TW, the youngest KW. Her name sign is the same as mine, she is KW there (at school) and I'm KW too (here). My (old) name sign is KA and so was hers. Then our names were changed to KW, so we have the same name.'

During a considerable part of the fragment, the non-dominant B hand of the name sign KW is held in place. This name sign is articulated several times here, with at most three signs intervening between two articulations. It is not clear whether the hold of the B hand is a case of perseverance for ease of production or whether it actually serves a discourse function, indicating that the names of KA and his daughter are the topic.

In (11), the sign EIGHT is held on the non-dominant hand, indicating that the eight children are the topic of the utterance (see Figure 18). In the latter part of this utterance, the signer seems to try to produce a simultaneous construction, but fails to.

(11)   R: IND-1 WOMAN BIRTH EIGHT EIGHT BIRTH EIGHT
       L: EIGHT EIGHT - - - - - - - - - -
       R: EIGHT FOUR DEAD(GSL)
       L: EIGHT   DEAD(GSL)
       'My mother gave birth to eight (children), three of whom died.'

The holds of the non-dominant hand as a discourse marker as in (10) and (11) fall under Miller's type three: 'holds of nouns on the non-dominant hand with proposition(s) on the other hand'.

Figure 18. The simultaneous construction in (11):
EIGHT BIRTH + hold_EIGHT EIGHT

4.6 Discussion

Finding only seven cases in more than half an hour of dense signing indicates an infrequent occurrence of simultaneous constructions. Moreover, the cases of ground incorporation as discussed in Section 4.3, may be free variants of a lexical sign, rather than full simultaneous constructions. Simultaneous constructions seem to occur much less frequently in AdaSL than in the signed languages studied so far on this topic.

A less intensive use of simultaneous constructions in AdaSL as compared to other signed languages also becomes evident in the number of signs that are produced during a hold. Most of the examples Miller (1994, 2000) gives contain holds of one of the hands that spread across several signs on the other hand. In our AdaSL cases, a sign was held during maximally three other signs as in (10).

Not only are fewer instances found, also the types of simultaneous constructions used in AdaSL appear to be limited. Miller (2000) considers the locative type of simultaneous construction involving classifiers to be the traditionally most widely recognised type of simultaneous construction. Looking at the AdaSL data however, we find no instances of this prototypical type of simultaneous construction. No examples of a locative construction using classifiers are found in the data. This absence is striking, but it can be explained on the basis of language internal properties. AdaSL differs from most signed languages in its use of space. Many signed languages use two major projection scales, real size signing as in character perspective and signing on a highly reduced projection scale on a limited plane in front of the signer making use of object classifiers. AdaSL uses only one projection scale, that of real-size signing. This restriction explains the absence of object or entity classifier predicates expressing motion or location in space, as these typically use spatial projection on a reduced scale. Instead of using an entity classifier construction, AdaSL uses a series consisting of a manner verb and a generic directional verb or a spatially modified whole body manner sign (Nyst 2007; Nyst & Perniss 2004).[4] As object classifiers in verbs of motion and location do not occur in simplex or isolated constructions, their absence in simultaneous constructions is no longer surprising.

In the data, no examples were found of simultaneous constructions of Miller's type 4 that is, no pointing signs were found simultaneously with other signs. From free observation, it seems that pointing signs behave differently in AdaSL as compared to other signed languages; this needs to be investigated in future research. Specifically, projecting referents on individual fingers in enumeration, *aka* the use of 'list buoys' (Liddell 2003), and consequently point at a specific enumerated finger for reference, is a strategy not attested for AdaSL (cf. Frishberg 1987). It was witnessed only once during a simultaneous interpretation of a church service from GSL into AdaSL, where it was a direct transfer from the GSL signing.

In summary, in the AdaSL data, only simultaneous construction of type two – 'holds of verbs or predicative adjectives with one or more proposition(s) on the other hand' – and of type three – 'holds of nouns on the non-dominant hand with (a) proposition(s) on the other hand' – are found. Interestingly, all the examples of holds of type two concern whole body signs. Debatably, a third type of simultaneous construction, not described by Miller, is found in the form of 'ground incorporation'. All in all, bimanual simultaneous constructions appear to be restricted in AdaSL in three respects: frequency, duration of holds, and types.

5. Conclusion

AdaSL uses simultaneous manual-mouthing constructions in the semantic domains of size and shape and colour, showing the integration of mouthings in the language system. Whereas these simultaneous manual-mouthing constructions are common in AdaSL, the use of bimanual simultaneous constructions is highly restricted in AdaSL in type, frequency and duration as compared to Quebec Sign Language. In the present study, AdaSL appears to use only two out of the five simultaneous constructions which Miller identified for LSQ. Contrary to LSQ, AdaSL uses neither simultaneous constructions involving classifiers predicates expressing motion or location in space, nor simultaneous constructions involving pointing. Simultaneous constructions contrasting two concepts are not reported either.

---

4.   As such, the expression of motion in AdaSL uses less simultaneous packaging than other signed languages of large Deaf communities. Relatively little simultaneous packaging is also attested in tracing signs (Nyst 2007).

The modality of signed languages creates the possibility of using simultaneous constructions. Yet, patterning differently from LSQ (and many of the signed languages discussed in this volume) with respect to simultaneous constructions, AdaSL shows that extensive exploitation of this possibility is indeed a possible, but not inevitable option for signed languages.

References

Amedofu, Geoffrey K., George Brobby, & Grace Ocansey. 1999. "Congenital Non-Syndromal Deafness at Adamarobe, an Isolated Ghanaian Village: Prevalence, Incidence and Audiometric Characteristics of Deafness in the Village (Part I)". *Journal of the Ghana Science Association [online]* 1:22.63–69.

Berlin, Brent & Paul Kay. 1969. *Basic Color Terms.* Berkeley, Calif.: University of California Press.

Branson, Jan, Don Miller, I Gede Marsaja & I Wayan Negara. 1996. "Everyone Here Speaks Sign Language, Too: A Deaf Village in Bali, Indonesia". *Multicultural Aspects of Sociolinguistics in Deaf Communities (=Sociolinguistics in Deaf Communities, 2)* ed. by Ceil Lucas, 39–57. Washington, D.C.: Gallaudet University Press.

Brobby, George W., Bertram Müller-Myhsok & Rolf D. Horstmann. 1998. "Connexin 26 R143W Mutation Associated with Recessive Nonsyndromic Sensorineural Deafness in Africa". *The New England Journal of Medicine* 338.548–550.

David, John B., Ben B. Edoo, J.F. Mustaffah & Ronald Hinchcliffe. "Adamarobe – A 'Deaf' Village". 1971. *Sound* 5.70–72

Frishberg, Nancy. 1987. "Ghanaian Sign Language". *Gallaudet Encyclopedia of Deaf People and Deafness* ed. by John V. van Cleve, vol. 3. S-Z, 778–779. New York: McGraw-Hill Book Company.

GNAD. Not dated, c. 2003. *Ghanaian Sign Language.* Accra: Ghana National Association of the Deaf.

Groce, Nora Ellen. 1985. *Everyone Here Spoke Sign Language: Hereditary Deafness on Martha's Vineyard.* Harvard: Harvard University Press.

Kisch, Shifra. 2001. *Deafness among a Bedouin Tribe in Southern Israel.* Unpublished master's thesis, Tel Aviv University.

Liddell, Scott K. 2003. *Grammar, Gesture, and Meaning in American Sign Language.* Cambridge: Cambridge University Press.

Miller, Chris. 1994. "Simultaneous Constructions and Complex Signs in Quebec Sign Language (LSQ)". *Perspectives on Sign Language Structure: Papers from the Fifth International Symposium on Sign Language Research. Volume 1* ed. by Inger Ahlgren, Brita Bergman & Mary Brennan, 131–147. Durham: International Sign Linguistics Association.

——. 2000. "Multi-channel Constructions and Universal Syntax". Paper presented at the 7th International Conference on Theoretical Issues in Sign Language Research. Amsterdam, July 23rd–27th 2000.

Nyst, Victoria. 2004. "Verb Series of Non-Agentive Motion in Adamorobe Sign Language (Ghana)". Poster presented at the 8th International Conference on Theoretical Issues in Sign Language Research, Barcelona, September 30th–October 2nd 2004.

—— & Pamela Perniss. 2004. "Classifiers or Verb Series: Motion in German Sign Language and Adamorobe Sign Language (Ghana)". Paper presented at ESF workshop "Modality Effects on The Theory of Grammar. A Crosslinguistic View from Sign Languages of Europe", Barcelona, November 2004.

—— 2007. *A Descriptive Analysis of Adamorobe Sign Language (Ghana)*. Doctoral Dissertation, University of Amsterdam.

Oteng, Florence S. 1988. *Give Them a Name*. Kumasi.

Sandler, Wendy, Irit Meir, Carol A. Padden & Mark Aronoff. 2005. "The Emergence of Grammar: Systematic Structure in a New Language". *Proceedings of the National Academy of Sciences of the United States of America* 102.2661–2665.

Talmy, Leonard. 1985. Lexicalization Patterns. *Language Typology and Syntactic Description*, ed. by Timothy Shopen, 57–149. Cambridge: Cambridge University Press

Washabaugh, William. 1986. *Five Fingers for Survival*. Ann Arbor: Karoma Publishers.

Zeshan, Ulrike. 2003. "The Use of Space in Kata Kolok, a Village-Based Sign Language in Bali". Paper presented at the workshop on Structuring of Space in Language and Cognition: What do Sign Languages Reveal?, Nijmegen, September 2003.

Mouthings and simultaneity
in British Sign Language

Rachel Sutton-Spence
Centre for Deaf Studies, University of Bristol

1. Introduction

Signed languages are often considered to be manual languages, in which one or both hands produce symbols with linguistic meaning. However, they also produce important linguistic information through non-manual channels, including the mouth. Just as it is possible to produce separate but related information on each of the two articulating hands in signed languages, so it is possible for the mouth to produce meaningful linguistic information that is separate from – but related to – the linguistic information articulated on the hands. This paper will describe some of the ways in which the mouth can operate with the hands in British Sign Language (BSL) to produce additional meaning.

Mouth movements have received some attention in the sign linguistics literature, especially in the edited volume by Boyes Braem & Sutton-Spence (2001) which presents research findings on the mouth from several different European signed languages. Sutton-Spence & Woll (1999) have also provided a detailed overview of the general use of mouth patterns in BSL.

Although the exact terms used by different researchers may vary, it is well established that mouth patterns fall into two main categories:

1. 'Mouthings', which are derived from a spoken language, and
2. 'Mouth gestures', which cannot be traced back to a spoken language but are idiomatic gestures produced by the mouth (Rainò 2001)

It is generally agreed that mouthings increase identification of a signed lexical item, and for this reason they tend to be associated especially with sentence and discourse topics, with nouns and with established lexical items. They may serve to increase the salience of, and so aid the foregrounding of, certain referents. In contrast, mouth gestures function more as part of the morphological system of a signed language (for example, Vogt-Svendsen 2001; Ebbinghaus & Heßmann 1996, 2001; but see also Woll 2001) and are more strongly associated with comments, verbs and productive lexical items. Although mouth gestures are an important part of all signed languages described to date, the focus here will be upon the simultaneous use of mouthings with manual signs.

Mouthings have their origins in the mouth patterns that are produced when a word is spoken. It is physically possible to speak an English word while articulating a BSL sign manually, and there are times when a signer might speak an English word, but this is not what is happening when a mouthing is used in BSL. When signers use these mouth patterns as part of BSL, they have been borrowed from the spoken language. Signers are not using English when they produce mouthings, but a feature of BSL that has been *derived* from English. Some signers use mouthings that have been less fully integrated into BSL (and might better be seen as some sort of simultaneous mixing of the two languages), and these will be considered here where necessary, but it is not possible to make a categorical distinction between those mouthings that are fully integrated into BSL and those that are not. In this paper any mouthing that is clearly derived from the English word and used during BSL signing will be considered.

Boyes Braem (2001), in her extensive description of mouthings in Swiss German Sign Language, has shown that they may be used lexically, grammatically, prosodically and for discourse and stylistic reasons. Analysis of the BSL data reported here leads to the same conclusions. In all cases, the simultaneity of the mouthing with the hands is an essential feature.[1]

Mouthings accompanied over two-thirds (69%) of all transcribed signs in the BSL data used for the exploration of mouth patterns.[2] This shows clearly that mouthings are a widespread feature of BSL. Of these mouthings, the majority were derived from the equivalent of the manual sign they accompanied. For example, the manual sign WAIT occurred with the mouthing '*wait*' and BOY with '*boy*'. This might be regarded as the simultaneous production of an element originating from outside BSL with the element of equivalent meaning native to BSL. In any study of simultaneity in languages, this is a remarkable phenomenon, and 69% is a remarkable figure.

However, the focus of this paper is consideration of the mouthings that did not correspond exactly with the transcription of the sign. These are termed 'mismatches' and they show that the simultaneous use of signs and mouthings is

---

1.   It should be noted, however, that 1% of the mouthings used here had no accompanying manual component. The majority of these mouthings were for interjections such as 'yes', 'no', 'well', 'of course' and 'oh'.

2.   See below for a description of the data used.

not restricted to direct English-BSL equivalences. This lack of exact one-to-one correspondence between sign and mouthing is another example of simultaneity occurring in signed languages, as information different in some way from that on the hands is simultaneously articulated with the hands. The phenomenon has been described in other signed languages, including Swiss-German Sign Language (DSGS, Boyes Braem 2001) and German Sign Language (DGS, Hohenberger & Happ 2001). In the BSL data described here, 15% (N = 1292) of all mouth patterns did not correspond exactly to the manual sign. At least 30 different types of mismatch were identified, of which a dozen of the most commonly occurring will be described here.

2.   Data corpus: Collection and analysis

This description of simultaneous use of mouthings with signs is based upon a large corpus of BSL data (see Sutton-Spence & Day 2001).

Twenty-four signers, aged between 18 and 69 years, contributed to the data corpus, which was collected between 1989 and 1997. All signers were Deaf and used BSL as their first language. Some had grown up in hearing, non-signing families, (termed 'DCHP' – Deaf child of hearing parents, after Day 1995) and others in Deaf, signing families ('DCDP' – Deaf child of Deaf parents). Some data were obtained from existing archive sources, and some collected specifically for this project. Almost all the signers addressed only other Deaf people (such as a Deaf interviewer, or a Deaf audience). The two exceptions were the signer appearing on television (who was aware of the existence of a hearing audience but targeted her BSL at the Deaf viewers) and the three signers who were signing stories designed to be teaching materials for advanced learners of BSL (and could thus be judged to be the language variety that was considered 'good BSL'). All signers knew that they were being filmed, but none knew at the time of data collection that their use of the mouth would be analysed.

Existing archive data used for this research were:

- 'Care-giver Register' – Two DCDP adults signing to Deaf children of different ages, telling stories and asking questions. (Transcription of 558 signs).
- 'Demographic interviews' – Twelve adults signing to a Deaf interviewer, in a structured, formal situation, describing their life history. (Transcription of 1557 signs).
- 'Teaching Stories' – Three adults (one DCDP and two DCHP) telling stories (personal vignettes) in BSL directly to a video camera to provide teaching material for advanced students of BSL. (Transcription of 620 signs).

- 'News Interpreting' – a DCDP signer interpreting the local BBC television afternoon news summary. (Transcription of 824 signs).
- 'Lectures' – Two members of University academic staff delivering lectures to all-Deaf classes of undergraduates, using BSL. One signer was DCHP and one DCDP. (Transcription of 392 signs).

Further data were collected specifically for the study of mouth patterns. Twelve Deaf BSL users (six DCDP and six DCHP) were filmed in interview sessions with a Deaf researcher known to them.

- 'News Story' – The participants individually recounted a recent news story about the safe rescue of a shipwrecked yachtsman (from which a total of 2389 signs were transcribed).
- 'Fantasy Story' – The participants individually retold part of the story of 'The Snowman' by Raymond Briggs, based on pictures from the book (from which a total of 2210 signs were transcribed).

Most of these stories lasted approximately two minutes, and for those who signed for longer, a minimum of two minutes' signing (usually approximately 200 signs) was transcribed, starting from the beginning of their stories.

The total number of transcribed signs used in this analysis was 8550.

3.   Data transcription

For each sign transcribed, the meaning of the sign was written down, with the accompanying mouth pattern, which was then categorised as either a mouthing or a mouth gesture or 'neutral' (see Table 1).

Mouthings were transcribed using the orthography of the complete English word, even though it was not always possible to determine that the full word was being articulated.[3] Where there was a mismatch between the meaning of the manual sign and the patterns on the mouth, this was noted. Where the mouthing linked to one sign extended over an adjacent sign, this extension was marked. In many

Table 1. Example of transcription from corpus

Mouth pattern	*Television*	m.g. lips closed firm	*wait*	Neutral	m.g. wide open
Sign meaning	-t-v-	WHAT-IS-IT	WAIT	TURN-ON-TV	PICTURE-BRIGHT

---

3. It became clear that the exact form of the mouthing is not always identical to the mouth pattern for the corresponding spoken word, but this aspect was not addressed by the project. See Keller (2001) for a critique of the practice of using orthography to represent the written form of the derived mouthing.

instances the mouthing over the second sign was the final mouth pattern of the mouthing. This was particularly true for monosyllabic English words. For example, in the construction DEAF HIM the /f/ from the mouth pattern 'Deaf' extended over HIM. An accurate gloss would be:

> *Deaf (cont) f*
> DEAF HIM

When this corpus was first analysed, before the era of widespread sign annotation software such as SignStream and ELAN, it was not practical to record the exact start and end points of the mouth movements making up the stretched mouthing across the two signs. Consequently, in the reporting of the data here, stretched mouthings are simply recorded as carrying the same mouthing as the previous sign.

Table 2 shows an example of the transcription of a section from the story of the shipwrecked yachtsman retold by one signer (manual signs are in small capital letters, and accompanying mouthings are in italics above each manual sign).

m.g.　　　*something*　*m.g.*　*don't-know*　*(cont)know what*　*why*　*what*
BOAT-SAIL SOMETHING BOAT DON'T KNOW WHAT　　　　　WHY WHAT

neutral m.g.　　*m.g.*　　*m.g.*　　　　*under*　*I think lucky*
SO　　BOAT-CAPSIZE BOAT-CAPSIZE STAY-FOR-LONG-TIME UNDER THINK LUCKY

under　*have*　*special*　*hull*　*can*　*breathe*　*(cont)breathe*
UNDER HAVE SPECIAL HULL CAN BREATHE SO

(cont)breathe m.g. think　*helicopter*　*or*　*plane*　*look*
UNDER　　STAY THINK HELICOPTER OR PLANE LOOK

(cont)look　*four*　*days*　*m.g.*　　　　*then*　*m.g.*　*found*
FLY-AROUND FOUR DAYS STAY-LONG-TIME THEN AT-LAST FOUND

don't-know　*who*　*found*　*helicopter*　　*plane*　*don't-know*　*(cont)know*
ME　　　WHO FOUND HELICOPTER PLANE DON'T-KNOW ME

who　*found*　*(cont)found don't-know*　*(cont)know then*　*found by*
WHO FOUND ME　　　DON'T-KNOW ME　　THEN FOUND

'He was sailing in his boat and – I don't know what happened – but it capsized and he stayed under the hull for a long time. I think he was lucky that it was a special hull so he could still breathe under there. He stayed under the hull. I think a helicopter or plane came to look for him. They searched for four days before they found him. I don't know if it was a helicopter or a plane that found him, but he was found by….'

Table 2. Transcription from a DCDP signer recounting the story of the shipwrecked yachtsman

4. Results

4.1 Stretching of mouth patterns

The most common type of mismatch was the stretching of a mouthing over one or more sequentially produced signs (N = 460). For example in ARMY BOAT, the component '*army*' extended over BOAT as well; in AUSTRALIA THERE, the component 'Australia' extended over THERE. These extended, stretched mouthings accounted for 37% of all the instances of a mismatch in the data.

The stretched mouthings were especially common for indexical signs. Almost two-thirds (63%, N = 287) of the extensions were over an indexical sign, as may be seen in Table 3.

Examples may be seen in Table 4.

These indexical signs, while often having lexicalised (albeit deictic) English equivalents, are not completely lexicalised in BSL, and rely heavily on context for their meaning. Deictic pronouns have no need for a mouthing to specify their meaning, because the referent is either present during the utterance or has been identified in a previous sign. This means that the mouth pattern of the specifying sign might be expected to co-occur with the indexical sign. (In fact, indexical signs rarely show any individual mouth pattern at all, including mouth gestures. Although a full analysis of all indexical signs is not complete, analysis of a subsection of the data showed that over half of them had a 'neutral' mouth pattern. Independent mouth patterns were used in some cases for emphasis).

Boyes Braem (2001:115) has argued convincingly that these 'stretched' mouthings serve to bind constituents of a sentence, saying "stretched mouthings seemed to act as an additional suprasegmental for binding sequences of manual signs [. . .] to bind constituents of noun phrases; to bind verbs and their subjects; to bind larger prosodic units." She suggests that the stretching of a mouthing over

Table 3. Percentages of all stretched mouthings over indexical signs

Type of indexical sign	Percentage of all stretched mouthings over indexical signs (N = 287)
Pointing locative	37% (103)
3rd person singular	27% (75)
1st person singular	11% (31)
3rd person plural	8.5% (24)
Two dimensional locative ("area")	7% (20)
2nd person singular	2.5% (7)
Possessive	1.5% (4)
ALL	1% (3)
"Self" (e.g. himself)	0.5% (2)

Table 4. Examples of stretched mouthings over indexical signs

Deaf (*cont*)	*Garden* (*cont*)
DEAF ALL	GARDEN AREA
Expect (*cont*)	*Sunday* (*cont*)
EXPECT HE	SUNDAY THAT
Braidwood (*cont*) *clever* (*cont*)	*Hear* (*cont*)
BRAIDWOOD HIM CLEVER HIM	HEAR THAT
School (*cont*)	*Australia* (*cont*)
SCHOOL ME	AUSTRALIA THERE
Seven (*cont*)	*Beds* (*cont*)
SEVEN ME	BEDS THERE
Think (*cont*)	*Asleep* (*cont*)
THINK ME	ASLEEP UPSTAIRS
Gloucester (*cont*)	*Thirty* (*cont*)
GLOUCESTER THEM	THIRTY HIMSELF
Hope (*cont*)	*Deaf* (*cont*)
HOPE THEM	DEAF HIMSELF
Cold (*cont*)	*Room* (*cont*)
COLD YOU	ROOM HIS
Man (*cont*)	*British* (*cont*)
MAN YOU	BRITISH OURS

the noun and the indexical spatial locus "might be a signed language equivalent of the marking of a prosodic word in spoken languages". Half (52%, N = 149) of all stretched mouthings in the data here were over the noun and indexical locus. However, additionally, a further 21% (N = 61) were over a verb and the indexical sign and another 12% (N = 35) were over an adjective and indexical sign.[4]

Of the remaining 37% of examples, the stretched mouthing covered a non-indexical sign. Table 5 shows the main classes of signs that led the bound constituents.

We can see in Table 5 that almost half of these pairs of signs had a noun followed by some other non-indexical sign. Nearly half of the noun pairs (49%) were followed by a verb, so these stretched mouthings could be categorised as serving to bind verbs to their associated nouns. Some showed the noun and its associated polycomponential verb, for example:

> *wreath* (*cont*)   *man* (*cont*)
> WREATH LAY-WREATH or MAN MAN-MOVE-TO-BOY

---

4. We should note that determining the word class of many BSL signs is not easy, and perhaps signed languages do not follow the same word class systems as English (see, e.g. Johnston & Schembri 1999). Judgements on word class here were based on the class of the English word from which the mouthing was derived.

Table 5. Word classes of the first sign in pairs of signs linked by a stretched mouthing

Word class	Percentage of classes of signs leading non-indexical bound constituents (N = 171)
Leading nouns	49% (84)
Leading verbs	19% (32)
Leading adjectives	12% (21)
Other classes (e.g. conjunctions or modal or aspectual auxiliaries)	20% (34)

Others simply bound the noun and established lexical verb together within a phrase, for example:

> *friend*   (*cont*)   *news*   (*cont*)
> FRIEND LAUGH or NEWS SEE

Where verbs led the sign pairs of bound constituents, the second signs of the pairs were usually of the 'minor' word classes, including negations (FEEL NOTHING with *feel*), rhetorical questions (SHOW WHAT with *show*) and time markers (BAN BEFORE with *ban*). Some, however, covered a second verb. The leading verb was usually an established verb, and the second verb was productively created, sometimes being a polycomponential verb, for example:

> *clash*   (*cont*)   *think*   (*cont*)
> CLASH ROUGH-WAVES-CLASH or THINK LOOK-AROUND

This evidence suggests that stretched mouth patterns frequently serve to bind the identifying established sign with the related productive sign, whether the leading sign is a noun, verb or other sign. Supporting evidence for this comes from the fact that although 49% (N = 149) of the leading signs in bound constituents are nouns, the nouns (the most common class of established signs) only make up 16% (N = 28) of the second constituents.

4.2 Anticipations

Stretched mouthings that represented anticipations of the following sign were less common than the perseverating mouthings considered so far. The forty-two occurrences of anticipatory mouthings accounted for only three percent of the mismatched mouthings over signs, compared to the 37% of perseverating mouthings. Examples of the anticipations included MY FATHER (where the mouthing *'father'* extended back over MY, as well as the equivalent sign FATHER); MAN WIFE (where *'wife'* extended over MAN as well as the following WIFE); and INSIDE WARM, (where *'warm'* extended over INSIDE).

Half (N = 20) of all the anticipatory mouthings covered indexical signs, supporting the observations made above that indexical signs may be bound to their 'identifying sign', whether the index occurs before or after it. Examples include:

feel (*cont*)	*bristol* (*cont*)
ME FEEL	HERE BRISTOL
cold (*cont*)	*have* (*cont*)
THAT COLD	THEY HAVE

Exactly what drives this type of extension is still unclear and needs further exploration. Their occurrence is spread throughout the registers (story-telling, interviews, lectures and news bulletins) and, while the signer delivering the news from an autocue was responsible for 31% of the anticipations (suggesting that this may have influenced her signing), nine other signers of various ages and signing backgrounds produced them.

4.3 Additional mouthings

Mouthings reflecting English grammar and morphology also occurred in conjunction with a manual sign, for example FOOD was accompanied by '*about his food*'; NOW by '*at the moment*'; BRISTOL by '*from Bristol*' and FILM by '*a film*'. These instances accounted for approximately 10% (N = 133) of all the mismatched mouthings. The addition of English grammar words (and their absence from the manual component) shows they are far less adapted to the phonology and morphology of BSL, so these occurrences might be better described as instances of code-switching into English or mixing the two languages simultaneously. Although these additional uses of English grammar were used by both DCDP and DCHP signers, the majority were produced by the DCHP signers, for whom we might expect English to be more dominant in their BSL.

lot of people	*from Bristol*	*rest of the world*	*pray for*
ALL	BRISTOL	WORLD	PRAY
(DCDP)	(DCDP)	(DCHP)	(DCHP)

Another use of this additional mouthing was the production of an English negation to support an entirely non-manual negation (N = 3). Although these negations were also shown through head movement and facial expression, there was no morphological information in the manual sign to show negation. For example:

never saw	*never watch*
SAW	WATCH

4.4 Incomplete relation to the sign

The use of a mouthing to represent just part of the English equivalence of the BSL sign also occurred, for a range of reasons.

The polycomponential verb could carry the mouthing related to the associated noun (N = 13), for example:

> *bed*   *light*
> ROLL-OVER-IN-BED LIGHT-SHINE-IN-FACE

Alternatively the mouthing of a verb that contains the subject or object agreement identifies the verb but not the agreement (N = 25), for example:

> *help*   *look*   *show*   *hit*
> HELP-ME LOOK-AT-HIM SHOW-YOU HIT-HIM

Where subject and verb appear in the same sign, either the subject alone may occur as the mouthing (e.g. BOAT-TURN-OVER with '*boat*'), or the verb alone (e.g. DOOR-OPEN with '*open*'). The same occurs when object and verb appear in the same sign (e.g. AMPUTATE-FINGER with '*amputate*' or RING BELL with '*bell*').

When noun and adjective information occur in the same sign, the data here implies that retention of the adjective in the mouthing is more common than retention of the noun (e.g. BRIGHT-SCREEN with '*bright*' and ROUND-WINDOW with '*round*') as the data contained no examples of adjective signs with the noun mouthing. It should be noted that these are productive signs and that the noun is not easily identified from the sign.

Phrasal verbs also occurred in which the mouthing was derived only from the adverb, showing that identifying the central part of the verb through the mouthing is not always essential (N = 70). GET-OFF, CUT-OFF, TURN-OFF, SWITCH-OFF and JUMP-OFF all had the mouthing '*off*'. GO-BACK and STEP-BACK had '*back*'; LIFT-OUT, THROW-OUT and GET-OUT had '*out*'; and LIE-ON, TURN-ON and SWITCH-ON used '*on*'.

4.5 Specific identification of a sign

There are times when one BSL sign could refer to several English words (although there are, conversely, times when one English word could refer to several BSL signs). Where the signer wishes to specify the exact English equivalence of a BSL sign, a mouthing can be used for this. Table 6 shows how mouthings used in the data can show the exact English meaning.

Table 6. Mouthings specifying the English meaning of a sign

ANGRY	*furious*
FACTORY	*manufacture*
SPREAD	*project (v)*
BOAT	*yacht*
CHILD	*boy*
QUIET	*peace*
HEAT	*radiator*
SURPRISED	*shocked*

4.6 Mouthings with simultaneous manual signs

Reference has been made in the other papers of this volume to the fact that signed languages can articulate separate signs on each hand. This option of producing simultaneous signs, also affects the relationship between the mouthings and manual components because having only one mouth and two hands means that mouthing could only possibly be related to one sign at a time. In the data here, the use of mouthings where there were two simultaneous manual signs was not extensive (perhaps because these constructions lend themselves more to the use of mouth-gestures, being frequently productive signs) but there were a few instances (N = 13). In most occurrences of simultaneous signs with a mouthing, one manual sign specified a lexical item and the other located it, and the mouthing reflected the specifying manual sign. For example:

mouth:	alive	Australia		hot	boy
dom:	ALIVE	AUSTRALIA		HOT	BOY
non-dom:	HIM	AREA-LOCATION		THAT	HIM

However in TALL/BOY the mouthing was linked to the adjective 'tall', perhaps to emphasise that it was a tall boy, rather than the fact that there was a boy. In HEAT/HAND-FEELS-HEAT, the mouthing was linked to the established sign HEAT, rather than the productive sign HAND-FEELS-HEAT.

4.7 Simultaneous production of phrases

Simultaneous signing may also occur with separate lexical items on the hands and mouth to produce phrases (N = 133).

guardian	*frightened*	*boy*	*push*
ANGEL	FEEL	LITTLE	BOAT
(Guardian angel)	(feel frightened)	(little boy)	(push the boat)

The mouthing could comment in some way upon the manual sign (e.g. PROTECT-HIMSELF with '*must*' and RUB-HANDS with '*warm*') and could provide an adjective or adverb for a manual noun or verb (e.g. TAP with '*cold*' and WATER-SPRAY with '*fast*').

There were also instances of a noun mouthing referring to the verb on the hands (e.g. TURN-ON-TAP with '*water*' and TURN-OVER with '*boat*') and a verb mouthing referring to a noun on the hands (e.g. FINGER with '*bite*' and BOTTLE with '*squeeze*').

Independent mouthings also specified the character performing an action described in the manual sign. For example, WALK with '*snowman*' showed it was the snowman who walked, and SHAKE-HANDS-AMAZED with '*boy*' was used to mean it was the boy who shook hands in amazement.

The mouthing could operate with head movement to negate a manual sign (e.g. BAD with '*no*' to create 'not bad' and HEAR with '*can't*' to create 'can't hear'). It was also used to specify the basic verb in a sign that was manually negated (e.g. DON'T-KNOW only with '*know*' and NOT-INTERESTED only with '*interested*').

A few indexical signs (N = 30) were accompanied by mouthings that provided more detailed 'content' information, rather than by the perseverating mouthing stretching from beyond that manual sign described above. For example, SHE occurred with '*girl*' and HE occurred with '*magistrate*' not as a perseverating stretched mouthing but simply as the pair of signs. In both these instances, the girl and magistrate had already been mentioned using manual signs, so this mouthing enabled the signer to refer to a previously established referent without the need to sign the full sign again. One especially common occurrence was the use of HERE with '*Bristol*' without any previous manual reference to Bristol. This was used by many of the interviewees, because HERE did indeed refer to Bristol where they were at the time, and the word 'Bristol' would have been highly activated in the minds of both parties. However, other examples of indexical signs with non-indexical mouthings did not follow this pattern. For example, THEY occurred with '*realise*' to mean 'they realised', but the manual sign REALISE was not articulated in the story. Similar occurrences included, HE with '*lucky*', and THOSE with '*see*'. These constructions rely upon the signer's lipreading knowledge of English, but they were rare occurrences and all produced by DCHP who might be expected to mix more English with their BSL signs. Where a mouthing has become almost lexicalised, this lack of manual equivalence is less of a problem. Several signers (both DCDP and DCHP) used mouthings to present direct speech, for example in THAT with '*what is it?*' to mean, 'What's that?'. The mouthing 'what is it?' has almost become lexicalised in BSL (looking more like '*woss*' or '*wossit*') and is recognised as the mouth pattern that can accompany a non-manual question.

4.8 Numerals and quantifiers

In many signs containing a numeral or quantifier as part of a morphologically complex sign, the mouthing articulated the numeral only. For example:

nine	*two*	*two*
AGE-NINE	TWO-KEELS-OF-BOAT	TWO-DAYS-AGO
four	*seven*	
FOUR-OF-US	SEVEN-POUNDS	

It was far less common for the mouthing to show the non-numeral morpheme, but it did occur, for example in:

fingers	*small*
TWO-FINGERS	BOTH-SMALL

4.9 Constructed speaking

Mouthings can occur as part of role-shift to report direct speech. The mouthing could be without any manual component, (for example in recounting a conversation with a non-signer: 'are you all right?' and 'yes, I'm fine') but also frequently co-occurs with a manual component.

what's that?
BOX
'He looked at the box and asked, "What's that?".'

all right
FEEL-SORRY-FOR-HIM
'I felt sorry for him, so I said, "all right".'

how do
HE-SHAKES-HANDS-WITH-MUM
'He shook hands with mum and said "How do you do?".'

off
HE-SHOUT-AT-ME
'He shouted at me to get off.'

no!
BACK-AWAY
'He backed away, saying "No!".'

4.10 Expression of sounds

The mouthing can also show the sound made by the action in the manual component (e.g. ALARM-SOUNDS with 'beep beep beep' and KNOCK-ON-HULL with 'bang bang bang').

4.11 Other mouthings

Some manual adjectives were also intensified using the mouthing of the English intensifier (e.g. HOT with 'too hot', LATE with 'very late' and GOOD with 'very good'). These English intensifiers were all produced by DCHP signers.

In another group of signs, the mouthing and manual components could be part of a compound noun, which is fully specified in the other component. For example, SNOW was accompanied by the full 'snowman' for some signers, while for others 'snowman' accompanied MAN. Other examples included EX with 'ex-husband' and SEE with 'See Hear!' (the name of a British Deaf magazine television programme). GAS-RING occurred with 'ring', AIRFORCE with 'air' and LIGHT-SWITCH occurred with 'light' but also with 'switch'.

Finally, there are signs which use a mouthing but not in a way that would be recognised by a monolingual English -speaker. For example, the sign LEARNER-DRIVER is accompanied by 'ell' and HIMSELF and MYSELF are made with 'self'. These are not errors or idiosyncrasies but rather an example of BSL borrowing a form from English and altering it as part of the language.

5.   Conclusion

Research on the simultaneous use of the multiple articulators available to signed languages needs to consider the simultaneous use of mouth and hands. The data reported here provide a detailed account of the range of categories of uses of mouthings with manual signs. Although alien to the manual language of BSL, mouthings are clearly not necessarily mere intrusions of spoken language. Instead, they have been incorporated into the language to serve specific purposes. For most occurrences, the mouthings are articulated simultaneously with the manual sign of the equivalent meaning to support its meaning. However, the interesting subgroup of 'mismatched' simultaneous mouthings with signs shows that BSL uses mouthings for far more than this. The data described here demonstrably support any claims that mouthings function in signed languages lexically, grammatically, prosodically and for discourse and stylistic reasons. There are still areas of this topic that need exploration, for example it would be very helpful to make a detailed analysis of the exact timing of movements of the mouthings in relation to manual movements of their accompanying signs. Additionally, further research in other signed languages would reveal the extent to which any or all of these patterns can be generalised cross-linguistically.

Acknowledgements

The research for this work was supported by ESRC Award Number R000221806. I would like to thank Jim Kyle, Lorna Allsop and Linda Day for their contributions.

References

Boyes Braem, Penny. 2001. "Functions of Mouthings in the Signing of Deaf Early and Late Learners of Swiss German Sign Language (DSGS)". *The Hands are the Head of the Mouth: The Mouth as Articulator in Sign Languages* ed. by Penny Boyes Braem & Rachel Sutton-Spence, 99–132. Hamburg: Signum Press.

—— & Rachel Sutton-Spence. 2001. *The Hands are the Head of the Mouth: The Mouth as Articulator in Sign Languages.* Hamburg: Signum Press.

Day, Linda. 1995. *Sign Language Acquisition of Deaf Adults in Deaf and Hearing Families.* Unpublished diploma dissertation, University of Bristol.

Ebbinghaus, Horst & Jens Heßmann. 1996. "Signs and Words: Accounting for Spoken Language Elements in German Sign Language". *International Review of Sign Linguistics. Vol. 1* ed. by William Edmondson & Ronnie B. Wilbur, 23–56. Mahwah, N.J.: Lawrence Erlbaum Associates.

—— & Jens Heßmann. 2001. "Sign Language as Multidimensional Communication. Why Manual Signs, Mouthings and Mouth Gestures are Three Different Things". *The Hands are the Head of the Mouth: The Mouth as Articulator in Sign Languages* ed. by Penny Boyes Braem & Rachel Sutton-Spence, 133–153. Hamburg: Signum Press.

Hohenberger, Annette & Daniela Happ. 2001. "The Linguistic Primacy of Signs and Mouth Gestures over Mouthings: Evidence from Language Production in German Sign Language (DGS)". *The Hands are the Head of the Mouth: The Mouth as Articulator in Sign Languages* ed. by Penny Boyes Braem & Rachel Sutton-Spence, 153–190. Hamburg: Signum Press.

Johnston, Trevor & Schembri, Adam. 1999. "On Defining Lexeme in a Signed Language". *Sign Language and Linguistics* 2:2.115–185.

Keller, Jörg. 2001. "Multimodal Representations and the Linguistic Status of Mouthings in German Sign Language (DGS)". *The Hands are the Head of the Mouth: The Mouth as Articulator in Sign Languages* ed. by Penny Boyes Braem & Rachel Sutton-Spence, 191–230. Hamburg: Signum Press.

Rainò, Päivi. 2001. "Mouthings and Mouth Gestures in Finnish Sign Language (FinSL)". *The Hands are the Head of the Mouth: The Mouth as Articulator in Sign Languages* ed. by Penny Boyes Braem & Rachel Sutton-Spence, 41–50. Hamburg: Signum Press.

Sutton-Spence, Rachel & Linda Day 2001. "Mouthings and Mouth Gestures in British Sign Language (BSL)". *The Hands are the Head of the Mouth: The Mouth as Articulator in Sign Languages* ed. by Penny Boyes Braem & Rachel Sutton-Spence, 69–86. Hamburg: Signum Press.

—— & Bencie Woll. 1999. *The Linguistics of British Sign Language. An Introduction.* Cambridge: Cambridge University Press.

Vogt-Svendsen, Marit. 2001. "A Comparison of Mouth Gestures and Mouthings in Norwegian Sign Language (NSL)". *The Hands are the Head of the Mouth: The Mouth as Articulator in Sign Languages* ed. by Penny Boyes Braem & Rachel Sutton-Spence, 9–40. Hamburg: Signum Press.

Woll, Bencie. 2001. "The Sign that Dares to Speak its Name: Echo Phonology in British Sign Language (BSL)". *The Hands are the Head of the Mouth: The Mouth as Articulator in Sign Languages* ed. by Penny Boyes Braem & Rachel Sutton-Spence, 87–98. Hamburg: Signum Press.

The non-dominant hand in a Swedish Sign Language discourse*

Anna-Lena Nilsson
Stockholm University

1. Introduction

Signers have two hands at their disposal to produce signs, and a stretch of signed discourse usually contains both one-handed and two-handed signing. As was pointed out by Battison regarding American Sign Language (ASL) "most people with strong hand preference will use their dominant hand to play the active role, and their non-dominant hand in the static role" (1974:8). The dominant hand will thus be used to produce most one-handed signs and fingerspellings, be the more active hand in asymmetric two-handed signs, and function as one of the active hands in symmetrical two-handed signs. The non-dominant hand will not be inactive though. Among its easily discernible functions are (1) being the base hand (Klima & Bellugi 1979:64) in asymmetric two-handed signs, (2) being one of the articulators in symmetric two-handed signs, and (3) to produce signs of its own. There are also instances where the non-dominant hand anticipates or perseverates from two-handed signs.

In the following, an attempt is made to describe the activities of the non-dominant hand when it does not participate in the production of a two-handed sign. The aim is thus not to describe e.g. the internal structure of two-handed signs or phonological processes within individual signs; several such studies have been published regarding different signed languages, e.g. Battison (1974) for ASL. Modified forms of signs, where the non-dominant hand is active due to some mor-

* I would like to thank Lena Johansmide for willingly allowing me to use this recording of her, and my colleagues at Stockholm University for interesting discussions about the material. I owe special gratitude to Brita Bergman for invaluable help in preparing this text.

phological process expressing, for example, plurality and/or repeated action (see e.g. Klima & Bellugi (1979) for ASL; Bergman (1983) for Swedish Sign Language) will not be included either. Constructions known as polysynthetic signs in descriptions of Swedish Sign Language (e.g. Wallin 2000), or as classifier constructions (e.g. Emmorey 2003), are also excluded.

The fact that signed languages permit simultaneous production of distinct elements by the two hands has frequently been observed. In a paper including studies covering five different signed languages (published from 1975 to the mid-nineties), Miller focuses on "non-classifier constructions involving the simultaneous production of distinct signs" (1994: 89). Simultaneous constructions such as, e.g. an enumeration morpheme, object incorporation, (topic) perseveration and Index$_{pro}$ are discussed, and they are also compared to similar constructions in Quebec Sign Language (LSQ). Some of the activities of the non-dominant hand described in the present study are discussed by Miller too, but from a different perspective and using different terminology.

Stretching the point, one could hypothesize that whenever the dominant hand produces a one-handed sign, the non-dominant hand is not required to take part in the production of that sign and thus will be inactive. No detailed analysis is needed, however, to note that the non-dominant hand is not inactive to such a large extent in normal signed discourse. In this study, the activities of the non-dominant hand in a whole discourse are described, something which, to the best of my knowledge is not found in any other study. As we will see, simultaneity is a key concept and there are several factors contributing to a markedly two-handed impression of this signed discourse.

2. Material and method

The material analyzed is a Swedish Sign Language discourse, consisting of a video recorded monologue (9 minutes 44 seconds long) where a deaf woman retells the contents of an autobiography she has read – *Livets hjul: En självbiografi i dödens närhet.* (original title *Wheel of life.*) – written by Elisabeth Kübler-Ross. There is a listener (a native signer) sitting by the camera.

In order to describe the activities of the non-dominant hand when it is not part of a two-handed sign, a list was made of the signs that occur in the material which are considered one-handed in citation form. The total number of occurrences of one-handed signs is 613, counting all instances regardless of whether the same sign has already previously occurred or not. The total number of instances of two-handed signs is 538, making the total number of instances of signs 1151. Thus, approximately 53% of the instances of signs are one-handed, and approximately 47% two-handed in citation form. This can be compared to the Swedish

Sign Language dictionary (*Svenskt teckenspråkslexikon* 1997) where approximately 45% of the main entries are one-handed signs.

Having identified all instances of one-handed signs, the activities of the non-dominant hand during the production of these signs were analyzed, and categorized. In the following, the activities of the non-dominant hand will be presented, starting with those where it is least active and adds least to the content of the discourse, and gradually moving towards more active participation and contribution to content. (All percentages have been rounded off to the nearest whole number.)

3. The non-dominant hand

3.1 In lap

There are sequences in the discourse where the non-dominant hand does not participate in the production of signs, but rests in the signer's lap. This position, illustrated in Figure 1, is referred to as 'in lap'.[1] Short sequences with 'in lap' occur

TO-INTERVIEW
in lap

Figure 1. Illustration of 'in lap'

---

1. Transcriptions consist of two lines, with or without photos to illustrate the signs. The top line represents the right (dominant) hand, the bottom line the left (non-dominant) hand. Glosses in capitals are used to identify Swedish Sign Language signs. Some glosses indicate the form of the sign, or the function, whereas most are chosen to represent the meaning of the sign. That does not imply that the sign has the same semantic, morphological or syntactic characteristics as the English word chosen. Glosses with hyphens between them are used when more than one word is used to identify a sign, glosses with a slash (/) between them are used to indicate compound signs. A gloss preceded by a '#' indicates a fingerspelled item. A line of hyphens (----) is used to indicate the duration of a sign, when that is of particular interest. Lower-case letters after glosses are used to indicate the direction of the movement of a sign; f-forward, fl-forward left, fr-forward right. The English translations below transcriptions give the meaning in that specific context.

at irregular intervals in the discourse, lasting one or a few signs. There are also seven longer sequences, one is 26 sec., where the non-dominant hand rests in the signer's lap during the one-handed signs, but actively takes part in the production of two-handed signs when they occur. Of the one-handed signs in the discourse, 19% ($n = 116$) co-occur with 'in lap'.

3.2 At chest

Another rest position of the non-dominant hand entails it being held still at chest height in a loose fist configuration. Sometimes the non-dominant hand is quite relaxed in this position, with a tendency for the index finger of this lax hand to be slightly extended. Two examples of 'at chest' are illustrated in Figure 2. Different forms of this position co-occur with a total of 22% ($n = 133$) of the one-handed signs in the material.

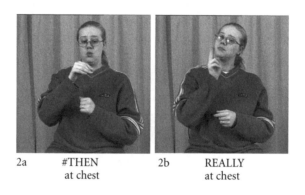

| 2a | #THEN
at chest | 2b | REALLY
at chest |

Figure 2. Illustrations of 'at chest'

3.3 Mirror at chest

In the positions of the non-dominant hand described so far, it is held still and the handshape is not influenced by that of the dominant hand. In 'mirror at chest', the non-dominant hand is also held still, in a position similar to that of 'at chest', but it mirrors the handshape and orientation of the dominant hand.[2] In the example in Figure 3, we see the one-handed sign GRADUATE, where the dominant hand is held at the contralateral side of the signer's chest, assuming a hand configuration where

---

2. Sandler (1993) also uses the term mirror in her paper on sign language phonology (ASL), but in a different way. According to her the non-dominant hand has two roles. "In one role, it is a mirror of the dominant hand, what I call an echo articulator. In the other role, it is not an articulator at all, but a place of articulation, like the head or the trunk" (1993:337–338).

GRADUATE
mirror at chest

Figure 3. Illustration of 'mirror at chest'

the thumb, index finger and middle finger are extended. The non-dominant hand is held still at chest height, but assumes the same handshape and orientation as the dominant hand. Since the non-dominant hand does not move the co-articulation is only partial. 'Mirror at chest' co-occurs with 6% ($n = 37$) of the one-handed signs.

'In lap', 'at chest', and 'mirror at chest' can all be described as rest positions of the non-dominant hand, since it does not participate in the sign production, and does not add to the content of the discourse. For 'at chest' and 'mirror at chest', however, the fact that the non-dominant hand does not rest in the signer's lap but is held at chest height makes it appear to take part in the discourse production, something we will return to in the discussion below.

3.4 Mirroring

In the rest positions of the non-dominant hand discussed in the previous sections, the non-dominant hand is held still, even though its position may contribute to a two-handed impression of the signing. In Figure 4, as the dominant hand pro-

TO-FAIL
mirroring

Figure 4. Illustration of 'mirroring'

duces the one-handed sign TO-FAIL, the non-dominant hand not only assumes the same handshape and orientation, but also performs the same movement (both the hand internal movement and the downward path movement) at a slightly lower location. This full co-articulation makes this instance of TO-FAIL look like a two-handed sign produced with the non-dominant hand slightly lower than the dominant. Even though the non-dominant hand is active here, this is a purely phonetic, sign-internal process, which does not add any content to the discourse. 'Mirroring' is the term used for instances of signs in the material which are considered one-handed in citation form, but are produced in this way. Of the one-handed signs in the discourse, 4% ($n = 22$) co-occur with 'mirroring'.

3.5 Doubling

The material also contains instances of signs that are one-handed in citation form, but produced with both hands active and performing the same movement at the same height. This is referred to as 'doubling', and there are two such instances in Figure 5 (which also illustrates other activities of the non-dominant hand), viz. the first and third signs in the first row. Both HOW and TO are one-handed in citation form, but in this example they are produced with 'doubling'. Instances of 'doubling', where we see active participation of the non-dominant hand, all occur in stretches of signing that are produced with a certain kind of intensity. In these stretches of signing, all signs, including signs that are one-handed in citation form, are produced with two hands. The intensity in the sign production combined with the two-handed sign production seems to reinforce what is said. There are 15 instances of 'doubling', co-occurring with 2% of the one-handed signs.

3.6 Sign fragments

'Sign fragments' are instances of a special kind of perseveration, where the non-dominant hand has been part of the production of a two-handed sign, and then remains in that position while the dominant hand continues to produce signs. Whereas phonological perseveration is non-meaningful, sign fragments are meaningful and indicate to the listener who/what the topic of the continued discourse is. In Figure 5 (below), the signer has told us that it is when people know they are soon going to die that they truly feel alive. This discourse topic is then kept constant with a fragment of the last sign LIVE (first sign in the last row of photos) on the non-dominant hand. Then the dominant hand produces the sign VIEW-OF-SOMETHING, which starts from the left and moves towards (and actually past) the sign fragment of LIVE. The direction where VIEW-OF-SOMETHING starts has previously been used for reference to the main character of the story, and we thus know that it is her view that is told.

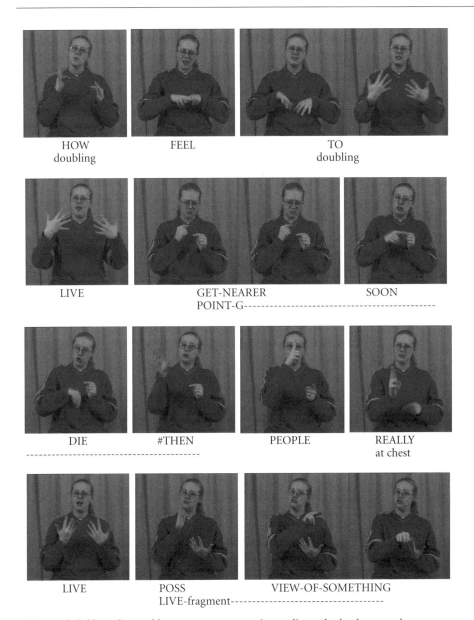

Figure 5. Illustration of 'doubling', POINT-G, 'at chest', and a 'sign fragment'

The analyzed material contains ten sequences with 'sign fragments', which all remain from symmetrical two-handed signs, co-occurring with 6% ($n = 37$) one-handed signs. No instances of 'sign fragments' from asymmetric two-handed signs have been found.

Similar use of the non-dominant hand has been noted in many studies of signed languages, using varying terminology and accounting for it in different ways. The use of the non-dominant articulator "to perform syntactic/semantic functions during simultaneous articulation" is one of the areas covered in Friedman (1975:953). Among the functions mentioned are e.g. maintaining topic or focus, maintaining locative, temporal or pronominal reference, and emphatic or contrastive stress. Gee & Kegl (1983:246), also for ASL, describe how a sign can perseverate on the non-dominant hand "as topic or background information for a number of lines", claiming that this is "an interesting device for topic marking and topic chaining unique to ASL". Ahlgren & Bergman (1994) have observed a phenomenon in Swedish Sign Language that they termed 'referential cue', which also involves maintaining a weak hand position to indicate the identity of a referent. (Also cf. Miller 1994, (topic) perseveration, mentioned above.)

Liddell (2003) uses the term 'sign fragments' for instances when the weak hand maintains its configuration from a preceding sign, while the strong hand continues to produce a one-handed sign, and this remaining 'sign fragment' does not appear to serve any semantic function. According to Liddell the signer can choose to assign semantic significance to a fragment of a preceding sign, though, in which case the fragment is no longer meaningless but constitutes a fragment buoy. (Buoys are discussed in the next section). In ASL, this is done by directing the index finger and the eye gaze at the fragment. The 'sign fragments' in the material of this study add to the content of the discourse, but as opposed to Liddell's fragment buoys they are not pointed at, and the gaze direction varies as a result of whether the story is told from the signer's perspective or from the perspective of a discourse participant. What also distinguishes these meaningful 'sign fragments' from other signs in this Swedish Sign Language discourse that indeed are treated as buoys, is that they are the result of the non-dominant hand remaining in position from several different two-handed signs, and thus do not have a fixed form.

3.7   Buoys

Whereas the 'sign fragments' described in the previous section were instances of a special type of perseveration, this section will look at signs that are independently produced by the non-dominant hand. The concept of a 'buoy' is introduced by Liddell (2003), in his description of American Sign Language. Buoys are signs produced with the weak hand, and held in a stationary configuration as the strong hand continues to produce signs. Semantically, buoys "help guide the discourse by serving as conceptual landmarks as the discourse continues" (2003:223). In the following sections, several types of signs in the material, produced by the non-dominant hand while the dominant hand continues to sign, will be compared to some of the buoys discussed by Liddell.[3]

3.7.1 *The POINTER buoy*

In Figure 6, a pointing sign on the non-dominant hand is directed to the left (earlier marked for reference to the main character of the story), and is then held stationary while the dominant hand produces the one-handed sign wow. The next sign is the two-handed sign STRANGE. In citation form, the handshape of the base hand would be either a fist or the flat hand. Here the non-dominant hand maintains the index finger handshape of the pointing sign, but the orientation of the hand is changed to that which the stationary hand would have in the citation form of STRANGE. The non-dominant hand then resumes its direction to the left, and it is kept like that while the one-handed sign CHILDHOOD is produced, and also during the sign TOO, which in citation form is a two-handed symmetrical sign.

at chest	WOW	STRANGE

POINTER---

CHILDHOOD	TOO

POINTER---------------------------------------

She had a really strange childhood too.

Figure 6. Use of the POINTER buoy

---

3. For a more thorough discussion of buoys see Liddell, Vogt-Svendsen & Bergman in this volume.

The form and use of the pointing sign in Figure 6 is similar enough to that of a sign in ASL that Liddell (2003) describes and refers to as the POINTER buoy, to warrant the use of the term POINTER buoy in Swedish Sign Language too.[4] It is the only buoy that actually points, and the non-dominant hand points toward an important discourse element, thereby directing attention to it, while the dominant hand continues to sign. This buoy co-occurs with 3% of the one-handed signs ($n = 20$).

The POINTER buoy in ASL frequently has a palm-down orientation, though, whereas in Swedish Sign Language the ulnar side of the hand is directed down when it is produced in the horizontal plane.[5] In this Swedish Sign Language discourse, the dominant hand can either produce one-handed signs (also one-handed variants of normally two-handed symmetric signs) while the POINTER is held, or the dominant hand can be active in a two-handed asymmetric sign, acting on the radial side of the non-dominant hand when it produces this pointing sign.[6] In Figure 6 the orientation of the non-dominant hand as base hand actually changes so much that it can hardly be claimed to still produce the POINTER buoy.

3.7.2 *The* THEME *buoy*

In Figure 7 below, the signer is introducing an important discourse theme – patients dying from cancer. The first two signs, NON-1ST-SING. and #SHE are directed forward, a direction that is now introduced for reference to the main character of the story. A hand configuration with a raised index finger then appears on the non-dominant hand, and is held stationary while the signer produces the perfect marker PERF.[7] and the one-handed sign TO-INTERVIEW with the dominant hand. The next two signs MANY and PATIENT are two-handed, and both hands are used to produce them. During the following one-handed sign CL-PERSON the handshape on the non-dominant hand changes to something resembling a pointing sign, but analyzed as an instance of the rest position 'at chest'. The next sign, ESPECIALLY, is two-handed and produced with both hands. It is followed by two one-handed signs: CANCER and NON-1ST-PLUR, and while they are produced by the dominant hand the raised index finger re-occurs on the non-dominant hand. It disappears

---

4. This pointing sign in Swedish Sign Language was first described as TEMA-PEK (THEME-INDEX), in lecture notes by Brita Bergman in 2001.

5. The only instance with more of a palm-down orientation in the material of this study is one where the THEME buoy is not produced in the horizontal plane, but directed forward and upward, with the palm directed slightly forward/downward.

6. Also noted in Liddell, Vogt-Svendsen & Bergman (2004).

7. The perfect marker is two-handed in citation form, but often produced with only the dominant hand.

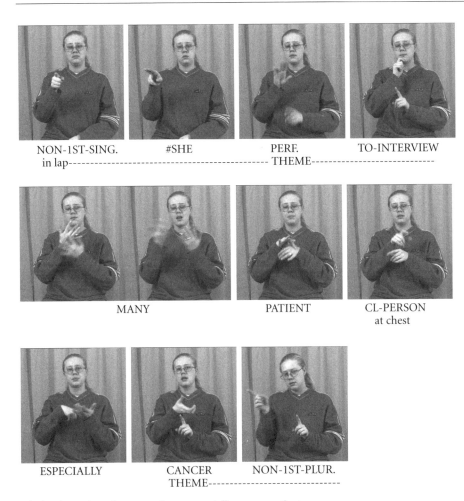

| NON-1ST-SING. | #SHE | PERF. | TO-INTERVIEW |

in lap--- THEME----------------------------

| MANY | PATIENT | CL-PERSON |

at chest

| ESPECIALLY | CANCER | NON-1ST-PLUR. |

THEME-----------------------------

She has interviewed many patients, especially cancer patients…

Figure 7. Use of the THEME buoy

again, however, during the next three, two-handed, signs, which are not shown in the example.

As can be seen in Figure 8, this discourse theme is mentioned again approximately five minutes later in the discourse, and the raised index finger re-occurs on the non-dominant hand precisely while the sign CANCER is produced with the dominant hand.

Both the form and the use of this raised index finger on the non-dominant hand very much resemble the THEME buoy in ASL, which is a buoy whose presence "signifies that an important discourse theme is being discussed" (Liddell 2003:242). The form and meaning of this buoy blend to produce a visible rep-

NON-1ST-SING. in lap	DO-RESEARCH	CANCER THEME	PATIENT

She had done research on cancer patients...

Figure 8. The THEME buoy reappears five minutes later in the discourse

resentation of that discourse theme. Liddell (2003:246) too has an example where the THEME buoy reappears after approximately five minutes. The Swedish Sign Language THEME buoy co-occurs with 5% ($n = 32$) of the one-handed signs.

The ASL THEME buoy can serve as the base hand in an asymmetrical two-handed sign (Liddell 2003:245). However, in this Swedish Sign Language discourse, the THEME buoy disappears when the signer produces two-handed signs. It is thus not used as base hand, but replaced by the two-handed sign. As the ASL sign, the Swedish Sign Language sign may have pronominal signs directed at it, but the signer can also actually touch it, something that is not mentioned by Liddell.

3.7.3 *List buoys*

List buoys are used to make conceptual associations between the extended digits of the hand and various entities (Liddell 2003). The described entities and the extended digits of the hand blend, and those extended digits are then no longer only an index finger, a middle finger, etc., but visual representations of that entity. The ASL list buoys use the handshapes corresponding to those of the numeral signs from ONE through FIVE. As opposed to numerals, list buoys are usually produced with the weak hand, which is not held as upright as when producing a numeral sign, but tilted slightly to the side, and often held ahead of the chest rather than ahead of the shoulder. The type of list buoy constructions described by Liddell has been termed static list buoy by Vogt-Svendsen (personal communication 2003).

3.7.3.1 *Static list buoys* The discourse of the present study only contains one static list buoy, glossed in example (1). It has three digits extended from the beginning, and is used to refer to three siblings (triplets), introduced as a group.

(1)   right   hand   SELF   /TWIN   touch-all-3-fingers ONE #OF
       left   hand   THREE/TWIN   **THREE-LIST** - - - - - - - - - -
       NON-1ST-PL-above-list touch-indexf OLDEST touch-indexf
       -

       BUT ONLY ONE KILO WEIGH BORN
       - BORN
       She was one of a set of triplets, the oldest of them, but she only weighed one
       kilo when she was born...

The introduction of the siblings is done with a compound sign consisting of the
one-handed form THREE (produced by the non-dominant hand, possibly anticipating the buoy) and the two-handed form TWIN (Figure 9a). The index finger is
associated with the oldest sibling, and pointed at several times for reference to that
sibling (Figure 9b), who is also the main character of the story. (In cases where
there is an age difference between the referents, the index finger is used for the
oldest referent). In the continued discourse, the list buoy on the weak hand is
used as one of the active hands in two two-handed signs which are symmetrical
in citation form; the signs BUT and KILO. The signs are produced with the citation form movement of both hands, but maintaining the handshape of the list
buoy on the non-dominant hand, while the dominant hand uses the citation form

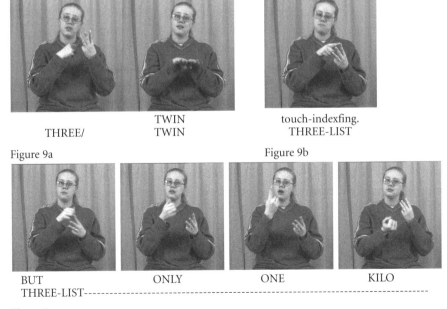

	TWIN	touch-indexfing.
THREE/	TWIN	THREE-LIST
Figure 9a		Figure 9b

| BUT | ONLY | ONE | KILO |
| THREE-LIST-- |

Figure 9c

Figure 9. Introduction of the referent 'triplets', returning to 'the oldest sibling' and use of
          the static THREE-LIST in the phrase 'but she only weighed one kilo'

handshape. Between those two signs, the list buoy handshape is maintained on the non-dominant hand while the dominant hand produces the two one-handed signs ONLY and ONE (Figure 9c). This only instance of a static list buoy co-occurs with 2% ($n = 9$) of the one-handed signs.

3.7.3.2 Sequentially built list buoys

The discourse that the present study focuses on mainly contains sequentially built list buoys, where a list is gradually built, with a maximum of five referents. Figure 10 shows a sequentially built list buoy. Note that the first six signs are not illustrated with photos, but are only glossed.

Sequentially built list buoys can serve the purpose of keeping track of referents that are described as they are enumerated. These entities are sometimes introduced in chronological order or some other logical order, but they may also simply be introduced in the order they come to the signer's mind. A particular referent can be kept constant by maintaining the handshape of the list buoy associated with it while the dominant hand produces one-handed signs. The referent can also be kept constant by maintaining the handshape of the list buoy on the non-dominant hand while it is used as base hand in an asymmetric two-handed sign or as one of the active hands in a symmetric sign (cf. Figure 10 below, the sign USA). The sequential list buoys in this discourse co-occur with 7% ($n = 44$) of the instances of one-handed signs.

Sequentially built list buoys do not always have a specific referent associated with every digit, and having begun to produce what looks like a sequentially built list buoy, the signer may sometimes not continue to build it. In the discourse examined here, the signer associates, for example, ONE-LIST with the signs meaning 'her research' by almost touching it. Then she produces TWO-LIST, which is followed by (and thus associated with) signs meaning 'her manner'. Finally, while she moves the right index finger to a fairly high starting position, she rapidly extends first the index finger, then the middle finger again, and lastly the other two fingers on the non-dominant hand (the preceding sign was a two-handed sign where both hands assumed the fist handshape) and then lets the dominant index finger move down – lightly touching the third and fourth finger of the non-dominant hand. This final sign sequence then, is used as a way of indicating that more referents could be given/named if needed, but that this is not deemed necessary for the specific purposes of the discourse.

3.7.4 Point buoys

Vogt-Svendsen and Bergman (this volume) describe another type of buoys referred to as point buoys, which they have identified in Norwegian Sign Language and Swedish Sign Language. There are two such buoys, POINT-G (index finger) and POINT-B (flat hand), which are described as a type of marker in space that help

NON-1ST-SING-f #SHE-f PERF DO-RESEARCH WORLD DIFFERENT

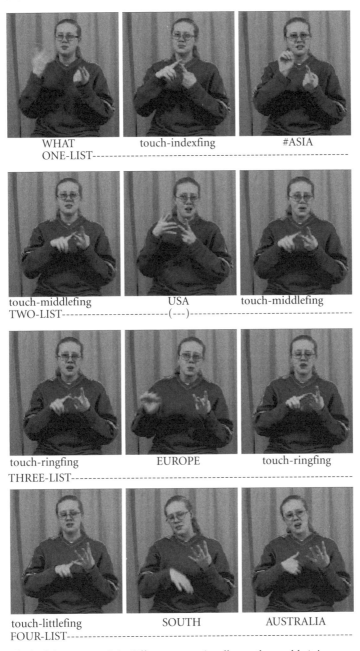

She had done research in different countries all over the world Asia,
the US, Europe, down in Australia, and what have you.

Figure 10. Example of a sequentially built list buoy. (First line without photos.)

visualize temporal and spatial relationships between entities. The material of this study contains one example of the POINT-G buoy, representing a point in time viz. 'the time that you are going to die'. It can be seen in Figure 5 above, where it is the base hand of GET-NEARER and SOON, and then remains in place during the one-handed signs DIE and #THEN. This single instance of a point buoy in the discourse co-occurs with approximately 0.33% ($n = 2$) of the one-handed signs.

3.7.5 Occurrences of buoys in the material

As has been noted in the descriptions of Swedish Sign Language buoys above, some buoys can occur with both one-handed and two-handed signs, whereas others will be replaced by a two-handed sign and may then reappear. When using list buoys, the digit associated with a particular referent can be touched both before and/or after that referent is mentioned, which means that their frequency can become very high. That is, because the signer may touch her finger both before and after articulating a referent, for every referent the list buoy may be touched twice. It is also typical that buoys are held for longer or shorter stretches of signing. We will therefore consider the number of sequences where buoys occur, in addition to the already presented number of one-handed signs they co-occur with. There are a total of six sequences where the POINTER buoy is used and another six sequences where the THEME buoy is clearly used. There are five sequences in the material where long lists are built, but there is only one static list buoy, and one point buoy. Together, these sequences with buoys co-occur with a total of 17% ($n = 107$) of the one-handed signs.

4.   Dominance reversals

The range of buoys described in the previous section are all typically produced with the non-dominant hand, while the dominant hand continues to produce other signs. The discourse examined also contains instances of one-handed signs produced with the non-dominant hand, where use of the dominant hand might have been expected and where no sign co-occurs on the dominant hand. For want of a better term, this is referred to as 'dominance reversal'.[8]

---

8. Frishberg (1985:79) uses the term in her study of hand preferences in signed languages and "the coordinated behaviour of the two hands within the flow of signs in running discourse". According to Frishberg, dominance reversal is never obligatory, but used to create semantic connections or contrasts within a narrative.

In the whole discourse, only 1% ($n = 8$) of the one-handed signs are produced by the non-dominant hand.[9] Seven of them are pointing signs (INDEX-x) produced with the non-dominant hand, and no sign co-occurring on the dominant hand. Five of those pointing signs occur at the end of a signed sequence and are followed by both hands assuming a two-handed variant of 'at chest', where the fist of the non-dominant hand is clasped by the dominant hand in front of the signer's chest, and the forearms rest against the body. Two of the instances of INDEX-x produced with 'dominance reversal' and followed by both hands in the 'at chest' position occur in the transcribed examples (2) and (3).

(2)   PLUS NON-1ST-SING-l GLADLY MUCH DISCUSS WITH PERSON
      PATIENT OBJ.pl DIE PATIENT WILL ON WAY DIE   at chest
                                              INDEX-f-fl at chest
      And she really enjoys discussing with patients who are going to die.

(3)   NON-1ST-SING-f DO-RESEARCH DIFFERENT HOSPITAL hook-index-fr-f
      both at chest #ABOUT INDEX-f DEATH ------- at chest
                                              INDEX-f at chest
      She has done research in many different hospitals – about death.

The other two of the seven instances of pointing signs produced with 'dominance reversal' are not followed by both hands being placed in the 'at chest' position. They are both instances of NON-FIRST-PL and co-occur with the signer changing perspective, which could be regarded as the end of something and/or a kind of contrast.

The use of 'dominance reversal' seems to be part of how the signer organizes the discourse structure, marking the end of something. It has earlier been noted for Swedish Sign Language that the end of a 'paragraph' can be marked by a one-handed sign where the signer switches active hand (Brita Bergman, personal communication).

There is one sequence in the material where change of active hand in a one-handed sign is used to indicate change of perspective and constructed dialogue (cf. Figure 11). Here, the signer describes something a dying patient wants to do, and produces NON-1ST-SING-f WANT-TO from the signer's perspective. Then a comment directed to that patient from a nurse is recounted. The signer switches from signer's perspective to the nurse's perspective using 'dominance reversal', but also by changing the position of her head (as seen in Figure 11). First, she produces the one-handed sign NO with the non-dominant hand. That one-handed sign then remains on the non-dominant hand (cf. the section above about sign

---

9. Producing a sign with the non-dominant hand as the active hand does not change the signer's hand dominance, and dominance reversal is thus in a sense actually a misnomer.

NON-1ST-SING   WANT-TO-------------------------------   WAIT
at chest---   NO------------------------

That was what she wanted. The nurse said "No, wait…"

Figure 11. 'Dominance reversal' in constructed dialogue

fragments keeping the referent constant) while the rest of the nurse's comment, the one-handed sign WAIT, is produced with the dominant hand.[10]

Interestingly, this 'reversal of roles' for the hands not only means that the non-dominant hand produces one-handed signs. The dominant hand takes on the role of the non-dominant hand, and is either held in the 'at chest' position, produces instances of assimilation, or (as we saw in Figure 11) it produces a 'sign fragment'.

5.   Discussion

In the introduction, it was mentioned that there are several factors contributing to a markedly two-handed impression of this stretch of signed discourse. As we have seen, looking only at whether a sign is one-handed or two-handed in citation form yields a distribution that is roughly fifty-fifty.

However, if we also include the activities of the non-dominant hand when not part of a two-handed sign, the impression we get is quite different. In Figure 12, a summary of what the non-dominant hand does when it is not part of a two-handed sign is illustrated as a continuum.[11] At the bottom left of the continuum are those instances where the non-dominant hand is least active, and where it does not contribute to the content of the discourse. The farther to the right and up, the more active the non-dominant hand is, and the more it contributes to the discourse production and to the content of the discourse.

---

10. The perseveration of WANT-TO on the dominant hand, in the third photo, may be due to the fact that the next sign to be produced by that hand uses the same handshape and place of articulation.

11. Assimilation, which is part of the production of a two-handed sign, has not been included in the continuum.

dominance reversals (1%)

buoys (17%)

sign fragments (6%)

doubling (2%)

mirroring (4%)

mirror at chest (6%)

at chest (22%)

in lap (19%)

Figure 12. Continuum of the activities of the non-dominant hand

In the 19% ($n = 116$) of instances of one-handed signs that co-occur with 'in lap', the non-dominant hand is maximally inactive, and does not take part in the discourse production at all. But, in the two rest positions – 'at chest' (22%, $n = 133$) and 'mirror at chest' (6%, $n = 37$) – the non-dominant hand is held at chest level, where many one-handed and two-handed signs are produced. Due to this, the non-dominant hand appears more involved in the discourse production than it does when it rests in the signer's lap, which is also true for one-handed signs co-occurring with 'mirroring' (4%, $n = 22$). Adding up these activities of the non-dominant hand, we find that 32% of the occurrences of one-handed signs in the discourse ($n = 192$), are produced with the non-dominant hand held in 'at chest', 'mirror at chest' or producing an instance of 'mirroring'. In these, the non-dominant hand does not contribute to the content of the discourse, and in a majority of the cases it does not move, but contributes to the two-handed impression of the sign production.

There are also a large number of instances of assimilation in the discourse, where the non-dominant hand is either anticipating or perseverating from a preceding or following two-handed sign, while the dominant hand is producing a one-handed sign. Assimilation co-occurs with 23% ($n = 141$) of the one-handed signs in the discourse. Even though assimilation is a result of the production of two-handed signs, it partly occurs during the production of one-handed signs and thus contributes to the impression of two hands being used simultaneously.

The use of the non-dominant hand in the present Swedish Sign Language discourse seems very different from what Klima & Bellugi (1979:217) claim regarding signed ASL discourse. According to them, "[i]n signed discourse, the base hand as a location frequently lags behind the active hand", and it is only in lexicalized compounds that anticipation is typical, rather than this delay. They also quote an unpublished manuscript by Friedman (1974), stating that the "hand configuration of the articulator of a given sign is formed first, and only then is the hand shape of the place of articulation hand shaped or even brought into the signing space".[12] The non-dominant hand as place of articulation is ready at the same time as the dominant hand in this discourse, or anticipates it, also in signs that are not lexicalized compounds.

Turning to instances where content is added and the non-dominant hand is active in the signing, a total of 25% ($n = 159$) of the one-handed signs co-occur with 'doubling', 'sign fragments' or different buoys. 'Dominance reversal' per definition means that the non-dominant hand is active. In the 1% ($n = 8$) of one-handed signs in the discourse that occur with 'dominance reversal', the dominant hand is either held in 'at chest' position, or assimilates with at preceding or following sign, or produces a 'sign fragment'. This reversal of roles also gives a two-handed impression.

Taken all together, a total of approximately 90% ($n = 1038$) of the 1151 instances of signs in the discourse are thus produced in a way that gives an impression of two hands participating simultaneously.

There is another interesting tendency in the material, however, which for parts of the discourse could be regarded as working against the impression of two-handedness discussed above. As mentioned earlier there are seven longer sequences where the non-dominant hand frequently rests in the 'in lap' position. During these sequences, the non-dominant hand is only used for a few instances of list buoys, assimilation and 'mirroring'. In general, though, the sequences give a markedly one-handed impression of the signing. 'In lap' co-occurs with 19% ($n = 116$) of the one-handed signs. (These, in turn, constitute the 10% of the signs in the discourse that do not give a two-handed impression.)

When the non-dominant hand adds content to the discourse, without being part of a two-handed sign, it often seems to help indicate to the addressee who/what the speaker is currently talking about. This is done in a number of different ways. The non-dominant hand can remain in place from a previous symmetrical two-handed sign as a 'sign fragment', thus maintaining the topic of the discourse. The different buoys in the discourse – the POINTER buoy, the THEME buoy, list buoys and point buoys – also help the listener understand who or what the current referent(s) is/are and the relationships between them, or that the referent is an important discourse theme. Finally, 'dominance reversal' seems to be part of how the signer structures the discourse, marking e.g. the beginning of something new or change of perspective.

---

12. The quote from Klima & Bellugi (1979:391) is in Note 12, Chapter 9, and refers to Friedman (1974). The list of references, however, lists Friedman 1974a and 1974b. They are both for unpublished manuscripts and I have not been able to tell which one is intended.

The present study provides us with more knowledge about simultaneity and the use of the non-dominant hand in Swedish Sign Language through the analysis of one signed piece of discourse. To find out more, we will have to analyze the use of the non-dominant hand in other kinds of discourse; monologues as well as dialogues, different styles and registers, and produced by different signers. As for the rest position, 'in lap', its existence is a consequence of the signer sitting down, and we do not know what happens if the signer is standing up. Analyzing more texts will also help us to better understand the use and meaning of 'mirroring', 'doubling', 'sign fragments', buoys, and reverse dominance. The existence, and to some extent also the frequency, of the rest positions, as well as their contribution to the two-handed impression that is so apparent in this signed discourse is of interest to others as well as to linguists. For example, for teachers of Swedish Sign Language, this can be of practical use to, helping them give their students more accurate advice than: "You need to use the other hand more".

6. Summary

In this paper, the activities of the non-dominant hand when not participating in the production of a two-handed sign have been described for one complete Swedish Sign Language discourse. These activities can be seen as a continuum (cf. Figure 12 above), starting from the bottom left with the activities where it is least active. First, there is a position where the non-dominant hand is resting 'in lap'. Then there are rest positions were the non-dominant hand looks more active, either held in the position 'at chest' where it is not influenced by the dominant hand, or in 'mirror at chest' where it mirrors the handshape and orientation of the non-dominant hand. In these positions, the non-dominant hand is still not actually moving, and does not add to the content of the discourse.

Next, the non-dominant hand begins to move and there are instances where the non-dominant hand mirrors the actions of the dominant hand when it produces one-handed signs. In 'mirroring' the handshape, orientation, and movement of the dominant hand are mirrored, but at a slightly lower location. This is a sign-internal, purely phonetic process, which does not add content to the discourse. In 'doubling', both hands are active, performing the same movement at the same height. Here, the non-dominant hand also begins to add content to the discourse, reinforcing what is said. Producing a 'sign fragment', the non-dominant hand remains in place after having been part of the production of a two-handed sign, and is held while the dominant hand produces signs, telling us who/what the topic of the discourse is.

In the top right corner of the continuum, the non-dominant hand independently produces signs. There are various kinds of 'buoys', which are normally produced by the non-dominant hand while the dominant hand also produces signs. All of the buoys contribute their own meaning to the discourse. Finally, in 'dominance reversals', a one-handed sign is produced with the non-dominant hand without any sign being produced simultaneously by the dominant hand. Dominance reversals seem to be part of how the signer organizes the discourse, marking, for example, the end of something.

Thus 90% of the signs in this discourse give the impression that both hands are being used simultaneously, when all the activities of the non-dominant hand are taken into consideration.

References

Ahlgren, Inger & Brita Bergman. 1994. "Reference in Narratives". *Perspectives on Sign Language Structure: Papers from the Fifth International Symposium on Sign Language Research* ed. by Inger Ahlgren, Brita Bergman & Mary Brennan, Vol. 1, 29–36. Durham: International Sign Linguistics Association.

Bergman, Brita. 1983. "Verbs and Adjectives: Some Morphological Processes in Swedish Sign Language". *Language in Sign: an International Perspective on Sign Language* ed. by Jim G. Kyle & Bencie Woll, 3–9. London/Canberra: Croom Helm.

Battison, Robbin. 1974. "Phonological Deletion in American Sign Language". *Sign Language Studies* 5.1–19.

Emmorey, Karen, ed. 2003. *Perspectives on Classifier Constructions in Sign Languages.* Mahwah, N.J./London: Lawrence Erlbaum.

Friedman, Lynn A. 1975. "Space, Time and Person Reference in American Sign Language". *Language* 51:4.940–961.

Frishberg, Nancy. 1985. "Dominance Relations and Discourse Structures". *SLR'83 Proceedings of the III. International Symposium on Sign Language Research. Rome, June 22–26 1983* ed. by William C. Stokoe & Virginia Volterra, 79–90. Silver Spring, Md.: Linstok Press Inc. and Rome, Italy: Instituto di Psicologia CNR.

Gee, James Paul & Judy Ann Kegl. 1983. "Narrative/Story Structure, Pausing, and American Sign Language". *Discourse Processes* 6.243–258.

Klima, Edward S. & Ursula Bellugi. 1979. *The Signs of Language,* with Robbin Battison, Penny Boyes Braem, Susan Fischer, Nancy Frishberg, Harlan Lane, Ella M. Lentz, Don Newkirk, Elissa L. Newport, C. C. Pedersen, & Patricia Siple. Cambridge, Mass.: Harvard University Press.

Liddell, Scott K. 2003. *Grammar, Gesture, and Meaning in American Sign Language.* Cambridge: Cambridge University Press.

——, Marit Vogt-Svendsen & Brita Bergman. 2004. *Crosslinguistic Comparison of Buoys: Evidence from American, Norwegian and Swedish Sign Language.* Paper presented at 26 Jahrestagung der Deutschen Gesellschaft für Sprachwissenschaft, an der Johannes-Gutenberg-Universität Mainz vom 25–27 Februar 2004.

Miller, Christopher 1994. "Simultaneous Constructions in Quebec Sign Language". *Word-order Issues in Sign Language. Working Papers* ed. by Mary Brennan & Graham H. Turner, 89–112. Durham: International Sign Linguistics Association.

Sandler, Wendy. 1993. "Hand in Hand: The Roles of the Non-dominant Hand in Sign Language Phonology". *The Linguistic Review* 10:4.337–390.

Svenskt teckenspråkslexikon. 1997. Leksand: Sveriges Dövas Riksförbund.

Wallin, Lars. 2000. "Two Kinds of Productive Signs in Swedish Sign Language: Polysynthetic Signs and Size and Shape Specifying Signs". *Sign Language & Linguistics* 3:2.237–256.

A crosslinguistic comparison of buoys

Evidence from American, Norwegian, and Swedish Sign Language

Scott K. Liddell, Marit Vogt-Svendsen and Brita Bergman
Gallaudet University / University of Oslo / Stockholm University

1.　An introduction to buoys

In vocally produced languages, once a word is produced, the speaker either stops talking or begins producing the next word. In either case the vocal signal for the just-uttered word is gone. It turns out that this is not a fact about language in general, but is merely a fact about vocally produced languages. In signed languages of the Deaf, each hand (and arm) can act as an articulator. Some signs are produced by only one hand while other signs are produced by the actions of both hands. The fact that each hand is capable of producing a sign means that each of the two hands could simultaneously produce independent meaningful signs. Such signs do exist and, in fact, are quite common. We will discuss signs normally produced by the weak hand and held in a stationary configuration as the strong hand continues producing signs. Semantically these physically maintained signs help guide the discourse by serving as conceptual landmarks as the discourse continues. Since they maintain a physical presence that helps guide the discourse as it proceeds Liddell (2003) calls them 'buoys'. Some buoys appear only briefly while others may be maintained during a significant stretch of signing. Thus, what is impossible in a vocally produced language turns out to be quite common in signed languages.[1]

1.　When speakers of vocally produced languages speak, it is not unusual to see buoy-like gestures produced while speaking. They appear similar to signed language buoys both in form and function. Marit Vogt-Svendsen has recorded a number of examples of speakers doing this, including using one hand to point at the buoy-like gesture. These buoy-like gestures, however, do not appear to be used in the same systematic ways they are used in signed language discourse – and obviously spoken language words are never directed toward them.

With the exception of fragment buoys, buoys are fixed forms with fixed meanings. They are part of the inventory of signs that a signer learns in acquiring a signed language. They are tightly integrated in the sign stream and it is even possible to direct some indicating verbs toward list buoys for referential purposes.

In this paper we examine the use of buoys in three signed languages with no clearly established historical connections: American Sign Language (ASL), Norwegian Sign Language (NSL), and Swedish Sign Language (SSL). While the historical connections between ASL and Old French Sign Language (OFSL) are sufficient to place ASL in the French sign language family, the same is not true for NSL and SSL. In the case of SSL, there is evidence for the existence of a signed language in Sweden as early as 1759 and Bergman (1979: 7) finds "no reason to assume that the Swedish sign language originated anywhere other than among the deaf themselves in Sweden". In the case of NSL, Schröder (1993) finds evidence for a connection between NSL and Danish Sign Language, but there appears to be insufficient evidence to place NSL in the French sign language family. There also appears to be some evidence that during the early parts of the twentieth century some German signs were brought to Norway both by a Norwegian headmaster of a school for the Deaf and by Deaf Norwegians visiting Germany (Fleischer 1944). Such connections, however, are not strong enough to put Norwegian Sign Language into any signed language family.

All three co-authors are interested in how buoys are used in the signed language studied by each. Since the three signed languages are not known to be related, a comparison of buoys across these three signed languages seemed like a natural place to begin the cross-linguistic study of buoys. Any commonalities found in the use of buoys in three unrelated languages would suggest not only that buoys serve important discourse functions, but that their development as weak-hand signs was natural in the context of signed languages.

Our aim is to illustrate the types of list buoys, THEME buoys, fragment buoys, and POINTER buoys used in these three languages, to describe how they are used in everyday discourse, and to compare and contrast the buoys found in these languages. Depicting buoys (see Liddell 2003) and point buoys will not be discussed here. (For a description of point buoys, see Vogt-Svendsen & Bergman, this volume.) Our description will be rather detailed since a detailed description is needed to understand when and how the buoys are used. In the case of list buoys, for example, it is important not only to see how the strong hand behaves in relation to the buoy, but also how the strong hand interacts with individual fingers of the buoy.

2. List buoys

List buoys are produced by the weak hand and provide a physical presence to ordered sets. Figure 1 illustrates list buoys from American Sign Language, Swedish Sign Language, and Norwegian Sign Language. All the signers in Figure 1 but one are right handed, and therefore produce buoys with their left hands. The ASL signer producing the ONE-LIST, FOUR-LIST, and FIVE-LIST, however, is left-handed and produces buoys with his right hand.[2]

In fourteen of the fifteen examples in Figure 1 the hand configurations of the list buoys are the same hand configurations as those found in the corresponding numeral signs. For example, the THREE-LIST buoys in ASL and NSL are each made with the thumb, index finger, and middle finger extended as illustrated in Figure 1. The signs for 3 in each of these languages are also produced with the same hand configuration. Similarly, the SSL sign THREE and the THREE-LIST buoy are both made with the index, middle, and ring fingers extended. The one exception to this generalization in Figure 1 is the ONE-LIST buoy in NSL. In NSL the numeral ONE is produced with the extended index finger while this ONE-LIST buoy is produced with the extended thumb. This can be seen in the first row of Figure 1.[3]

Even though list buoys are generally produced with the same hand configuration as the corresponding numeral sign, their forms are nevertheless distinct from numeral signs. We have already pointed out that it makes a difference which hand produces the sign. Numeral signs are produced by the strong hand and list buoys are produced by the weak hand. In addition, list buoys are oriented differently than the numeral signs. The difference in orientation can be seen by comparing the ASL sign TWO (Figure 2a) with the ASL TWO-LIST buoy (Figure 2b). The ASL numeral TWO is produced by the strong hand with the fingers oriented upward. The TWO-LIST buoy, on the other hand (literally), is produced with the fingers in a more horizontal orientation.

Figure 2b also illustrates the signer holding the TWO-LIST buoy in place as the right hand directs the index finger toward the index finger of the TWO-LIST

---

2. The ASL photos appearing in Figures 1, 2, 11, 18, 21, and 22, are from Liddell (2003) and are reprinted here with permission of Cambridge University Press.

3. We have not attempted to include every list buoy in these three languages. For example, in NSL the numeral TWO is produced with the index and middle fingers extended. The corresponding TWO-LIST buoy with the index and middle fingers extended is illustrated in Figure 1. There is also a TWO-LIST buoy with the thumb and index finger extended, but not illustrated in Figure 1. Similarly, NSL has two different versions of the numeral THREE. One is produced with the thumb, index and middle fingers extended. The other has the index, middle, and ring fingers extended. There are corresponding list buoys with both hand configurations.

Figure 1. Common list buoys in ASL, SSL, and NSL

buoy, thereby making reference to the first item on the list. This illustrates a third difference between the numeral and the list buoy. List buoys can remain in place as the active hand continues signing.

a.   TWO

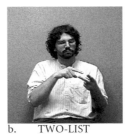

b.   TWO-LIST

Figure 2. The ASL numeral TWO and the TWO-LIST buoy

There are also grammatical and semantic differences between numerals and list buoys. Numerals can be used to quantify nouns, but list buoys cannot. Numerals express numerical values, but list buoys express the existence of a list of a certain length. There are also spatial differences between numerals and list buoys. Numerals do not have the spatial properties associated with list buoys. That is, list buoys exist as part of spatial representations that can be maintained during several grammatical constructions (e.g. phrases or clauses). Their function is to provide a physical presence to the list. Through mental space blending, the tips of the fingers 'become' the items on the list.[4] The result is a visible list in the form of a list buoy. Given the existence of a visible list in which extended digits become items on a list, signers can easily refer to the items on the list by touching, tapping, or directing signs toward the appropriate finger or thumb.

One property shared by all three signed languages is that the numeral signs signifying values from 1 to 5 are produced using handshapes with the corresponding number of extended digits. That is, the signs signifying 'one' in ASL, SSL, and NSL all have a single digit extended. The signs signifying 'two' have two extended digits, and so on up to five. If the goal is to create a physically present list by individually associating items on the list with extended digits, then it is not surprising that the handshapes used in producing the corresponding numerals are also used in list buoys. There are two reasons for this. First, numeral incorporation is quite common not only in these three signed languages, but also in signed languages generally. Numeral incorporation works by incorporating the hand configurations found in numeral signs into numeral incorporating 'stems' (Liddell 1996).[5] The numeral incorporation process demonstrates that the hand configurations themselves are symbolic (i.e. they signify numerical values). Thus, using the very same

4.   For more information about blending in general see Fauconnier & Turner (1996, 2002). For more details about how blending applies in the case of signed languages see Liddell (2003).

5.   For an analysis of numeral incorporation in Swedish Sign Language see Wallin (1994). For an analysis of numeral incorporation in American Sign Language see Liddell (1996).

handshapes in list buoys makes sense since the hand configurations can be understood as symbolically representing the number of items on the list. In addition, for list buoys with values from one to five, since the number of extended digits corresponds exactly to the number of items on the list, it is also possible to make correspondences between each extended digit and a specific item on the list. Thus, the high correspondence between the hand configurations used in producing the numerals ONE to FIVE and the hand configurations used in producing the ONE-LIST through the FIVE-LIST should not be surprising.

2.1 Sequentially built lists vs. single fixed-length lists

List buoys can appear in two different ways. In ASL it is common for a signer discussing four sequential entities to first mention that four entities will be discussed followed by signing the FOUR-LIST buoy. The signer then generally identifies the entities one at a time, making sequential associations with the extended digits of the FOUR-LIST buoy and each of the four entities. The ASL signing in Figure 3 took place in a context in which the signer had already mentioned that he had four Deaf nieces and nephews. He then uses the FOUR-LIST buoy to represent the four nieces and nephews in the order of their ages. The oldest would normally be associated with the index finger and the youngest with the baby finger. He begins making the associations by first contacting the index finger of the FOUR-LIST with his extended index finger. We are treating this as a simple act of touching something to identify it, just as one might touch a book on a table to identify it as the thing being talked about. Liddell (2003) uses the convention of identifying the first extended digit as D1, the second as D2, and so on. We will also use that convention here.

After touching D1 he signs GIRL. This identifies the oldest of his nieces and nephews as a girl. Next he signs BOY while simultaneously raising the FOUR-LIST buoy such that D2 is now roughly in the physical location that D1 used to occupy. The combination of signing BOY second and raising D2 makes the association between D2 and a nephew. That is, D2 now physically represents the oldest male nephew. He then signs BOY again, but now D3 has been raised to roughly the positions previously occupied by D1 and D2. This associates D3 with a younger nephew. He makes the final association by signing GIRL then touching D4.

At the conclusion of the signing in Figure 3 the FOUR-LIST buoy is no longer merely a list of four entities. It has become a list of his four Deaf nieces and nephews in the order of their birth. D1 has become his oldest niece, D2 has become the oldest nephew, D3 has become the youngest nephew, and D4 has become the youngest niece. Once such associations have been made a signer can direct other signs toward the now elaborated entities that the digits of the list buoy have become. For example, the signer later was talking about the ages of his nieces and nephews. Producing the sign SIX on D3, as illustrated in Figure 4 further elabo-

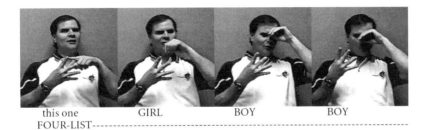

this one   GIRL   BOY   BOY
FOUR-LIST---

GIRL   this one
FOUR-LIST----------------------------

Figure 3. 'The oldest (of four) is a girl, the next a boy, another boy, and the youngest, a girl'

SIX (on D3)   FOUR (on D4)
FOUR-LIST------------------------------------

'This one is six (years old), this one is four'

Figure 4. Adding the ages of the two youngest nieces and nephews

rates D3. The addressee will now understand that the nephew (D3) is six years old and that the youngest niece (D4) is four years old.

It is interesting to note that when the signer produces the numeral FOUR with his left hand against D4 on his right hand, he produces the numeral in a nearly palm up orientation. In spite of the unusual orientation of the hand, it is nevertheless an instance of FOUR produced in contact with D4.[6]

---

6.   If the heel of the hand producing FOUR contacts the tip of D4 with the fingers oriented upward, the sign FOUR would be partially behind the FOUR-LIST buoy. Producing FOUR as illustrated may be a way of avoiding this awkward relationship between the two hands.

The signing in Figures 3 and 4 illustrate the use of a single list buoy to talk about four nieces and nephews. The signer began by producing a FOUR-LIST buoy and used it throughout the description without changing it. Figure 5 illustrates the use of sequentially built list buoys in SSL. In this example the SSL signer says that ECRS (European Community Regional Secretariat) has bought a building in Brussels and that they are going to employ three people: a director, a consultant, and a secretary who will also be an interpreter.

In the previous ASL example the signer uses the FOUR-LIST buoy in a context where the number of nieces and nephews being talked about is already clear. The SSL signer begins similarly by mentioning that three people will be hired by signing THREE with his right hand at face level (see Figure 5). But now he begins with a ONE-LIST buoy, which begins to appear as he is signing PERSONx2 ('persons'). The ONE-LIST buoy is ready in its position when PERSONx2 is finished. He then contacts D1, the pad of the left hand's index finger[7] with his right hand index finger and signs DIRECTOR while the ONE-LIST buoy remains in place. After DIRECTOR he contacts D2, the pad of the middle finger of the TWO-LIST buoy, then signs CONSULTANT.

As the signer contacts D3, the pad of the ring finger, he looks down at his hands. Next he signs SECRETARY, a two-handed sign normally produced against the palm of the flat weak hand. Since his left hand is already performing another role by maintaining the presence of the THREE-LIST buoy, he uses the THREE-LIST buoy as the base hand for SECRETARY. Note that the right hand does not contact the ring finger in producing SECRETARY, but rather the hand as a whole, more specifically the side of the palm.

Next the signer directs the verb BE-IN$^{\rightarrow y}$ and his gaze at D3.[8] Directing BE-IN$^{\rightarrow y}$ toward D3 signifies that the secretary position to be filled contains something within it. He immediately identifies what that is by signing ALSO FUNCTION AS INTERPRETER.

If we exclude the preceding statement that three people are to be hired, a buoy is present during all of the next eleven signs or contacting gestures. Some of the signs produced in the presence of buoys are two-handed. We have already discussed how the THREE-LIST became the base hand for SECRETARY. Similarly, INTERPRETER would normally have the palm of the flat hand as place of artic-

---

7.   Swedish Sign Language also has list buoys with all four fingers extended starting 'from below', i.e. the little finger is D1, the ring finger D2, etc. They are used when talking about entities at different levels, such as levels in an educational system, starting with the lowest and moving up. Similar buoys for educational levels are also used in ASL and NSL.

8.   We have adopted the notations conventions in Liddell (2003) for signs that are directed or located meaningfully in space. The notation$^{\rightarrow y}$ in BE-IN$^{\rightarrow y}$ is used to show that the sign is directed toward some entity y.

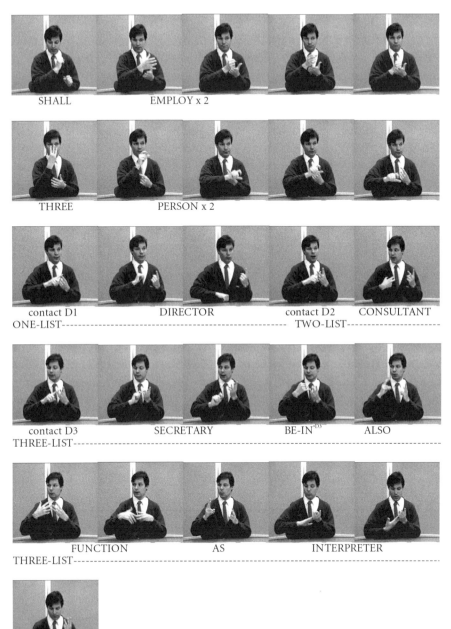

(rest position)
THREE

Figure 5. ONE-LIST, TWO-LIST, and THREE-LIST buoys produced sequentially in SSL

ulation, but the handshape from the buoy is retained and serves as the base hand for INTERPRETER.

ALSO, FUNCTION, and AS are symmetrical signs in which both hands move. In these signs the left hand participates as the second hand, but maintains the 'three' handshape from the buoy rather than handshapes that match the active hand in these two-handed symmetrical signs.[9]

The sequence finishes with the left hand being raised to a higher position, while the right hand goes down to a rest position. It seems as if the signer has switched the roles of the hands, making his left hand the strong hand. The vertical orientation of the hand and the level to which it is moved, suggests that the final sign in Figure 5 is the sign THREE, produced by the weak hand, rather than the THREE-LIST buoy.

In Figure 6 the signer is listing six countries. Although he appears to begin with a ONE-LIST buoy, what he has actually done is maintain the presence of a POINTER buoy from his previous discussion of the founding of EFTA (European Free Trade Association). For that reason we have glossed it ambiguously as POINTER/ONE-BUOY.

Figure 6 shows that sequential list buoys are also not always touched or pointed at by the strong hand. In this example the TWO-LIST and THREE-LIST buoys appear simultaneously with the signs referring to the enumerated entities without being touched at all. Only D4 on the FOUR-LIST buoy is contacted by the index of the strong hand. The FIVE-LIST buoy appears when the strong hand makes a transitional movement between AUSTRIA and SWITZERLAND, but is not contacted by the strong hand.

Another ambiguity arises during PORTUGAL, the sixth country listed. Even though it is the sixth country listed, a FIVE-LIST buoy appears to be present as PORTUGAL is signed. The reason for our inability to identify this definitively as a FIVE-LIST buoy is that the sign following PORTUGAL is the two-handed sign SIX, produced as the final sign in Figure 6. The weak hand has a 5 hand configuration in the two-handed sign SIX, which is produced by moving both hands outward followed by a hold. Thus, the hand configuration during PORTUGAL could either be a buoy or it could be the weak hand anticipating the production of the two-handed sign SIX.

In Figure 7 an NSL signer uses a THREE-LIST buoy to talk about his two youngest children. Previous to the sequence in Figure 7 the signer has explained that on National Day one of his three sons was struck by a bamboo cane while sleeping in a baby carriage. The addressee then interrupts him, asking if the signer

---

9.   Note that the weak hand in these examples is not held in a 'stationary configuration', but 'phonologically active'.

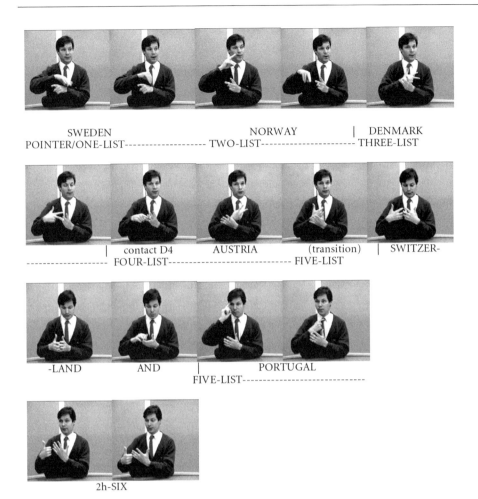

SWEDEN   NORWAY | DENMARK
POINTER/ONE-LIST-------------------- TWO-LIST---------------------- THREE-LIST

| contact D4   AUSTRIA   (transition) | SWITZER-
-------------------- FOUR-LIST---------------------------- FIVE-LIST

-LAND   AND | PORTUGAL
FIVE-LIST-----------------------------

2h-SIX

Figure 6. 'It was Sweden, Norway, Denmark, Austria, Switzerland, and Portugal, those six'

meant his second son. The signer answers by saying 'the oldest one', then sets up the THREE-LIST buoy representing his three sons as shown in Figure 7. He mentions the oldest one to explain that that son was not with him on that day. He continues by saying that he had the two youngest sons, the second and third of his children, with him.

The signs in Figure 7 identify the two youngest sons. Figure 7 also shows that after directing both TWO and SON toward D2 and D3, he then contacts D2 then D3 at or close to the fingertips, followed by YOUNG. By now he has made it clear that D2 and D3 represent the signer's middle and youngest sons. In this context the thumb would represent the oldest son.

The addressee then responds by saying 'Oh yes, those two'. The signer replies, 'Yes, those two'. He expresses this by nodding and directing PRO-DUAL$^{D2 \leftrightarrow D3}$ to-

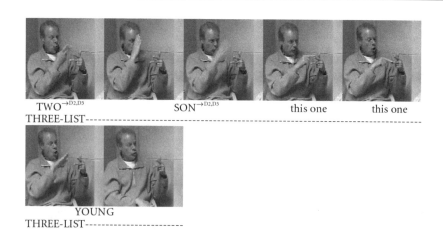

TWO→D2,D3   SON→D2,D3   this one   this one
THREE-LIST--

YOUNG
THREE-LIST-----------------------

Figure 7. 'The two youngest sons' (the second and third of my three sons)

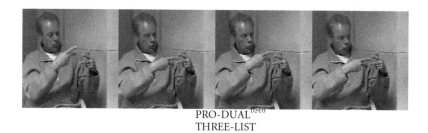

PRO-DUAL D2-D3
THREE-LIST

Figure 8. 'The two of them' (second and third sons)

ward D2 and D3 using the down-up-down movement shown in Figure 8. Note that the THREE-LIST buoy representing the signer's three sons remains in place during the entire sequence of signing shown in Figures 7 and 8. Additionally, only D2 and D3 are contacted and pointed at since he is only talking about the two youngest sons who were with him on the day he is talking about. He identifies those two sons by pointing out D2 and D3. He goes on to identify the youngest son by contacting D3, identifying him as the one who was in the baby carriage that was struck by the bamboo cane.

The same signer talking about the National Day states that the TV usually makes film recordings from four places. Then he mentions each place in turn. After contacting D1 on the ONE-LIST buoy (Figure 9a) he mentions Oslo. He then contacts D2 on the TWO-LIST buoy (Figure 9b) and mentions Ål. While maintaining the TWO-LIST in place he states that he was very surprised and pleased to see Ål there and that he recognized people that he knew since he had previously lived at Ål. He does all this while keeping the TWO-LIST buoy in place and before he contacts D2 a second time. He then produces the THREE-LIST buoy (Figure

a	b	c	d
this one	this one	this one	this one
ONE-LIST	TWO-LIST-SEQ	THREE-LIST	FOUR-LIST-SEQ
'first'	'second'	'third'	'fourth'

Figure 9. A sequence of list buoys to list four places

9c) and touches D3, states that it was Kristiandsand, and touches D3 a second time. Next he produces the FOUR-LIST-SEQ buoy (Figure 9d), contacts D4, states that it was a place in the north of Norway that he didn't know, and also contacts D4 a second time. We use the glosses TWO-LIST-SEQ and FOUR-LIST-SEQ to distinguish the sequentially produced list buoys in Figure 9b, d from the TWO-LIST and FOUR-LIST buoys illustrated in Figure 1.

After the signing in Figure 9 he states, 'Those four, it is so fun that Ål was among them.' To represent the four different places, the signer uses four list buoys, here glossed ONE-LIST, TWO-LIST-SEQ, THREE-LIST and FOUR-LIST-SEQ respectively (see Figure 9a–d). The buoys are presented sequentially and incrementally in that the size of each subsequent list is one greater than the size of the preceding list. It is also interesting to note that once the man discussing the four places introduces the ONE-LIST buoy, he signs continuously for 16 seconds while his left hand produces the four list buoys. During those sixteen seconds of signing there is always a list buoy present.

Toward the end of the discussion of the four places, the signer made reference to all four at once. He did this using the sign FOUR-OF-THEM$^{⊃y}$.[10] In doing so he replaced the incremental four list buoy (FOUR-LIST-SEQ) with a four list buoy typically used without preceding incrementally smaller list buoys. The difference between these two buoys can be seen in Figure 10.

The incremental four-list buoy (Figure 10a) is produced with the thumb, index, middle and ring fingers extended. The non-incremental four-list buoy (Figure 10b) is produced with only the four fingers extended. The reason for replacing one list buoy with the other is not yet clear. One possibility is that the primary function of the incremental list buoys is to refer to the final element of a list, at that stage in the development of the list. In contrast to the ASL signer using a FOUR-LIST buoy and making reference to each of his four Deaf nieces and nephews in Figure

---

10. The notation $^{⊃y}$ is used to show that the path movement of the sign identifies some set of entities (y). In this example the path of the movement identifies D1-D4.

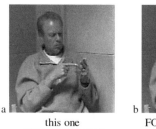

a this one   b FOUR-OF-THEM$^{\supset D1\text{-}D4}$
    FOUR-LIST-SEQ   FOUR-LIST

Figure 10. Comparing FOUR-LIST-SEQ with FOUR-LIST

3 and explaining the ages of two of the nieces and nephews in Figure 4, the signer only makes reference to the final element of each list buoy in his entire description of the four places. It is possible that the non-incremental FOUR-LIST buoy is used at the end of this description because it more easily allows reference to elements other than the final element of the list.

2.2 Lists as spatial representations

The final point we wish to make about list buoys is that the visible list buoy may make only part of the list visible. The spatially represented list may in fact have elements between or beyond the extended fingers. In Figure 11 the ASL signer is talking about weeks during which she has meetings already scheduled and weeks in which she is free to meet. She associates the individual fingers of the FOUR-WEEK-LIST buoy with four non-consecutive weeks and maintains the buoy in place throughout the sequence of illustrated signs. Although the FOUR-WEEK-LIST buoy has the same form as a FOUR-LIST buoy, Liddell (2003) makes a distinction between the two since the hands contact the two buoys differently.

As she has conceptualized the buoy and the space around it, there is one week between each of the weeks represented by the fingers. Thus, even though the fingers of the FOUR-WEEK-LIST buoy only represent four weeks, when the spaces between her fingers are included, she is actually representing seven weeks since there are weeks conceptualized in the gaps between adjacent extended fingers. Evidence for this comes during the first picture in Figure 11. The signer uses a V handshape to point toward both sides of the D3 of the FOUR-WEEK-LIST buoy (i.e. she points toward the gaps between the middle and ring finger and between the ring and baby finger). In doing so she identifies the weeks before and after that week. These are the weeks available for meetings. Then she leaves the buoy in place as she explains that she can (meet) during those weeks.

In the following NSL example, the signer builds a list that eventually extends well below his hand. This list is expressed (i.e. constructed) sequentially. The signer

'these two weeks'   CAN   PRO-1
FOUR-WEEK-LIST---

Figure 11. 'I can (meet with you) on either of these two weeks'

is enumerating a large, but unspecified number of complaints about the EU. Since the end result is unspecified, but includes the significance 'many', the final hand configuration is glossed here as a MANY-LIST buoy.[11]

Just before the signer starts using the incremental buoys in this example, he mentions some taxes – like road taxes and annual taxes – that he has to pay to the EU. Then he says that 'EU controls' and places his weak hand in a B hand configuration with thumb out as shown in the first photo of Figure 12a. Next he says that he must pay 'this one, and this one, and this one, and this one and this one'. The first unmentioned item is presented by contacting the pad of D1 (the thumb) with his index finger, then an arc movement down to contact with the nail of D2 that appears to push D2 down into contact with D1. He similarly contacts D3, D4, and D5 in the same way with the same kind of movements resulting in all fingers placed in contact with each other creating what appears to be a 'stacked' O hand configuration, as illustrated in the final photo of Figure 12a.[12]

Then he continues by saying 'and this one, and this one, and this one'. Now he extends the list in Figure 12b, not by pointing at each of the fingers as it closes (since the fingers are all already bent over), but by pointing at three different places on the baby finger of his buoy-hand, each contact made further toward the base of the baby finger than the previous contact. When he comes to the bottom of the baby finger, he extends the list further by depicting a line from the base of his baby finger downward in space several inches below the buoy, as shown in the final picture in Figure 12b.[13]

As a result of the signs produced in Figure 12 the signer has created a lengthy conceptual list in the space ahead of him. The first several items on that list are

---

11. In NSL there are different kinds of list buoys with the significance 'many'.

12. See Johnson (1990) for a description of 'stacked' hand configurations.

13. The movements of the strong hand in building up this MANY-LIST, are all very fast, and the way the index finger of the strong hand contacts the fingers of the list buoy seem to not only point out each unspecified tax, but also to mean 'done with'.

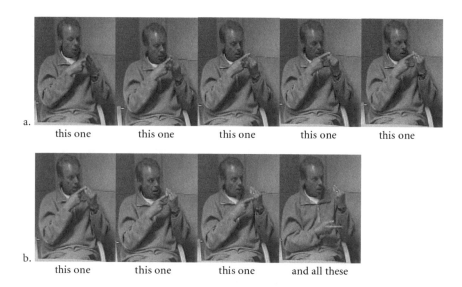

Figure 12. A list extending below the hand

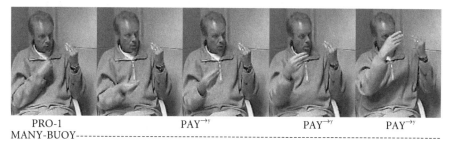

Figure 13. The MANY-BUOY becomes a mass of money

associated with the weak hand buoy, but there are also several items conceptualized as being beneath the buoy. Next the signer 'packs' all those listed items into the buoy hand itself. He states that the EU controls these things, then produces the sequence in Figure 13.

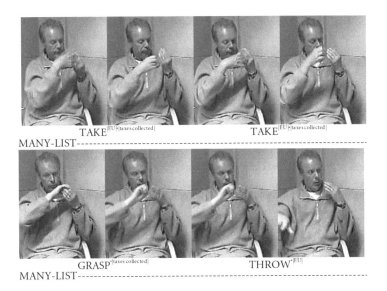

TAKE$^{|EU|}$|taxes collected| TAKE$^{|EU|}$|taxes collected|
MANY-LIST--

GRASP$^{\downarrow}$|taxes collected| THROW$^{\rightarrow|EU|}$
MANY-LIST--

Figure 14. 'The EU takes and takes (the money). It is all thrown away at the EU'

He states that he pays each of them, directing the final instance of PAY$^{\rightarrow y}$ toward the list of taxes associated with the visible MANY-BUOY. He then extends the MANY-BUOY outward toward the addressee and pauses, staring at her for more than a second. It is almost as if he were saying, 'look at all the taxes I pay' because during that second the visible buoy has become the money associated with the payment of those taxes.

He states that 'it is like EU takes my entire budget; for example food – they take and take. It is all thrown away on the EU.' He had earlier associated the EU with an area of space on his right. This type of spatial association, where an area of space is associated with some entity and where that association is not part of a larger topographical spatial representation, is called a token by Liddell (2003).[14] He points at the |EU| token, previously associated with the space on his right, uses the MANY-LIST as the second hand in AS-IF and then produces TAKE$^{x \leftarrow y}$ by directing this (backward) verb (cf. Padden 1988) from the MANY-LIST to the token |EU|. He maintains the buoy ahead of him (though the hand configuration becomes more lax during FOR-EXAMPLE and FOOD) and uses it as the second hand in ALL and BUDGET.

In Figure 14 he twice directs TAKE$^{x \leftarrow y}$ from the MANY-LIST (all the taxes collected) toward the |EU| token. Then he signs GRASP$^{\downarrow|\text{taxes collected}|}$ and THROW$^{\rightarrow|EU|}$ in a nearly continuous sequence. In fact, in order to illustrate both signs it was nec-

---

14. Liddell identifies a number of types of spatial representations including token spaces, surrogate spaces, and depicting spaces. See Liddell (2003) for more detailed descriptions.

essary to use the picture ending GRASP$^{↓|\text{taxes collected}|}$ again as the beginning picture illustrating THROW$^{→|\text{EU}|}$.

By grasping the entire MANY-LIST buoy with his strong hand, he appears to show that all the collected taxes are thrown at the EU. If that were the case, there would be no money left. As evidence for this, note that at the conclusion of GRASP$^{↓|\text{taxes collected}|}$ the hand configuration that had been forming the MANY-LIST buoy loses its form.[15] The fingers have opened up. We take this as support for the interpretation that all the money was thrown at the EU and none is left. After this, the MANY-LIST is no longer relevant and does not reappear.

2.3 List buoy summary

We have illustrated two ways of presenting list buoys. Some are presented as a complete list from the very beginning. For example in Figure 3 the ASL signer produced a FOUR-LIST buoy in describing his Deaf nieces and nephews. There were four of them and he produced a FOUR-LIST buoy in talking about them. We also illustrated a number of examples of list buoys used where the first item on the list was introduced with a ONE-LIST buoy, the second with a TWO-LIST buoy, etc. Regardless of which type is used, both types have the ability to remain in place as other signs are produced. They remain in place precisely because they have a spatial significance. D1 is associated with the first item on the list, D2 with the second, etc. In Figure 5, for example, the SSL signer directs BE-IN$^{→y}$ toward D3, the |secretary position to be filled|, to express that that position would also include interpreting duties.

We also showed that not all digits must be contacted. When the NSL signer was talking about his two youngest sons he only directed signs toward D2 and D3. D1 was understood to be the oldest of his children, but he did not contact or direct signs toward D1. In addition, the spatial significance of list buoys may extend beyond the visible hand configuration. In Figure 11, for example, the ASL signer directs the fingertips of a V hand configuration on either side of D3 to indicate the week prior to and the week after the week associated with D3. Similarly, the NSL signer in Figure 12 extended the list he created well below the visible list buoy. These properties are common to buoys in ASL, SSL, and NSL.

The differences between the buoys in these three languages are mostly differences in hand configuration. That is, each language has its own unique set of hand configurations used to produce list buoys. But these lexical differences in

---

15.   We are treating THROW$^{→|\text{EU}|}$ as only indicating the recipient of the throwing. What is thrown is understood from the context in that he has just signed GRASP$^{↓|\text{taxes collected}|}$. This sign tells us that the hand has grasped all the taxes collected. Since that is what the hand contains, that is what is thrown at the EU.

hand configuration are slight compared to the commonalities described above. The one unique type of list buoy encountered in the three signed languages appears to be the MANY-LIST buoy in NSL. The closing of the fingers associated with the growing list appears to be unique to NSL.

3.   THEME buoys in ASL, SSL, and NSL

A THEME buoy signifies that "an important discourse theme is being discussed" (Liddell 2003:242). In the narratives examined to date there is tentative evidence in SSL for a THEME buoy, with strong evidence supporting the existence of a THEME buoy in ASL and NSL. So far, in NSL a THEME buoy has only been observed in the signing of a few younger signers. Signers who say they do not use the THEME buoy themselves do, however, understand the THEME buoy and explain its meaning with expressions like 'it means that this is what the signer is talking about; that one must not forget', 'keep to it', 'this is the theme' and so on.[16] A spontaneous reaction from a group of Swedish students studying Liddell (2003) was that Swedish Sign Language does not have a THEME buoy. More research is needed before a definite answer can be given for SSL, but a few examples of what might be a THEME buoy in SSL have been identified.[17]

Figure 15 illustrates examples from ASL, SSL, and NSL. The examples found in all three languages are highly similar both in form and function. In each of the examples in Figure 15 the weak hand maintains a 1 hand configuration with the index finger elevated from the horizontal as the other hand produces an independent sign. Each of the signers is producing a sign related to the description of a theme of the discourse with the strong hand while the weak hand maintains the elevated index finger.

The ASL signer in Figure 15a is introducing a new character into the narrative. The character is the aunt of an architect who lives in Italy. She is one of the main characters in the narrative and he introduces her with the phrase POSS[→|man from Italy|] AUNT ('his aunt') while maintaining the THEME buoy ahead of his chest. The presence of the THEME buoy identifies her as a significant discourse theme. The SSL signer in Figure 15b maintains the tentatively identified THEME buoy for a much longer stretch of discourse. She is introducing Tolkien's

---

16.   Naturally saying that one does not use a particular linguistic form must be understood as a statement about what signers are consciously aware of. Since much of language use is beneath conscious awareness, the extent of the use of the THEME buoy will only become apparent after the analysis of additional NSL discourse.

17.   See Nilsson (this volume), who describes an additional instance of a THEME buoy in SSL.

Figure 15. THEME buoys in ASL, SSL, and NSL

Figure 16. A candidate for a THEME buoy in SSL

book *The Lord of the Rings*. As she finishes the preceding sentence with the sign PRO-1, her weak hand produces something that looks like a THEME buoy and which seems to represent the central theme, which is *The Lord of the Rings*. She then points at the tentatively identified THEME buoy. She apparently realizes that she has not yet mentioned the name of the author and she inserts the comment 'Tolkien wrote the book'. The beginning of that parenthetical insertion is illustrated by the final two pictures in Figure 16, where she signs T-O-L-K-I-E-N and then DETERMINER. During those final two signs she maintains the THEME buoy in place directly ahead of her.

A more extensive use of the THEME buoy is illustrated in Figure 17. Here the NSL signer is describing problems she is having with an alarm clock. In Figure 17 she says that in one week the alarm clock ran two to three minutes fast; the next week four minutes fast. The THEME buoy is maintained in place during 10 of the 11 signs following the initial contact with the THEME buoy. The THEME buoy made its appearance after a long description of all the trouble the signer had had with her alarm clock. We get to know that the clock did not show the correct time, and the description gets more and more complex. The signer is explaining how it came to be that she had had trouble with the clock. The THEME buoy seems to help the addressee not to lose the fact that she is still dealing with the theme: the alarm clock.

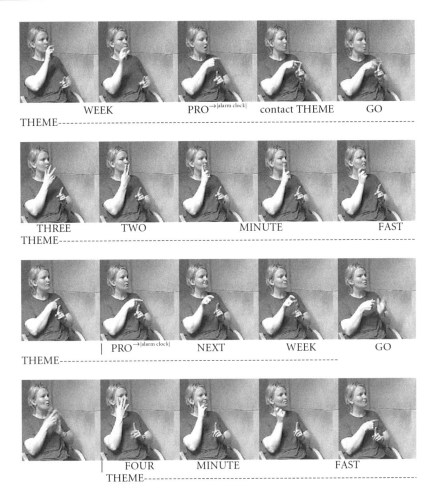

'In one week the alarm clock went two to three minutes fast,
the next week four minutes fast.'

Figure 17.   An example of extended discourse with the NSL THEME buoy

The NSL verb GO is normally produced against a horizontal B hand. Note that in the first row of pictures, GO is produced using the more vertically oriented THEME buoy as the base hand. Interestingly, during the second instance of GO (third row of pictures) the THEME buoy disappears and GO is produced with a B base hand, as it would normally be produced, except that the B hand has maintained the upright orientation of the buoy.

Then the signer produces the THEME buoy again during the signs FOUR MINUTE FAST. She lowers the THEME buoy (not illustrated) and rests it in her lap while she pauses and appears to talk to herself by saying 'No, it went slow – slow'. It is interesting that when she appears to be talking to herself the THEME buoy drops to her lap. At that moment she is no longer signing to the addressee. After this interruption, she begins signing again to the addressee by saying 'Actually slow, not fast, but slow.' Once again the THEME buoy returns and is present during the final few signs of this narrative (not illustrated).

Note also that the signer creates a token |alarm clock| to the left of the THEME buoy. This can be seen in the first and third row of pictures where the pronoun PRO$^{\rightarrow x}$ is directed toward the |alarm clock| token rather than toward the *theme* 'alarm clock' in the form of the THEME buoy. Interestingly, the same occurs in the ASL example shown in Figure 15a. When the signer later created a token |aunt|, the token was located to the right of the signer just above the height of his shoulder.

As with list buoys, the commonalities across the three signed languages with respect to the THEME buoy are striking. In each case the THEME buoy is produced with a 1 hand configuration with the index finger raised from horizontal as a discourse theme is being discussed. The NSL example just discussed shows that the entity being discussed (i.e. the alarm clock) was both associated with the THEME buoy as well as a separate token |alarm clock|. The signer was able to make pronominal reference to the alarm clock by directing PRO$^{\rightarrow x}$ toward the |alarm clock| while simultaneously maintaining the THEME buoy ahead of her at a distinct location.

4.   Fragment buoys

Fragment buoys are created by associating the meaning of a sign with all or part of its final state of production. In Figure 18a, b the signer produces the sign CULTURE. It is a two-handed sign in which the strong hand makes an arc around the weak hand. The signer creates a fragment buoy by her actions in Figure 18c. She leaves her strong hand in place, gazes at it, and also points at it with her weak hand. This associates the meaning 'culture' with the C hand configuration as placed in Figure 18c.

a. CULTURE (start)   b. CULTURE (end)   c. creating a fragment buoy

Figure 18. Pointing and gazing in the production of a fragment buoy

Unlike the other types of buoys we cannot list all possible fragment buoys since they are created spontaneously. Creating the fragment buoy in Figure 18 makes the concept 'culture' much more prominent than simply signing CULTURE.[18]

Because fragment buoys do not have lexically fixed forms, sign fragments may be difficult to distinguish from instances of (phonological) preservation (Dudis 2000). If the strong hand acts relative to the weak hand in a meaningful way, however, we take that to be evidence that the signer has created a fragment buoy. In the following SSL examples the strong hand acts relative to the weak hand, thereby providing evidence that the weak hand contributes to the meaning.[19]

The signed sequence illustrated in Figure 19 contains two different fragment buoys. The first fragment stems from a sign glossed as 2h-SIX. This sign is special in that it does not conform to the symmetry condition identified in Battison (1978). That is, both hands move, in spite of the fact that they have different handshapes. The strong hand has an extended thumb configuration and the weak hand has a 5 configuration. The more commonly used sign SIX is a one-handed sign.[20] Just prior to the signs in Figure 19 the signer has enumerated the member states of EFTA (see Figure 6). After mentioning the last state, PORTUGAL, he directs 2h-SIX at the |EFTA| token ('those six').

The weak hand then remains in its configuration and the signer points toward it, moving his strong hand from a location to the right of the little finger to a location above the thumb. The weak hand here looks like a FIVE-LIST buoy, but the fact that the pointing directed at the weak hand refers to all six member states, indicates that it is a fragment from 2h-SIX. That it is a fragment, and not an example of phonological preservation, is clear since the strong hand is directed toward the weak hand, thereby showing that it contributes to the meaning.

The second sign fragment in Figure 19 comes from THAT-GROUP$^{\rightarrow|EFTA|}$ and remains in that configuration when the signer points with his strong hand at the token |EFTA|. In this case the token |EFTA| is bounded on one side by the fragment buoy from the sign THAT-GROUP$^{\rightarrow|EFTA|}$. The fragment buoy disappears during WHY$^{\rightarrow|EFTA|}$ and CREATE$^{\rightarrow|EFTA|}$ and appears again when the signer spells E-F-T-A. The reappearance is especially interesting in that it provides evidence that the fragment buoy takes on an independent existence once it has been formed. It can reappear even though the sign THAT-GROUP$^{\rightarrow|EFTA|}$ has not been signed again.

---

18. This example is unusual since buoys are normally associated with the weak hand. By using her weak hand to contact the fragment of CULTURE, the signer makes her strong hand into a fragment buoy.

19. It is not yet clear if there are any (formational or other) restrictions regarding from which signs fragment buoys are created.

20. The signs for numbers 6–9 have such double forms with a weak five hand in SSL.

points at fragment   CREATE$^{|\rightarrow\text{EFTA}|}$ | THAT-
fragm 2h-SIX$^{\cdot|\text{EFTA}|}$----------------------

-GROUP$^{\cdot\rightarrow|\text{EFTA}|}$ points at |EFTA| WHY$^{\rightarrow|\text{EFTA}|}$ CREATE$^{\cdot|\text{EFTA}|}$
     fragmTHAT-GROUP$^{\cdot\rightarrow|\text{EFTA}|}$

E-$^{\cdot\rightarrow|\text{EFTA}|}$ -F-$^{\cdot\rightarrow|\text{EFTA}|}$ -T-$^{\cdot\rightarrow|\text{EFTA}|}$ -A$^{\cdot\rightarrow|\text{EFTA}|}$
fragmTHAT-GROUP$^{\cdot\rightarrow|\text{EFTA}|}$---

Figure 19. 'Those (six) countries founded the organization. Why did they found EFTA?'

Note that the two fragment buoys described above are used in slightly different ways. When the fragment buoy from 2h-SIX$^{\rightarrow|\text{EFTA}|}$ (with the five handshape) is created, signs are directed at the fragment buoy itself. The signer does not direct signs toward the fragment buoy created from THAT-GROUP$^{\rightarrow|\text{EFTA}|}$. Instead, the fragment buoy appears to identify a boundary of the token |EFTA|, which is contained inside that boundary and signs are directed toward the token |EFTA| in the interior of that boundary.

In Figure 20 the NSL signer is talking about reading the lips of his teachers as they spoke Norwegian – without really understanding what the teachers were saying. He states that he could recognize a specific word (i.e. he knew the word), but he did not know its meaning.

The sign WORD in NSL is normally made with or without an initial contact at the jaw near the mouth with a 'baby-C' hand configuration followed by an outward movement. In Figure 20 the signer produces WORD well ahead of his ipsilateral shoulder, then leaves the fragment of WORD in place. The fragment becomes the word the signer 'knows' but whose meaning he does not know. This is a fragment buoy involving the strong hand since the signer produces the one-handed sign WORD with his strong hand. For two-handed signs the signer has a

'There was one word that I knew, but I didn't know its meaning.'

Figure 20. An NSL fragment buoy from the sign WORD

choice as to which hand to use as the fragment. The ASL signer in Figure 18, for example, uses the strong hand of the two-handed sign CULTURE to form the fragment buoy while the Swedish signer in Figure 19 uses the weak hand of the sign THAT-GROUP$^{\rightarrow|EFTA|}$ to form the fragment buoy.

After the sign WORD is produced, the fragment buoy remains in place for five consecutive signs. He even directs PRO$^{\rightarrow|word|}$ toward the fragment to identify the word he is talking about. After the pronoun he also uses the fragment as the base hand for MEAN. The fact of directing the pronoun toward the fragment and additionally using the fragment as a base for the sign MEAN demonstrates that the fragment is serving a significant role in this short stretch of discourse.

ASL   SSL   NSL

SOMETHING   E-C   CHEAP
POINTER$^{\to |thing|}$ POINTER$^{\to |EC|}$ POINTER$^{\to |Esso\ station|}$

Figure 21. POINTER buoys in ASL, SSL, and NSL

5. The POINTER buoy

The POINTER buoy is also a weak hand sign maintained while the strong hand produces other signs. The POINTER buoy differs from the list buoys, the THEME buoy, and fragment buoys in that the POINTER buoy does not acquire any new significance through blending. Instead, it *points toward* an important element in the discourse. It points at an element of real space or a real space blend. The fact that the POINTER is not a blended entity, explains its idiosyncratic properties, such as the fact that other signs, like pronouns and verbs, do not point at it, something which is characteristic of list buoys, for example.

In Figure 21 the ASL signer is describing a child noticing something and wanting it. This POINTER buoy is present during SOMETHING and the next sign WANT. The SSL signer is talking about the EC and maintains the POINTER during nine consecutive signs discussing the EC (Note: only the final hand configuration of E-C is illustrated in Figure 21b). The NSL signer is describing an Esso gas station with low prices. He maintains the POINTER buoy during seven consecutive signs.

It is common, then, in all three signed languages to keep the POINTER buoy directed toward some conceptualized entity as the other hand continues signing about it. In Figure 22 the ASL signer is explaining that a group of visitors must arrive as their host's home. She directs the POINTER buoy toward the conceptualized location of the host's home and keeps it directed toward that location during the four signs illustrated.[21] After signing the sequence in Figure 22, she repeats MUST ARRIVE$^{\to location\ of\ |home|}$. The POINTER buoy is still present during MUST, but is not present during the two-handed sign ARRIVE. As a result, she produces

---

21.   Since the host is at his home it is difficult to distinguish between directing the POINTER buoy toward the home and toward the host. If both are at the same place, then there really is no difference.

THAT$^{\rightarrow|host|}$ H-O-S-T   POSS$^{\rightarrow|host|}$ HOME

POINTER---

Figure 22. Seven of eight signs accompanied by the POINTER buoy

19-HUNDRED$^{\rightarrow|EFTA|}$ FIVE$^{\rightarrow|EFTA|}$ NINE$^{\rightarrow|EFTA|}$ STOCKHOLM   HERE

POINTER$^{\rightarrow|EFTA|}$--

Figure 23. '(And so EFTA was founded.) It was in 1959 here in Stockholm'

all the signs in Figure 22 and one additional sign while simultaneously directing the POINTER buoy toward the destination.

In Figure 23 the SSL signer is talking about the foundation of EFTA. Earlier on he has used the token |EFTA| in the area in front of him slightly to the right when referring to EFTA. The handshape of the base hand in NINETEEN-HUNDRED is the 1 hand configuration, not the expected fist hand. It may be an anticipation of the handshape of the POINTER buoy, or it may in fact already be the POINTER buoy, which is the analysis chosen here. The POINTER is directed at |EFTA| and remains in the same configuration during the whole sentence.

In Figure 24 the NSL signer is talking about an Esso gas station that sold really cheap gasoline. Just prior to these signs he says DRIVE-TO$^{\rightarrow|gas\ station|}$ GAS^STATION, with both signs directed left and forward. Figure 24 illustrates the subsequent signs. He begins by signing THERE$^{\rightarrow|gas\ station|}$ with his strong hand while the weak hand produces POINTER$^{\rightarrow|gas\ station|}$. The result is both hands pointing toward the gas station.

The POINTER buoy remains in place as the strong hand produces THERE$^{\rightarrow|gas\ station|}$ E-S THERE$^{\rightarrow|gas\ station|}$ PRO$^{\rightarrow|gas\ station|}$ REALLY CHEAP. He spells E-S, short for 'Esso' (Note: only the final hand configuration of E-S is illustrated in Figure 24), just above the POINTER buoy. Then he directs the next two signs toward the same location the POINTER buoy is directed toward. In addition, the two-handed sign REALLY uses the POINTER buoy as its place of articulation.

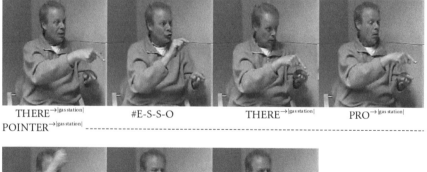

THERE$^{\rightarrow|gas\,station|}$ #E-S-S-O   THERE$^{\rightarrow|gas\,station|}$ PRO$^{\rightarrow|gas\,station|}$
POINTER$^{\rightarrow|gas\,station|}$ ---

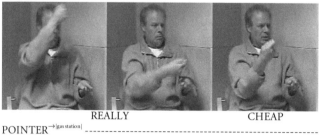

                              REALLY   CHEAP
POINTER$^{\rightarrow|gas\,station|}$ ---

Figure 24. The POINTER buoy directed toward a |gas station|

6. Conclusions

In this paper we examine list buoys, THEME buoys, POINTER buoys, and fragment buoys in American Sign Language, Norwegian Sign Language, and Swedish Sign Language. We find evidence for each type of buoy in each of the three signed languages. In fact, the similarities we find across the buoys in these three languages far outweigh the differences. Aside from some phonological differences in handshapes, and some forms that exist in one language but not another (such as the MANY-LIST buoy in NSL), list buoys appear to function in essentially the same ways in each language. The evidence found for the THEME buoy is even more uniform. The hand configurations and orientation of the weak hand are virtually the same in all three signed languages. The same uniformity is also found with respect to POINTER buoys. Finally, we would not expect uniformity of form with fragment buoys since they are formed from fragments of signs from each of the three signed languages. Nevertheless, the mere fact that sign fragments can function as buoys is demonstrated by the data from these three signed languages.

The existence of these similarities across three mutually unintelligible signed languages raises the question of why these buoys should be so similar without providing an obvious answer.

While possible historical connections, including language contact, could help explain the commonalities we have found, we do not have sufficient evidence to support this explanation. While there is a well-known historical connection between ASL and Old French Sign Language (OFSL), it does not appear that a common historical connection with OFSL is a likely explanation for the commonalities found in all three signed languages. It is possible that there are language functions that naturally develop in specific ways in a manually produced language. Directional pronouns, indicating verbs, and depicting verbs, for example, are widely found across unrelated signed languages. The various types of buoys may also be examples of such phenomena that naturally develop in signed languages. When the existence and nature of buoys has been studied in a much larger set of signed languages we may be in a better position to address the interesting issues raised concerning the strong similarities in the form and use of buoys.

References

Battison, Robbin. 1978. *Lexical Borrowing in American Sign Language.* Silver Spring, Md.: Linstok Press.

Bergman, Brita. 1979. *Signed Swedish.* Stockholm: National Swedish Board of Education / Liber UtbildningsFörlaget.

Dudis, Paul. 2000. "Tokens as Abstract Visible Blended Elements". Paper presented at the conference Conceptual Structures in Discourse and Language 5, University of California, Santa Barbara, May 2000.

Fauconnier, Gilles & Mark Turner. 1996. "Blending as a Central Process of Grammar". *Conceptual Structure, Discourse and Language.* ed. by Adele Goldberg, 113–130. Stanford, Calif.: CSLI Publications.

—— & Mark Turner. 2002. *The Way We Think: Conceptual Blending and the Mind's Hidden Complexities.* New York: Basic Books.

Fleischer, Axel. 1944. "Redegjørelse for Tegnspråkets Tilblivelse". *Tegn og Tale* 25:1.10.

Johnson, Robert E. 1990. "Distinctive Features for Handshapes in American Sign Language". Paper presented to the Third International Conference on Theoretical Issues in Sign Language Research, Boston.

Liddell, Scott K. 1996. "Numeral Incorporating Roots and Non-Incorporating Prefixes in American Sign Language". *Sign Language Studies* 92.201–226.

—— 2003. *Grammar, Gesture, and Meaning in American Sign Language.* Cambridge: Cambridge University Press.

Padden, Carol A. 1988. *Interaction in Morphology and Syntax in American Sign Language.* New York & London: Garland Publishing.

Schröder, Odd-Inge. 1993. "Introduction to the History of Norwegian Sign Language". *Looking back. A Reader on the History of Deaf Communities and their Sign Languages (International Studies on Sign Language and Communication of the Deaf, vol. 20)* ed. by Renate Fischer & Harlan Lane, 231–248. Hamburg: Signum Press.

Wallin, Lars. 1994. *Polysyntetiska Tecken i Svenska Teckenspråket. [Polysynthetic Signs in Swedish Sign Language].* Stockholm University: Institute of Linguistics, Department of Sign Language.

Point buoys

The weak hand as a point of reference for time and space

Marit Vogt-Svendsen and Brita Bergman
University of Oslo / Stockholm University

1. Introduction

Buoys are signs (typically) produced by the weak hand "held in a stationary configuration as the strong hand continues producing signs" and whose physical presence "helps guide the discourse as it proceeds" (Liddell 2003:223). The types of buoys identified by Liddell in American Sign Language (ASL) include list buoys, fragment buoys, the THEME buoy, and the POINTER buoy. The same types of buoys have also been observed in the two unrelated languages discussed here: Norwegian Sign Language (NSL) and Swedish Sign Language (SSL) (Vogt-Svendsen 2003a; Liddell, Vogt-Svendsen & Bergman 2004; Liddell, Vogt-Svendsen & Bergman, this volume).

Buoys typically represent discourse entities and, as such, can be pointed at, and have verbs and pronouns directed towards them. The POINTER buoy (an extended index finger), however, is special in that it *points* towards an entity, rather than represents it.

In the present paper we argue that Norwegian Sign Language and Swedish Sign Language have yet another category of buoys, henceforth referred to as 'point buoys'.[1] In contrast to other types of buoys a point buoy neither represents, nor points at, a prominent discourse entity. Instead, a point buoy represents a point in time or space and is used for visualizing temporal and spatial relations between entities. A point buoy serves as a prop (cf. the distinction participants – props (Grimes 1975)) in relation to which other signs can be located.

---

1. This type of buoy was first identified in NSL (Vogt-Svendsen 2003b).

Using data from videotaped dialogues (Norwegian Sign Language) and monologues (Swedish Sign Language) we will show that point buoys, though sharing
some properties with other types of buoys, do constitute a category of their own,
a category of crucial importance when talking about time and space.

2.   POINT-G and POINT-B

Two point buoys with identical forms in the two languages have been identified,
POINT-G and POINT-B. POINT-G is an extended index finger, with fully extended middle and distal joints, but, depending on the orientation of the buoy
hand, the proximal joint may be either extended or flexed. A POINT-G buoy
with the finger directed to the side is typically bent in the proximal joint, while
a POINT-G buoy directed up or forward is extended in the proximal joint. In
POINT-B, which takes the form of a flat hand, the position of the thumb is either
radial or palmar. Both languages use POINT-G and POINT-B, identical not only
in form, but, judging from the present data, also in function. Before discussing
the characteristic properties of point buoys, a detailed description of seven sequences containing point buoys will be given. Examples (1)–(3) represent points in
space and examples (4)–(7) represent points in time. (Transcription conventions
are outlined in the Appendix).

3.   Buoys representing points in space

3.1 Example one

The sequence illustrated in Figure 1 (from Norwegian Sign Language) shows a
prototypical example of POINT-G used for representing a point in space. The example, which means 'it is a very short distance from where I live to the airbus
(stop)', is from a discourse where the signer tells how she was considering whether
to take the train or the bus to the airport. After PRO-1 LIVE she signs CLOSE-TO,
which is a two-handed sign with flat hands (third photo). The hands then change
from B-hands to extended index fingers. The weak hand produces a POINT-G
buoy with the index finger directed to the right and placed in front of the signer
(fourth photo). It remains in place while the strong hand moves between two locations relative to it. First, the strong hand starts from a location close to the tip of
the buoy finger (fourth photo). From the three first signs we know that the location close to the tip of the buoy finger represents the place where the signer lives.
Next, the strong hand moves along a path forward, slightly to the left, and stops at
a location in front of POINT-G (fifth photo). Immediately after this the buoy hand

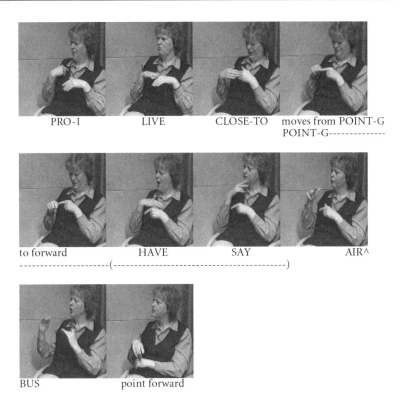

PRO-1	LIVE	CLOSE-TO	moves from POINT-G POINT-G-------------
to forward ---------------------(---------------------------------------)	HAVE	SAY	AIR^
BUS	point forward		

Figure 1. 'It is a very short distance from where I live to the airbus (stop).' (Norwegian Sign Language)

first goes down to a lower position where it does not seem to have any significance any more (indicated by parenthesis in the transcription), and then it disappears. It is only after the buoy is gone, that it becomes clear that the location in front of POINT-G represents the stop for the airport bus: the lax index finger following the two-handed sign AIR^BUS is directed towards the same forward location previously used in relation to the buoy.

In Figure 1 POINT-G represents an unspecified point in space in the signer's neighbourhood, and is not explicitly talked about. The strong hand does not point *at the buoy*, but moves along a path between *locations relative* to it: close to the tip of the buoy finger and in front of the finger.

3.2 Example two

A slightly different use of POINT-G representing a point in space is shown in Figure 2 (Swedish Sign Language). POINT-G appears in the illustration in Figure 2 in the second row, fifth photo. However, whereas the citation form of AVIATION

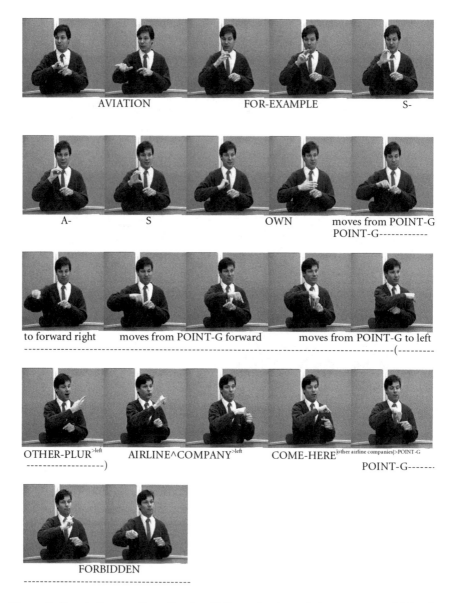

AVIATION   FOR-EXAMPLE   S-

A-   S   OWN   moves from POINT-G
                                                   POINT-G------------

to forward right   moves from POINT-G forward   moves from POINT-G to left
---(---------

OTHER-PLUR>left   AIRLINE^COMPANY>left   COME-HERE[other airline companies]>POINT-G
------------------)   POINT-G-------

FORBIDDEN

Figure 2. 'In aviation, e.g. Scandinavian Airlines, they have their own routes which other companies are not allowed to use.' (Swedish Sign Language)

has a flat hand as base hand, it is produced here with a lax index hand. This could be a partial assimilation of the left hand to the handshape of the right hand, or an anticipatory assimilation to the handshape of POINT-G. During the signs that follow, the left hand remains in a relaxed form and at a slightly lower location. After OWN the left hand is raised to a higher location and the index finger now has the full extension in the middle and distal joints characteristic of POINT-G. POINT-G is used as the starting point of the movement of the right hand (second row, fifth photo), which outlines three paths in different directions: forward to the right, forward, and to the left. This is how the signer expresses the concept of 'routes'. POINT-G, which begins to appear again after AIRLINE^COMPANY, is back in its former location in the final phase of COME-HERE, so that the movement of COME-HERE ends close to POINT-G. Whereas in Figure 1 the signer uses different *locations* relative to the buoy, the present signer uses the buoy as the starting point of *movement* in three different *directions*. The buoy does not represent a specific discourse entity, rather an unspecified starting point for a route. It is a prop in relation to which the strong hand acts, making it possible to show routes sharing the same point of departure.

3.3 Example three

The third example, which is from Norwegian Sign Language, differs slightly from the two first examples, in that POINT-G is used in a spatially more complex context. The signer uses locations that have been established before POINT-G appears, and she uses the buoy not only as the starting and end point of movements, but also to point out locations relative to it. Focus will here be on what is most relevant in relation to the buoy.

Previous to the sequence illustrated in Figure 3, the signer says that she and her husband had been waiting for a train to Oslo Airport at Oslo Sentralbanestasjon (Oslo S), first at one track, then at another track and finally, they returned to the first track. In this part of the discourse, the signer relates a series of events from the perspective of the acting participants,[2] using several locations in the signing space to represent the places she is talking about (without using a point buoy). Some of these locations are included in the glosses in Figure 3. As can be seen in the figure, POINT-G remains in place during 20 signs while the signer explains what made them wait for the train at two different tracks at Oslo S.

After ONLY FROM OSLO SENTRAL (four first photos, Figure 3) both hands change handshape to produce index fingers. The left hand is set up as POINT-G far in front of, slightly to the right of the signer, and the strong hand signs HERE close to and in front of the buoy (first photo, second row). From now on this location, close to and in front of the buoy, represents the point of departure of the airport train at the first track at Oslo S. This is the first location established relative to POINT-G in Figure 3. The second location is established behind the buoy (third

---

2. In terms of Liddell's model (2003): the signer uses surrogates.

photo, second row) and represents the place or platform at the first track where they were first waiting for the train.

The signer used the location 'far in front of her' (where POINT-G now is placed) also in the first part of the discourse, but there she did not differentiate spatially between the place of departure of the train and the place where they had

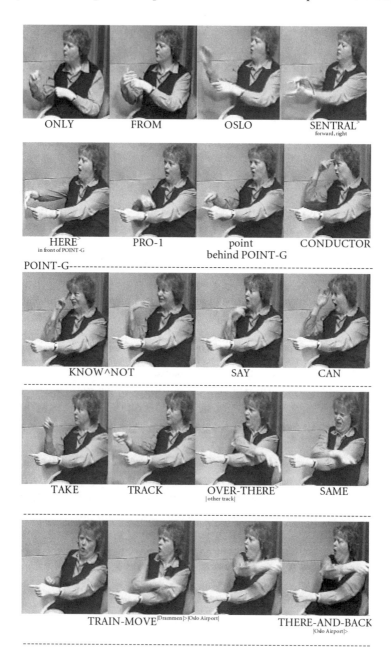

| ONLY | FROM | OSLO | SENTRAL⌐ forward, right |

| HERE⌐ in front of POINT-G | PRO-1 | point behind POINT-G | CONDUCTOR |

POINT-G--

| KNOW^NOT | SAY | CAN |

| TAKE | TRACK | OVER-THERE⌐ | other track | | SAME |

TRAIN-MOVE|Drammen |> |Oslo Airport| THERE-AND-BACK |Oslo Airport |>

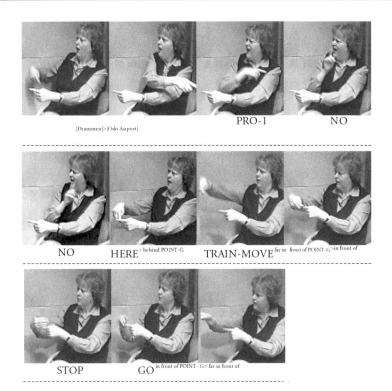

Figure 3. ('The airport trains from Oslo S that day departure) only from the track where we were standing, but the conductor did not know that. He said we should go to the track on the other side where the train from Drammen (via Oslo S) to Oslo Airport arrives. I said no, we have to stay here! The train arrives here, stops here and departures from here (to Oslo Airport).' (Norwegian Sign Language)

been waiting. In order to explain what happened, however, she makes this spatial distinction, and is able to do so by using POINT-G and relating signs to the buoy. POINT-G represents an unspecified point at the first track at Oslo S where they were waiting.

The third location used, far to the left of the buoy, has already been used in the preceding context and represents another track at Oslo S. The conductor had said they should go to that track since that is where the train from Drammen (to Oslo Airport) arrives (which it did not do on that day). This location is reactivated by OVER-THERE directed to the far left of POINT-G (third photo, fourth line). Note that OVER-THERE in its final position has the form of an index pointing in the same horizontal plane as the buoy.

The citation form of the following sign, SAME (last photo, fourth row), is a sign with two active G-hands signed in front of signer, but as the left hand in this example is used in POINT-G and the right hand is already placed to the left because of the previous sign, SAME is signed as a one handed sign contacting the left upper arm.

The fourth location used while POINT-G remains in place can be seen in the starting point of the verb TRAIN-MOVE[|Drammen|>|Oslo Airport|], which is to the right, far behind the buoy (first photo, fifth row). The right hand moves from |Drammen| along a path to |Oslo Airport| through the location far to the left in the signing space representing the other track at Oslo S (second photo, fifth row). This is significant and means that the train from Drammen (bound for Oslo Airport) always stops at the other track at Oslo S. The final location of TRAIN-MOVE, which represents Oslo Airport, is the fifth location used in this part of the discourse, and is even further to the left than the location used for the other track (the utmost part of the hand is outside the screen). It is also higher in the signing space than the horizontal plane used up till now. The height distinction does not mean that the train moved uphill, but that it went far away (to Oslo Airport). Height can be used to show distance.

When the signer then says 'I said no, we have to stay here!' she locates HERE just behind POINT-G (second photo, seventh row), which still represents the place at the first track where they stood waiting.

The sixth location is established by the starting point of the verb TRAIN-MOVE (third photo, seventh row), far in front of and also higher than POINT-G, meaning that it came from far away.[3] The end point of TRAIN-MOVE is in front of and close to the buoy. It is clear that this location, which already has been established as the place of departure of the train, now also represents the place of arrival at the first track. It is a shuttle-service train between Oslo Airport and Oslo S.

When the signer signs STOP (first photo, eight row) in 'the train stops here', the strong hand moves downwards and ends in contact with the radial side of the index finger. The left hand is here used as place of articulation in the two-handed sign STOP. The fact that a buoy hand is used as the other hand in a two-handed sign is not unique to point buoys, but has also been shown for other types of buoys (Liddell et al., this volume).

In GO, which is the last sign produced while POINT-G remains in place, the signer once more uses the two locations close to, in front of POINT-G and higher than, far away from POINT-G.

In this example we have seen that the signer makes use of locations that were established in the signing space before the buoy appeared, but that she also establishes new locations. Setting up POINT-G in the signing space, makes the signer able to be more precise when referring to the places of departures and arrivals of

---

3.   The buoy hand is here moved slightly closer to the signer's body, probably for articulatory reasons.

trains and where they were waiting. At the same time the buoy serves as a spatial 'placeholder' keeping *all* reestablished and new locations active during its presence.

4.   Buoys representing points in time

While the buoys described in the previous examples represent space, the examples to follow demonstrate that buoys may also represent points in time. This is a natural extension of spatial expressions: they are commonly found as metaphorical devices for time in both spoken and signed languages (see e.g. Lakoff & Johnson 1980; Taub 2001).

4.1 Example four

In the sequence from Swedish Sign Language illustrated in Figure 4 the signer describes the process of changing the legislation before a nation may join the European Community. During the sign GOAL (first row, second and third photos), which is a one-handed sign starting at the forehead, the signer begins to move his

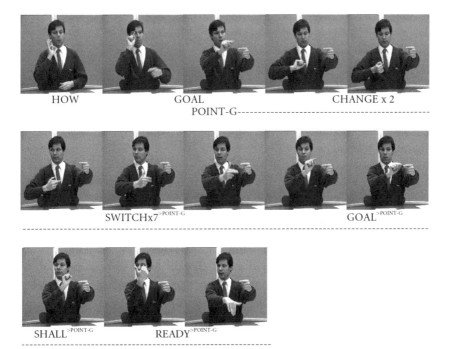

Figure 4. '(It is up to each state to decide) how to make the required changes (in their respective legislation) in time.' (Swedish Sign Language)

left hand up to a forward position at shoulder level (with almost full extension of the elbow), so that the movement of GOAL ends close to the left hand. The left hand, a POINT-G buoy, represents the point in time when the legislative changes must be completed. The signs that follow can all be said to be produced in relation to POINT-G, in that they either move towards it or are located near it. In the reduplicated form CHANGEx2, which is signed here with only one hand, the second cycle is made slightly further away from the signer's torso in the direction of POINT-G (not shown in the illustration). Similarly SWITCH is repeated seven times while the hand moves towards POINT-G. The movement of the second token of GOAL does not start near the forehead as would be expected, but close to the left hand. SHALL and READY, both normally two-handed citation forms, are articulated with only one hand, close to the left hand (as can be seen from the fact that the elbow is more extended than in their respective non-directed forms).

Summarizing, the verb forms, CHANGEx2 and SWITCHx7, move along a path in the direction of POINT-G and the other signs GOAL, SHALL and READY, are located near it. Similar use of space has been described by Engberg-Pedersen (1993) in her analysis of time lines in Danish Sign Language. The use of space in the present SSL example can be seen as an instance of the 'mixed time line'. It "can be thought of as a line perpendicular to the signer's body, and it seems to be used for expressing a sequence of moments in time or a period of time seen from a point before its start" (Engberg-Pedersen 1993:88). The function of POINT-G in this example is to mark the endpoint of the time line, i.e. it represents the point in time, "the temporal goal," when the changes must be completed. The movements of CHANGE and SWITCH along the mixed time line express the process of making the changes seen over time and approaching the deadline.

4.2   Example five

A similar example from Swedish Sign Language, demonstrating the use of POINT-B representing a point in time, is illustrated in Figure 5. In the preceding context the signer has said that some of the countries that have applied for membership in the European Community, have been very fast in changing their laws. He then goes on to compare this with some other countries and says that Italy and Greece are very slow to change their laws, having, until now, made only 14 changes out of 225, and he notes that they have only two more years in which they can make the outstanding changes.

The signer makes a spatial distinction between the countries that are fast and those that are slow to implement change: the fast countries are represented by a location to his left, and the slow ones to his right. In the sequence about the slow countries he also uses another spatial device, similar to the 'deictic time line' in Danish Sign Language, which "can be thought of as a line from behind the signer's

PERIOD-FROM-TO[>]^{|now to 1993|}   point behind POINT-B   UNTIL^{from behind>POINT-B}
(both hands move down)

POINT-B[>]^{|now|}--

FROM-TO^{POINT-B>|1993|}   ON   TWO   YEAR
moves forward from POINT-B

Figure 5. '(Only 14 laws out of 225 have been changed) up till now and only two more
years (for all the outstanding changes).' (Swedish Sign Language)

dominant-hand shoulder and forward" (Engberg-Pedersen 1993: 84). It has a fixed
reference point of time near the signer's body of which the "*default meaning is the
utterance time*" (ibid. p. 84; italics ours). The sign glossed as PERIOD-FROM-
TO$^{>|now\ to\ 1993|}$, which is produced with two active hands making a short downward
movement (as can be seen in the first and second photos), sets up a period of time
on the deictic time line.[4] The left hand, located near the signer's body slightly to
his right, marks the beginning of the period. Since it marks a location near the
signer's body, it refers to the point in time of the utterance, 'now', which in the
present example is October 14th, 1991 (the date of the recording of the lecture).
The right hand in PERIOD-FROM-TO$^{>|now\ to\ 1993|}$ is further out from the body
(approx. 90° extension in the elbow joint) and marks the end of the period. It is
known from the previous context that the changes must all be made by the end
of 1993, thus, PERIOD-FROM-TO$^{>|now\ to\ 1993|}$ sets up a period of time extending
from the time of the lecture (1991) to two years beyond that time (1993).

The left hand remains in its position as a POINT-B buoy representing the
time of the utterance. The signer points behind POINT-B (third photo) and then
his right, flat hand moves forward to contact with the left hand, conveying the
meaning that this is what has happened until now. Starting in front of POINT-B
the right hand then moves along the deictic time line to the location representing
the end of the remaining two-year period (two first photos, second row).

---

4.   PERIOD-FROM-TO is different in form and function from the noun PERIOD, which is a
two handed sign with one active hand.

POINT-B is located on the deictic time line and because it is located close to the signer's body, it represents the time of the utterance, which is the default meaning of that location on this time line.

4.3 Example six

Figure 6 shows a POINT-B buoy in Norwegian Sign Language representing a point in time. The signer says that 'the decision (that she should get a computer) was made just before they (the Centre for Technical Aids) moved to Strømmen.' After DECISION (first photo, Figure 6), both hands change into B-hands (with the thumb in the palm). While the weak hand moves to the location where it will remain as a POINT-B buoy, the strong hand takes its position to the left of the weak hand, and makes two small, rapid movements towards the buoy hand (second photo). The movement of the strong hand towards the buoy shows a location close to the left of the buoy representing a point in time: 'just before'. Next, the strong hand in the shape of an index finger points towards |just before|. Also the starting point of the following verb MOVE is at a location to the left of POINT-B representing 'before', while the final location of MOVE to the right of POINT-B represents 'after'.

POINT-B in Figure 6 activates what can be seen as the 'sequence line', which for Danish Sign Language is described as

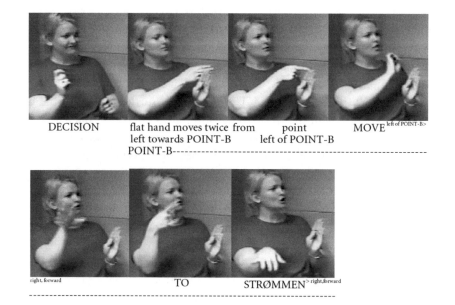

DECISION   flat hand moves twice from   point   MOVE ^{left of POINT-B>}
              left towards POINT-B   left of POINT-B
              POINT-B--

right, forward   TO   STRØMMEN^{> right,forward}

Figure 6. 'The decision (that I should get a computer) was made just before they (the Centre for Technical Aids) moved to Strømmen.' (Norwegian Sign Language)

a line parallel with the signer's surface plane from her left to the right. For right-handed signers, it has a left-to-right orientation in the sense that if A is a locus to the left of another locus B, then A is used for an earlier point in time than B.

(Engberg-Pedersen 1993:86)[5]

In Figure 6 the movement of the strong flat hand, the direction of the index finger, and the starting point of MOVE are at locations to the left of the buoy, locations used for an earlier point in time than the final location of MOVE (to the right of the buoy). The sequence line

> does not have a reference point with a spatially fixed locus. Instead, it is possible to establish reference points by representing time referents by loci of the line and talk about moments or periods before, after or between reference points.
>
> (Engberg-Pedersen 1993:86)

In Figure 6 POINT-B is established as a 'reference point' on the time line making it possible to talk about moments and periods before and after that reference point. POINT-B in our example is a visible partition separating 'before' and 'after'. It is not explicitly mentioned which point in time POINT-B represents, but it is clear from the context that it represents a point in time shortly after the decision was made.

The starting point of MOVE in Figure 6 is not only to the left of POINT-B, but is also higher than the buoy, and the final location of MOVE is not only to the right, but also forward of POINT-B. These locations are located outside the sequence line, and do not represent points in time, but places. The high location in MOVE (to the left of the buoy) represents the place where the Centre for Technical Aids moved from, and the forward location of MOVE (to the right of the buoy), represents the place to which the Centre moved. The example shows that when a POINT-B buoy is used as a referential point of time, reference to places can still be made simultaneously. By using the left, high initial location of MOVE, the signer simultaneously refers to both 'before' and 'the place where the Centre moved from', and by using the right, forward final location of MOVE, the signer refers to both 'after' and 'the place where the Centre moved to'.

4.4 Example seven

The point buoy in Figure 7 (Norwegian Sign Language) also activates the sequence line, but it differs from the sequence in Figure 6 in at least three respects. Firstly,

---

5.   See also Malmquist & Mosand (1996) on time lines in NSL. Note that Engberg-Pedersen's description of time lines in Danish Sign Language appears to apply not only to NSL, but as shown in previous examples, also to SSL. For a recent, alternative analysis of similar temporal expressions in NSL, see Selvik (2006).

in Figure 6 the signer uses POINT-B while in Figure 7 she starts with POINT-G. Secondly, the point in time that POINT-B represents in Figure 6 is not explicitly specified, but in Figure 7 it is specified as 'Sunday'. Thirdly, in Figure 6 both sides of the buoy are used, but in Figure 7 only the right side of the buoy is used. Below the example illustrated in Figure 7 is described in detail.

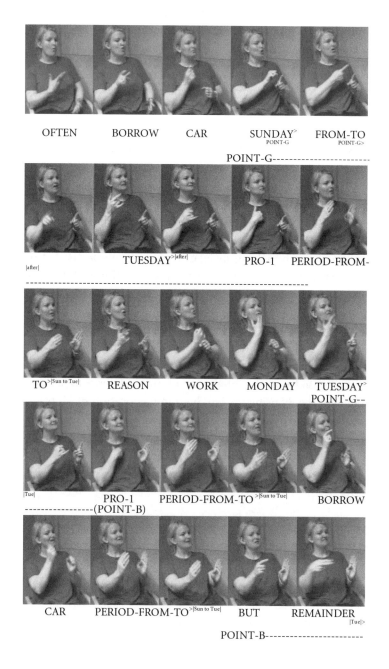

OFTEN   BORROW   CAR   SUNDAY$^>$ FROM-TO

                                                  POINT-G   POINT-G$^>$

POINT-G-----------------------

|after| TUESDAY$^{>|after|}$ PRO-1   PERIOD-FROM-

TO$^{>|Sun\ to\ Tue|}$ REASON   WORK   MONDAY   TUESDAY$^>$

                                                         POINT-G--

|Tue| PRO-1   PERIOD-FROM-TO$^{>|Sun\ to\ Tue|}$ BORROW

----------------(POINT-B)

CAR   PERIOD-FROM-TO$^{>|Sun\ to\ Tue|}$ BUT   REMAINDER

                                                         |Tue|$^>$

                            POINT-B-----------------------

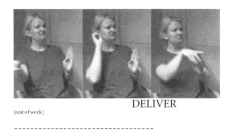

DELIVER

|rest of week|

Figure 7. 'I often borrow the car from Sunday through Tuesday because I work on Monday and Tuesday. I borrow the car during those days, then deliver it back and don't use it the rest of the week.' (Norwegian Sign Language)

In reply to a question asked by her interlocutor, the signer says that she often borrows her father's car from Sunday through Tuesday, because she works on Monday and Tuesday. After OFTEN BORROW CAR the POINT-G buoy is set up (fourth photo, first row). SUNDAY is directed towards POINT-G making it represent 'Sunday'.[6] In FROM-TO$^{\text{POINT-G>|after|}}$ the right hand moves along a path from POINT-G to a location to the right where the signer then locates TUESDAY, making that location on the sequence line represent 'Tuesday' (second and third photos, second row).

During PERIOD-FROM-TO$^{>|\text{Sun to Tue}|}$ the buoy is gone, but the locations of |Sunday| and |Tuesday| are still in use: The weak hand in PERIOD-FROM-TO$^{>|\text{Sun to Tue}|}$ is located at |Sunday| and the strong hand at |Tuesday|. POINT-G turns up again simultaneously with TUESDAY (last photo, third row and first photo, fourth row). The signer then repeats PERIOD-FROM-TO$^{>|\text{Sun to Tue}|}$ and goes on by saying that she borrows the car during those days, but delivers it back and does not use it during the rest of the week. During this part of the discourse POINT-G is not used. Instead the weak B-hand remains in its position as a POINT-B buoy after the third instance of PERIOD-FROM-TO$^{|\text{Sun to Tue}|}$ in the same place, with the same orientation and with the same function as the previous POINT-G (see fourth photo, fifth row and onwards).

In the very last sequence of this example, which begins with a one-handed form of BUT (fourth photo, fifth row), another segment of the sequence line is used. REMAINDER moves from |Tuesday| to a location further to the right (the hand is partly outside the screen). It is not a point on the sequence line, but the part extending from |Tuesday| to the final location of REMAINDER, that now represents 'the rest of the week'. After DELIVER, POINT-B does not show up again.

---

6. Put differently, in terms of Liddell's model (2003): POINT-G becomes 'Sunday' through blending.

5.   Use of signing space in relation to point buoys

In spite of the similarities, a point buoy representing a point in space and a buoy representing a point in time seems to use the signing space in different ways. A point buoy representing a point in *time* evokes a time line along which the strong hand may move or be located. As can be seen from the examples described, the orientation of the finger(s) of the point buoy is perpendicular to the time line, thereby indicating which time line is used. A point buoy directed forward or up activates the sequence line, which extends from side to side parallel to the signers body (Figure 6 and 7). The strong hand acts on either side of the point buoy, i.e. to the left and/or to the right, but not in front of or behind it. A point buoy directed contra-laterally (Figure 4 and 5) uses a time line where the strong hand moves in front of or behind, but not to the left or the right of, the buoy. The difference between the mixed and the deictic time lines is shown by the position of the weak hand in relation to the signer's body, in front of, or on the dominant hand side respectively. The use of signing space in relation to a point buoy representing a point in time is along a line, i.e. it is restricted to *one* dimension.

A point buoy representing a point in *space* evokes a plane, typically a horizontal plane, and serves as a prop on a stage around which the strong hand acts (see Figure 1, 2, 3). The strong hand may move or be located in any direction in that plane, but vertical distinctions are not used to indicate, for example, height distinctions. Thus, point buoys representing points in space restrict the use of signing space to *two* dimensions.

In conclusion, *point buoys seem to restrict the use of signing space* to one and two dimensions, thereby structuring signing space differently compared to the three dimensional, topographical use of space, which may characterize other sequences of signed discourse.

6.   Discussion

A point buoy is set up at the same time as the strong hand produces a sign relative to the buoy. It then remains in place as the strong hand continues to produce signs, but as Liddell (2003:224) points out, a buoy may temporarily disappear, so that signs requiring both hands can be produced normally. Such examples can be found in e.g. Figure 2 (line four) where POINT-G is dropped during AIRLINE^COMPANY[>left] and in Figure 7 where POINT-G is dropped during PERIOD-FROM-TO[>|Sun to Tue|] REASON WORK MONDAY.

In other cases, the buoy is not dropped, and instead, the strong hand produces a sign that normally would demand two active hands, as is the case with SAME in Figure 3 and SHALL in Figure 4. It also happens that a point buoy remains in place and serves as place of articulation, base hand, of two-handed signs in which one hand is active and the other passive (see STOP in Figure 3 and READY in Figure 4).

When using a location in relation to a point buoy, the signer seems to look in the direction of the strong hand, but when the hands are close to each other it is often not possible to decide which hand the gaze is directed towards. However, in those instances when the active hand moves away from the buoy, the gaze tends to follow the active hand. This is actually to be expected, in view of the function of the buoy as a prop, as it does not represent a prominent discourse entity.

Point buoys have formal and functional characteristics that distinguish them from other types of buoys. POINT-G resembles the POINTER buoy in that it uses the index finger, but whereas the POINTER buoy "*points towards* an important element in the discourse" (Liddell 2003: 250), POINT-G represents a point in space or a point in time. Because the POINTER does not represent anything, signs cannot be directed at it. In addition, whereas the POINTER buoy points out only *one* location at a time, *more than one* location can be used in relation to POINT-G.

When the strong hand points near the fingertip of the weak hand, it may sometimes be difficult to tell whether it is a POINTER or POINT-G. However, when POINT-G represents a point in space, the movement of verbs and points stops in the same plane as that of the buoy, but with the POINTER, points (and other signs) may very well move below or above that plane. Moreover, when POINT-G represents a point in space, the locations are established near the distal part of the palmar or dorsal side of the buoy finger (see Figure 1, 2 and 3). Locations near the base of the buoy finger and radial side of the finger are not used.

POINT-G, with extension in the proximal joint (Figure 7), also resembles the THEME buoy in that the hand configuration is similar, but in the THEME buoy the index finger is directed up, and in POINT-G it may have different orientations. They also function differently. As the name suggests, the THEME buoy represents a central theme of the discourse (Liddell 2003: 242), and therefore, can be pointed at to refer to the entity with which it is associated. In contrast, when the strong hand points in relation to a point buoy it is not directed at the buoy, but at locations relative to it. This can be seen e.g. in Figure 2 (third to last photo) and Figure 3 (seventh photo) where the active finger is in contact with and is close to the buoy finger respectively, but is not pointing at it.

Some occurrences of point buoys may look similar to fragment buoys, i.e. to buoys that typically consist of the weak hand remaining from a two-handed sign (Liddell 2003). However, a thorough analysis reveals that point buoys function differently. Whereas a fragment buoy signifies the entity referred to by the sign it stems from (Liddell 2003), a point buoy does *not* maintain the significance of the just produced sign. For example, if the weak hand in the form glossed as PERIOD-FROM-TO[>|now to 1993|] in Example 5 had been a true fragment buoy, it would have represented the whole two year period (1991–1993). This is not the case. The weak hand only represents the point in time that is the time of the utterance ('now'). For a similar example in Norwegian Sign Language see Figure 7 where the weak B-hand represents Sunday, not the whole period Sunday through Tuesday.

Finally, Liddell also briefly mentions a type of buoy referred to as 'depicting buoys'. One of his examples is from a depicting verb in which the weak flat hand depicts a broad surface "which can remain in place as other depicting signs are produced" (Liddell 2003:263). What distinguishes a depicting buoy from other types of buoys is that it is part of a depicting space, which is described as "a topographical real-space blend separate from the signer" (ibid. 2003:367). Because point buoys restrict the use of space to only one or two dimensions, they are not depicting buoys.

In summery, a point buoy serves as a prop in relation to which the strong hand acts, and through its physical presence, it helps in structuring the signing space. Point buoys represent points in time or space and may be more or less specified. The examples presented here show that the degree of specification varies from less specified points, like 'starting point of route', to more specified points, such as 'Sundays' and 'now'. However, regardless of the degree of specification, a point buoy does not represent a prominent discourse entity. It is a prop and as such, differs from other types of buoys.

References

Engberg-Pedersen, Elisabeth. 1993. *Space in Danish Sign Language: The Semantics and Morphosyntax of the Use of Space in a Visual Language*. Hamburg: Signum Press.

Grimes, Joseph E. 1975. *The Thread of Discourse*. The Hague: Mouton.

Lakoff, George & Mark Johnson. 1980. *Metaphors We Live by*. Chicago: The University of Chicago Press.

Liddell, Scott K. 2003. *Grammar, Gesture, and Meaning in American Sign Language*. Cambridge: Cambridge University Press.

———, Marit Vogt-Svendsen & Brita Bergman. 2004. "Crosslinguistic Comparison of Buoys: Evidence from American, Norwegian and Swedish Sign Language". Paper presented at the 26. Jahrestagung der Deutsche Gesellschaft für Sprachenwissenschaft in Mainz, 25–27 February 2004.

Malmquist, Ann Kristin & Nora Edwardsen Mosand. 1996. *Se mitt Språk! Språkbok – en Innføring i Norsk Tegnspråk*. Bergen: Døves Forlag AS.

Selvik, Kari-Anne. 2006. *Spatial Paths Representing Time. A Cognitive Analysis of Temporal Expressions in Norwegian Sign Language*. Doctoral dissertation, Department of Linguistics and Scandinavian Studies, University of Oslo.

Taub, Sarah F. 2001. *Language from the Body: Iconicity and Metaphor in American Sign Language*. Cambridge: Cambridge University Press.

Vogt-Svendsen, Marit. 2003a. "'Buoys' – One Role of the Weak Hand. Work in Progress on Norwegian Sign Language". [Abstract and handout.] Presentation at Department of Language and Communication Sciences, City University London, 28 November 2003.

——— 2003b. "A 'New' Type of Buoy?" Ms., University of Oslo.

Appendix

Transcription conventions

CONDUCTOR, HAVE	a word in capitals represents a sign
COME-HERE, TRAIN-MOVE	words separated by hyphens represent a sign
S-A-S	capital letters separated by hyphens indicate fingerspelling
AIR∧BUS, KNOW∧NOT	∧ indicates compounds and contractions
PRO-1	first person pronoun, singular
CHANGEx2	x followed by a figure indicates number of repetitions
OTHER-PLUR>left	> indicates that a sign is meaningfully directed
HERE>behind POINT-G	or located
TRAIN-MOVEfar in front of POINT-G>in front of	> between descriptions of locations indicates movement from one location to another
OVER-THERE>|other track|	a location representing an discourse entity is marked with vertical brackets (cf. the use of vertical brackets for indicating *blended entities* in Liddell 2003)

Simultaneous use of the two hands in Jordanian Sign Language

Bernadet Hendriks

Holy Land Institute for the Deaf, Salt (Jordan)

1. Introduction

This paper provides an overview of manual simultaneity in narrative discourse in Jordanian Sign Language (LIU), showing that there is a strict phonological rule for manual simultaneity, and that simultaneity can have different functions in discourse and syntax. In terms of formal features, the focus is on the apparent lack of a distinction between 'perseveration' and 'full simultaneity' (Miller 1994) in LIU.

Since manual simultaneity often interacts with dominance reversal in LIU, the different functions of dominance reversal and the environments in which it takes place will also be discussed in this paper. From my own observations, dominance reversal seems to be particularly common in younger LIU signers (students in their late teens), who have provided most of the data for this paper. Although there are examples in LIU where both dominance reversal and simultaneity have a very clear function, there are also cases where these processes are used for no apparent reason. Further analysis of the syntax and discourse of LIU will be needed to explain some of the data and to fine-tune the analysis below.

2. Jordanian Sign Language (LIU)

Jordanian Sign Language (or Lughat il-Ishaara il-Urdunia, LIU) is closely related to the signed languages of Lebanon, Syria, and the Palestinian areas. Preliminary results from my research show that it is also related to the signed languages of other Arab countries in the Middle East (such as Yemen and Iraq), albeit to a lesser degree. Very little research has been done on any of the signed languages in the Arab world. Publications are limited to dictionaries, which are typically not much more than wordlists, though an introductory grammar of Jordanian Sign Language, written for learners of the language, has been published recently (Hendriks 2004).

LIU has several dialects, none of which can be considered a 'standard' variety. Deaf people in Jordan often make a distinction between the signed language used in schools and that used in the Deaf clubs. The creation of a dictionary of around 5000 signs, published in 2006, already has some standardizing influence. The data in this paper is based on the dialect used at the Holy Land Institute for the Deaf in Salt (Jordan).

The Holy Land Institute for the Deaf was the first school for the Deaf to be established in Jordan. It was opened in 1964 and is currently the only residential school for the Deaf in Jordan and the only school where most of the teaching takes place using signs (often a mix between LIU and sign supported Arabic). Over the years this institute has grown to become the main research and training institute for signed languages and Deaf people in the Middle East. The present author has worked at the Holy Land Institute for the Deaf for more than five years.

3.   Data and methodology

The data used for this paper is taken from five stories videotaped at the Holy Land Institute for the Deaf. Four of the stories are informal stories told by Deaf students aged between seventeen and twenty years old. All of these students learned LIU at a very young age, having a Deaf parent and/or Deaf brothers and sisters. The content of these stories varies from students' own experiences to a ghost story and the re-telling of a movie seen on television. Three of the stories were told to another Deaf student who sat next to the video camera. The fourth story was told to the author of this paper, who is a fluent signer of LIU. For two of the students their right hand is their preference hand[1] the other two have a left hand preference. One of the left-handed signers is particularly ambidextrous and uses dominance reversal much more often than any of the other signers.

---

1.   In this paper I will refer mostly to a signer's preference or non-preference hand, rather than to the dominant or non-dominant hand, because the terms dominant and non-dominant hand may cause confusion for the reader when dominance reversal takes place and the signer's non-preference hand becomes dominant at the phonological level. In such constructions the term 'dominant hand' can apply to either hand, depending on which hand moves. I will therefore refer to a signer's preference hand when referring to the hand that the signer usually uses in one-handed signs. The other hand will be referred to as the non-preference hand. The term 'dominant hand' will be used to refer to the hand that is moving. This may be either the preference or the non-preference hand.

The fifth story was told by a 36-year old Deaf signer, who is a staff member at the school. Although he went to residential school and learned LIU from other students at a young age, education at that time was much more oral than it is at present. The story he tells is a fragment of a biblical story that he had learned by heart. This story differs from the other stories in the way it is told. It is less casual and signed much more slowly and deliberately. Although this older signer uses some dominance reversal and also some simultaneity, these phenomena are much less prominent than in the other stories. This difference may be due to the different style of the story. Klima & Bellugi (1979) have suggested that style may play a role in the occurrence or non-occurrence of simultaneous constructions in American Sign Language (ASL). They suggest that simultaneity is limited to formal register, whereas the LIU data indicates that it is more prominent in informal story-telling (cf. also Kyle & Woll 1985). However, it is also possible that the difference between the four stories signed by students and the more formal biblical story is less related to style than to the fact that the signer of the latter story is of an older generation, which makes less use of these constructions. Further research is needed to establish which of these factors is the most important.

The analysis presented here is based on stories because they provide the most natural data. Signed language stories, however, are difficult to analyze because of the many different articulators that can be used in a signed language and the way they all contribute to the meaning of the utterance, Thus, facial expression, eye gaze, head position, body lean, and the two hands may all simultaneously convey different aspects of the signers' communication. Although all these aspects are important in the analysis of discourse, this paper will focus on manual activity. A transcription of the other articulators will only be presented in examples if they make a crucial contribution to the analysis.

4.   Phonological restrictions on simultaneity

Several different types of manual simultaneity in signed languages have been described. It would seem from these descriptions that in the most common type of simultaneity the two hands are involved in the production of different signs, but are not moving simultaneously (cf. Miller 1994; Engberg-Pedersen 1994). In other words, one hand is holding a sign, or the end state of a sign, which it produced earlier, while the other hand makes a different sign. Liddell (2003) refers to ASL constructions in which the non-preference hand holds the end state of a two-handed sign while the preference hand continues signing as 'fragment buoys', and says that they do not "appear to serve any semantic function [although] a signer may choose to assign semantic significance to a fragment" (Liddell 2003:148). Miller (1994:98) talks about 'perseveration' and states that in Quebec Sign Language (LSQ) "[a] perseveration may involve either a one-handed sign [...] or one hand of a two-handed sign". This chapter will show that in LIU, perseverations can be held on either the preference or the non-preference hand and that they can have different syntactic, prosodic and discursive functions. When remnants of signs are held on the preference hand, a reversal of dominance takes place whereby the non-preference hand becomes dominant and continues signing (see Frishberg (1985) for a discussion of this process in ASL). Dominance reversal does not always coincide with simultaneity, however, and may have its own functions in the discourse.

The type of simultaneity in which a remnant of a sign is held on one of the hands while the other hand continues signing has been contrasted with full simultaneity, in which two distinct signs are produced with independent but simultaneous movement. Miller (1994) notes that these fully simultaneous constructions are less common than the examples of perseveration, in which one hand holds the end state of a sign (without moving), while the other hand continues signing. Although similar examples of full simultaneity seem to be present in LIU, a closer look reveals that most of these examples do not differ much from the more commonly occurring kind of simultaneous construction (see Section 6 for further discussion). In fact, it will be suggested here that manual simultaneity in signed languages is limited by very strict phonological criteria and that perseveration is one of the strategies used to fulfil these criteria. It is therefore not necessary to distinguish between fragment buoys or perseveration on the one hand and full simultaneity on the other hand.

Miller (1994) suggests that in simultaneous constructions the two hands have different functions. In his analysis, the non-preference hand (which Miller refers to as the non-dominant hand) conveys background information while the preference (or dominant) hand expresses information that is in focus. This explains why in simultaneous constructions it is usually the preference hand that moves, while the non-preference hand is held still. Miller prefers this explanation to a phonological analysis stating that movement should be confined to the dominant hand. In this paper I will show that the functional analysis provided by Miller does not work for LIU. Instead, I propose a phonological rule that leaves room for dominance reversal. The functional properties of dominance reversal will be discussed in Section 7.

I propose the following rule for simultaneity in LIU

(1) Manual simultaneity can only take place when at least one of the hands makes no lexically specified movement, or when the movement of the two hands is symmetrical.

This rule makes it impossible for signs to be made simultaneously when they both have a different inherent movement. Inherent movement is movement that is specified in the lexicon as belonging to a specific sign, or that is the result of a productive morphological form such as a classifier construction (Emmorey 2003). It is not allowed (and articulatorily almost impossible), for instance, to produce a sign with up-and-down movement and simultaneously produce a sign with a side-to-side movement on the other hand.

Thus, when one hand produces a sign with a certain inherent movement, the other hand can only produce a sign that has symmetrical movement, or no movement, or a very simple phonetically inserted movement from one location to another (i.e. not a lexically specified movement). The LIU numerals one to five are examples of signs that have no movement. Thus, numbers can occur simultaneously with any (one-handed) sign on the other hand. Liddell (2003) mentions 'list buoys' as a special kind of construction on the non-dominant hand, as different from numbers. In LIU, however, both lists and numbers in their regular form can occur simultaneously on either the preference or the non-preference hand. I assume that this is because they both are well-formed under the phonological simultaneity condition.

Signs with only a phonetically inserted movement are those that make a straight movement towards a certain location in the signing space, or from one location to another (as represented in many phonological models since Liddell (1984)). Pointing signs are examples of signs that move towards a certain 'locus' in the signing space. According to Liddell (1990), a locus is a point in space representing either a referent or the location of an entity. An index pointing at a locus does not have an inherent movement. It simply makes a 'transitional' movement towards that locus. These movements resemble the transitional movements between two signs, in not being lexically specified. Once an index has reached the position where it points at a certain locus it can be held there without movement. This makes pointing signs another set of forms likely to be found in simultaneous constructions. As we will see in the LIU data below, indexes do indeed occur in simultaneous constructions and, like numbers, may be held on either the preference or the non-preference hand.

Classifier constructions express the location or the movement of an entity in the signing space. When both hands simultaneously produce a classifier it is often the case that only one of these classifiers expresses a path movement, whereas the other hand simply makes a phonetic movement to a certain location. One classifier may be located at a certain point in the signing space, while the other classifier moves in relation to that position (cf. the BRIDGE classifier in example (3) below). Constructions in which a classifier is made simultaneously with a sign that does not involve a classifier also occur. In these cases the classifier construction normally does not move in LIU.

Under the phonological rule for simultaneity presented in (1), the only examples of simultaneity in which there is more than just a short phonetic movement on both hands are classifier constructions in which both hands make a simul-taneous path movement. The LIU data show that in these cases the two hands make the same movement or mirror each other's movement. Where this is not the case, a perseveration tends to occur. Thus, these constructions seem to adhere to a strict symmetry rule for movement, similar to Battison's (1978) 'symme-try condition' for two-handed signs, which states that if both hands are moving, the non-dominant hand makes the same movement as the dominant hand (or an alternating movement). It may even be analyzed as an extension of Battison's symmetry constraint, in which case this would have wider application than just two-handed lexical signs. However, Battison includes a restriction on the articula-tors, the lexical symmetry condition whereby the two hands should have identical handshapes and identical or symmetrical orientations. This restriction is not ap-plicable to the rule proposed here.

5.   Simultaneity in classifier constructions in LIU

Simultaneity has often been discussed in connection to classifier constructions, which Engberg-Pedersen (1994) calls 'polymorphemic verbs'. Discussing Danish Sign Language, she says that "[t]he 'central' type of simultaneous construction is two polymorphemic verbs articulated simultaneously and expressing a loca-tive relation between two or more referents" (Engberg-Pedersen 1994:85). For an overview of the different classifiers used in LIU, cf. Hendriks (2004) and Van Dijken (2004). We have already observed that in LIU it seems that such construc-tions are only possible if the two hands move in a symmetrical way, or if one of the classifiers only has transitional movement or no movement at all. An example of a simultaneous classifier construction with symmetrical movement in LIU can be seen in (1). An overview of the conventions used here for transcription is given in the appendix

(2)   TOGETHER   SCHOOL   PERSON-class$^{go around in circles}$
      (2-handed)   (2-handed)   PERSON-class$^{go around in circles}$
      "together they walked around the school"

In this example the two classifiers move around together, representing two people walking next to each other. The two hands make the same movement, thus pro-viding evidence for the generalization in (1). In constructions where both hands move simultaneously, it is not evident that the information on one hand is more in focus than the information on the other hand.

      There are, however, also constructions in which one hand holds a classifier, while the other hand produces signs that are not classifiers. One LIU example of

Figure 1. The LIU vehicle classifier

this kind of 'non-central' simultaneity (cf. Engberg-Pedersen 1994) is presented in (3).

(3) BRIDGE-class   KNOW BRIDGE-class STAY WHAT
     VEHICLE-class^{forward} hold _ _ _ _ backward-forward_ hold _ _ _ _ _ _

     "The car passed under the bridge, you get it? It passed under the bridge and stayed there. What could he do?"

     VEHICLE-class^{move-forward-repeatedly} index-towards-class.
     VEHICLE-class^{hold} _
     "That parked car was passed by other cars."

In this example the non-preference hand produces the LIU vehicle classifier (Figure 1), which moves forward, while the preference hand first produces a classifier depicting a bridge under which the vehicle passes. Since the classifier representing the bridge only has transitional movement (i.e. it moves to the point in the signing space where the bridge is located), the two signs can be produced simultaneously. The vehicle classifier on the non-preference hand is then held still in its final location, while the preference hand signs the verb KNOW, slightly tapping the forehead. Again, these two signs can be made simultaneously, because the vehicle classifier has stopped moving. After this, the signer repeats the earlier classifier construction, during which the vehicle classifier appears with the same movement pattern as before. When it stops (in the same location as previously), the preference hand continues signing STAY WHAT.

Note that in this example the two hands move in alternation. If the movement of a particular hand indicates that the information presented on that hand is in focus, as suggested by both Miller (1994) and Engberg-Pedersen (1994) for some of their examples, this would mean that foregrounding of information can occur on both the preference and the non-preference hand in LIU. However, in example (3) it would seem that the vehicle classifier on the non-preference hand is in focus throughout the construction.[2] This vehicle plays an important role in the story because the hero of the story is trapped inside. The idea that this vehicle is in focus even when it does not move is confirmed by the final index on the preference hand in (3), which points to the vehicle classifier, making sure that the addressee understands it is still this vehicle that forms the centre or focus of the discourse, rather than any of the vehicles passing it.

Thus, this example from LIU shows that the non-preference hand does not necessarily hold background information and that it is also not necessarily the case that the non-moving hand in a simultaneous construction conveys background information, at least in classifier constructions. In fact, I propose that in this particular classifier construction it is the classifier on the non-preference hand that is in focus throughout the construction, whether it moves or not. The fact that it is held on the non-preference hand, rather than the preference hand, may be the result of a phonetic preference for movement to occur on the preference hand. Note, however, that this is a tendency rather than a rule, since the vehicle classifier on the non-preference hand does move. If movement in these constructions were confined to the preference hand, the vehicle classifier would have to switch hands repeatedly. This would not only slow down the story, but might also lead to confusion on the part of the addressee. Instead, a repeated reversal of dominance takes place. In this example, then, dominance reversal is simply a part of the simultaneous construction and does not seem to have a meaning or function of its own. In Section 7, however, we will see that dominance reversal can also occur with its own discursive functions.

The two examples of classifier constructions that were presented in this section are typical of LIU: the two hands can be used flexibly, creating two-handed classifier constructions, or combining lexical signs and classifier constructions, but the flexibility in creating these combinations, is limited by the phonological restriction in (1).

6.   Do buoys exist in LIU?

Liddell (2003:223) describes buoys as "signs [produced] with the weak hand that are held in a stationary configuration as the strong hand continues producing signs". He also says that the function of buoys is that "they maintain a physical

---

2.   The term 'focus' is not used here to express the idea of new or contrastive information, but rather to refer to information that is active or foregrounded in the discourse (discourse focus).

presence that helps guide the discourse" (ibid.). Liddell distinguishes four different kinds of buoys: the list buoy (numbers ONE to FIVE held with the fingers sideways rather than upward), the THEME buoy (a vertical index), the fragment buoy (a perseveration of a two-handed sign on the weak hand), and a POINTER buoy (an index pointing towards an important element in the discourse, like the final index in example (3)). The buoys Liddell mentions are also found in LIU. However, I will attempt to show in this section that these buoys are not special kinds of constructions in terms of their phonological characteristics, that they do not have to be held on the non-preference hand, and they are by no means limited to the categories listed in Liddell (2003). In the analysis presented here, buoys are simply permitted simultaneous constructions under the phonological simultaneity rule in (1), and their function of 'guiding the discourse' is considered a function of simultaneity in general.

6.1 Simultaneity involving determiners and pronouns

LIU has a pronoun which I describe as an 'emphatic pronoun'. It has a fist handshape and can be used as a possessive pronoun with alienable possessions (i.e. possessions that do not inherently belong to the possessor), especially with contrastive emphasis ('that is *my* book'). In contrast, the index is normally used for inalienable possessions, like someone's name or body-parts. The emphatic pronoun can also be used as a pronoun glossed as SELF or OWN. It can be seen as the emphatic version of the index when it is used as a pronoun. Both indexes and emphatic pronouns can occur in simultaneous constructions, because they do not have lexically specified movement.

An example of an index in a simultaneous construction is given in (4), an example of the emphatic pronoun in (5).

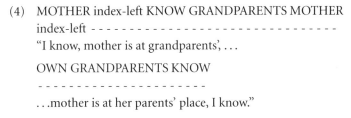

> (4)   MOTHER index-left KNOW GRANDPARENTS MOTHER
>   index-left -
>   "I know, mother is at grandparents', ...
>
>   OWN GRANDPARENTS KNOW
>   -
>   ...mother is at her parents' place, I know."

In (4) the locus of the mother (index-left) in the signing space is held on the non-preference hand, while the preference hand signs where she might be (GRANDPARENTS). At this point in the story, the mother is the focused element in the discourse, and the index is held in position as long as she is in focus (and as long as no two-handed sign occurs to break up the sequence). In this example, therefore the index could be seen as a POINTER buoy.

In (5) a similar example is given with an emphatic pronoun.

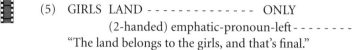

(5)   GIRLS LAND - - - - - - - - - - - - - ONLY
              (2-handed) emphatic-pronoun-left - - - - - - - -
        "The land belongs to the girls, and that's final."

In (5) the girls are located on the left-hand side of the signing space. Although this example is not as long as (4), it is clear that the emphatic pronoun (used here as a possessive) is purposely held by the signer until the end of the utterance. This is especially clear, because the sign glossed as ONLY is normally a two-handed sign, but is here produced with one hand so that the pronoun can be left in its position. This seems to give additional emphasis to the statement. Thus, both the index and the emphatic pronoun can point to important elements in the discourse, functioning in a similar way. Combined with dominance reversal, they can also occur on the preference hand, as will be shown in (15) below.

6.2 Numbers in simultaneous constructions

Three different kinds of simultaneously produced numerals were found in the LIU data. The first example is what Liddell (2003), discussing ASL, refers to as a 'list buoy'. Other than for cardinal number signs, the fingers are held to the side and the fingertips are associated with referents. Enumeration of referents starts at the thumb in ASL. The list buoy in LIU can be produced in the same way. An example of the hand configuration for the second item in a list is given in Figure 2. However, lists are not the only types of numerals that can occur in a simultaneous construction in LIU. The cardinal number TWO, which compared to the list numeral has both a different handshape (index and middle finger extended) and a different orientation (palm outward, fingers upward), also occurs simultaneously on the non-preference hand. A picture of this example is given in Figure 3. In this example the sign TWO modifies the noun GIRL in a simultaneous construction, meaning 'the two girls'.

    An example of a numeral which is held on the preference hand, while the non-preference hand continues signing is given in (6).

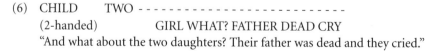

(6)   CHILD   TWO -
        (2-handed)   GIRL WHAT? FATHER DEAD CRY
        "And what about the two daughters? Their father was dead and they cried."

A very interesting example of a simultaneous construction involving a numeral is shown in (7). This seems to be a cross between the list numeral in Figure 2 and the cardinal number in Figure 3. Although the hand orientation is like that of the number TWO, the counting starts at the thumb, like the list numeral. This numeral is used to modify a verb. The signer is talking about a person who keeps sending

Figure 2. The number two used in a list

Figure 3. The cardinal number two in a simultaneous construction

e-mails but gets no reply. She then signs the verb SEND several times, each time adding a finger to the numeral on her non-preference hand, as shown in (7).

(7)   E-MAIL SEND neg.   SEND neg.   SEND SEND neg.
                      TWO - - -   THREE FOUR-FIVE
       "He sent an e-mail, no (reply). He sent another one, but no (reply). He sent again and again, but no (reply)."

Example (7) and Figure 3 show that in LIU the list numeral, in which the fingertips are associated with referents is not the only type of numeral that can occur in a simultaneous construction. Under the phonological rule given in (1), certain numerals (including 1 to 5) can always be produced simultaneously because they have no inherent movement, and this is borne out by the data. Thus, I conclude that the 'list buoy' in LIU is not a special kind of construction as far as simultaneity is concerned.

6.3 The use of perseverations

Perseverations (which include Liddell's class of 'fragment buoys') occur when two signs with inherent movement occur together in a simultaneous construction for functional and/or syntactic reasons, but are not allowed to move simultaneously because of the simultaneity rule in (1). In these cases, one hand moves first and the end state of that sign is held while the other hand produces the other sign. Engberg-Pedersen (1994) mentions perseverations in polymorphemic verbs (classifier constructions) in Danish Sign Language and says that these verbs have a 'hold morpheme'. She assumes that this hold morpheme occurs on the hand that expresses information that is not in focus. In the phonological analysis presented here for LIU, however, perseverations are not a special kind of buoys, and do not need to be analyzed as having hold morphemes. They are simply a phonological strategy that allows simultaneity (for syntactic or discursive purposes) to take place when two signs that do not obey the rule in (1) are involved. Perseverations can be held on one hand while the other hand produces several signs. In this way they are the same as signs that have no inherent movement, such as numbers, indexes, and classifiers.

Although the grammatical function of perseveration is often not clear, it would seem that they can mark phonological or syntactic domains (see also Nespor & Sandler (1999) and Sandler (1999) for delineation of phonological domains by the non-dominant hand in Israeli Sign Language). Examples of perseverations and their function in combination with dominance reversal will be given in Section 8.

Perseverations, when consciously held by the signer, and signs with no inherent movement can function in the same way, as shown in the following examples. Example (8) shows the perseveration of the sign CAR on the non-preference hand, while the preference hand signs what happens during the driving.

(8)   DRIVE   GO index-forward RECOGNIZE index BUILDING
      (2-handed) -(2-handed)
      "She drove around and recognized the building over there."

Example (9) shows the one-handed sign TO-PHONE, which has no inherent movement and is held on the non-preference hand, while the preference hand signs what is said on the phone.

(9)   headshake
      ASK^right NO   ASK HELLO
      TO-PHONE - - - - - - - - - - -
      "He phoned and asked, but no, he asked someone else and said 'hello'…"

Both (8) and (9) are examples of an almost iconic type of simultaneity, expressing simultaneous action. In both examples the simultaneity ends when a two-handed sign is produced.

Examples (8) and (9) show that perseverations of two-handed signs and one-handed signs with no inherent movement can function in the same way. Therefore, I conclude that they are not a special kind of construction in LIU with regard to simultaneity.

7.   Functions of dominance reversal

Dominance reversal in LIU tends to occur mainly to express contrasts or transitions in the discourse. The two hands may, for instance, represent two different participants in the story. They may also mark a transition from narration to the direct speech of one of the characters in the story, or from narration to interjections addressed directly to the addressee. An example of an interjection that is marked by dominance reversal is given in (10). Note that there are also non-manual markers (in particular head position) that show that the verb on the non-preference hand is addressed directly to the person listening to the story, rather than being part of the narrative. The story tells about someone who is guilty of hurting someone else. The daughters of the victim want to know who has done it.

(10)   PERSON WHO? index-forward EXIST WHO? - - - - -
                                                   KNOW?
       "Which person did it? Someone did it, but who? Do you know?"

The dominance reversal in (10) seems to mark a transition in the discourse, and is independent of simultaneity (there are similar constructions where no simultaneity occurs). In this example, the dominance reversal does, however, interact with simultaneity. The preference hand holds a perseveration of the sign WHO, while the non-preference hand produces the interjection. It is not entirely clear what the function of the perseveration in this example is. It may tie the interjection to the previous utterance, or establish a certain prosodic domain within which spreading of phonological features is allowed.

An example of dominance reversal for contrastive purposes is given in (11). One of the characters is having a meal, while the other character is leaning on the table and staring at her. The person eating gets nervous and wants to know why the other person is staring. She offers him some food, but he declines.

(11)   LEAN STARE WHAT STARE-AT-ME WHAT FOOD - - - - - - - - - -
      TABLE-class   WHAT - NO-THANKS

"He leaned on the table and stared at her. What is he staring at me for? (She said:) 'Some food?' (He replied:) 'No thanks.'"

In this example, too, the preference hand holds the end state of the sign FOOD while the non-preference hand signs the reply. This may be done to establish a link between the question and the answer, but similar constructions without simultaneity are also found, as in (12).

> (12)   YESTERDAY COME   (2-handed)
>   YESTERDAY PRESENT
>   "(She said:) 'I came yesterday.' (They replied:) 'But we were here yesterday!'"

An example of dominance reversal marking a contrast between narration and direct speech can be seen in (13), which relates to a situation where the relatives of two young girls, who have lost both their parents, want them to give up ownership of their land.

> (13)   GIRLS STUBBORN
>   NEVER
>   "The girls were stubborn (and said:) 'Never!' "

Note that the construction with dominance reversal can be replaced by a longer construction which does not contain dominance reversal. In such a construction the sign for the person uttering the direct speech is normally repeated (i.e. GIRLS STUBBORN GIRLS [SAY] NEVER). A few longer examples illustrating this same phenomenon are presented by the same signer.

A fourth use of dominance reversal seems to mark the transition from subject to predicate (or possibly, more generally, from topic to comment). Although dominance reversal is not the only or most common way to mark this transition, it is regularly used in this way, and is used by the older signer in a more formally told story, as shown in example (14).

> (14)   MULTI-COLOURED-COAT
>   BEAUTIFUL GOOD
>   "The multi-coloured coat was beautiful and good."

Although this use of dominance reversal often occurs when the predicate is an agreement verb or a classifier directed to, or located at, the non-preference hand side of the signing space, it can also occur with body-anchored verbs or predicates made in neutral space. A perseveration of the subject can be held on the preference hand, creating a simultaneous construction (cf. also Section 8).

In addition to marking transitions or contrasts, dominance reversals may also be used to locate something on the side of the non-preference hand in the signing space, using a pointing sign, a classifier or an agreement verb. In these cases, dominance reversal does not appear to be a discourse strategy, but rather seems to be used to make articulation easier and faster, because the dominant hand does not have to cross to the other side of the signing space.

Finally, it has become clear that there is quite some variation between LIU signers regarding the extent to which dominance reversal is used. As was noted earlier, younger signers appear to use dominance reversals more frequently than older signers, but there is also variation within these generations. It is not always apparent what the linguistic function of this is for signers who switch hands very frequently.

In the next section we will see that, when combined, dominance reversals and simultaneity can have very interesting syntactic and discursive functions.

8.   The interaction of simultaneity and dominance reversal

The most interesting examples of simultaneity in LIU occur in interaction with dominance reversals. We have already seen an example of dominance reversal and simultaneity interacting in classifier constructions in Section 5 (example (3)). In such examples, the locative relation between two elements (like the bridge and the car) is expressed simultaneously, leading to dominance reversal if the classifier on the preference hand is held for a longer stretch of discourse (in this example, the classifier referring to the car). In the constructions presented in this section, it is not always clear whether the signers use a dominance reversal in order to create a simultaneous construction, or whether simultaneity is merely a side effect of a dominance reversal (which some signers use more than others, and which does not always appear to have a clear linguistic function).

Example (15) shows that both the emphatic /possessive pronoun and the index can occur simultaneously on the preference hand, when combined with a dominance reversal, as stated in Section 6.1. In this case a dominance reversal is used to contrast the location of two referents in the story; a mother and her sister, who have had a fight.

> (15)   REMEMBER index-right - - 1st person-poss. - - - - - - - - FIGHT
>   (2-handed)   MOTHER - - index-left   RELATIVE (2-handed)
>   "They remembered: our mother and her relative had a fight."

In this example the dominance reversal also seems to be phonetically motivated. The signer uses a large signing space and the pointing signs are made with out-stretched arms. Because the locus for the mother is on the right-hand side of the signing space, the signer uses her right hand (her preference hand) to point to it. She uses her non-preference hand to indicate a locus on the left side of the signing space, making articulation easier. Note, however, that the nouns MOTHER and RELATIVE are both signed on the non-preference hand. The sign RELATIVE is normally a two-handed sign, but is produced here with one hand. Although the noun MOTHER is signed simultaneously with its determiner (the index), the sign RELATIVE is signed on the same hand as its determiner and follows it. It would also have been possible, and even more clearly contrastive, to also sign the two nouns on different hands, or to use the preference hand for both. I suggest that the reason the signer does not do this, and signs both MOTHER and RELATIVE on the non-preference hand, is that she intentionally creates a simultaneous construction. The fact that the two-handed sign RELATIVE is only signed with one hand also suggests this. If the simultaneous construction is indeed created intentionally, it must have a function.

I would like to suggest that in this example simultaneity aids the addressee in interpreting the syntactic structure of the clause. Note that the NP [det. MOTHER poss.] is complex, because the sign MOTHER is modified by both a determiner (the index) preceding it and a possessive pronoun following it. In order to make sure that the addressee understands that both these signs belong to the same syntactic constituent, the signer uses a simultaneous construction linking the three signs together. The last sign of the constituent is then held as a perseveration of the constituent as a whole, while the other hand signs the next NP. Because the prolonged possessive pronoun represents the entire previous constituent, it is clear that it is 'my mother's sibling' who is the other party in the conflict, rather than the signer's or someone else's sibling. This type of simultaneity may be an alternative strategy to localization, which appears to be used less in LIU than in many documented Western signed languages.

A similar example of the use of simultaneity is found in (16).

(16)   MOTHER poss. - - - - SIBLING - - - LAND   TAKE
                         DEAD - - - - - - BOY (2-handed) - - - -
          "The brother of their mother who had died, took the land...
                  <u>lean forward</u>
          SAY OUT GIRL TWO
          - - - - - -
          ...and told the two girls to get out."

This example has a very complex NP 'the brother of their mother who had died', the structure of which is clarified by simultaneity and a dominance reversal. As there is no ambiguity as far as the possessive pronoun is concerned (it can only modify the noun MOTHER) simultaneity is not needed to disambiguate the syntactic structure. The sign DEAD is used as a relative clause, as is shown by the facial expression (cf. Hendriks 2004). The dominance reversal may mark the transition between the main clause and the relative clause. A perseveration of the sign DEAD is held on the non-preference hand, while the preference hand continues with the main clause, indicating that this is still the same noun phrase and that the brother who is mentioned next is the brother of the woman who had died. It is not clear why dominance reversal takes place between the signs SIBLING and BOY (meaning 'brother'), unless this is a parenthetic comment ('a sibling, a brother, of their mother who had died').

In this example simultaneity does not only occur in the complex NP, but also with the two-handed sign LAND. The non-preference hand perseverates this sign, while the preference hand continues signing what the brother did to the land (he took it and told them to get out). It is interesting to see how the perseveration of the sign LAND drops before the last two signs of the utterance and the hand is put on the knee. This may be caused by the fact that the NP 'two girls' is a constituent that is post-positioned for reasons of focus (indicated by a strong body lean forward), and therefore does not form a syntactic unit with the preceding signs. It could also be true, however, that this body lean makes it phonetically difficult to keep the perseveration in place, and that this is the reason for dropping the non-preference hand. A translation of (16) which takes into account all the instances of simultaneity and dominance reversal would then look like this (italics indicate emphasis): 'a sibling, a brother, of their mother, who had died, took the land and said 'get out!' *to the two girls*!'

Although in the examples of complex noun phrases presented here simultaneity seems to have a semantic or syntactic function, this is not always very clear. Many instances of simultaneity in the data do not appear to be as deliberate as the ones presented in (15) and (16), and the remnant of a sign (in Liddell's terms 'fragment') may be held on the non-preference hand for phonetic reasons only (ease of articulation). It is precisely the presence of dominance reversal that makes the intentional use of a simultaneous construction clearly visible. When perseverations of two-handed signs occur on the non-preference hand (like LAND in example (16)) it is less clear that they clarify syntactic structure. In fact, they often cross syntactic boundaries and seem to be constrained more by prosodic boundaries or other phonological contexts, such as a subsequent two-handed sign. Investigations into the prosodic structure of Israeli Sign Language (Nespor & Sandler 1999; Sandler 1999) have revealed that the non-dominant hand functions as a delineator of boundaries of the phonological word and the phonological phrase, but more research is needed into the prosodic structure of LIU before similar claims can be made.

9.   Conclusion

This paper has presented several examples of manual simultaneity in LIU. The examples illustrate that manual simultaneity commonly occurs in various types of constructions, but is restricted in its possible forms by a clear phonological rule in LIU. Thus, full simultaneity, with both hands moving at the same time, is only possible when one of the signs produced does not have inherent movement. In all other cases, perseverations are found. I have also shown that there does not seem to be a good reason for proposing a special category of 'buoys' in LIU. Rather, these constructions can be seen as well-formed instances of simultaneity and are closely paralleled by structures that contain elements that would not be considered buoys. In this respect, LIU appears to differ from ASL as described by Liddell (2003).

Although the function of simultaneity is not always completely clear, some examples have been presented where simultaneity, often in combination with a dominance reversal, may aid the addressee in understanding the syntactic structure of complex phrases. Further research will be necessary to investigate whether this hypothesis can be confirmed. Simultaneity can also be iconic, representing two things happening at the same time on different hands. This is particularly true for classifier constructions, but examples of this kind of use of simultaneity outside of classifier constructions also occur. More research on dominance reversal and simultaneity, as well as research into other grammatical and discourse structures in LIU, is needed in order to verify and elaborate on the analysis presented here.

References

Battison, Robbin. 1978. *Lexical Borrowing in American Sign Language*. Silver Spring, Md.: Linstok Press.

Emmorey, Karen, ed. 2003. *Perspectives on Classifier Constructions in Sign Languages*. Mahwah, N.J./London: Lawrence Erlbaum Associates.

Engberg-Pedersen, Elizabeth. 1994. "Some Simultaneous Constructions in Danish Sign Language". *Word order Issues in Sign Language. Working Papers* ed. by Mary Brennan & Graham H. Turner, 73–88. Durham, England: International Sign Linguistics Association.

Frishberg, Nancy. 1985. "Dominance Relations and Discourse Structures". *SLR' 83. Proceedings of the 3rd. International Symposium on Sign Language Research. Rome, June 22–26 1983* ed. by William C. Stokoe & Virginia Volterra, 79–90. Silver Spring, Md.: Linstok Press/Rome: CNR.

Hendriks, Bernadet. 2004. *An Introduction to the Grammar of Jordanian Sign Language*. Salt, Jordan: Balqa' University.

Klima, Edward S. & Ursula Bellugi. 1979. *The Signs of Language*. Cambridge, Mass.: Harvard University Press.

Kyle, Jim G. & Bencie Woll. 1985. *Sign Language. The Study of Deaf People and Their Language*. Cambridge: Cambridge University Press.

Liddell, Scott K. 1984. "THINK and BELIEVE: Sequentiality in ASL". *Language* 60:2.372–399.

——. 1990. "Four Functions of a Locus: Re-examining the Structure of Space in ASL". *Sign Language Research: Theoretical Issues* ed. by Ceil Lucas, 176–198. Washington, D.C.: Gallaudet University Press.

——. 2003. *Grammar, Gesture, and Meaning in American Sign Language*. Cambridge: Cambridge University Press.

Miller, Christopher. 1994. "Simultaneous Constructions in Quebec Sign Language". *Word order Issues in Sign Language. Working Papers* ed. by Mary Brennan & Graham H. Turner, 89–112. Durham, England: International Sign Linguistics Association.

Nespor, Marina & Wendy Sandler. 1999. "Prosody in Israeli Sign Language". *Language and Speech* 42:2–3.143–176.

Sandler, Wendy. 1999. "Cliticization and Prosodic Words in a Sign Language". *Studies on the Phonological Word* ed. by Tracy Hall & Ursula Kleinhenz, 223–254. Amsterdam: Benjamins.

Van Dijken, Lianne. 2004. *Creating Perspective: Hand Classifiers and Referent Projections in Lughat il-Ishaara il-Urdunia*. MA Thesis, University of Amsterdam.

Appendix

Descriptions of simultaneous constructions are represented on two lines. The upper line represents the preference hand and the lower line the non-preference hand. If two glosses are written directly above each other, this indicates that the signs are produced simultaneously.

Manual signs are glossed in English using capital letters. Any additional information about the sign (e.g. that it is a classifier) is added in lower case letters and abbreviated. In some cases a description of a sign is given instead of a gloss (e.g. index-left, neg.). These descriptions are also presented in lower case letters and may be abbreviated. Hyphens between words indicate that they refer to a single sign.

If a sign, or perseveration of a sign, is held on one of the hands while the other hand simultaneously produces several signs, the duration of that prolonged sign is indicated by means of a series of hyphens following the gloss. Any significant changes in the movement of such a sign are presented in superscript.

Sign + gesture = speech + gesture?

Comparing aspects of simultaneity in Flemish Sign Language to instances of concurrent speech and gesture

Myriam Vermeerbergen and Eline Demey

Research Foundation-Flanders & Vrije Universiteit Brussel /
Ghent University

1. Introduction: Definition of gesture and aim of this contribution

The starting point for this paper is simultaneity, particularly manual simultaneity, as observed in Flemish Sign Language (VGT). VGT is used by approximately 6,000 signers living in Flanders, the northern part of Belgium. Research on this signed language began circa 1990 and initially the focus was on descriptive work with the aim of describing and documenting a wide variety of grammatical structures and mechanisms with regard to form and use. As part of that work, dominance reversals and simultaneity were investigated (see e.g. Vermeerbergen 1996, 1997, 2001).

From the examples and discussions in the international signed language literature, it becomes clear that many – if not all – of the structures found in Flemish Sign Language are also described as occurring in various other signed languages. Many of these structures are discussed in detail elsewhere in this volume, which is why we have decided not to present a full account of a wide range of simultaneity and dominance reversals in VGT here. Instead, we concentrate on a smaller range of structures and on the hitherto less discussed topic of the (possible) parallels between the simultaneous use of different articulators by signers and the simultaneous use of speech and manual gestures by speakers.

In modern gesture research the term 'gesture' refers to a wide variety of hand and arm movements. Kendon (1988) describes and categorises various types of manual gestures, which has led McNeill (1992) to establish a continuum distinguishing between co-speech gestures (or 'gesticulation') and other types of manual activity. He calls this continuum 'Kendon's continuum'.

Gesticulation $\rightarrow$ Language-like Gestures $\rightarrow$ Pantomimes $\rightarrow$ Emblems $\rightarrow$ Sign Languages

McNeill (2000) points out that Kendon's continuum can actually be subdivided into four continua, on the basis of specific characteristics of these gesture types, such as their relationship to speech, their conventionality (or lexicalisation), their semiotic character, and the presence of linguistic properties. Leaving aside the elaborate 'gesture systems' that constitute signed languages, McNeill makes a useful distinction based on the conventionality of gestures. On the one hand, there are conventional gestures with a fixed and conventional form, generally called 'emblems'. Examples are the 'OK' and the 'thumbs up' gestures. On the other hand, there are unconventional gestures "that are created spontaneously by the speaker during the act of speaking and adhere to no standards of form" (McNeill 1998:12). Four types of nonconventional gestures are recognised: iconics, metaphorics, deictics and beats.

In order to facilitate the comparison between certain simultaneous structures in VGT and the simultaneity of speech and gesturing, it is necessary to point out some properties of co-speech gestures as characterised in the gesture literature. Firstly, all authors agree on the close relationship between speech and gesture in communication. Speech and gestures are produced synchronously and are semantically and pragmatically co-expressive. In many cases co-speech gestures illustrate the spoken utterance, but very often the gestures present different aspects of the meaning expressed in discourse, by adding specific information to a linguistic expression or by providing meanings other than those expressed in speech. For these reasons, gesture researchers consider speech and co-speech gesture as "two aspects of a single process" (Kendon 1997:111; cf. also McNeill 1992; Goldin-Meadow 2003).

Secondly, while gesture is acknowledged as being co-expressive with spoken utterances, it is said to be structured in a wholly different way from language. Unconventional co-speech gestures are global and synthetic (e.g. McNeill 1992). In linguistic expressions, small meaningful parts (such as morphemes and words) combine to create greater wholes (such as sentences), whereas, according to McNeill (1992:19), the direction in gesture is from "whole to part": "The whole determines the meanings of the parts (thus it is 'global')." Moreover, gestures are synthetic, in that they combine different meaning elements, which in speech would be represented in an analytical and segmented way. McNeill (1992:21) further considers gestures to be non-combinatoric, which means that gestures do not combine to form larger, more complex structures.

Following McNeill (and others, e.g. Gullberg 1998), spoken language may be viewed as an expression of thought by means of two distinct representational systems: speech tends to be categorical, arbitrary and conventionalised, while gesture is mostly gradient, iconic, and synthetic. This view on spoken language communication raises questions as to whether – and if so how – this can be applied to signed language communication. In signed languages, the manual channel 'takes over' from the oral modality – with the result that language 'moves' from the mouth to the hands. Theoretically, this may result in the gesture being 'pushed aside' and disappearing. Indeed, in an important part of the signed language literature, it seems to be taken for granted that there is no room for gesture in signed language use. We would like to argue here that gesture does not disappear. Again in theory, there are three possible outcomes that arise when the hands take over from the mouth: (1) gesture and sign come to co-exist in the manual modality; (2) gesture and sign are integrated into one structure; (3) gesture and 'speech' trade places, resulting in the manual articulators producing the linguistic component and the mouth producing the gestural component of a message.

In Flemish Sign Language, these three theoretical possibilities seem to be realised. In Section 2 of this paper we will begin by briefly discussing both the integration of sign and gesture and provide some examples of a 'gesturing mouth'. Most of the paper will however be devoted to the first of the above-mentioned possibilities, i.e. the possible co-production of sign and gesture in signed language use. In line with the focus of this volume we will concentrate on the simultaneous use of the two *manual* articulators. Three different simultaneous constructions that frequently occur in VGT and other signed languages, will be considered in Section 3 of this paper: (1) simultaneous constructions involving the use of a numeral sign; (2) simultaneous constructions involving pointing signs, and (3) examples where a lexical sign is 'held' on one hand, while the other hand produces gesture. In all three cases we first extensively discuss VGT examples in order to facilitate cross-linguistic comparison with data presented elsewhere in this volume. After that, these constructions are compared to speech+co-speech gesture combinations which at first sight seem similar. The aim here is to explore whether some examples of manual simultaneity might be (to some extent) equated to speech-with-gesture as produced by speakers of oral languages and whether these then can be analysed as combinations of a linguistic (sign) component and a gestural component.

The topic of this paper is on the interface between sign linguistics and gesture research. As signed language researchers, we approach this issue from the perspective of sign linguistics. This implies that there will be some imbalance between the 'two sides of the story'. First, the discussion of Flemish Sign Language is based on the analysis of examples selected from a relatively large corpus of data that has been used in a number of previous studies on aspects of the linguistics of VGT, whereas the gesture examples are taken from the literature or from personal, unsystematic observations. Second, especially in Section 3, the discussion concerning simultaneity in Flemish Sign Language will be more extensive compared to the discussion of related constructions used by speakers of a spoken language.

2.   Gesture integrated and gesture having 'moved out'

2.1   Gesture integrated

Some recent publications on signed languages have related properties of signs and signed language grammar to gesture. Liddell (2003a), for instance, argues that the use of space in 'spatialised syntax' is not linguistic in the strict sense. He analyses spatially modified signs in American Sign Language as being composed of a linguistic part, expressed by the handshape, the type of movement and certain aspects of the hand's orientation, and a gestural part relating the sign to a locus, i.e. an area or 'direction' (cf. Engberg-Pedersen 1993) in the signing space used to represent a locus.

Especially with respect to so called 'classifier constructions', researchers also more frequently consider the possibility of dealing with mixed forms, i.e. structures involving both linguistic and non-linguistic components (Schembri 2002; Liddell 2003a, 2003b; Schembri, Jones & Burnham 2005). Schembri et al. (2005) report on a study comparing the representation of motion events by sign-naive gesturers and by native signers of three different signed languages (American Sign Language, Australian Sign Language and Taiwan Sign Language). This study reports that the classifier constructions in the three signed languages compared are strikingly similar, and notes that the motion events produced by the hearing gesturers also correspond in a significant way to the signed constructions. Moreover, in both cases, the location and movement are alike and the handshape component shows most differences. These data are consistent with the claim that classifier verbs of motion and location are blends of gestural and linguistic elements (Liddell 2003a). Schembri et al. (2005:287) conclude that

> there is a need for all serious scholars to rethink assumptions about the relationship between signed languages and gesture, and to seek further evidence of the extent to which movement and location in classifier constructions may be grammaticalized gestures, or whether they involve blends of linguistic and gestural elements.

2.2   Gesture on the mouth

In some signed utterances the mouth seems to produce the gestural component of the message. When describing a picture showing a truck towing a car, one VGT signer imitates the sound of a truck while producing the sign TRUCK. In another example a signer refers to the sound of running water by means of an fffffff-sound when producing the sign construction meaning 'fill-with-water-from-tap'. Goldin-Meadow (2003:207) writes: "Several years ago, David McNeill and I, convinced of the importance of gesture to all human languages, including sign languages, speculated that mouth movements might be serving a gestural function for signers." She refers to Sandler's (2003) description of how the mouth works in Israeli Sign Language. Sandler (2003:398–403) presents an overview of the variety of linguistic tasks the mouth performs and discusses examples of the mouth producing gestures. She claims that all these mouth gestures are iconic, "representing some physical aspect of an object or event" (2003:399). Interestingly, one of the three examples she considers is similar to the 'water running' example from VGT. When signing an utterance meaning 'he emptied the water out of the pool', the signer creates "friction as the air passes through the constricted lips, and represents the draining water through a small opening" (2003:400). Sandler claims that this mouth gesture complements the signed message, just like manual gestures may be used to complement messages conveyed in speech. She also points out that mouth gestures often accompany classifier constructions, which is an interesting observation and can be related to the above-mentioned discussion concerning the status of the component parts of classifier constructions.

3. Sign + gesture, one hand for each?

3.1 'Enumeration'

3.1.1 *Enumeration in Flemish Sign Language*
Previous work on manual simultaneity in VGT (Vermeerbergen 1996, 2001) includes examples of 'enumeration' (Miller 1994a, 1994b) or 'digital enumeration' (Pinsonneault & Lelièvre 1994). These examples involve the use of a numeral handshape, usually produced by the non-dominant hand, in which (the fingertip of) each extended finger is associated with one referent, all referents together forming a list or an ordered set. The fingertips of the extended digits of the numeral hand are thought of as representing or 'becoming' the referents discussed. As such, enumeration may be compared – be it not in all respects, cf. Liddell (1990:191–192) – to the establishment and use of loci in the signing space.

In Flemish Sign Language, the numeral handshape can disappear immediately after the items in the list have been identified, but more often the handshape remains in place and items on the list are referred to in the subsequent discourse; in VGT this is most often done by touching or tapping the relevant fingertip, although pointing at it is also possible. Sometimes the numeral handshape disappears but becomes re-activated later in the discourse.

Vermeerbergen (2001:78) mentions the following example of enumeration (see the Appendix for transcription conventions). Here, the signer talks about three children from the same family. She first signs the clause HAVE THREE CHILD followed by the numeral handshape THREE. She then lists the three children and goes on to indicate which child is deaf.

(1)   Right hand: indexfinger-touches-D1-
       Left hand: HAVE THREE CHILD THREE-LIST - - - - - - - - - - - - - - - -
       Right hand: L-hand SON indexfinger-touches-D2-L-hand DAUGHTER
       Left hand: -
       Right hand: indexfinger-touches-D3-L-hand SON // indexfinger-touches-D1-
       Left hand: -
       Right hand: L-hand DEAF
       Left hand: - - - - - - - -
       'He/she has three children, one son, one daughter and another son. The first son is deaf.'

This example is in many ways comparable to the ASL example discussed by Liddell, Vogt-Svendsen and Bergman (this volume, Figures 3 and 4). The form and function of list buoys in VGT indeed appear to be very similar to what has been described in the literature, not only for American Sign Language, but also for a number of other signed languages. Given that the Liddell et al. paper (this volume) is an up-to-date cross-linguistic account involving three different signed languages, we take that as the starting point for presenting some characteristics of simultaneous constructions involving enumeration or listing in VGT. We will adopt both the notion 'list buoy' and the convention of glossing these buoys as NUMERAL-LIST, e.g. TWO-LIST, FOUR-LIST.

In example (1) above, the signer first mentions how many items are in the list. As with ASL, it is very common for VGT signers to do this. It seems a bit odd here that the signer uses the same hand to sign the preceding clause and then successively produce the buoy, as buoys are usually produced by the non-dominant hand. This particular signer, however, can be considered ambidextrous: although she shows a slight preference for her left hand, she uses her right hand almost as easily. This implies that it is possible to consider the left hand as the non-dominant hand in this entire stretch of signing. As pointed out by Liddell (personal communication, May 2005), the signer may have chosen to sign HAVE THREE CHILD with her left hand in anticipation of using the buoy (cf. also Nilsson, this volume).

In example (1) the signer touches the relevant extended digit immediately before the production of the sign for the referent associated with that fingertip. There are also examples where only one or some of the fingers are physically referred to (i.e. by touching, tapping or pointing) in the process of 'setting up a list'. In example (2) the signer lists the three languages his former remedial teacher used to practise with him. He touches the fingertip of the extended digit of the ONE-LIST but there is no contact between the dominant hand and the non-dominant hand when he continues signing, thereby producing TWO-LIST and THREE-LIST.

(2)   Right hand: ONLY LANGUAGE indexfinger-touches-D1-L-hand ENGLISH
      Left hand: ONE-LIST -
      Right hand: FRENCH   DUTCH   THOSE-THREE
      Left hand: TWO-LIST THREE-LIST - - - - - - - - - - -
      '(He) only (practised) languages: English, French and Dutch.'

As becomes clear from the comparison of the two examples discussed so far, like American, Norwegian, and Swedish Sign Language, VGT shows both static list buoys (or: single fixed-length lists) and sequentially built list buoys. When establishing the association between the digits of a static list buoy and the items on the list, touching – or otherwise physically referring to – the related fingertip immediately before or after producing the sign for the relevant item is common, and may even be obligatory. As already said, this is not the case for sequentially built list buoys. When signing for example the utterance that may be rendered as '(It has got) three colours, red, white and yellow', one signer produces the numeral handshapes ONE, TWO and THREE one after another with his non-dominant hand while simultaneously signing RED, WHITE and YELLOW with his dominant hand. In this example, there is no physical contact between the hands.

Interestingly, when we asked one of our informants whether it is possible to set up a list using a list buoy but without the dominant hand touching the fingers of the non-dominant hand, she said yes and subsequently produced an example summing up three items of a list with her dominant hand and simultaneously signing lexical items looking like ONE-LIST, TWO-LIST and THREE-LIST. However, these were produced with a rotating movement, as if she was signing the ordinal numerals FIRST, SECOND and THIRD. We did find examples in our corpus where this movement was absent, i.e. examples where the non-dominant hand is 'counting' while the dominant hand signs the referents associated with the digit 'last added'. We are not 100% sure whether the production of the non-dominant hand should be considered a sequentially built list in all of these cases. Nevertheless, examples such as these constitute one of the reasons why at this stage we are not inclined to make such a clear-cut distinction between list buoys and the corresponding numeral signs as other authors have done (cf. Pinsonneault & Lelièvre 1994: 160 for Quebec Sign Language and Liddell et al. this volume).

Many VGT signs are two-handed, but when a signer is maintaining a stationary hand configuration forming a list buoy, this hand does not seem available for the production of two-handed signs. In this case, signers may decide to use only one hand to form the sign (as they also often do when one hand is occupied doing other things, e.g. holding something). However, as Liddell et al.'s example from Swedish Sign Language (this volume, Figure 5) shows, it is also possible to involve the buoy in the production of the two-handed sign and use the non-dominant hand either as the base or one of the active hands in the production of a symmetrical two-handed sign.

In Flemish Sign Language the buoys ONE-LIST, TWO-LIST and THREE-LIST each come in two forms, either with or without extended thumb. This means that TWO-LIST may be signed with extended thumb and index finger or with the index finger and middle finger stretched out. The same can be said for the numerals ONE, TWO and THREE.

In all VGT examples we have seen so far, the first item on the list is associated with the 'top extended digit' (i.e. with the thumb in cases where the thumb is functioning as one of the digits, or with the index finger in examples where the thumb does not take part in the formation of the buoy). Often, the order that items on a list buoy are presented in mirrors some sort of inherent – often chronological – order between the referents in the real world, but this need not always be the case. We have asked some Flemish signers whether it would also be possible to 'turn the list around' and relate the first item on a list to the bottom extended finger. Apparently, this does seem to be possible for Flemish Sign Language; in most cases there is a motivation for the reversed order. One signer replied saying that she would use a 'reversed order' to describe a situation where four people lived (or stayed) on four different floors in a building. She claims she would form a FOUR-LIST and would first relate the ground floor to the little finger, second, the first floor to the ring finger, etc. Another example (from a different informant) would be where the result of a sports competition is discussed. Signers might start off by telling who was third and associate this referent with the middle finger (i.e. the bottom finger) of a THREE-LIST, continue signing who was second, and finally relating the winner to the top finger. The result here is of course that the first one (i.e. the winner) is associated with the top digit after all. According to this signer, the 'reversed presentation' is chosen to create suspense.

3.1.2 *Speakers enumerating on their hand(s)*

Following a suggestion from Marianne Gullberg, we invited family and friends for an 'I am going on a trip and in my suitcase I put...' game. In this game, the first player says what she puts in the suitcase, the second player repeats this first item and adds a second one, the third player repeats items 1 and 2 and adds another, and so on. When players cannot recall all items named so far, they are 'out'. We played the game four times with a different group of (5 to 7) people. Most participants were adults, though one game involved a four-year-old and two teenagers.

Speakers employ different manual mechanisms when trying to remember all the items in the suitcase. One such mechanism involves the use of pointing gestures; each time the player tries to remember an item, she points at the player who put that item on the list. We also observed people 'pointing' with their eyes, i.e. looking at the relevant person in the circle. As expected by Marianne Gullberg, several players used enumeration when recalling the items. Most often, the lists were sequentially built, i.e. the speaker first extended one digit when naming the first item, added a second digit when naming the second etc. When setting up a list for more than five items, players used their two hands and extended more than five fingers. We did not see examples where the speakers re-started using the same five digits on one hand to list items 6 to 10, but we would not exclude that possibility. During the game the 4-year-old child was participating in, she named the first item. By the time it was her turn again, there was a list of six items to be recalled. Her uncle, sitting on her left hand side, wanted to help her. He said the sentence 'I am going on a trip and in my suitcase I put...', which she repeated. She did not continue naming the items however. Her uncle, in an attempt to help her further, took hold of her left hand and formed a 'number one' handshape. This shows that, although few people are aware of their manual activity when playing this game, they do seem to realise that when trying to remember items on a list, forming 'numeral handshapes' may help.[1]

The examples we witnessed during these games are in many respects comparable to what happens when signers relate back to the digits of their hand(s) in order to prompt items of a list. In one example taken from our VGT-data a signer talks about a visit to a deaf school. He tries to recall the people who went on the visit and when doing this produces a sequentially formed list containing 6 items. The 'numeral signs' ONE to FIVE are simultaneously formed by the non-dominant hand each time the associated referent is signed by the dominant hand. (He uses the two-handed version of SIX which he signs before naming visitor number six.) The form and function of this enumeration look very similar to most instances of listing items on the hand(s) during the game. Of course, it is possible that, whereas both signers and speakers form manual numeral gestures/signs when retrieving items (from memory), only signers use true list buoys. This would imply that only signers produce handshapes that look like, but may not exactly be the same as numeral signs, and hold these signs in a stationary position so that their physical presence helps in guiding the discourse as it proceeds. We did, however, also notice *speakers* produce examples of the non-dominant hand being held stationary with the fingers pointing sideways, i.e. the non-dominant hand displaying a typical list buoy form. In one instance, the speaker first said 'I want to take three', formed a static THREE-LIST buoy (not involving an extended thumb) on the non-

---

1.   The reason we claim that most speakers are unaware of their manual activity while playing this game, is that very often, when they were afterwards told that the purpose of the game was to observe what they were doing with their hands, many of them did not realise that they had been using their hands at all.

dominant hand, and held the hand stationary while continuing: 'one for me, one for Ben and one for Maarten'. Both form and function here are very similar, if not completely identical, to examples involving list buoys in VGT.

Although we have not come across gesture literature concerning speakers using their hands to enumerate items, Gullberg notes that speakers do this very frequently in co-speech gesture (personal communication, April 2005). Our own – unsystematic – observations confirm that when speakers are not involved in a memory game, but are referring to a number of entities or ideas ordered in a list, they also frequently simultaneously combine naming these referents with setting up a static or sequentially built list buoy on their hand(s). These list buoys include both numeral handshapes with extended thumb and numeral handshapes only involving the fingers. Again just as with the signers, speakers may physically refer to the tip of the relevant finger when naming the referent associated with that finger, but equally, they may produce a list buoy on one of their hands without using the other hand to point at or touch the fingertips. 'Mixed forms' also occur, e.g. when speakers touch the first digit, then only extend but do not touch the second digit, touch the third digit etc.

As we have indicated earlier, signers can, after setting up a list, refer back to the fingers in that list to give further information about some of the items in the list (cf. example (1)). Likewise, speakers may also point to one or more of the extended digits in order to expand on the referents these digits are representing. As opposed to signers, however, it seems that they cannot do this without simultaneously using a co-referential expression in speech that takes up the aforementioned referent. Signers are free either to only point to the digits in the list or to combine this with (re)naming the referents. This could be an important difference between 'list gestures' and 'list signs'.

Descriptive work of 'list buoys' in co-speech gesture could bring to light yet other similarities and differences in both form and function between lists on the non-dominant hand of a signer and lists set up in co-speech gesture. Furthermore, such work could show whether the spoken language influences the specific use of co-speech list buoys. It could be the case that for speakers of pro-drop languages, as for signers, the fingers in the list buoy can have a truly and purely pronominal function by themselves (Gullberg, personal communication, April 2005).

3.2 Pointing signs and pointing gestures

3.2.1 *Introducing pointing signs in Flemish Sign Language*
An extensive discussion of pointing signs, even when limited to pointing signs in Flemish Sign Language, would require a separate volume. Signers use pointing signs very frequently and these pointing signs come in different forms which serve a number of different functions. Here, we will first summarise some information

on the form and function of VGT pointing signs in general, and continue to discuss examples of pointing signs that feature the simultaneous use of both hands. The brief general introduction to pointing signs below is based on Vermeerbergen (1996), which in turn is inspired by Engberg-Pedersen's (1993) analysis of pointing signs in Danish Sign Language. We note that when we use the notion 'pointing sign', we are referring to prototypical pointing i.e. pointing with an extended index finger. In other words, we exclude all forms of non-manual pointing as well as indicating signs showing a different hand configuration.

Signers may point at the actual location of entities or to places in the context of an utterance. When discussing a non-present referent, a signer may also choose to relate that referent to a locus. This locus may then be pointed at, e.g. for the purpose of anaphoric reference. Pointing signs may also be directed towards (a part of) the other hand, for example when referring to a referent 'depicted' by a classifier handshape produced by that other hand.

Often, but not always, the choice of a locus in space is motivated, for example when a signer associates her absent father with his now empty chair at the dinner table or when the president of an association is attributed a higher locus than the vice-president (cf. Vermeerbergen 1996:142–143; Engberg-Pedersen 1993:71–74; Schermer, Fortgens, Harder & de Nobel 1991:151–158). One locus may refer to more than one referent, at least when there is a connection between these referents (for example, a person and the town the person lives in) and when there is no need to keep them separated in the discourse.

Some VGT pointing signs are analysed as predicates, i.e. they are used to predicate the location or the direction of the movement of a referent. However, in most cases, predicates meaning something like 'be located at', 'be directed towards', 'move towards' show a hand configuration different from that of the prototypical pointing sign. Non-predicative pointing signs can be combined with a noun to form a constituent or can have 'constituent status' by themselves. Engberg-Pedersen (1993, 2003) for Danish Sign Language, coins these two types of pointing signs as determiners and pronouns respectively. We adopt this approach here (cf. also Vermeerbergen 1996). However, we would like to point out that it is not always easy to distinguish between the two (cf. the discussion in Liddell (2003a:331) concerning the difficulty in distinguishing between (1) a pronoun followed by an appositive and (2) a determiner plus a noun in American Sign Language). As noted earlier, pointing signs functioning as determiners or pronouns are often directed at a specific locus but this is not necessarily the case. When not associated with a specific locus, the direction in which the signer points is irrelevant. Especially when undirected, the production of pointing signs may be extremely brief and informants often do not immediately notice their presence in videotaped data. Engberg-Pedersen (2003:274) considers the frequent occurrence of undirected pronouns and determiners in Danish Sign Language to be strong evidence for the integration of pointing signs in (the syntax of) the linguistic system.

Within the group of non-predicative pointing signs, Engberg-Pedersen (1993, 2003) further distinguishes the 'proform'. This form is usually produced by the non-dominant hand and is "used as a carrier of information which is otherwise expressed in spatial modifications of manual signs" (2003:275). An example of a pointing sign functioning as 'proform' can be seen in the following example from Danish Sign Language (Engberg-Pedersen 1993:124).

(3)   1.p. POSS FAMILY   DEAF+redupl.
                    PROFORM+'sideways-movement'
      'In my family everyone is deaf.'

In this example, the pointing sign produced by the non-dominant hand and occurring simultaneously with the production of DEAF by the dominant hand, cannot be analysed as a determiner – since it occurs along with a predicate. According to Engberg-Pedersen (1993:124) it cannot be a pronoun either, because "it is not possible to use the reduplicated form of DEAF with a plural form of the pronoun (expressed by a sideways movement of the index hand)". Engberg-Pedersen's informants reject the combination of a "pronoun with sideways movement" followed by the reduplicated form of DEAF when both are signed with the same hand. If the pointing sign produced by the non-dominant hand in the example above is analysed as a pronoun, this would mean that it is possible to combine the plural form of the pronoun with the reduplicated predicative sign in a simultaneous construction, but that the same combination is not possible in a non-simultaneous structure. Because of this, Engberg-Pedersen prefers to distinguish proforms from pronouns and determiners. Vermeerbergen (1996:148) rejected this distinction, but in this paper we reviewed Engberg-Pedersen's argumentation. In some cases (e.g. examples (10) and (13) in Engberg-Pedersen 1993:124) there may be good reasons for not analysing the pointing sign as a pronoun, at least not in Danish Sign Language. However, not every argument presented for Danish Sign Language also holds for VGT. For instance, the fact that the argument position is already occupied by another (pro)nominal is seen as a reason not to analyse a simultaneously produced pointing sign as a pronoun in Danish Sign Language (Engberg-Pedersen 2003:276), but we are not inclined to say the same for similar examples in VGT. Moreover, as Engberg-Pedersen (1993:125) herself points out, in many examples we have no means for deciding whether a pointing sign carrying spatial information and 'held' by the non-dominant hand should be seen as a proform or as the continuation of a pronoun. To sum up, the current state of the art regarding the research on pointing signs in VGT does not allow us to decide on the need for a separate category for these pointing signs which occur in simultaneous constructions and carry some sort of spatial information 'taken over' from other signs.

However, we clearly do not wish to agree with Liddell (2003a: 253–254) and totally exclude an analysis in terms of pronominal reference for pointing signs that are held stationary on the non-dominant hand during the production of other signs (see further).

3.2.2 *Simultaneous constructions involving pointing signs in Flemish Sign Language*

As noted earlier, Flemish signers may relate a non-present referent to a locus in the signing space. Establishing a locus is often done by means of a pointing sign indicating the locus before, after, or simultaneous with the production of the sign(s) for the referent. In the latter case, the pointing usually, but not always, ends immediately after articulating the associated sign(s). This type of 'localising pointing signs' produced simultaneously with the sign(s) for the referent may be analysed either as proforms or determiners, depending on the definition of these categories. The status of the pointing sign produced with the non-dominant (left) hand in the following example is ambiguous:

(4) Right hand: WHERE Ps-loc$_a$ GIRL
     Left hand: SAY WHERE Ps-loc$_a$ - - - -
     'I say: Where is the girl?' or: 'I say: Where is she, the girl?'

In the next example (example (5)), the signer narrates a scene from an animated movie. The signer first explains that the two main characters are driving in one car and are being followed by two men in a second car. The final sign in this utterance is FOLLOW, which is produced with two 'fist-with-thumb-up' hand configurations, each representing one car. After the production of this sign, the non-dominant hand remains in place, while the dominant hand continues to sign:

(5) Ps KNOW NOTHING BEHIND FOLLOW // Ps STOP
     'They/the men in the first car don't know they are being followed. They/this car stop/stops.'

Both pointing signs produced by the dominant hand are directed towards the non-dominant hand. Interestingly, another signer, talking about the same episode, also first produces a sign involving two classifier handshapes referring to the two cars. However, this signer does not hold the configuration of the non-dominant hand, instead, she points at the exact location the hand was occupying:

(6) Ps YELLOW CAR KNOW NOTHING FOLLOW BEHIND RED FOLLOW
     'The men in that car (or: The men in that car, the yellow one) don't know they are being followed by the red car.'

In another example three pointing signs occur, each used to point at a referent present in the context of the utterance. Five people, four deaf and one hearing, are standing together, talking about deaf education. The signer explains to the hearing person that they all went to different schools. He first signs: WE SCHOOL DIF-FERENT+++ // I ANTWERP ('We went to different schools. I went to Antwerp'). Then he explains where the other three went to school, each time pointing at the relevant person with his non-dominant hand, while simultaneously signing the town where they went to school with his dominant hand:

(7)   Right hand: GHENT HASSELT BRUGES
Left hand: Ps - - - -   Ps - - - - -   Ps - - - - -
'He went to Ghent, he to Hasselt and he to Bruges.'

According to our informants, this utterance is equally well-formed when the pointing signs are directed at loci associated with non-present referents.

In many cases, the production of the pointing sign accompanies more than one sign. Often, but not always, their form and (overall) function seem to fit Liddell's definition of buoys; they are produced by the non-dominant hand, held in a stationary configuration and their physical presence helps guide the discourse as it proceeds (Liddell 2003a: 223). We give some examples of pointing signs that co-occur with more than one sign. In the first example, example (8), the pointing sign is directed towards a locus previously associated with a specific boy.

(8)   Right hand: GRAND^PARENTS DEAF GRAND^PARENTS
Left hand: Ps - - - - - - - - - - - - - - -
'His grandparents are deaf.' or 'He has deaf grandparents.'

The context for example (9) relates to a signer who is referring to a recent visit he made to a school for the deaf. The school housed two groups of children: children educated orally and children educated through signed language. He says that he wanted to ask how the decision was made regarding the placement of the children in one section of the school as opposed to the other, and he says:

(9)   Right hand: IF PARENTS Ps-loc_a TRY SCHOOL FIRST TRY Ps-loc_a
Left hand: Ps-loc_a - - - - - - - - - - - - - - - - - -
                                                    neg_____
Right hand: SIGNING ... OR FIRST   ORAL   CAN-NOT FOLLOW
Left hand: SIGNING   Ps-loc_b - - - - - - CAN-NOT FOLLOW
Right hand: loc_b-TRANSFER-loc_a
Left hand:
'(...) whether the parents wanted to try it ('education in sign') and so the school did, or whether they were first placed in an oral program and trans-ferred in case they could not keep up.'

Both pointing signs produced by the dominant hand as well as the first pointing sign on the non-dominant hand are directed towards the previously established locus for 'education involving the use of signs'. The second pointing sign on the non-dominant hand relates to the locus already associated with oral education while the movement of the sign TRANSFER starts in relation to the second locus and ends in relation to the first.

The next example, example (10), begins with two simultaneously produced pointing signs, both pointing in more or less the same direction. The last sign in the utterance is produced (by the non-dominant hand) in relation to the locus pointed at.

(10)   t _____

    Right hand: Ps TWO MAN   ENVELOPE

    Left hand: Ps-   ENVELOPE GONE-loc$_b$

    Mouthing: from

    'The two men with the envelope depart.'

Following Liddell (2003a: 250–260; cf. also Liddell et al. this volume), the pointing sign produced by the non-dominant hand in (10) might be analysed as a POINTER buoy. POINTER buoys are used to point at an important element in the discourse. Vogt-Svendsen & Bergman (this volume) set apart POINTER buoys from point buoys for Norwegian and Swedish Sign Language. They claim that "a point buoy neither represents, nor points at, a prominent discourse entity. Instead, a point buoy represents a point in time or space and is used for visualizing temporal and spatial relations between entities." In our corpus, we have a number of interviews conducted in VGT. In every interview the interviewer asks whether the person he is interviewing would choose a different type of education if she were 16/17 again. When asking this question the signer often directs his non-dominant hand toward a locus in front of him (representing 'now') and produces most of the following signs in relation to this hand/locus:

(11)   Right hand: E.G. BACK SIXTEEN SEVENTEEN BACK WHAT

        Left hand: Ps -

        'Suppose, if you were sixteen, seventeen again, what (would you study)?'

Both renderings of the sign BACK are produced with a movement starting above the non-dominant hand and ending at a locus left-front. This is also where the signs SIXTEEN and SEVENTEEN are signed. In this example the handshape of the non-dominant hand is not that of a typical pointing sign but rather a B-handshape. It seems that VGT-point buoys used to visualise temporal relations usually take this handshape. This does not seem the case for spatial point buoys, where the index hand is more common.

A pointing sign held by the non-dominant hand throughout the production of (almost) a whole sentence is also seen in interrogative structures where the non-dominant hand points at the addressee.

(12)   Right hand: FINISH SCHOOL GO-TO FINISH Ps-addressee
       Left hand: FINISH Ps-addressee - - - - - - - - - - - - - - - - - -
       'You have been in that school, haven't you?'

Miller (1994a: 104) claims that for Quebec Sign Language this type of pointing sign functions as a marker for a yes/no-question. We hypothesise that this may be a valid analysis for the VGT examples as well.

3.2.3 *Abstract deixis in gesture*

Kita (2003a) offers a cross-disciplinary collection of various studies of pointing that shows that pointing during communication is a ubiquitous and universal phenomenon. However, as Gullberg (2004: 235) points out, the studies in Kita's book also indicate that "pointing is anything but simple". It occurs not only in diverse forms, as speakers may use their hands, eyes, heads and other body parts to point at entities and locations in space, but also with a rich variety of functions. Within the limits of this paper we focus on those uses of pointing gestures which show correspondences with pointing signs in signed languages (cf. §3.2.1–2).

It is often assumed that when speakers point, they point at things, people or places that are present. Apparently, "when communicating about referents locatable in the speech situation, pointing is almost inevitable" (Kita 2003b: 1). We have observed several examples of this, e.g. someone pointing at the phone that starts to ring and saying 'Listen, phone' and someone else saying 'That comes from this' pointing at the spilled water at the floor when saying 'that' and at the wet washcloth she is holding in her other hand when saying 'this'. As this last example illustrates, pointing signs may be crucial in order to understand the message.

Research on pointing gestures has shown that in speech (especially in narratives) exophoric pointing to present objects or persons is far less frequent than endophoric pointing, i.e. pointing to non-present entities. Such pointing at 'empty space' is also called 'abstract pointing' or 'abstract deixis' (for example, McNeill 1992; McNeill, Cassell & Levy 1993). "In concrete pointing there is a demonstrable target, but in abstract pointing the target is created by the speaker and concretely instantiated as a locus or direction." (McNeill et al. 1993: 5) In other words, in abstract deixis, pointing to a location assigns meaning to that location. According to Gullberg (1998: 140) these locations – or loci – "can be referred back to anaphorically, such that a referent can be tracked by pointing to the locus associated with it in space". In the words of McNeill et al. (1993: 11): "Deixis at the narrative level often establishes coreferential chains where successive references are linked by virtue of occupying the same locus in space", as exemplified in this example:

(13)   and in fact a few minutes later we see [the artist]
                              Points to left side of space.
       and uh she [looks over] Frank's shoulder at him
              Points to the left side of space again.   (McNeill et al. 1993:11)

The (potential) co-referential use of pointing is yet another striking correspondence between deictic signs and deictic gestures.

In our observations of pointing gestures we have noticed that many instances of pointing are motivated, in that the locus pointed at has a certain semantic link with the referent being talked about. These examples encompass characteristics of both concrete and abstract deixis. An example is the following, where the speaker refers to his student days at the *Vrije Universiteit Brussel*, simultaneously pointing at one of the people participating in the conversation who currently is working at that university. In another example, the speaker points at the person working in a primary school while saying 'and in primary education...'. Kita (2003b:4) presents a similar example where there is "an associative link from the direct referent to the inferred referent". Interestingly, his example of someone pointing at an empty chair to refer to the person who normally sits in that chair is an example frequently used in the signed language literature to illustrate that the choice of a locus is often motivated (cf. §3.2.1).

It is often assumed that whereas in signed languages the pointing sign may carry the full burden of personal pronominal reference, this is not possible in co-speech pointing. We have seen at least one example where pointing was the sole identification of the subject. In this example, the speaker points at himself, leaves out the subject (I) and auxiliary (have), and says 'also played outdoors a lot'. We have not seen examples where the speaker points at a locus for a non-present referent without also naming the referent in speech, but we imagine this is also possible.

We have witnessed speakers accompanying their speech with undirected pointing signs where it is not very clear what the function of the pointing may be. Similar examples can be found in signed language discourse; here, signers use their non-dominant hand to 'point' without any obvious reason while signing with their dominant hand.

To conclude, we cite Gullberg (2004:245) who raises the question as to whether pointing signs are conventionalised signs or spontaneous co-speech gestures and claims:

> The difficulties in distinguishing that which is linguistic, conventional, and grammaticised, from that which is gestural, non-conventionalised, yet systematic, are the same for Sign and gesture research. The view of how pointing or indexical movements fit into this perspective is of course of interest to both Sign and gesture research.

We could not agree more.

3.3 Concurrent lexical items and gesture(s)

3.3.1 *Examples from Flemish Sign Language*

Emmorey (1999: 145) presents an example of an ASL signer holding a sign on the one hand while producing a gesture with the other when describing a scene from the 'Frog, where are you?' story. In this scene, a dog is running alongside a deer and wants the deer to stop. The signer first fingerspells 'dog', then forms a two-handed classifier construction meaning 'run', continues holding the classifier handshape of the dominant hand stationary while producing a gesture meaning 'stop' with his non-dominant hand, and subsequently returns to the classifier construction. In another example taken from the same narrative the signer first produces the sign LOOK, holds this sign on his left hand while producing a string of gestures with his other hand and then continues the story with a classifier construction involving the use of both hands. According to Emmorey (1999: 146), "this is as close as one gets to simultaneous gesture and signing".

We have discussed these examples from American Sign Language with some of our informants and they seem to think combinations such as these may equally well be produced by VGT signers. When going through our corpus in order to see whether we could find VGT examples, we did indeed come across instances of what looks like a gesture simultaneously occurring with a sign. In the next example, the signer first claims there are a hundred deaf children, he then stops and thinks about this (while holding his dominant hand and sort of wiggling his fingers) and then continues producing a sign (WRONG) + gesture (meaning 'wait' or 'stop') combination.

(14)   Right hand: 100 Ps 'wiggling-fingers' .... WRONG I 162 DEAF
       Left hand: 'wait/stop'
       '(There are) one hundred.... no, wait, I am mistaken, one hundred sixty two deaf.'

When looking at the data, one of our informants frequently pointed out utterances involving what is called 'constructed action' (see discussion below) as possible illustrations of simultaneous sign plus gesture combinations. One example is the following:

(15)   Right hand: DRIVER   WAIT   vc: "read-newspaper" SMOKE/vc: "smoke"
       Left hand: DRIVER - - - - - vc: "read-newspaper" - - - - - - - - - - - - -
       'The driver is waiting, he reads his newspaper and smokes a cigarette.'

Emmorey (1999) refers to the gestures in her examples using Clark's notion of 'component' iconic gestures. According to Clark (1996), such iconic gestures are embedded as part of the utterance, as in 'The boy went [rude gesture] and ran away', i.e. the speaker (or signer) stops speaking (or signing) when producing the gesture. Emmorey points out that Liddell & Metzger (1998) describe such gestures as 'constructed action'. In the sign linguistics literature this notion is used to refer to the signer re-enacting a character's actions or pose. Liddell & Metzger (1998:660) write:

> The idea is that just as constructed dialogue is not a direct copy of the speech being reported, but is the current speaker's construction of another person's speech (Tannen 1986, 1989), constructed action is also not a direct copy of a character's actions. It is the narrator's construction of another's actions (Metzger 1995).

Furthermore, they present an example from McNeill (1992) where a native speaker of English illustrates the actions of the cartoon character he talks about through (co-speech) gesture. They explicitly state that examples such as these are comparable to instances of constructed action in signed language use. It is interesting to see that both signers and speakers 'construct action' and it would be exciting to conduct an in-depth comparison. However, this falls outside the scope of this paper.

3.3.2 *Holding gesture for discursive reasons*

Both Emmorey's (1999) ASL examples and our own VGT examples show that a signer can hold a lexical sign on one hand, while simultaneously producing a gesture with the other hand. In spoken language use, however, the articulation of a word may be lengthened, but it does not seem feasible to 'hold' (part of) a word, simultaneously produce a gesture, and then later return to the word. Conversely, it is possible for speakers to produce a (two-handed) gesture, hold one hand stationary while producing one or more other gestures, and then return to the first gesture. Enfield (2004) describes many examples of such combinations of gesture-in-hold and other gestures in his data from speakers of Lao (a South-Western Tai language of Laos). He calls these combinations 'symmetry-dominance constructions' (Enfield 2004:57):

> Phase 1 is a two-handed symmetrical gesture; in the subsequent phase 2, one hand holds in position (representing given/topical/backgrounded information from phase 1), while one hand executes a new gesture (representing new/focal/foregrounded information).

We would like to explain one example of a symmetry-dominance construction from Enfield (2004) in which different speakers expand on two types of traditional Laotian fish-trapping mechanisms. One speaker describes the fluted shape of one particular fish trap by combining a spoken utterance with a symmetrical iconic gesture representing the fluted opening of the trap. In the subsequent dominance phase the speaker holds his left hand in position, while indicating with his right hand a fish going into the mouth and body of the trap. This example illustrates the typical use of symmetry-dominance constructions in co-speech gesture, showing the twofold function of the non-dominant hand. Firstly, it "provides a stable spatial reference point (or ground) facilitating the depiction of complex three-dimensional spatial representations by the dominant hand" (Enfield 2004:61). Secondly, Enfield stresses the discourse pragmatic function of the non-dominant hand, as it signals "that certain background information continues to be relevant to what is being said" (ibidem). For sign linguists acquainted with the literature on buoys, this and similar examples look very familiar.

Enfield himself points out that the non-dominant hand shows similar functions in signed languages (he refers to Sandler 2002 and Liddell 2003a among others), which indicates that both signed languages and co-speech gesture make use of the same structures. As he puts it, the symmetry-dominance constructions in his data "reveal semiotic effects arising systematically from affordances of the manual/visuospatial modality which are *not* 'unique to signed languages'" (2004:119).

We would like to point out here that, whereas in the Enfield examples there is a close semantic relation between both hands, this need not always be the case in examples of speakers' gesture+gesture combinations. Gullberg (personal communication, April 2005) informs us that it is also possible to produce a (two-handed) iconic gesture, hold one hand stationary while producing one or more other, unrelated, gestures, such as beats, and then return to the first gesture. This often happens when there is some sort of interruption in the spoken message, e.g. when a speaker stops a narrative to utter a comment aside and later returns to the narrative.

4. Discussion

From the gesture research it becomes clear that gestures are an integral part of linguistic communication. Apparently, speakers must gesture when they speak and they primarily use the manual channel to do so. In contrast, researchers seem to assume that signers do not use the manual channel to produce (similar) gestures. This assumption can be found in the signed language literature and is equally expressed by some gesture researchers. The following quotations illustrate this. Sandler (2003:405) argues:

> If the oral channel is used for the purely linguistic signal, then the hands supply the gestural complement. If the manual channel is the medium for language, then the mouth provides the complementary gestures.

McNeill (1993:156) states that

> one supposes that for the deaf and others who make use of conventional signed languages the primitive stages of their sentences also include global-synthetic

images, just as in the case of spoken languages, but their signs, unlike the spontaneous gestures of the hearing, do not, cannot, reflect this stage. The kinesic-visual
medium is grammatical and socially regulated for the deaf, and this shifts the overt
performance of deaf signers to the final stage of the internal temporal evolution
of utterances.

The general idea seems to be that in signed languages, gesture either moves away
from the manual channel and/or (partly) loses its true gestural character and becomes part of or integrated in the linguistic system. Both options, (1) gesture
moving from the manual to the oral channel and (2) the integration of sign and
gesture have been discussed in part 2 of this paper. However, we also explored the
possible presence of ('non-integrated') gesture in the manual production of signers. In line with the general theme of this volume, we have chosen to approach
this issue by a comparison of (1) simultaneous constructions in signed languages,
as exemplified by Flemish Sign Language, with (2) various, possibly comparable,
types of speech combined with gesture.

Our preliminary comparison reveals many more similarities than we had expected, both in form and in function. We are also struck by the relatively high
degree of systematicity in (co-speech) gesture. We found it very interesting to
confront our knowledge of signed language structure with the results of gesture
research and we hope to have shown that cooperation between sign linguists and
gesture researchers may lead to a more profound understanding in both research
domains. Such cooperation may for instance result in a clearer view on the delineation of the different forms of speakers' and signers' "visible bodily action that
play a part in the process of the utterance" (Kendon & Blakely 1986: 1).

Our excursion into the domain of gesture studies raises some general questions as to the relation (1) between signs and gestures, (2) between different forms
of language/communication, and (3) between signed language research, spoken
language research and gesture studies. We want to conclude this contribution by
giving the initial impetus to some answers.

In some (more) recent work on signed language structure, researchers exploit
the possibility of elements of the manual signal being gestural. Often, gesture is
then defined according to the criteria presented in McNeill (1992). Interestingly,
within the gesture literature, some of these criteria are being contested. McNeill
(1992: 21) considers gestures to be non-combinatoric, for example, which means
that gestures do not combine to form larger, more complex gestures. However,
Kendon (1997: 119) refers to Webb (1996) who recognises stable form-meaning
relationships in the metaphoric gestures of different speakers and who therefore
speaks of a 'morphology' of gesture. Furthermore, other researchers do consider
'combinatorics' in co-speech gesture (e.g. Enfield 2004), thus suggesting structural similarities between co-speech gesture and signs of linguistic systems, such
as signed languages. Kendon (1997: 123) therefore points out that gestures are

equivalent to lexical units in speech not only at a functional level (i.e. in communicating meaning), but also at a formal level: "there may be in gesture a spectrum of forms, more or less linguistic, rather than a sharp break". Thereby he implies that some gestures, like (signed) linguistic forms, are analytic, compositional and combinatoric.

As mentioned in the introduction, Kendon (1988) observed that gestural phenomena can be categorised in different types, which led McNeill (1992) to introduce the notion of 'Kendon's continuum', an organisation of gestures/manual activity according to their language-like properties, their relationship to co-occurring speech, and their degree of conventionalisation. Gullberg (2004:246) writes:

> Roughly, primary Sign Language is placed at one end of the continuum (+language-like, +conventional, –co-occurring speech) and spontaneous co-speech gestures at the other (–language-like, –conventional, +co-occurring speech) with things like emblems/quotable gestures in the middle.

For us, the idea of characterising manual activity in relation to a continuum (or continua, cf. McNeill 2000: 1) seems justifiable, not only for speakers, but for signers as well. Thus, we propose that not all manual production from signers be considered as belonging to one end of the continuum. Instead, we suggest that we leave open the possibility that signers make use of a whole range of forms. As becomes clear from the collection of papers in Kita's *Pointing* volume (2003a), pointing exists both as spontaneous co-speech gesture and as conventionalised, language-like structure, which means that what looks like, and may be, the same thing, shows characteristics of both ends of the continuum (Gullberg 2004:246). We suggest that the idea that some instances of pointing may be characterised as (more) language-like, whereas others display gesture-like and non-language-like qualities, also applies to signed languages.

Following Taub, Pinar & Galvan (2002) and Enfield (2004:119) we would also like to suggest that when the communication of signers and speakers is being compared, it is speech in combination with (co-speech) gesture – and not speech by itself – that constitutes the appropriate level for cross-linguistic analysis. Moreover, we want to argue that just as gesture should be seen as an integral part of a speaker's communicative output, for signed languages as well, gesture may be part of the system:

> Rather than being homogeneous systems as commonly assumed (i.e., all major elements of signing behaviour are equally part of a morphosyntactic system), signed (and spoken) languages may be best analysed as essentially heterogeneous systems in which meanings are conveyed using a combination of elements, including gesture.   (Johnston, Vermeerbergen, Schembri & Leeson, in press)

From the above, it follows that when studying natural language one should take into consideration the output of all different 'channels' involved. Moreover, as we already pointed out, for both signed languages and spoken languages, it should be taken into consideration that each channel can contain +language-like elements as well as −language-like elements. For instance, one should not *a priori* assume that the manual channel in signed languages is purely linguistic nor that the manual channel in oral languages contains nothing but −language-like elements.

Thus, we state that human communication, in signers and speakers alike, should be seen as a primarily multi-channel activity. This, of course, implies that simultaneity is omnipresent.

Acknowledgments

For the preparation of this paper, we are grateful to Marianne Gullberg for orienting us within the body of literature on gesture and for generously sharing her knowledge of the field. Further, our thanks go to Mieke Van Herreweghe for providing helpful and insightful comments on earlier drafts and to Diane Boonen for recording the examples referred to in the paper.

References

Clark, Herbert. 1996. *Using Language*. Cambridge: Cambridge University Press.

Emmorey, Karen. 1999. "Do Signers Gesture?" *Gesture, Speech, and Sign* ed. by Lynn S. Messing & Ruth Campbell, 133–159. Oxford: Oxford University Press.

Enfield, Nick J. 2004. "On Linear Segmentation and Combinatorics in Co-Speech Gesture: A Symmetry-Dominance Construction in Lao Fish Trap Descriptions". *Semiotica* 149:1–4.57–123.

Engberg-Pedersen, Elisabeth. 1993. *Space in Danish Sign Language*. Hamburg: Signum Press.

———. 2003. "From Pointing to Reference and Predication: Pointing Signs, Eyegaze, and Head and Body Orientation in Danish Sign Language". *Pointing. Where Language, Culture, and Cognition Meet* ed. by Sotaro Kita, 269–292. Mahwah, N.J./London: Lawrence Erlbaum Associates.

Goldin-Meadow, Susan. 2003. *Hearing Gesture: How Our Hands Help Us Think*. Cambridge, Mass.: Harvard University Press.

Gullberg, Marianne. 1998. *Gestures as a Communication Strategy in Second Language Discourse. A Study of Learners of French and Swedish*. Lund: Lund University Press.

———. 2004. "Review of Sotaro Kita (ed.) (2003). Pointing. Where Language, Culture, and Cognition Meet". *Gesture* 4:2.235–248.

Johnston, Trevor, Myriam Vermeerbergen, Adam Schembri & Lorraine Leeson. In press. "'Real Data are Messy': Considering Cross-Linguistic Analysis of Constituent Ordering in Australian Sign Language (Auslan), Vlaamse Gebarentaal (VGT), and Irish Sign Language (ISL)." *Sign Languages: A Cross-Linguistic Perspective* ed. by Pamela Perniss, Roland Pfau & Markus Steinbach. Berlin: Mouton de Gruyter.

Kendon, Adam. 1986. "Some Reasons for Studying Gesture". *Semiotica* 62:1–2.3–28.

——.1988. "How Gestures Can Become Like Words". *Cross-Cultural Perspectives in Nonverbal Communication* ed. by Fernando Poyatos, 131–141. Toronto: Hogrefe.

——.1997. "Gesture". *Annual Review of Anthropology* 26.109–128.

—— & Thomas D. Blakely. 1986. "Preface to the Special Issue of Semiotica". *Semiotica* 62:1–2.1.

Kita, Sotaro. ed. 2003a. *Pointing. Where Language, Culture, and Cognition Meet*. Mahwah, N.J./London: Lawrence Erlbaum Associates

——. 2003b. "Pointing: A Foundational Building Block of Human Communication". *Pointing. Where Language, Culture, and Cognition Meet* ed. by Sotaro Kita, 1–8. Mahwah, N.J./London: Lawrence Erlbaum Associates.

Liddell, Scott K. 1990. "Four Functions of a Locus: Reexamining the Structure of Space in ASL". *Sign Language Research. Theoretical Issues* ed. by Ceil Lucas, 176–198. Washington D.C.: Gallaudet University Press.

——. 2003a. *Grammar, Gesture, and Meaning in American Sign Language*. Cambridge: Cambridge University Press.

——. 2003b. "Sources of Meaning in ASL Classifier Predicates". *Perspectives on Classifier Constructions in Sign Languages* ed. by Karen Emmorey, 199–220. Mahwah, N.J./London: Lawrence Erlbaum Associates.

—— & Melanie Metzger. 1998. "Gesture in Sign Language Discourse". *Journal of Pragmatics* 30:6.657–697.

McNeill, David. 1992. *Hand and Mind. What Gestures Reveal about Thought*. Chicago/London: The University of Chicago Press.

——. 1993. "The Circle from Gesture to Sign". *Psychological Perspectives on Deafness* ed. by Marc Marschark & M. Diane Clark, 153–183. Hillsdale, N.J.: Erlbaum.

——. 1998. "Speech and Gesture Integration". *The Nature and Functions of Gesture in Children's Communication. (New Directions for Child Development, No. 79)* ed. by Jana M. Iverson & Susan Goldin-Meadow, 11–27. San Francisco: Jossey-Bass.

——. 2000. "Introduction". *Language and Gesture* ed. by David McNeill, 1–10. Cambridge: Cambridge University Press.

——, Justine Cassell & Elena T. Levy. 1993. "Abstract deixis". *Semiotica* 95:1–2.5–19.

Metzger, Melanie. 1995. "Constructed Dialogue and Constructed Action in American Sign Language". *Sociolinguistics in Deaf Communities* ed. by Ceil Lucas, 255–271. Washington D.C.: Gallaudet University Press.

Miller, Chris. 1994a. "Simultaneous Constructions in Quebec Sign Language". *Word-Order Issues in Sign Language. Working Papers* ed. by Mary Brennan & Graham Turner, 89–112. Durham: International Sign Linguistics Association.

——. 1994b. "Simultaneous Constructions and Complex Signs in Quebec Sign Language". *Perspectives on Sign Language Structure. Papers from the Fifth International Symposium on Sign Language Research. Volume 1* ed. by Inger Ahlgren, Brita Bergman & Mary Brennan, 131–147. Durham: International Sign Linguistics Association.

Pinsonneault, Dominique & Linda Lelièvre. 1994. "Enumeration in LSQ (Québec Sign Langage): The Use of Fingertip Loci". *Perspectives on Sign Language Structure. Papers from the Fifth International Symposium on Sign Language Research. Volume 1* ed. by Inger Ahlgren, Brita Bergman & Mary Brennan, 159–172. Durham: International Sign Linguistics Association.

Sandler, Wendy. 2002. "From Phonetics to Discourse: The Non-dominant Hand and the Grammar of Sign Language". Paper presented at the Eighth Conference on Laboratory Phonology (LabPhon 8), Yale University, New Haven, Conn.

——. 2003. "On the Complementarity of Signed and Spoken Languages". *Language Competence across Populations: Toward a Definition of Specific Language Impairment* ed. by Yonata Levy & Jeanette C. Schaeffer, 383–409. Mahwah, N.J./London: Erlbaum.

Schembri, Adam. 2002. "The Representation of Motion Events in Signed Language and Gesture". *Progress in Sign Language Research. In Honor of Siegmund Prillwitz* ed. by Rolf Schulmeister & Heimo Reinitzer, 99–126. Hamburg: Signum Press.

——, Caroline Jones & Denis Burnham. 2005. "Comparing Action Gestures and Classifier Verbs of Motion: Evidence from Australian Sign Language, Taiwan Sign Language, and Non-Signers' Gestures without Speech". *Journal of Deaf Studies & Deaf Education* 10:3.272–290.

Schermer, Trude, Connie Fortgens, Rita Harder & Esther de Nobel, eds. 1991. *De Nederlandse Gebarentaal*. Twello: Van Tricht.

Tannen, Deborah. 1986. "Introducing Constructed Dialogue in Greek and American Conversational and Literacy Narratives". *Reported Speech across Languages* ed. by Florian Coulmas, 311–332. The Hague: Mouton.

——. 1989. *Talking Voices: Repetition, Dialogue, and Imagery in Conversational Discourse*. Cambridge: Cambridge University Press.

Taub, Sarah, Pilar Pinar & Dennis Galvan. 2002. "Comparing Spatial Information in Speech/Gesture and Signed Language". Manuscript. Paper presented at the "Gesture: The Living Medium" conference, Austin, 5–8 June 2002.

Vermeerbergen, Myriam. 1996. *ROOD KOOL TIEN PERSOON IN: Morfo-syntactische Aspecten van Gebarentaal*. Doctoral dissertation, Vrije Universiteit Brussel.

——. 1997. *Grammaticale Aspecten van de Vlaams-Belgische Gebarentaal*. Gent: Cultuur voor Doven.

——. 2001. "Simultane Constructies in de Vlaamse Gebarentaal". *Handelingen LIV (2000)* ed. by Rita Beyers, 69–81. Brussel: Koninklijke Zuid-Nederlandse Maatschappij voor Taal- en Letterkunde en Geschiedenis.

Webb, Rebecca. 1996. *Linguistic Features of Metaphoric Gestures*. Doctoral dissertation, University of Rochester.

Appendix: Transcription conventions

Only minimal transcription and glossing are given for the signed language examples in this paper. The top line in a transcription represents the production of the dominant hand; the second line refers to the non-dominant hand. In other words: if the production of the left hand is written down in the top line of the transcription, this means the left hand functions as the dominant hand.

Other conventions used include:

GIRL	English gloss for a manual sign.
DOOR-OPEN	A gloss consisting of more than one word, but standing for one sign only.
DOOR----	Lengthened production of a sign, e.g. when the sign is held in a stationary configuration.
GRAND^MOTHER	^ separates the parts of a compound
Ps	Pointing sign, sometimes the referent or locus pointed at is included in the transcription: Ps$_{-addresssee}$; Ps-loc$_a$
vc: "walk"	The abbreviation 'vc' stands for 'verbal construction'. A verbal construction is a predicate that belongs to the productive lexicon. This group of predicates include 'classifier constructions' as well as 'constructed actions'. Verbal constructions are transcribed here only in terms of their meaning.
WALK/ vc: "walk"	When the status of a predicate is not clear, both interpretations (lexical verb sign/ verbal construction) are given.
"stop"	A gesture is represented by its meaning written between quotation marks.
...	A pause, hesitation in the production, e.g. when a signer stops to think.
//	Clause boundary.
D1, D2	Digit 1, digit 2 (in a list buoy).
neg___	Nonmanual marking for negation, the line following neg indicates the scope of the negation.
t___	Nonmanual marking for topic, the line indicates the scope of the nonmanual marking.

When concurrent speech and gesture examples are presented, we follow the convention to indicate the extent of the meaningful part of the gesture by enclosing the concurrent word(s) the gesture co-occurs with in square brackets. The gesture itself is described in italics.

Acquisition of simultaneous constructions by deaf children of Hong Kong Sign Language

Gladys Tang, Felix Sze and Scholastica Lam
Centre for Sign Linguistics and Deaf Studies, Chinese University
of Hong Kong

1. Introduction

Signed languages are well known for their complex morphology, which can be represented by a set of morphemes articulated simultaneously. Typical examples that surface in many signed languages are the rich inflectional system of verb agreement and verbal aspect, as well as classifier predicates (Klima & Bellugi 1979; Meir 1998, 2001; Meier 2002; Lam 2003). That morphemes are combined compositionally in a simultaneous fashion poses a very interesting research question from a language acquisition perspective. Specifically, how do deaf children acquire the knowledge that some signs are not conventional and their component parts are predictably meaningful? What is more, some of these component parts can be 'stacked up' simultaneously with spatial configurations to encode predicative relations between objects and entities. Previous signed language acquisition literature reports that aspects of grammar involving space like verb agreement or classifier predicates tend to develop late (Schick 1990; Slobin, Hoiting, Kuntze, Lindert, Weinberg, Pyers, Anthony, Biederman & Thumann 2003) While inflectional verb agreement involves a lexical category (i.e. a verb) simultaneously superimposed by direction of movement or palm orientation to mark various pronominal arguments in space, classifier predicates involve the adoption of one or two specific meaningful handshapes embedded in a form of movement that encodes certain predication.

Our focus is the acquisition of simultaneous constructions that incorporate classifiers. These include typical classifier predicates as well as other simultaneous constructions that combine a lexical sign with a classifier (see also Section 2.2). On the basis of the data collected from fourteen deaf children whose signed language development was charted along three levels: elementary (Level 1), pre-intermediate (Level 2) and intermediate (Level 3), we attempted to establish a developmental sequence of these simultaneous constructions in Hong Kong Sign Language (HKSL). In the following sections, we will first provide a working definition of simultaneity in signed language research, with particular reference to the grammatical representation of classifier predicates. Then, we will summarize the previous literature on how deaf children acquired this grammatical construction. This is followed by a report on our current study, its methodology, results and a final discussion.

2.   Simultaneity in signed language

Signed language research in the past decades has shed light on our understanding of the origin and nature of signed languages, in particular, how modality of communication interacts with organization of grammar in natural language. Meier (2002) discusses whether modality has an effect on linguistic structure. Pertinent to our discussion is the hypothesis that the signing modality may induce qualitative differences due to the number of articulators adopted as well as the perceptual cues generated by the visual-gestural system of communication. Given these characteristics, information transmission in a signed language is prone to be multi-channel and this factor provides a potential source for simultaneity as an organizing principle of signed language grammars.

2.1 Simultaneity: A definition

There has been some discussion on simultaneity and sequentiality at the level of phonology (Stokoe 1960; Liddell & Johnson 1989); morphosyntax (Padden 1988; Emmorey 2002) and signed language discourse (Morgan 2002; Morgan & Woll 2003). Miller (1994a) represents the first attempt to provide a systematic analysis of the types of simultaneous constructions, quoting data from American Sign Language (ASL), British Sign Language (BSL), Danish Sign Language and Sign Language of the Netherlands (SLN). He puts forward a definition of simultaneous constructions whereby "(a) distinct lexical elements are produced independently and simultaneously in autonomous channels, and (b) these elements are bound together in some kind of syntactic relationship." (Miller 1994: 133). This definition is too narrow in the context of our investigation because, while it discusses a broad range of simultaneous constructions, it excludes classifier predicates. We propose to revise this working definition of simultaneity by incorporating the analysis of classifier predicates while not losing sight of Miller's contribution.

In our working definition, a simultaneous construction is a set of morphemic units set up in a sign articulation, which may be free or bound. These units may be lexical or morphological, simultaneously produced in autonomous channels.

They are either bound in some kind of morphosyntactic relationship, or they co-exist with other morphemic units for discourse purpose. This definition allows us to investigate a classifier predicate as an independent morphosyntactic unit or the occurrence of classifiers in other simultaneous constructions.[1]

2.2 Classifier constructions in Hong Kong Sign Language

Classifier constructions are good exemplars demonstrating simultaneity in the grammars of signed languages. Typical constructions are classifier predicates that involve combinations of distinct handshape and movement morphemes in the formation of various types of predicates, stative or process (Carlson 1981). Their unique properties have led to both interesting accounts and controversy, in particular, in relation to the grammatical properties of handshape and movement components (Supalla 1990; Schembri 2003; Tang 2001, 2003; Tang & Gu in press; Benedicto & Brentari 2004).[2] Nevertheless, closer scrutiny of classifier predicates also suggests that simultaneity and sequentiality are at play in the organization of the grammars of signed languages. In predicating an event of motion in HKSL, it is common to find a locative predicate preceding a motion predicate, in accord with Talmy's (2000) conceptual model of a motion event where a spatial reference for ground is necessarily established before figure is introduced in a motion predicate. This can be seen in example (1) below:

(1)   The cat steps into a box.

    BH: BOX

    LH: CL:CONTAINER-BE-LOCATED-AT$_i$ - - - - - - - - - - - -
    "A box is located here"

    RH: CAT CL:ANIMATE-ENTITY-STEP-INTO-A-CONTAINER$_i$

    LH: -
    "The cat steps into a container (i.e. box)."

---

1.   A caveat of this definition is the role ascribed to gesture in signed articulation. This definition by no means undermines the importance of gesture in signing, particularly when classifier predicates are regarded as depictive and iconic, strewn with stylized but phonologically conditioned handshape and movement components (Schick 1990; Slobin et al. 2003).

2.   The analysis of this construction has been controversial. This is in part due to associating the handshape configuration with classifiers in spoken languages of the Athapaskan family (Schembri 2003; Slobin et al. 2003). As for movement, unlike agreement verbs where the directionality of movement serves to distinguish grammatical subject and object, movement of the classifier can be stylized, as in handling an object entity; or gradient, as in locating the motion of an entity through space; if not depictive of the qualitative dimension of a referent object through a path and/or local movement of the classifier. As such, classifier constructions are said to be iconic, gestural and analogous to visual imagery in depicting real world properties (DeMatteo 1977).

BH: BOX

BH: CL:CONTAINER-BE-LOCATED-AT_i

LH: CL: CONTAINER-BE-LOCATED-AT_i - - - - -
RH: CAT

LH: CL: CONTAINER-BE-LOCATED-AT_i - - - - - - - - - - - - -
RH: CL:ANIMATE-ENTITY-STEP-INTO-A-CONTAINER_i

In (1), a locative predicate for box is signed first at a locus in space.[3] The classifier for box on the non-dominant hand is sustained while the dominant hand denoting an agentive subject encodes the verbal root of step-into through a translational movement of the dominant hand to the spatial locus (i.e. cl:container)

---

3.   Emmorey (2003) and Engberg-Pedersen (1993) make similar observations in American Sign Language and Danish Sign Language respectively.

occupied by the non-dominant hand. Example (1) also demonstrates how the verb root STEP-INTO differs from other lexical verbs in HKSL. While a lexical sign like RUN is decomposable at phonological level, one cannot analyze these sub-lexical units at the morphosyntactic level because they are not meaningful morphological units. In contrast, (1) shows that the sub-lexical units of a classifier predicate are decomposable because both the movement, and the classifier handshapes are meaningful morphological units. Its decomposability is evident when the classifier on the non-dominant hand in the locative predicate is retained for the subsequent motion predicate. The original figure entity for the locative predicate now becomes ground in the motion predicate. The classifier is a constant for both predicates (i.e. a container) referring to the lexical antecedent BOX, suggesting that it is possible to incorporate other morphemic units in the formation of a simultaneous construction. Newport (1982) suggests that a classifier would lose its morphemic status in the process of lexicalization and become a phoneme of the derived sign. Our data from HKSL suggest that the grammatical status of a classifier predicate and a corresponding, derived lexical sign is not as clear cut as we may have originally thought. In HKSL at least, our data show that even a lexicalized verb sign derived from a classifier predicate may resume this morpho-syntactic property and behave like a classifier predicate in a natural signing stream.

Besides the typical classifier predicates reported above, there are other simultaneous constructions in HKSL that involve a classifier on the non-dominant hand and a distinct lexical sign articulated by the dominant hand. Our data show that there is a syntactic relation between the classifier and the lexical sign. The classifier may be a complement of the lexical verb sign, as in example (2), or a complement of the determiner realized by the index sign, as in example (3). These examples show that a classifier morpheme is not restricted in terms of occurrence to classifier predicates, but may also impact on other grammatical relations in signed languages like HKSL. To what extent this is a universal phenomenon is still subject to debate. The HKSL data show that classifier morphemes can be incorporated in some other constructions. Alternatively, the classifier can be retained over a long stretch of signing for discourse regulatory function as reported in the literature (Friedman 1975; Engberg-Pedersen 1993; Liddell 2003), as in example (4).[4]

---

4.   Liddell (2003) calls this classifier on the non-dominant hand a 'depicting buoy', which is sustained either briefly or over a long stretch of discourse as the other classifier predicates are produced.

(2)   The referee examined the injured person, dropped his flag and blew the whistle.

RH: IX-DET_i REFEREE COME LOOK-AT_j DROP-FLAG
LH: CL:LEGGED-PERSON_j   -
RH: BLOW-WHISTLE
LH: - - - - - - - - - -

LH: CL:LEGGED-PERSON_j - - - - -
RH: COME

LH: CL:LEGGED-PERSON_j - - - - - - - - -
RH: LOOK-AT_j

(3) A player kicked the leg of another player who then fell down. He was in pain.
RH: KICK-PERSON'S-LEG IX-DET$_i$ PAINFUL
LH: CL:PERSON(LEG)-HERE$_i$ CL:PERSON-FALL-DOWN -----------

LH: CL:PERSON(LEG)-HERE$_i$
RH: KICK-PERSON'S-LEG

RH: KICK-PERSON'S-LEG-----------------
LH: CL:PERSON-FALL-DOWN

LH:CL:PERSON-FALL-DOWN-----
RH: IX-det$_i$

LH:CL:PERSON-FALL-DOWN-------
RH: PAINFUL

(4)   The plane flew (in the sky). Many birds flew together with the plane.
      RH: CL:PLANE-FLY -
      LH: HAVE MANY BIRD CL:MANY-BIRDS-FLY-BY

Miller (1994a) argues that simultaneous constructions involving classifiers are accessible to syntax due to the principle of compositionality at the morphological level. We argue that it is this linguistic principle of compositionality in classifier predicates that leads to the many instances of simultaneous constructions cited above. The classifier morpheme is accessible to syntax as an argument in the predicate. As an argument, the morpheme is grammatically a complement in many syntactic structures. For example, Benedicto & Brentari (2004) argue that classifier morphemes are associated with different types of arguments on the grounds of their grammatical behaviours in both transitive and intransitive predicates. Hence, it is understandable why certain simultaneous constructions may potentially violate the symmetry or dominance conditions put forward by Battison (1978) to account for the ASL lexicon. In our observations in HKSL, the grammar may require that the articulators encode different predicates subsumed under the same event in one complex sign, as in examples (5)–(7).[5]

(5) (The man) was drinking while driving.
  RH: CL:DRINK - - - - - - - - - -
  LH: CL:DRIVE - - - - - - - - - -

RH: CL: DRINK – – – – – – – – – – – –
LH: CL: DRIVE – – – – – – – – – – – –

---

5. This argument by no means implies that classifier constructions do not conform to the two phonological conditions of two-handed signs. On the contrary, they usually do but may violate them when the grammar of predication requires that the two articulators encode meaning differently (cf. Supalla 1982). We predict that conjoined or temporal embedding of clauses are sites for such potential 'violations'.

(6)   (The plane and the birds) flew alongside each other.
      RH: CL:PLANE-FLY - - - - - - - - - -
      LH: CL:BIRDS-FLY - - - - - - - - - -

RH: CL:PLANE-FLY – – – – – – – – – – –
LH: CL:BIRDS-FLY – – – – – – – – – – –

(7)   The football player carried the stretcher away with his own leg on it.
      RH: CL:PERSON-MOVE-FORWARD$_i$ -
      LH: CL:PERSON$_j$-WITH-LEG-ON-STRETCHER-MOVE-BEHIND-(PERSON)$_i$

RH: CL:PERSON-MOVE-FORWARD$_i$ –
LH: CL:PERSON$_j$-WITH-LEG-ON-STRETCHER-MOVE-BEHIND-(PERSON)$_i$ – – – – –

Examples (5)–(7) are not typical classifier predicate constructions but they do occur in signed discourse. Example (5) involves two conjoined predicates over a single argument while (6) and (7) involve a single predicate over two conjoined arguments. These data would be hard to explain if we did not resort to morphological compositionality in classifier predicate constructions.

3.   Implications for signed language acquisition

3.1   Classifier predicates: Previous acquisition findings

Despite the fact that classifier predicates are iconic in their representation, full mastery of this grammatical domain can be as late as age 8–9 (Schick 1990; Slobin et al. 2003). Earlier studies of ASL acquisition showed that different components of the predicates were not acquired in a holistic and analogue fashion; rather, they showed different developmental sequences, and errors of handshape, movement and location were found in the acquisition process (Kantor 1980; Supalla 1982; Newport 1981; Newport & Meier 1985). In Schick's (1990) study, the developmental sequence of American Sign Language classifiers is semantic > SASS (size and shape specifier) > handle.[6] However, in terms of the development of different predicate types, predicates with handle classifiers encoding locative transfer of a direct object in space occurred developmentally earlier than those predicates involving semantic classifiers, and SASSs were most difficult because they required an accurate depiction of spatial configuration of entities through different handshape configurations. A recent study by Slobin et al. (2003) reports that knowledge of morphological handshapes may emerge as early as age 2–3. They also observe that deaf children learn how to 'pare down' gestures adopted in adult signing and incorporate them into their interim grammars. However, coordinating the two articulators to represent predicate relations between entities in space is developmentally late because it entails a concomitant development of movement and location morphemes. Also, full mastery of classifiers for ground is later than that of figure and errors include omission of handshapes or adoption of inappropriate ones, as well as inconsistent assignment of ground to locations in space. In classifier predicates, ground is usually represented by the non-dominant hand (Tang 2003), to which we shall now turn.

3.2   The non-dominant hand in the acquisition of classifier constructions

A canonical mapping in HKSL, possibly in other signed languages too, is that the dominant hand encodes figure while the non-dominant hand encodes ground. Thematically, figure encodes agent, causer or theme arguments. Ground is associated with location in locative predicates, source and goal in motion predicates, as well as affected theme in transitive causative predicates (Tang & Gu in press). Hence, the non-dominant hand is crucial because it is fundamental to the devel-

---

6.   She argues that handle classifiers are more complex compared with semantic classifiers because deaf children have to learn to manipulate the hand internal configuration to reflect the size and shape of the direct object being manipulated.

opment of some relatively more complex predicates like the transitive causative predicates. CL:PERSON-WALK requires a theme argument and is a morphologically less complex structure than CL:PERSON-WALK-INTO-AN-ENCLOSURE because the latter involves ground configured in space to express a relation (i.e. WALK-INTO) between a theme and a location argument. In terms of signed language acquisition, deaf children need to develop knowledge that specific thematic information is assigned to the two articulators independently. Also, the learners need to develop knowledge that the dominant hand that bears the movement component encodes the root of the predicate while the non-dominant hand is responsible for other linguistic information required for predication, as in example (8):

(8)   A person dived from the boat.

> RH: CL:PERSON-DIVE-FROM
> LH: CL:BOAT - - - - - - - - - - - - - -

BH: CL:BOAT

RH: CL:PERSON-DIVE-FROM
LH: CL:BOAT - - - - - - - - - - - - - - -.

In example (8), the verb DIVE requires an agentive argument and selects a prepositional phrase (PP) with a Noun Phrase (NP) complement (i.e. cl:BOAT). Where the non-dominant hand consistently presents the conceptual ground, we might see this as constituting positive evidence for acquiring the morphology of this construction. Without the non-dominant hand, grammatical constituents like PP or NP as direct object would be hard to realize overtly in classifier constructions.

3.3 Triggering experiences in language acquisition

It is generally assumed in the language acquisition literature that positive evidence to children provides triggering experiences in the acquisition of a target structure (Crain & Lillo-Martin 1999). Triggers are defined as robust linguistic data inducing a language learner to reformulate her hypothesis about the structure she is acquiring, which allows her to revise her current hypotheses in the course of language development (Lightfoot 1991). In the English language child data, it has been claimed that the child's development of functional categories triggers a corresponding development from a stage of null subject to overt subject in finite sentences (Valian 1990; Hyams 1986, 1996).

By the same token, one may ask what triggers deaf children to realize that classifier predicates are morphologically compositional, given the assumption that their previous acquisition experiences probably involve development of conventional lexical items articulated sequentially. One plausible trigger is the development of verb agreement where the direction of movement of the articulator marks person and number agreement (Padden 1988; Meir 1998). Lillo-Martin (1999) argues that linguistic development of verb agreement morphology is independent of the development of spatial memory (i.e. associating non-present referents with locations in space). Her data show that development of verb agreement may be as early as age 3 or 3;6, but representing this knowledge in signing space is not fully mastered until age 5.

Classifier predicates are more intriguing because, in addition to a conceptual use of space for grammatical representation (i.e. surrogate and token space in Liddell's (1994, 1995) sense of the word), a reanalysis of the sub-lexical handshape and movement components into a set of meaningful, morphemic units is also required. How do deaf children come to such a state of knowledge? Surely native deaf signers have knowledge of these complex structures, and access that knowledge in sign articulation. At some stage of signed language development, deaf children need to learn that handshape is morphological in some constructions, and can be 'stacked up' simultaneously with the movement and location morphemes. We argue that developing knowledge of the morphological properties of classifiers helps children realize that classifier predicates are compositional. Second, use of the non-dominant hand is a crucial determinant for developing other types of simultaneous constructions that incorporate classifiers. Hence, developing knowledge of the morphological composition of classifier predicates enables deaf children to 'extract' the classifier from the predicates for some other simultaneous constructions. Therefore, we predict that simultaneous constructions involving a combination of a classifier and a lexical sign are acquired later developmentally than typical classifier predicates.

3.4 Research questions

On the basis of the acquisition issues discussed above, we put forward the following research questions:

1. What is the developmental sequence of the different types of simultaneous constructions? We predict that predicates involving one argument are acquired earlier than those involving two because predicates involving two arguments reflect a higher degree of morphological complexity, requiring a more elaborate form of spatial configuration by the two articulators.[7]
2. What is the developmental sequence of classifiers in HKSL? Given sufficient positive evidence, deaf children will realize that certain handshapes are associated with noun categories and are reflective of the thematic roles of the arguments in the predicate.
3. What types of errors would occur when learners are developing classifier predicates in HKSL? Do they produce a similar set of errors such as handshape, movement and location as reported in the literature for ASL? (Slobin et al. 2003; Schick 1990; Supalla 1982)
4. What is the role of the non-dominant hand in the acquisition of simultaneous constructions?

4. The present study

4.1 Subjects

Fourteen deaf children ranging in age from six to thirteen were invited to participate in the study. They were students of a deaf day school with hearing abilities ranging from moderately severe to profound hearing loss. With one exception, all the children were born to hearing parents and did not develop a signed language until they joined the deaf school. This happened at different ages for each of them. Table 1 shows the background of the subjects.

The students were categorised on the basis of their HKSL proficiency into one of three groups. They were assessed by two native signers who were instructed

---

7. A reviewer suggests that this research question may also be related to the development of transitivity with verbs and arguments. While agreeing that there is a very close relation between categories of classifier constructions and transitivity, we would like to leave this topic to a separate discussion on how deaf children acquire verb structure in HKSL.

Table 1. Age and background of the subjects

Subject Codes	Age	Years of exposure to HKSL	Averaged score	Levels of proficiency
001	10	5	1.1	Level 1
002	8	1	1.3	Level 1
003	11	3	1.4	Level 1
004	8	3	1.4	Level 1
005	9	5	1.9	Level 2
006	9	2	2.1	Level 2
007	12	8	2.2	Level 2
008	9	5	2.4	Level 2
009	12	4	2.5	Level 2
010	6	2	3.2	Level 3
011	11	4	3.4	Level 3
012	9	2	3.4	Level 3
013	13	4	3.6	Level 3
014	13	Since birth	4.1	Level 3

to judge the subjects' general performance on a production task that involved a retelling of a story from a comic strip along a scale from 0–5.[8] The native signers were not told the aims of the study but were encouraged to give their judgment of the degree of native signing and clarity of content demonstrated by the deaf child subjects. The scores awarded were then averaged out for each student, and on the basis of this score, each subject was allocated to one of the three categories of proficiency.

4.2 Methodology

The subjects were invited to narrate six comic strip stories. Each story had no more than four pictures to ensure a clear and straightforward story line. They were instructed to study the comic strips one by one and to narrate them to a deaf research assistant. Two native deaf signers were invited to narrate the same set of comic strips to provide baseline data for comparison. All video recordings were

---

8. Assessing HKSL proficiency in signing was adopted because these children entered the deaf school at different ages, hence different years of exposure to the target language. In addition, in Hong Kong, years of exposure shows no direct relationship with signed language proficiency either because the school environment is not conducive to HKSL acquisition because it adopts an oral approach and students are discouraged from using HKSL in the classroom, not to mention that some parents prohibit signing at home. A reviewer suggested that the results of the current study could be hampered by the failure to control for either age or years of exposure to HKSL. While it may be the case, the use of proficiency assessment in HKSL with guidelines given to the native deaf signers at least provides some objective measures for categorizing the subjects proficiency at different levels.

later transcribed using ELAN, a software package developed by Max Planck Institute of Psycholinguistics, Nijmegen. The coding of the data adopted the following criteria:

a. Types of simultaneous constructions
To address research question (1), which relates to the developmental sequence of different types of simultaneous constructions, where we predict that predicates involving one argument are acquired earlier than those involving two due to their higher degree of morphological complexity, we coded the simultaneous constructions into five categories:

1. S1: Classifier predicates that involved one classifier. They included intransitive motion predicates usually with semantic classifiers or transitive predicates with handle classifiers. Use of the dominant hand was expected and the non-dominant hand was not required. Examples such as CL:PLANE-FLY, CL:PERSON-WALK-AROUND, CL:HOLD-UMBRELLA, CL:PLACE-HAT-ON-NEST.

2. S2: Classifier predicates that involved two classifiers to encode the spatial configuration of the entities. They included both intransitive motion predicates and locative predicates. Examples such as:
   – Motion – CL:CAR-FALL-FROM-HILL, CL:BIRD-ENTER-PLACE
   – Locative – CL:PANEL-ON-PLANE, CL:HANDLE-HOOKED-ON-NEST

3. S3: Simultaneous constructions that used a classifier as a discourse 'buoy' (Liddell 2003) while articulating some other distinct lexical signs on the dominant hand. Example (4) cited above belongs to this category.

4. S4: Simultaneous constructions that combined a classifier with some distinct lexical signs to form a grammatical constituent. Examples are locative existentials: CL:NEST // HAVE BIRD ('The nest has birds in it'); or verb phrases: SEE$_i$ // CL:ROCK$_i$ ('saw the rocks'), LOOK-AT$_i$ // CL:LEGGED-PERSON$_i$ ('looked at the person')

5. S5: Classifier predicates that involved two conjoined predicates of the same event, comprising either one or two arguments. Examples are: CL:DRINK-AND-DRIVE-AT-THE-SAME-TIME, CL:BIRDS-AND-PLANE-FLY-ALONGSIDE-EACH-OTHER, CL:PERSON-WITH-LEG-ON-STRETCHER-MOVE-BEHIND-ANOTHER-PERSON

b. Types of classifiers
To address research question (2), regarding identifying the developmental sequence of classifiers in HKSL, we focused on the three types of classifiers reported in the acquisition literature: (a) semantic classifiers for animate objects such as humans and birds; (b) handle classifiers for humans and objects and (c) SASS for inanimate objects.

c. Types of errors observed in S2s

To address research question (3), which asked what types of errors would occur when learners are developing classifier predicates in HKSL, we focused on the learners' development of the morphological properties of S2, namely, classifier predicates that involved two classifiers to encode the spatial configuration of the entities, including both intransitive motion predicates and locative predicates. We isolated S2 type constructions in our analysis because they involved a combination of figure and ground, which allowed us to compare our results with those of the previous analysis. We examined the types of errors produced by the learners at all levels.

d. Development of use of the non-dominant hand in simultaneous constructions

To address research question (4), which asks what role the non-dominant hand plays in the acquisition of simultaneous constructions, we examined the learners' performance on the dominant and non-dominant hands by comparing the errors they produced in S2 (i.e. classifier predicates involving two classifiers to encode the spatial configuration of entities). We also analyzed the frequency of retention of the non-dominant classifier in subsequent signing. We coded the occurrence of the classifier handshape on the non-dominant hand according to whether it was sustained while the other signs were produced. We predicted that the number and types of simultaneous constructions increased as a function of the learners' development of retaining the non-dominant hand in subsequent signing.

5. Results

5.1 Production of simultaneous constructions

Figure 1 shows the average number of simultaneous constructions produced by the two adult native signers and the learners based on the six comic strips in our analysis. The adult data show a high occurrence of S1 (classifier predicates that involved one classifier), S2 (classifier predicates that involved two classifiers to encode the spatial configuration of the entities, including both intransitive motion predicates and locative predicates) and S3 (simultaneous constructions that used a classifier as a discourse 'buoy'), some S4 (simultaneous constructions that combined a classifier with some distinct lexical signs to form a grammatical constituent) but few S5 (classifier predicates that involved two conjoined predicates of the same event, comprising either one or two arguments).

S1 and S2 represent typical classifier predicates with varying degrees of morphological complexity, i.e. one argument as against two argument predicate types. That a classifier serving as a 'discourse buoy' (Liddell 2003 for ASL) in a narrative

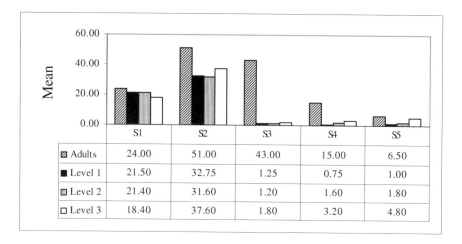

	S1	S2	S3	S4	S5
Adults	24.00	51.00	43.00	15.00	6.50
Level 1	21.50	32.75	1.25	0.75	1.00
Level 2	21.40	31.60	1.20	1.60	1.80
Level 3	18.40	37.60	1.80	3.20	4.80

Figure 1. Simultaneous constructions produced by adults and learners

discourse features prominently in the adult data (i.e. S3) shows that using a classifier to sustain a prolonged narrative discourse is characteristic of adult signing in HKSL. This finding is in line with Morgan & Woll's (2003) analysis of British Sign Language in which they also report a significant proportion of body/semantic classifiers (i.e. around 30%) for reference maintenance in discourse. There are some instances of S4 that use a classifier and a lexical sign to form a single grammatical constituent. The low distribution of S5 that involves two simultaneous events in one classifier predicate sign may be due to task specific reasons.[9]

On the other hand, the average number of S3, S4 and S5 produced by the learners is significantly lower than that produced by the native signers, suggesting that these three types of constructions could be acquired at a developmentally later stage. In fact, retaining a classifier for subsequent simultaneous constructions as demonstrated by S3 and S4 proved remarkably difficult for the learners.

Figure 2 shows the percentages of target production produced by the subjects at each level, based on the tokens observed in Figure 1.

S1 generally receives a higher score because of the relatively simple morphosyntactic structure (i.e. one-place predicate). Although the target production rate for categories S3, S4 and S5 can be as high as between 60%–80% in some cases, note that the actual number of production tokens is extremely low, some as low as 1 to 1.8 tokens on average (cf. Figure 1). One reason why the percentage score of S5 is quite high for all three levels is that the score comprises mainly the classifier predicate, CL:DRINK-AND-DRIVE-AT-THE-SAME-TIME, which involves two handle

---

9. The comic strips did not elicit many classifier predicates that involve two simultaneous events as described in S5.

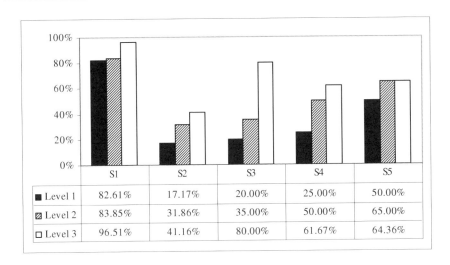

Figure 2. Learners' target performance of simultaneous constructions

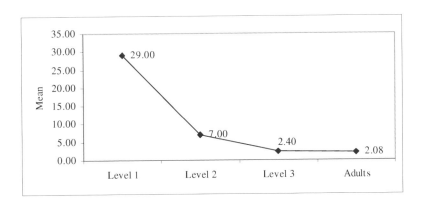

Figure 3. Use of gesture

classifiers and a depictive movement of gestural origin, thus explaining its early mastery by the learners. If tokens of this classifier predicate were removed from the set, the average percentage of target S5 produced by the learners as shown in Figure 2 would be reduced drastically to 25%, 33.33% and 29.33% for Level 1, 2, and 3 respectively.

Figure 3 shows that the average tokens of gesture are highest among Level 1 learners who had limited knowledge of lexical signs. While the adults gestured within signing space, on most occasions, our subjects' gestures extended beyond the signing space (e.g. a subject lay on the floor to stand for CL:PERSON-SLEEP-ON-BED). This echoes Slobin et al.'s (2003) argument that gestures are default production strategies used by learners at the initial stage of signed language acquisition. In the current elicitation, these gestural productions were adopted to substitute the classifier predicates. In many of these instances, the learners assumed the role of figure and/or ground and some Level 1 learners even gestured the entire plot. More interestingly, using their body to represent ground, some learners also performed the action of figure on their own body (i.e. ground). This is typical of those learners who produced a predicate that involved a handle classifier to transfer an object to ground.[10] Nevertheless, as HKSL proficiency improved, these learners gradually replaced gestures with lexical signs or classifier predicates, albeit inaccurately.

5.2 Performance on classifiers

Figure 4 shows the averaged tokens of classifiers produced by the adult signers and the deaf learners. Occurrences of SASS are highest in the adult data, followed by semantic classifiers, while handle classifiers are lowest.

Figure 4 shows that the production of handle classifiers is similar across the three levels of proficiency. The production of SASS is the lowest but increases as proficiency improves. The production of semantic classifiers is highest in terms of frequencies of occurrence but Level 1 and Level 2 learners show no obvious increase in production. Compared with the adult signers, the deaf learners across

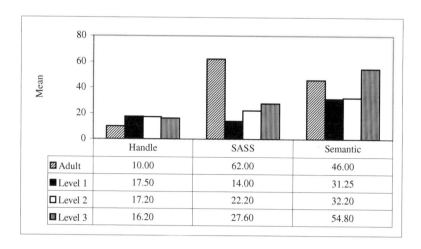

	Handle	SASS	Semantic
▨ Adult	10.00	62.00	46.00
■ Level 1	17.50	14.00	31.25
□ Level 2	17.20	22.20	32.20
▥ Level 3	16.20	27.60	54.80

Figure 4. Production of classifier types

10.   One reviewer queried whether gesture was just an alternative strategy of these learners while they might have already acquired the grammatical knowledge of classifier predicates. This possibility of performance error can be ruled out because most of these learners were observed to gesture the entire plot quite consistently and did not display any systematic articulation of other lexical signs in the study.

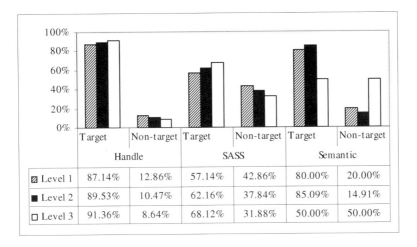

	Target	Non-target	Target	Non-target	Target	Non-target
	Handle		SASS		Semantic	
▨ Level 1	87.14%	12.86%	57.14%	42.86%	80.00%	20.00%
■ Level 2	89.53%	10.47%	62.16%	37.84%	85.09%	14.91%
□ Level 3	91.36%	8.64%	68.12%	31.88%	50.00%	50.00%

Figure 5. Performance on classifier types

all three levels produced relatively fewer SASSes. In addition, given the fact that our narratives typically represent ground with SASSes, and figure with semantic classifiers, the low production rate of SASSes among the learners at all three levels suggests that this category of classifiers poses learning difficulty. This may be due to the initial difficulty in developing ground for S2, or in acquiring the various features for SASSes to encode the objects' size and shape, as well as dimensionality.

Figure 5 shows the percentage scores of the target classifiers recorded in each category. Overall, there is more target formation with handle classifiers, implying that they pose little difficulty to the learners. Note that all handle classifiers elicited in this study involve a gestural depiction of holding an object through the use of S-handshape, G-handshape, and open-5-handshape. Slobin et al. (2003) make a similar observation for American Sign Language and Sign Language of the Netherlands, and they ascribe it to the gestural advantage in signed language acquisition. On the contrary, against the backdrop that the production of SASSes among the HKSL learners is low (cf. Figure 4), the much higher rate of non-target formation suggests that SASSes are relatively more difficult to develop than other classifier types. In sum, based on the data recorded, the developmental sequence of HKSL classifier thus observed is handle > semantic > SASS.

At first glance, this finding differs from what Schick (1990) reported for her deaf subjects acquiring ASL. In her study, the developmental sequence thus established was semantic > SASS > handle. However, Schick's study focused on those handle classifiers that incorporated a transfer movement path, which she referred to as 'locative transfer'. In our study, only a subset of the handle classifiers produced by the deaf learners involves such spatial displacement; this explains why

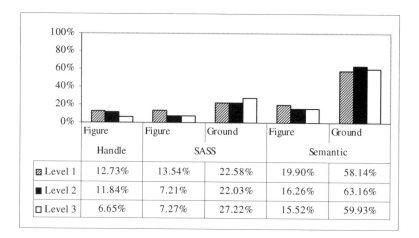

	Figure	Figure	Ground	Figure	Ground
	Handle	SASS		Semantic	
▨ Level 1	12.73%	13.54%	22.58%	19.90%	58.14%
■ Level 2	11.84%	7.21%	22.03%	16.26%	63.16%
□ Level 3	6.65%	7.27%	27.22%	15.52%	59.93%

Figure 6. Errors of classifier handshapes for figure and ground

our finding is not compatible with that of Schick (1990). We will come back to this issue in the discussion section below.

Figure 6 shows that there are more errors associating with ground than figure for SASSes and semantic classifiers, suggesting that developing the use of the non-dominant hand to encode ground in classifier predicates poses difficulty to the learners. This finding accords with our expectation that the development of simultaneous constructions rests upon the learners' knowledge of encoding ground with the non-dominant hand. In the next section, we will focus on a description of the errors produced by the learners with respect to the dominant and non-dominant hands in S2 constructions (i.e. classifier predicates with two arguments to encode figure and ground).

5.3 Morphological development of dominant and non-dominant hands in S2 constructions

S2, which involves two arguments in the predicate, is usually realized as two-handed signs in HKSL. Generally speaking, the learners' performance in encoding figure with the dominant hand is better than in encoding ground with the non-dominant hand, where more errors arise. Of the 477 tokens of S2 constructions in our data,[11] 125 and 198 errors were identified for figure and ground respectively.

---

11.   The number of errors here includes those S2 that were actually produced by learners during the process of elicitation. Apart from these instances, however, learners sometimes adopted a range of simplification strategies in places where an S2 or S5 was normally expected. These include the use of gestures, role shift, locative pointing, lexical signs or the sequential production of series of S1 or lexical signs in place of a more complex S2 or S5.

Table 2. Error production on dominant and non-dominant hands

Levels of Proficiency	# of S2 produced	Errors of dominant hand as figure	Errors of non-dominant hand as ground
Level 1	131	26.0% (34/131)	43.5% (57/131)
Level 2	158	15.8% (25/158)	57.0% (90/158)
Level 3	188	35.1% (66/188)	27.1% (51/188)

For learners at Level 1 and Level 2, errors of ground outnumber those of figure significantly. For Level 3 learners, the error rate of figure is higher than that of ground. The decrease in errors of ground at Level 3 indicates an improved mastery of the non-dominant hand in simultaneous constructions. Note that due to an increase in the number of attempts made by learners at Level 3 to produce S2, we observed more errors for figure at this level because these learners failed to configure figure and ground in space to express the underlying conceptual relationship between the entities morphologically.

Figure 7 below provides a summary of the error types recorded in the learners' production grouped between the dominant hand (dh) and the non-dominant hand (ndh). The percentages are based on the total number of errors produced by the three groups of learners. The results show that most of them are orientation errors of the dominant hand against the non-dominant hand (i.e. dh of E-O), in line with our expectation. Interestingly, there are few errors of location and movement, which suggests that the learners have already developed the concept of using space to assign loci to the referents by the time they develop classifier predicates.

Among the types of errors recorded for all three levels, most errors involve an absence of ground (i.e. E-ABSe) in an obligatory S2 context.[12] This error constitutes a major proportion of all the errors produced and is most noticeable at Level 1 and 2. Although there is improvement at Level 3, the proportion of errors remains highest of all non-dominant hand errors at this level. In (9), for instance, the ground classifier for 'canopy of a tree' (i.e. goal argument) is absent in the predicate, which adult native intuition judged as ungrammatical.

(9)   A car plunged down (the cliff into a tree canopy)
        *CAR CL:CAR-PLUNGE-DOWN

This result suggests that the non-dominant hand for encoding a ground object emerges at a later stage of the acquisition process. Interestingly, absence of figure does not surface in our data.

When the learners managed to realize ground overtly, they generated numerous instances of inappropriate handshapes (i.e. E-H), both for figure and ground. Preliminary observation suggests that before an accurate SASS for ground was

---

12.   Adult signers were recruited to judge if the absence of ground constituted an error.

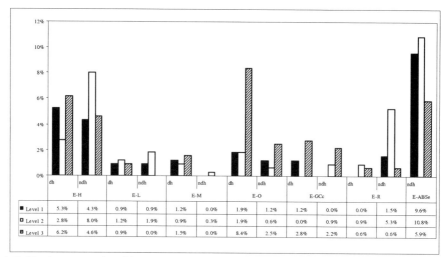

* E-H =inaccurate handshape; E-L=inaccurate location; E-M=inaccurate movement; E-O=inaccurate spatial orientation; E-GCc=use of a lexical handshape as classifier; E-R=reduction of multiple figures or grounds to one only; E-ABSe=absence of a ground object

Figure 7. Types of error in S2

adopted, tracing with a 1-handshape as a production strategy was common at Level 1. This is understandable, as tracing is gestural in nature and resorting to gesture is always a default simplification strategy. Dimensionality also appears to be a factor determining the development of SASSes. It seems that a two-dimensional flat surface to refer to the wingspan of an airplane or a road is relatively easier than a three-dimensional round object such as 'canopy of a tree', or 'boulders in a river'. To refer to three-dimensional objects, learners at Level 1 and Level 2 used a B-handshape or a relaxed spread-5 that are usually reserved for two-dimensional objects.

Another major source of handshape errors came from the semantic classifiers. While the learners were able to identify a Y-handshape for human entities at an early stage of development, they failed to extend it to the category of birds; instead, unmarked handshapes like S-handshape or O-handshape were adopted. Alternatively, some learners simply adopted the handshape of the corresponding lexical antecedent as classifiers. Examples are observed in using the handshape of TREE for cl:CANOPY and that of BIRD for cl:ANIMATE-ENTITY, as shown in example (10):

(10) (Some) birds were located under the panel. The plane then flew away.
      LH: CL:PANEL - - - - - - - - - - - - - - - CL:PLANE-FLY-AWAY
    *RH: CL:BIRDS-BE-LOCATED

Spatial orientation errors (i.e. E-O) refer to either an erroneous orientation of an independent classifier for figure or erroneous spatial configuration of figure and ground. In fact, this type of error is more prominent for figure than ground. This pattern is expected, as figure generally exhibits more variation in spatial orientation than ground in classifier predicates when encoding information such as manner of location or spatial configuration. In example (11), a Level 3 learner was describing a picture in which several birds landed under the wingspan of an airplane. He mistakenly placed the classifier representing the birds on top of the classifier representing the wingspan of the plane rather than under them:

(11)   An array of birds entered the plane and landed under the wingspan.
    *LH: PLANE -
    *RH: AN-ARRAY-OF-BIRDS-BE-LOCATED

As reported in Tang (2003), semantic classifiers for animate entities in HKSL can be further decomposed into smaller meaningful manner components through different palm orientations. As such, they pose a great challenge to learners and this language-specific reason accounts for a high occurrence of errors. Moreover, the data show that errors involving spatial orientation are an advanced error as it is more prominent among learners at Level 3. This also seems to apply to the spatial orientation between the dominant and non-dominant hand.

Another common error observed in our data is the reduction of multiple classifier predicates to a single construction in contexts where a series of identical classifier predicates are required to express the predication such as CL:PERSON-MOVE-FROM-ONE-BOULDER-TO-ANOTHER.

Our observation is that multiple classifier predicates obligatorily involving ground are more prone to this process of simplification than multiple figures, as shown in example (12):

(12)   A man stood there. He jumped from one boulder to another.
    *LH: CL:PERSON-STAND CL:ROUND-OBJECT - - - - - - - - - -
    *RH: HAVE   CL:PERSON-WALK
    *LH: - - - - - - - - - -
    *RH: CL:PERSON-FALL

In sum, learners across all levels produced more errors for ground than for figure. Nonetheless, the error types associated with ground and figure differ in a number of respects, reflecting the different grammatical functions of figure and ground in the predication. Figure, especially when encoded by semantic classifiers, allows a much wider range of spatial and orientation possibilities than ground, and this leads to a higher occurrence of orientation errors associated with the dominant hand. Nevertheless, while absence of ground is prevalent in the data, especially at Level 1 and 2, absence of figure is not observed. This may be attributable to the conceptually more prominent role of figure in a motion event (cf. Talmy 2000) and semantically, it assumes the role of agent or theme in the predication, thus making omission impossible.

Despite the fact that ground is conceptually less salient to the learners, as it typically encodes source, goal, or location, it still contributes to grammatical information essential to the well-formedness condition of predication. The priority of figure over ground in the acquisition timetable inevitably highlights the role of the dominant hand in the process towards acquiring adult-like competence in the production of simultaneous constructions.

5.4 The non-dominant hand in the acquisition process

In this analysis, we examined the extent to which the learners had developed the knowledge that associated the non-dominant hand with classifiers. We argue that such knowledge has the potential to support the development of the different types of simultaneous constructions identified in the current study.

In order to examine this issue, we attempted to adopt a coding system where classifiers occurring on the non-dominant hand were coded according to whether they supported one (i.e. –continuous) or more signs (i.e. +continuous). When a classifier construction was coded as [–continuous], the classifier was observed not to be retained in subsequent signing. We further divided this group of [–continuous] classifier constructions into two subgroups, depending on whether or not there was a lexical antecedent referring to a referent in the discourse context (i.e. [±referent]). Classifier constructions having an antecedent were coded as [+referent], otherwise [–referent]. Example (13) contains no referent for the classifier, and is a typical learner error:

(13)   The ducks entered (the airplane) and landed under (the wings).
    RH: BIRD
    *BH: (CL:PANEL)   CL:BIRD-LANDED-UNDER-WINGS(OF-PLANE)

In example (13), neither a lexical sign for AIRPLANE nor a classifier cl:PANEL (flat object) was introduced into the discourse to support the motion predicate CL:BIRD-LANDED-UNDER-WINGS(OF-PLANE).[13] Only the lexical sign BIRD, but not AIRPLANE, was mentioned in the preceding discourse. Hence, the figure classifier

---

13.   This phenomenon also occurs with the classifier for figure. However, in the current analysis, we only focus on the classifier on the non-dominant hand that was being retained in the subsequent signing stream.

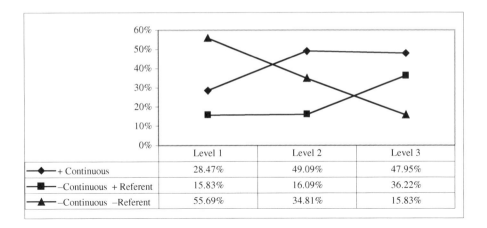

	Level 1	Level 2	Level 3
+ Continuous	28.47%	49.09%	47.95%
–Continuous + Referent	15.83%	16.09%	36.22%
–Continuous –Referent	55.69%	34.81%	15.83%

Figure 8. Use of non-dominant hand in simultaneous constructions

for BIRD was marked as [+referent], whereas the ground classifier for PANEL is [–referent].[14]

Figure 8 presents the frequency of incorporating the non-dominant hand in the simultaneous constructions produced by the learners. The percentage scores were generated by dividing the total number of tokens produced that involved the non-dominant hand in each of the three identified categories within each subject. As shown, the use of [+continuous] classifiers increased steadily from Level 1 to Level 2, which suggests an incrementally increasing ability on the part of the learners to retain a classifier in space in a narrative discourse. However, there is little difference in performance between Level 2 and Level 3. Given findings that there are very few S3, S4 and S5 produced by the learners (i.e. Figure 1), this result means that most of the retained classifiers are used to support the production of S2, which requires a figure-ground configuration.

[–continuous] classifiers are also common in the data, that is, classifiers that only occur once and are seldom retained in the subsequent signing stream. As mentioned earlier, this category is also analyzed in terms of whether the learners also bind the classifier to a proper antecedent. The results show that the learners show an increasing knowledge of introducing an antecedent in the discourse (i.e. [–continuous +referent] before associating it with a classifier; as such, the percentages for [–continuous –referent] decrease as a function of increasing proficiency. In sum, the improvement in sustaining the non-dominant hand in a narrative discourse suggests that the learners are gradually acquiring the knowledge

---

14. Referent identification was based on whether the lexical antecedent (a) immediately preceded the classifier predicate, or (b) appeared in the preceding discourse and was therefore recoverable.

that classifier constructions can be decomposable into meaningful morphological units, which can be 'sustained and stacked up' with some other morphological or syntactic units in the construction.

This improvement also shows that the learners are developing knowledge of the referential properties of classifiers, which are potentially [+definite] and [+referential] through a binding relation between the classifier and the antecedent. This semantic knowledge also enables the learners to develop classifier constructions in token space, as suggested by Liddell (1995).

6. Discussion

The findings reported above suggest that the acquisition of simultaneous constructions in HKSL is contingent upon whether the learners have developed knowledge that the handshape component is morphological, hence decomposable. This knowledge is crucial: without it learners have no way of knowing that they can treat the non-dominant hand as an independent morphological unit and incorporate it into the different types of simultaneous constructions identified in this study. Engberg-Pedersen (2003) cautions against an 'over-simplistic' assumption that learners are behaving like adults in embarking on the acquisition process with a well-developed knowledge of decomposition. She observes that producing lexicalized classifier predicates for FALL as a verb may form the first stage of the developmental sequence. Our data provides further support to her observation, namely that lexicalized classifier predicates that select a single argument may represent an intermediate stage towards the production of morpho-syntactic classifier predicates that encode two arguments (i.e. figure and ground).

In our data, a majority of the early adult-like S1 produced by Level 2 learners have corresponding lexicalized forms. Examples are verbs such as SWIM, JUMP, WALK, FOOTBALL (frozen legged classifiers), FALL, SIT, STAND, JUMP (frozen semantic classifiers for animate entities), CAR and AIRPLANE (frozen semantic classifiers for vehicles and planes). Interestingly, the lack of a lexicalized counterpart often made the Level 2 learners in our study resort to gesture.

We might then ask what causes the learners in our study to eventually reanalyze these 'conventionalized' verb signs into morphologically decomposable units? Although handle classifier predicates pose little difficulty initially, as reported in Slobin et al. (2003), we argue that they do not provide unique linguistic information about the morphological status of handshape; they are too ambiguous to act as triggers because linguistic and communicative gestures tend to blend to some extent. Note that while showing little difficulty in developing handle classifiers, Level 1 learners produced few other classifier types and replaced a lot of classifier predicates with gestures. This suggests that while gesture has the role of providing a 'latch' for developing classifier predicates, the handle classifiers, if combined with simple body actions, do not trigger formal grammatical reanalysis.

Instead, semantic classifiers are good candidates for triggering a reanalysis of the grammatical status of handshape at this initial stage of development. Emmorey & Herzig's (2003) study shows that location or depictive use of signing space is gradient while handshape for size and shape is categorical. Semantic classifiers are equally, if not more, categorical, and have the potential for uniquely associating generic classes such as humans, animals, vehicles and the like with specific hand-shapes. They can be ascribed with specific referential properties (i.e. +referential, +definite) as discussed in Tang & Sze (2002). These semantic properties would trigger a grammatical reanalysis of the classifier predicates, turning the handshape component from a purely phonological sub-unit to a morphophonemic sub-unit. Given this, we suggest that the handshape and orientation errors observed in S2 are output evidence of this linguistic process where the learners are consistently testing the hypotheses of mapping a particular handshape onto a noun category, or mapping a specific orientation onto a certain manner as a meaning component. Therefore, the reanalysis is semantically driven by the learners' perception of the morphemic status of classifiers, which can be triggered by the anaphoric nature of semantic classifiers because these handshape classifiers are consistently bound to an antecedent in the signing discourse.

As argued, the acquisition of morphological decomposition in classifier pred-icates has implications for the development of incorporating the non-dominant hand in other simultaneous constructions. Hence, another triggering experience may be obtained from reanalyzing the classifier on the non-dominant hand in S2 because it satisfies some grammatical relations (e.g. a complement of the main verb) in those constructions. Conservatism as a learning principle also shows that these learners initially refrained from extending the knowledge of morphological decomposition to the non-dominant hand to encode grammatical relations as well as discourse functions, as demonstrated in their performance in S3–S5. S2 seems to provide the 'window of opportunity' in the acquisition of simultaneous con-structions, resulting in a high concentration of developmental errors. Therefore, the acquisition of ground encoded by the non-dominant hand in S2 may serve as a precursor for developing other functions in other more complicated simultaneous constructions like S3, S4, and S5 (cf. Section 3.2).

Another possible explanation rests upon our assumption that simultaneity is a processing principle rather than a linguistic principle in signed language gram-mar. Conceptually speaking, these learners had already demonstrated knowledge of ground in their performance through production of certain lexical signs or ges-tures. Moreover, even at Level 1, they had displayed knowledge of how to configure objects in space for location even at Level 1, albeit through gesture or gesture su-perimposed with classifiers. The difficulty appears to be one of spatial mapping; in other words, processing linguistic information simultaneously in space. To couch the analysis in Liddell's (1994, 1995) discussion of mental spaces and signed languages, learners have to map different linguistic constructions onto the various types of mental spaces. Except for handle predicates that invoke surrogate space, classifier predicates generally invoke token space representations. Since initial acquisition adheres to the 'here-and-now-principle', we assume that deaf learners of a signed language will first adhere to real space. Handle classifiers are easy because they are associated with role shift and gesture in surrogate space. As acquisition of S2 involves learners' development of representing figure and ground relationships in token space, where, regardless of how depictive they may appear, the classifiers formally encode the referent as an argument in predication. In token space, classifiers for ground are necessary because they provide crucial thematic information about source, goal or location. When the learners' intermediate knowledge of morphological decomposition is developing, they may experience a heavy cognitive processing load in coordinating this linguistic information simultaneously through multiple channels (e.g. the two articulators, the body and space types). Therefore, economy of labour would stipulate that less prominent information encoded by ground tends to be ignored, if not simplified, or, in the initial stages, grappled with difficulty.

Therefore, we observed that some learners resorted to sequential production to bypass the difficulty in presenting a complex configuration of figure and ground. In fact, the learners from all three levels tended to adopt avoidance strategies, producing a series of simple S1 or lexical signs instead of a simultaneous construction. However, there are qualitative differences: Level 1 learners typically produced lexical signs and gestures in sequence in contexts where classifier predicates were called for. Level 2 and Level 3 learners chose to 'break up' S2 or S5 into series of S1 (i.e. figure only predicates) articulated at appropriate locations in space. For a classifier predicate glossed as CL:PUT-HAT-ON-BIRD'S-NEST which was articulated as a two-handed sign in token space by native adults, the learners would first produce a one-handed sign CL:BIRD'S-NEST-BE-LOCATED$_i$, followed by another one-handed sign, an S1 with a single handle classifier to refer to the figure, and lastly another one-handed sign CL:PUT-HAT-AT$_i$. These examples suggest that the learners were attempting to reduce the processing load by simplifying the sign from a two-handed sign to a series of one-handed signs and by assuming surrogate space in their production. In sum, the learners' progression from real/surrogate space to token space is evident by a decrease in gestures and a concomitant increase in developing classifier handshape as a morphological unit in a classifier predicate. This is in line with Zeshan's (2003) proposal that evolution from depictive gestures to conventional classifier predicates is a process of grammaticalisation. The data shows that gesture plays a pivotal role in the initial stages in the development of classifier predicates. Volterra & Iverson (1995) suggest that at the early stage of signed language development, the gestural modality provides a powerful resource for communication before the emergence of the first sign. In the HKSL data, gesture pervades the course of acquiring simultaneous constructions as a resource to support formal grammatical development. An example of transition from surrogate to token space is shown by signs that show that the learners attempted to combine gesture with a semantic classifier for figure. In one instance, a Level 2 learner gestured a fall but both his hands carried a semantic classifier typically used to encode cl:PERSON. We take this as evidence that the learner was gradually becoming aware of the semantic and morphological function of classifier handshapes.

7. Conclusion

The current study provides some preliminary findings concerning how deaf learners of HKSL developed various types of simultaneous constructions that involve classifiers. We have described the process of acquisition in terms of developmental sequence and triggering experiences and have identified the important role played by the semantic classifiers of HKSL in triggering grammatical reanalysis of the handshape component from a phonological unit to a morpho-syntactic unit. We have also made some preliminary observations that apart from gesture, deaf learners of HKSL may have recourse to lexicalized classifier predicates at the initial stage of acquisition. They may assume from the outset that predicate constructions are lexical in nature, resulting in many instances of seemingly accurate classifier predicates in the absence of an associated antecedent. A break from this incorrect hypothesis seems to come from their reanalysis of the handshape component of the classifier predicates, as in S2 of the adult input, which always occur in combination with other morphological handshapes. To conclude, what we have projected is a plausible working assumption, which awaits further analysis and verification in future research, particularly from cross-linguistic comparison with data from other signed languages.

Notation conventions

In this paper, HKSL signs are glossed in capital letters. Glosses are hyphenated when they combine to form one sign. The list below provides an explanation of the notation conventions adopted in the paper:

1st tier:	glosses in capital letter
2nd tier:	English translations
BH:	both hands
LH:	left hand
RH:	right hand
----	the hand articulator is sustained in space
CL:	classifier predicates
cl:	classifiers

References

Battison, Robbin. 1978. *Lexical Borrowing in American Sign Language*. Silver Spring, Md.: Linstok Press.

Benedicto, Elena & Diane Brentari. 2004. "Where did All the Arguments Go?: Argument-changing Properties of Classifiers in ASL". *Natural Language and Linguistic Theory* 22:4.743–810.

Carlson, Lauri. 1981. "Aspect and Quantification". *Syntax and Semantics Vol 14: Tense and Aspect* ed. by Philip Tedeschi & Annie Zaenen, 31–64. New York: Academic Press.

Crain, Stephen & Diane Lillo-Martin.1999. An Introduction to Linguistic Theory and Language Acquisition. Malden, Mass.: Blackwell Publishers.

DeMatteo, Asa. 1977. "Visual Imagery and Visual Analogues in American Sign Language". *On the Other Hand: New Perspectives on American Sign Language*. ed. by Lynn A. Friedman, 109–136. New York: Academic Press.

Emmorey, Karen. 2002. "The Effects of Modality on Spatial Language: How Signers and Speakers Talk About Space". *Modality and Structure in Sign and Spoken Languages* ed. by Richard P. Meier, Kearsy Cormier & David Quinto-Pozos, 405–421. Cambridge: Cambridge University Press.

——& Melissa Herzig. 2003. "Categorical Versus Gradient Properties of Classifier Predicates in ASL". *Perspectives on Classifier Constructions in Sign Languages* ed. by Karen Emmorey, 311–332. Mahwah, N.J./London: Lawrence Erlbaum Associates

Engberg-Pedersen, Elizabeth. 1993. *Space in Danish Sign Language: The Semantics and Morphosyntax of the Use of Space in a Visual Language*. Hamburg: Signum Press.

——. 2003. "How Composite Is a Fall? Adults' and Children's Descriptions of Different Types of Falls in Danish Sign Language". *Perspectives on Classifier Constructions in Sign Languages* ed. by Karen Emmorey, 311–332. Mahwah, N.J./London: Lawrence Erlbaum Associates

Friedman, Lynn. A. 1975. "Space, Time and Reference in American Sign Language". *Language* 51:4.941–961.

Hyams, Nina. 1986. *Language Acquisition and the Theory of Parameters*. Dordrecht: Reidel.

——. 1996. "The Under-Specification of Functional Categories in Early Grammar". *Generative Perspectives on Language Acquisition* ed. by Harold Clashen, 91–128. Amsterdam: John Benjamins.

Kantor, Rebecca. 1980. "The Acquisition of Classifiers in American Sign Language". *Sign Language Studies* 28.193–208.

Klima, Edward S. & Ursula Bellugi 1979. *The Signs of Language*. Cambridge, Mass.: Harvard University Press.

Lam, Wai-sze. 2003. *Verb agreement in Hong Kong Sign Language*. Unpublished MPhil Thesis, Chinese University of Hong Kong.

Liddell, Scott. 1994. "Tokens and Surrogates". *Perspectives on Sign Language Structure: Papers from the Fifth International Symposium on Sign Language Research Vol. 1* ed. by Inger Ahlgren, Brita Bergman & Mary Brennan, 105–119. Durham: ISLA.

——. 1995. "Real, Surrogate, and Token space: Grammatical Consequences in ASL". *Language, Gesture and Space* ed. by Karen Emmorey & Judy Reilly, 19–41. Hillsdale, N.J.: Lawrence Erlbaum Associates.

——. 2003. *Grammar, Gesture, and Meaning in American Sign Language*. Cambridge: Cambridge University Press.

—— & Robert E. Johnson. 1989. "American Sign Language: The Phonological Base". *Sign Language Studies* 64.197–277.

Lightfoot, David. 1991. *How to Set Parameters: Arguments from Language Change*. Cambridge, Mass.: The MIT Press.

Lillo-Martin, Diane. 1999. "Modality and Modularity in Language Acquisition: The Acquisition of American Sign Language". *Handbook of Child Language Acquisition* ed. by William C. Ritchie & Tej K. Bahtia, 531–567. San Diego, Calif.: Academic Press.

Meier, Richard. 2002. "Why Different, Why the Same? Explaining Effects and Non-Effects of Modality upon Linguistic Structure in Sign and Speech". *Modality and Structure in Sign and Spoken Languages* ed. by Richard P. Meier, Kearsy Cormier & David Quinto-Pozos, 1–26. Cambridge: Cambridge University Press.

Meir, Irit. 1998. *Thematic Structure and Verb Agreement in Israeli Sign Language*. Doctoral dissertation, Hebrew University of Jerusalem.

——. 2001. "Verb Classifiers as Noun Incorporation in Israeli Sign Language". *Yearbook of Morphology 1999* ed. by Geert Booij & Jaap van Marle, 299–319. Kluwer Academic Publishers.

——. 2002. "A Cross-Modality Perspective on Verb Agreement". *Natural Language & Linguistic Theory* 20.413–450.

Miller, Christopher, 1994. "Simultaneous Constructions in Quebec Sign Language". *Word Order Issues in Sign Languages* ed. by Mary Brennan & Graham H. Turner, 89–109. Durham: ISLA.

Morgan, Gary. 2002. "Children's Encoding of Simultaneity in British Sign Language Narratives". *Sign Language & Linguistics* 5:2.131–165.

—— & Bencie Woll. 2003. "The Development of Reference Switching Encoded Through Body Classifiers in British Sign Language". *Perspectives on Classifier Constructions in Sign Languages* ed. by Karen Emmorey, 297–310. Mahwah, N.J./London: Lawrence Erlbaum Associates

Newport, Elissa. 1981. "Constraints on Structure: Evidence from American Sign Language and Language Learning". *Aspects of the Development of Competence. Minnesota Symposium on Child Psychology, Vol. 14*, 93–124. Hillsdale, N.J.: Lawrence Erlbaum Associates.

——. 1982. "Take Specificity in Language Learning? Evidence from Speech Perception and American Sign Language". *Language Acquisition: The State of the Art* ed. by Eric Wanner & Lila R. Gleitman, 450–486. Cambridge: Cambridge University Press.

—— & Richard Meier. 1985. "The Acquisition of American Sign Language". *The Cross-linguistic Study of Language Acquisition. Vol. II, The Data* ed. by Dan Slobin, 881–938. Hillsdale, N.J.: Lawrence Erlbaum Associates.

Padden, Carol. 1988. *Interaction of Morphology and Syntax in American Sign Language*. New York: Garland Publishing.

Schembri, Adam. 2003. "Rethinking Classifiers". *Perspectives on Classifier Constructions in Sign Languages* ed. by Karen Emmorey, 3–34. Mahwah, N.J./London: Lawrence Erlbaum Associates.

Schick, Brenda. 1990. "Classifier Predicates in American Sign Language". *International Journal of Sign Linguistics* 1:1.15–40.

Slobin, Dan, Nini Hoiting, Marlon Kuntze, Reyna Lindert, Amy Weinberg, Jennie Pyers, Michelle Anthony, Yael Biederman, & Helen Thumann. 2003. "A Cognitive/Functional Perspective on the Acquisition of Classifiers". *Perspectives on Classifier Constructions in Sign Languages* ed. by Karen Emmorey, 271–296. Mahwah, N.J./London: Lawrence Erlbaum Associates.

Stokoe, William. 1960. *Sign Language Structure: An Outline of the Visual Communication Systems of the American Deaf (Studies in Linguistics, Occasional Papers 8).* Silver Spring, Md.: Linstok Press.

Supalla, Ted. 1982. *Structure and Acquisition of Verbs of Motion and Location in American Sign Language.* Doctoral dissertation, University of California, San Diego.

——. 1990. "Serial Verbs of Motion in ASL". *Theoretical Issues in Sign Language Research, Vol 1. Linguistics* ed. by Susan D. Fischer & Patricia Siple, 127–152. Chicago/London: The University of Chicago Press.

Talmy, Leonard. 2000. *Toward a Cognitive Semantics. Vol. I, Concept Structuring Systems.* Cambridge, Mass.: MIT Press.

Tang, Gladys. 2001. "Classifiers of Hong Kong Sign Language: A Semantic Universals Perspective". *12th North American Conference on Chinese Linguistics* ed. by Zheng-sheng Zhang, 187–207, San Diego State University, California.

——. 2003. "Verbs of Motion and Location in Hong Kong Sign Language". *Perspectives on Classifier Constructions in Sign Languages* ed. by Karen Emmorey, 143–165. Mahwah, N.J./London: Lawrence Erlbaum Associates.

—— & Felix Sze. 2002. "Nominal Expressions in Hong Kong Sign Language: Does Modality Make a Difference?". *Modality and Structure in Signed and Spoken Languages* ed. by Richard P. Meier, Kearsy Cormier & David Quinto-Pozos, 296–319. Cambridge, Mass.: Cambridge University Press

—— & Gu, Yang. In press. "Events of Motion and Causation in Hong Kong Sign Language". *Lingua.*

Valian, Virginia. 1990. "Syntactic Subjects in the Early Speech of American and Italian Children". *Cognition* 40.21–81.

Volterra, Virginia & Jana Iverson. 1995. "When do Modality Factors Affect the Course of Language Acquisition". *Language, Gesture and Space* ed. by Karen Emmorey & Judy S. Reilly, 371–390. Mahwah, N.J./London: Lawrence Erlbaum Associates.

Zeshan, Ulrike. 2003. "'Classificatory' Constructions in Indo-Pakistani Sign Language: Grammaticalization and Lexicalization Processes". *Perspectives on Classifier Constructions in Sign Languages* ed. by Karen Emmorey, 113–142. Mahwah, N.J./London: Lawrence Erlbaum Associates.

Simultaneity in atypical signers

Implications for the structure of signed language

Martha E. Tyrone
Haskins Laboratories

1. Introduction

Because signed languages employ the complex, coordinated movements of multiple articulators, and those articulators can be controlled independently of one another, it is possible for signers to produce separate streams of information simultaneously. The independent control of sign articulators also allows the breakdown of independent articulatory movements in atypical signers. For instance, following damage to one cerebral hemisphere, a signer may experience weakness or loss of movement on one side of the body. As a result, the simultaneity of the movements of the two limbs by typical signers may be disrupted or eliminated in atypical signers, and this disruption of articulatory simultaneity in turn may disrupt the information carried in the linguistic signal.

This paper will explore how simultaneity in signed language is lost or preserved in different groups of atypical signers. No study to date has focused on the breakdown of the types of linguistic (e.g. lexical, syntactic, semantic) simultaneity and linguistic-gestural simultaneity emphasized in this volume, so this paper will review what is known about the breakdown of articulatory simultaneity and suggest how linguistic simultaneity is likely to be affected by particular neural pathologies. The first two sections will examine the physical structure and neural basis of signed language, because these are possible loci of disruption in atypical signing. The following section will discuss specific neural pathologies and how they are likely to impact simultaneity, and the final section will discuss what disruptions to simultaneity can reveal about the structure of signed language.

2.   Modality differences inherent to the physical production mechanism

Speech is produced via the vocal tract, whereas sign uses the hands and arms as its primary articulators. (Secondary sign articulators include the shoulders, trunk, head, mouth, eyes, and eyebrows.) The details of the primary articulators greatly influence the structure of sign and speech in a variety of ways (Klima & Bellugi 1979; Meier 2002). First of all, the primary articulators for sign production are paired: each articulator has a corresponding mirror-image articulator on the opposite side of the body. By contrast, the speech articulators are mostly single organs located along the midline of the body. Additionally, the sign articulators are spread across different parts of the body (e.g. the face and the hands), in contrast to the speech articulators which form a contiguous region in the vocal tract. As a result, the sign articulators can move largely independently of each other; whereas the movement of one speech organ tends to influence or constrain the movements of other speech organs.

The sign articulators consist of groups of large muscles organized around bones, whereas the speech articulators are not arranged in these types of agonist/antagonist configurations. In order for the sign articulators to move, one set of muscles has to relax while the opposing set contracts. Additionally, sign articulators move large distances and have many degrees of freedom: they move easily in all three spatial dimensions and can take an infinite number of paths in moving from one location in space to another. The result of these factors is that movements for sign production are larger and slower than movements for speech (Bellugi & Fischer 1972; Klima & Bellugi 1979). Bellugi & Fischer (1972) measured the durations of individual signs in American Sign Language (ASL) and the durations of individual spoken English words, both produced by hearing speakers from Deaf households. In that study, subjects produced between 4 and 5.2 English words per second, and between 2.3 and 2.5 ASL signs per second.

Speech can be described as a source-filter mechanism with an energy source (the vibrating vocal folds) which generates pulses that are modified by the filter that they pass through (the supralaryngeal vocal tract). By contrast, sign does not have an apparent energy source independent of the excitation of the muscles themselves. In addition, sign is not obviously dependent on or structured by respiration patterns, which could mean that the limitations on utterance length or articulation/pause ratio will be different for the two modalities.

The sign production mechanism is configured such that the articulators that can perform rapid, precise movements (i.e. the hands) are attached at the ends of articulators that make only gross movements (i.e. the arms). The result of this is that signs are composed of precise movements superimposed on the gross movements of the same limb. The two sets of movements (gross and precise) are coordinated to overlap in time. When a typical signer produces a sign with an internal handshape change and a path movement of the arm, for example, the movement of the hand begins after arm movement has begun, and the two types of movement end at the same time (Brentari, Poizner & Kegl 1995). There is no equivalent coupling of gross and precise movements for the speech production mechanism.

3.   Brain, motor control, and language

Little is known about brain function for sign articulation; however, there has been a great deal of research on motor control for the limbs and how it differs from motor control for the vocal tract. So it is possible to extrapolate slightly to discuss how brain function is likely to be different for sign vs. speech, given their primary articulators.

The human motor control system is composed of the portions of the brain, brainstem, spinal cord, and peripheral nerves controlling movement, as well as the striated muscles that execute movements. At the highest level of the nervous system, there are two cerebral hemispheres on the left and right sides of the brain. The outermost layers of cells in the two hemispheres are known as the cerebral cortex. Motor areas of the cerebral cortex are divided somatotopically, i.e. specific cortical motor areas control movement for specific parts of the body. Cortical areas that control movement are located in the medial and posterior frontal lobe. The primary motor cortex is the main source of movement commands to peripheral muscles; and the supplementary motor area and premotor area, which are just anterior to the primary motor cortex, are activated prior to movement onset and serve a role in movement planning.

The fibres that descend from the cortex can be subdivided into the corticospinal and corticobulbar tracts. The corticospinal tract descends through the cerebral hemispheres and brainstem, and ultimately terminates in the spinal cord. Along the way, in the lower part of the brainstem, the majority of corticospinal fibres cross (or decussate) to the contralateral side of the brainstem (see Figure 1). Consequently, one hemisphere of the brain controls movements for the opposite side of the body. The corticobulbar tract also originates in motor areas of the cortex, but rather than projecting to motor nerves in the spinal cord, it projects to motor nuclei in the brainstem. The cranial nerves arise from these motor nuclei and control the movements of the head, neck, eyes, and vocal tract. Unlike the corticospinal tract, the projections of the corticobulbar tract are largely bilateral. In other words, with few exceptions, both cerebral hemispheres control movements of both sides of the vocal tract in almost equal proportions.

There are also structures outside the cerebral neocortex that are involved in the control of voluntary movement. The two largest and most important are the cere-

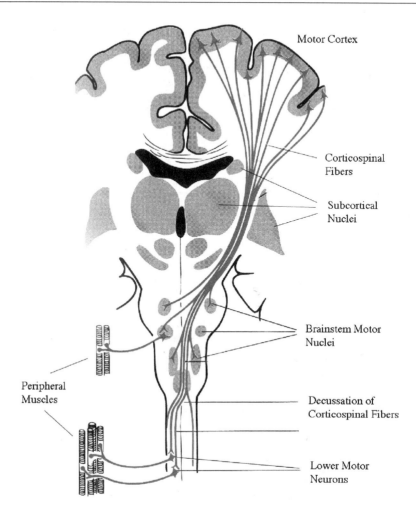

Motor Cortex

Corticospinal
Fibers

Subcortical
Nuclei

Brainstem Motor
Nuclei

Peripheral
Muscles

Decussation of
Corticospinal Fibers

Lower Motor
Neurons

Figure 1. Motor pathways from the primary motor cortex to the muscles (adapted from Brodal 1998)

bellum and basal ganglia. There are no common pathologies associated with the cerebellum in humans, whereas the basal ganglia are affected by both Parkinson's disease and Huntington's disease. Neither the cerebellum nor the basal ganglia are directly responsible for movement generation, but rather for shaping voluntary movement so that it is accurate, natural, well-timed and coordinated (Jueptner, Jenkins, Brooks, Frackowiak & Passingham 1996; Lang & Bastian 2002; Timmann, Citron, Watts & Hore 2001; VanGemmert, Teulings, Contreras-Vidal & Stelmach 1999). Additionally, both structures play a role in modifying muscle tone, balance, and posture, probably through projections to brainstem nuclei. Both the cerebellum and the basal ganglia receive input from and project back to cortical motor areas.

From this it seems likely that neural damage to the basal ganglia or cerebellum would have the same effect on articulation for sign as for articulation for speech. On the other hand, damage to motor areas of the cortex or to the corticospinal/corticobulbar tracts may have different effects for the two modalities. This follows from the fact that the cerebellum and basal ganglia do not have effector-specific functions, so they tend to affect movements of different parts of the body in the same way. By contrast, specific cortical motor areas can control specific parts of the body. Moreover, damage to motor areas in one hemisphere often has a dramatic effect on the contralateral limb, but less effect on the ipsilateral limb, and also less effect on the vocal tract.

In general, the brain structures most relevant to language are located in the left cerebral cortex. The two language areas identified earliest were Broca's area (left inferior frontal lobe) and Wernicke's area (left posterior temporal lobe) in the posterior and anterior left hemisphere. More systematic analysis of patients' language abilities following stroke later showed that some right hemisphere structures are important for language as well, particularly at the level of discourse. Since new technologies have allowed more precise localization of brain areas relevant to specific cognitive functions, it has become clear that additional cortical areas in the left and right hemispheres are recruited during language production and processing (Stowe, Haverkort & Zwarts 2005). A discussion of particular cortical areas and their role in language is beyond the scope of this paper, but a short list of those areas includes the left inferior frontal gyrus, superior temporal gyrus, posterior temporal lobe, and supplementary motor area, and the left and right supramarginal gyrus and angular gyrus. (For a review of research on the neural basis of language, see Stowe et al. 2005.)

Other studies have suggested that non-cortical areas are also important to language function. In particular, it has been suggested that the basal ganglia play a role in syntax (Arnott, Chenery, Murdoch & Silburn 2005; Lieberman, Friedman & Feldman 1990); however, the evidence for this is somewhat equivocal, and there is no consistent pattern of syntactic deficits in subjects with damage to those areas (Murray & Lenz 2001; Patterson & Bly 1999). In addition, various studies have suggested that parts of the cerebellum are activated during language processing (Fiez, Raife, Balota, Schwarz, Raichle & Petersen 1996), and that damage to the right cerebellum can cause aphasia (Fabbro, Moretti & Bava 2000; Marien, Engelborghs, Pickut & DeDeyn 2000). Anatomically, this makes sense because there are strong connections between the right cerebellum and the left frontal lobe, where many important language areas are located. Because of their importance both to motor control and to other cognitive functions, the role of the cerebellum or the basal ganglia in language as opposed to articulation remains largely unclear.

4.   Signed language and the brain

On the basis of extensive research, it seems clear that neural damage results in the same linguistic deficits in sign and in speech. Several studies have examined ASL signers with various types of brain damage (Corina, Vaid & Bellugi 1992b; Poizner, Klima & Bellugi 1987), in order to determine how the brain processes sign in comparison to speech, given that the two systems use different articulators, different sensory perception channels, and, to some extent, different grammatical structures (e.g. use of word order vs. physical space to express grammatical relations). Particular issues addressed by studies of signers with brain damage include: the function of traditional language areas and visuospatial cognition areas in processing spatialized grammar; and the relationship between sign aphasia and limb apraxia.

Poizner et al. (1987) studied four Deaf subjects who had either left or right hemisphere damage, in order to determine whether language deficits following stroke would pattern similarly in signed and spoken language. They found a double dissociation in the language and visuospatial abilities of signers with left hemisphere and right hemisphere damage. The signers with left hemisphere damage retained their ability to perceive spatial relations of objects but lost their use of space for signed language grammar; whereas signers with right hemisphere damage lost their ability to perceive spatial relations but retained their ability to use space grammatically.

In addition, Poizner et al. (1987) as well as Corina, Poizner, Bellugi, Feinberg & O'Grady-Batch (1992a) found a dissociation between disruption to language (aphasia) and disruption to symbolic gesture (apraxia). Damage to left anterior cortical areas often causes both of these disorders to occur, and it had been claimed that aphasia and apraxia were the same phenomenon in signed language (Kimura 1981). However, there have been reported cases of Deaf subjects who could understand gestures but not signs (Corina et al. 1992a; Marshall, Atkinson, Smulovitch, Thacker & Woll 2004), indicating that apraxia and aphasia are separate phenomena irrespective of language modality.

Most research on signed language and the brain has focused on signed language as a linguistic or cognitive task; however, a few studies have sought to understand sign articulation. The majority of these studies collected data from subjects who had motor control disorders, primarily Parkinson's disease, but one research group also described sign articulation in a subject with right hemisphere damage (Loew, Kegl & Poizner 1997; Poizner 1990; Poizner & Kegl 1993), and a more recent study has examined sign production across a broad range of movement disorders (Tyrone 2005).

A few brain imaging studies of healthy Deaf signers have explored questions related to movement or articulation in signing and fingerspelling. One study explicitly designed to investigate articulation explored a basic but neglected issue: whether left-handed signing activates left hemisphere frontal structures and other structures relevant for motor control for speech articulation (Corina, San Jose-Robertson, Guillemin, High & Braun 2003). In principle, given that motor cortical areas in the right hemisphere control movements of the left arm, one might hypothesize that left-handed signing would primarily activate the right hemisphere. In fact, Corina et al. (2003) found left inferior frontal (and right cerebellar) activation during sign production in right-handed subjects, even when productions were made with the left hand. This finding is consistent with earlier studies which suggested that the anterior left hemisphere plays an important role for speech articulation (Dronkers 1996; Wise, Greene, Buchel & Scott 1999). In speech it is not possible to test how closely this function is tied to the lateralization of motor control, since speakers cannot control the two sides of the vocal tract completely independently.

5.   Simultaneity and specific neural pathologies

Typically, brain injury or stroke affects some portion of one of the cerebral hemispheres, but not both hemispheres. Consequently, injury or stroke may cause weakness or paralysis on one side of the body (i.e. hemiplegia or hemiparesis). When hemiplegia or hemiparesis occurs, the normal simultaneity of limb movements during signing can be disrupted, thereby altering two-handed signs or precluding simultaneous production of two different signs by the two hands. In a recent study of British Deaf signers with movement disorders, one subject with right hemisphere damage had a disruption to simultaneous movements of the two limbs during signing, but simultaneous bimanual movements were not eliminated from his signing altogether. In particular, he produced two-handed signs, but lowered his left hand during signing, while his right hand was not lowered.

In the same study, a subject with left hemisphere damage, whose signing was severely disrupted, produced only one-handed signs (Marshall, Atkinson, Woll & Thacker 2005; Tyrone 2005). While she could copy some signs, when asked to copy a two-handed sign, she would shrug and gesture to her left arm, indicating that she could not produce the sign since she could not move both arms. Deaf subjects with unilateral brain damage whose signing was similarly disrupted by hemiparesis have been reported elsewhere (Atkinson, Campbell, Marshall, Thacker & Woll 2004; Kegl & Poizner 1997; Poizner et al. 1987).

5.1   Left hemisphere damage

Either left or right hemisphere damage can cause hemiparesis and disrupt two-handed signing, as discussed above. Left hemisphere damage can additionally cause aphasia, which is the breakdown of language function. This is so because the brain areas that are most important for both spoken and signed language are in the left hemisphere. The use of space to show grammatical agreement in signed languages causes the verb and its subject or object to be presented in the same lexical item in many cases. Signed language also uses facial expression concurrently with movements of the hands to show grammatical and prosodic information. Because signed languages allow grammatical information to be produced simultaneously with lexical information, if there is a breakdown of grammar, then an aspect of sign simultaneity may be lost as a result. Interestingly, some studies have reported the breakdown of grammatical but not affective facial expression in cases of aphasia (Kegl & Poizner 1997). In other words, signers who have aphasia have exhibited a disruption in manual-facial simultaneity purely resulting from their language deficit, and not from any difficulty coordinating limb movements with facial movements. Additionally, Kegl & Poizner (1997) reported an aphasic subject who preferred to use word order rather than grammatical agreement – which in effect reduces the simultaneous production of lexical and syntactic information.

5.2   Right hemisphere damage

As discussed above, the brain structures most important to language are located in the left hemisphere. As a result, right hemisphere damage does not usually cause aphasia, but it can disrupt prosody, affective facial expression, and pragmatic components of language. Loew et al. (1997) described a signer with right hemisphere damage who experienced a disruption to role-shift in particular. (Role shift is the use of body orientation and gaze to differentiate roles in a narrative.) He had difficulty assuming the perspective of the agents in his discourse, so he continually referred to them in the third person, as points in the signing space. In his case, it was not syntactic simultaneity that was disrupted, but the ability to present multiple viewpoints in his signing.

A recent study in the UK identified a signer with right hemisphere damage who experienced what may have been a deficit in language prosody. In particular, he had an impairment in processing information on the face during signing. On tests of sign perception, he showed difficulty identifying negation when it was presented on the face as eyebrow wrinkling (Atkinson et al. 2004). So in addition to his production deficits, this signer had a deficit in perceiving simultaneous streams of information in signed language, if one stream of information was presented via facial expression. His case is an interesting contrast to the signers with aphasia, because he exhibited a particular deficit in manual-facial simultaneity irrespective of the nature of the facial information.

There are also sign articulation deficits which result from right hemisphere damage, but these tend to be quite varied. Poizner & Kegl (1993) and Loew et al. (1997) described the effects of right hemisphere damage on one individual's signing. When the subject produced two handed signs, movement initiation was delayed in the left hand relative to the right hand, which Poizner & Kegl (1993) analyzed as a deficit in motor neglect. Given that his simultaneous bimanual movements within signs were so severely disrupted, it is unlikely that he would use many two-handed simultaneous constructions. Poizner & Kegl (1993) do not report their being used at all.

The articulatory deficits of a Deaf signer with right hemisphere damage in the UK ('James') were described in Tyrone (2005). Like the subject reported by Poizner & Kegl (1993), James had incoordination of the two hands during sign production and tended to delay the movements of his weak arm at the onset of two-handed signs. However, his incoordination was not very pronounced. Additionally, he had no difficulties using his affected hand as a base hand in two-handed signs, despite his left-side hemiparesis. This study did not explicitly examine the use of the non-dominant hand as a buoy or a placeholder, but based on broader patterns in his sign production, it seems likely that James would be able to produce these and other simultaneous constructions with no difficulty.

5.3 Parkinson's disease

Research on signers with Parkinson's disease suggests that their language deficits are articulatory rather than linguistic in nature (Brentari & Poizner 1994; Poizner 1990). Broadly speaking, signers with Parkinson's disease (PD) tend to hypo-articulate: their sign production is smaller, slower, and prosodically reduced. In particular, signers with PD have reduced and lowered signing space (Loew, Kegl & Poizner et al. 1995; Poizner & Kegl 1992; Poizner & Kegl 1993). Relative to neurologically-intact control subjects, signers with PD do not use as much of the space in front of the body to produce signs, even though they are capable of reaching distant locations with their hands and arms.

Signers with Parkinson's disease produce signs with more distal articulators; for example, in a sign that is normally initiated from the elbow, a signer with PD might produce it from the wrist or from the fingers (Brentari & Poizner 1994; Tyrone, Kegl & Poizner 1999). Additionally, signers with PD often lax the distal articulators of the hands and wrist during sign production, so that the hand-shape and orientation of signs are less articulatorily contrastive than they would be normally (Brentari & Poizner 1994; Brentari et al. 1995; Loew et al. 1995).

Figure 2. ASL sign ASK

Several studies indicate that signers with PD show a disruption in the simultaneous movement of multiple articulators, including articulators on the same limb (e.g., the fingers and elbow) (Brentari & Poizner 1994; Brentari et al. 1995; Poizner & Kegl 1993; Tyrone et al. 1999). In some cases, signers with PD delete handshape or orientation change from a sign or a fingerspelled word (Brentari & Poizner 1994; Tyrone et al. 1999). In other cases, signers with PD may completely synchronize or completely serialize handshape change and arm movement, rather than produce them in a partially overlapping manner, as control signers do (Brentari et al. 1995). For example, the ASL sign ASK requires a forward movement of the arm while the index finger flexes (see Figure 2). Based on research on ASL, this type of sign seems to be particularly difficult for signers with Parkinson's disease. Interestingly, given that ASL signers with Parkinson's disease sometimes serialize, sometimes synchronize, and sometimes delete distal movements, the normal inter-articulator simultaneity in signs can be either increased or decreased, depending on which tendency an individual subject exhibits.

Another atypical signing pattern found in signers with Parkinson's disease was handshape mirroring on the non-active hand in one-handed signs or fingerspelled words (Loew et al. 1995; Poizner, Brentari, Tyrone & Kegl 2000; Tyrone et al. 1999), which effectively creates a type of simultaneity not present in typical signing. For example, in producing the ASL sign BIRD, which is a one-handed sign, a signer with Parkinson's disease produced the sign's handshape and hand-internal movement on both his left hand and his right (Poizner et al. 2000). Signers with Parkinson's disease were not reported to produce fully-articulated two-handed signs in place of one-handed signs. Rather, they produced the movements of the active hand in a reduced form on the non-active hand.

Finally, signers with Parkinson's disease showed a reduction in their use of facial expression (Kegl, Cohen & Poizner 1999). As a result of this, they exhibited less manual-facial simultaneity, for both grammatical and prosodic facial expression.

Unlike signers with aphasia, their facial movement deficit was related to motor control rather than language, and hence it was present for non-linguistic as well as linguistic facial expression.

A recent study of a Deaf man with Parkinson's disease in the UK had somewhat different results from earlier studies in the US (Tyrone & Woll in press). Specifically, the subject in the UK study, 'John', had no more coordination deficits than the control subject, and thus no particular deficit in articulatory simultaneity. In fact, John's signing was relatively similar to that of a typical signer. Static components of his signs were often laxed, which is common during relaxed, informal signing. John had no difficulty with coordination of the two limbs or of proximal and distal articulators on the same limb. In addition, his facial expressions were somewhat reduced, but he was still able to produce the correct oral and facial movements simultaneously with their lexical correlates on the hands. Further study would be needed to determine what differentiates John from other signers with Parkinson's disease whose signing is more severely disrupted.

5.4 Cerebellar damage

While it is clear that the cerebellum serves an important role in motor control, there is still debate as to what exactly it does. In general terms, cerebellar damage causes intention tremor, impairments in movement scaling, and coordination deficits. There has been little research specifically on signed language and the cerebellum, because cerebellar damage is comparatively rare in humans. To date, only one signer with cerebellar damage has been identified and studied (Tyrone 2005).

The subject in that study, 'Robert', experienced severe damage to the right cerebellum following hemorrhaging during an operation to correct an arteriovenous malformation. Broadly speaking, Robert's signing was oversized and uncoordinated. Additionally, his signing, like his limb movement more generally, was slow and often disrupted by intention tremor. In contrast to signers with Parkinson's disease, Robert's movements were proximalized on some signs; in other words, he would produce a sign using articulators proximal to those normally used for its production (e.g. in producing the BSL sign HAMMER, which normally has a repeated downward movement of the wrist, he might instead produce the downward movement from the elbow). In addition, he had an overall pattern of enlarged signing: large movements, distant sign locations, and hyperextended articulators. In a number of ways, Robert's signing was the opposite of what was reported in signers with Parkinson's disease; his signs were large, proximalized, and sometimes included movements which were not required.

Robert's simultaneity difficulties took a variety of forms. In particular, he had difficulty making simultaneous movements of his hands to produce two-handed signs. He was not always able to make his hands begin moving at the same time,

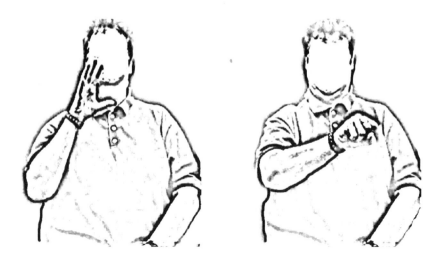

Figure 3. BSL sign BITE

come to the same place, or produce the same movement. His bimanual coordination was so severely disrupted that he did not attempt to produce buoys or place holders, or to produce separate signs simultaneously with the two hands. Because Robert could not suppress involuntary movements during signing, his hands sometimes appeared to be producing different signs even though he did not intend them to be doing so.

Robert also had difficulty with simultaneous movements of the independent articulators on a single limb: both correctly timing separate movements relative to each other and suppressing involuntary movements that emerged during voluntary movement. For example, the BSL sign BITE requires a downward movement of the arm at the same time that the fingers close to make a fist (see Figure 3). What Robert would do instead was to produce the two movements serially, by moving his arm down first, then pausing, then closing his fingers.

Robert had a tendency to produce one-handed signs with two hands without obvious intent to place linguistic emphasis. Unlike signers with Parkinson's disease, Robert would produce a fully two-handed form of one-handed signs, adding a component of simultaneity to signs that would not normally be present. The production of two-handed forms of one-handed signs has also been documented in normal Deaf children in the early stages of acquiring signed language (Cheek, Cormier, Repp & Meier 2001). For example, one child from that study produced a two-handed version of the ASL sign DOG, which is one-handed in its citation form. It may be that the children studied by Cheek et al. (2001) were relying on descending brainstem tracts which enable simple, symmetrical, two-handed movements (Wiesendanger, Kazennikov, Perrig & Kaluzny 1996). The children in that study ranged in age from 5 to 17 months, at which stage the corticospinal tract and the connection between the cerebellum and cerebral cortex, both of which are necessary for precise, coordinated movements, would not yet be fully developed (Brodal 1998). This could explain the similarity between the children's signing and Robert's signing.

5.5   Progressive supranuclear palsy

Progressive supranuclear palsy is a disease that is similar to Parkinson's disease in pathology and symptomatology, but occurs less frequently. Like Parkinson's disease, progressive supranuclear palsy causes neuronal loss in the brainstem, affecting projections to the basal ganglia and causing movements to be slow and small (or hypokinetic). In addition, progressive supranuclear palsy causes atrophy in the frontal lobes and damages projections from the brainstem to the cerebellum (Cordato, Duggins, Halliday, Morris & Pantelis 2005). One of the characteristic symptoms of the disease, which is used to distinguish it from Parkinson's disease, is the loss of eye movements, or ophthalmoplegia. A recent study on movement disorders and signed language included a British signer with progressive supranuclear palsy. 'Joseph' had severely disrupted facial expression and limited use of eye gaze, which affected both prosodic and grammatical information carried on the face during signing. However, he had no difficulty understanding grammatical or affective facial expressions used by other signers (Tyrone 2005). As a result of his disease symptoms, both his manual-facial and manual-oral simultaneity were drastically reduced in all forms.

Broadly speaking, Joseph's signing was reduced in size and speed, and was characterized by laxed articulation. In this way, his deficits were similar to those reported in signers with Parkinson's disease (Brentari & Poizner 1994; Brentari et al. 1995). In addition, Joseph had great difficulty coordinating multiple sets of articulators during signing. Consequently, he had a reduction in simultaneous movements of the two arms, as well as in the simultaneous movements of multiple articulators on the same arm. However, he had no difficulty with sign-internal movement change as long as those movements were confined to a localized set of articulators. This suggests that at some level, groups of sign articulators (specifically the fingers) are acting together as a unit, which is consistent with findings from studies on sign and Parkinson's disease (Brentari et al. 1995; Tyrone et al. 1999), and consistent with models of hand configurations and finger movements (Iberall & Fagg 1996; Schieber 1996). Despite the fact that the fingers can move independently, during sign production in both typical and atypical signers, the fingers seem to move as a unit.

6.   Implications for the structure of signed language

Research on atypical signers consistently suggests that neurological disorders do not disrupt sign and speech substantially differently, whether the deficits being examined are linguistic or articulatory in nature (Tyrone 2005). For users of either spoken language or signed language, for example, left hemisphere damage causes aphasia, right hemisphere damage causes disrupted prosody, and Parkinson's disease causes disrupted articulation, despite the fact that the two modalities use different sets of articulators with different anatomical and physiological properties. This paper has outlined a variety of neural pathologies that can all disrupt simultaneity in signed language; however, each of these pathologies disrupts simultaneity differently, depending on the underlying nature of the sign articulation deficit.

Simultaneity is affected in a variety of ways in atypical signers with aphasia or with movement disorders. Moreover, neither of these categories of disorders affects sign simultaneity in a uniform way. Some aspects of simultaneity do not seem to be inherently linguistic in nature; instead, they provide redundant information in the communication stream which may facilitate language perception or production, although they are not crucial to the linguistic signal. By contrast, there are aspects of simultaneity that are fundamentally linguistic in nature, as evident from the fact that they are preserved in individuals with articulatory disorders but not in those with aphasia. The fact that simultaneity can be either a linguistic or an articulatory phenomenon in signed language suggests that more research should focus specifically on the nature of sign articulation, so that the aspects of the language that result from motor control can be teased apart from those that are linguistic and arbitrary in nature. The idea that sign is by nature more simultaneous and less sequential than speech should be probed further to explore the extent to which this modality difference (assuming it is real) is purely articulatory.

Investigations of atypical language can provide useful insight into language structure, as illustrated by research on atypical signing. For instance, studies in the UK and in the US suggest that particular sets of sign articulators (e.g. the fingers) tend to move simultaneously, while other sets of articulators (e.g. the elbow and fingers) move in a coordinated, overlapping fashion, but slightly asynchronously (Brentari et al. 1995; Tyrone 2005; Tyrone et al. 1999). These findings support the idea that handshape, orientation, movement, and location are the formational primitives of signed language production (Battison, Markowicz & Woodward 1975; Stokoe 1960). Given that the fingers move simultaneously, they might form a single production unit at the level of motor planning. Conversely, since the relative movements of the elbow, wrist, and fingers are slightly asynchronous over the course of a sign's production, they can be modeled as three different production units, namely, movement, orientation, and handshape, respectively.

There is a form of signed language which has not been included here as a type of atypical signing, but it provides an interesting contrast to the forms of atypical signing that have been discussed. Tactile signing is used by people who are both Deaf and blind, and requires signers' hands to remain in contact as signs are produced. As with visually-perceived signing, the physical form of tactile signing can influence its structure in numerous ways. Because Deaf-blind signers must maintain physical contact with an interlocutor during signing, their use of space and of nonmanual articulators is more constrained, which may limit the occurrence of simultaneity in sign production. As a result, Deaf-blind signers develop alternative means of expressing the grammatical information that is usually conveyed by use of space or nonmanual articulators for sighted Deaf signers. For instance, a Deaf-blind signer might use fingerspelling in place of referential pointing (Quinto-Pozos 2002). Similarly, Deaf-blind signers have been reported to use lexical signs rather than facial expressions to mark questions (Collins & Petronio 1998). By contrast, atypical signers whose use of grammatical facial expression is disrupted do not seem to compensate by adding lexical signs for questions. These reported differences between atypical and tactile signing suggest that the former is a disruption to normal sign production which may or may not cause the deletion of simultaneous grammatical information, whereas the latter is an established system which provides a means of encoding grammatical information manually.

7. Directions for future research and methodological development

There remains a great deal that is not known about atypical signing in general, and about the effects of atypical signing on simultaneity in particular. What is known suggests a number of areas of research to be explored. First, it would be interesting to do kinematic studies of simultaneity in typical and atypical signers, in which the relative timing of movements of multiple articulators such as the dominant and non-dominant hands, the trunk, and the head could be compared. In this way, it would be possible to distinguish normal articulatory variation from disrupted signing. Similarly, high speed video recording could be used to investigate the relationship between signing and mouthing during typical and atypical sign production.

Another open research question is whether there are mechanisms that can compensate for loss of simultaneity. It may be that if one channel of information transfer were disrupted (e.g. facial expression), that signers might use another channel to transmit the same information (e.g. lexical signs). In a more basic scenario, if a signer loses the use of one arm, will she attempt to avoid two-handed signs, or will she produce two-handed signs with just one hand?

Finally, this paper has primarily addressed simultaneity as a production phenomenon – it would be interesting to also examine the role of simultaneity in typical and atypical sign perception to determine whether redundant information in the sign stream facilitates or impedes sign perception. It is unclear what aspects of signs or simultaneous constructions can be dropped or reduced and the utterance still be comprehensible. We know from research on typical signers that movements of the non-dominant hand can be deleted from a two-handed sign or added to a one-handed sign in everyday discourse (Battison 1978; Padden & Perlmutter 1987). However, beyond this, it is difficult to say which aspects of a sign (e.g. handshape, relative timing of articulatory movements, nonmanual sign components) can be modified and to what extent for the sign to remain intelligible.

Further exploration of simultaneity and sequentiality in signed language could be facilitated by improved methodologies and measures in sign phonetics. To date, there is no consistent set of measures, methods, or technologies for describing sign productions below the level of the phonological parameter. Development of methodologies for analyzing sign phonetics would allow researchers to better compare natural variation that occurs across phonetic contexts, across signed languages, and across individual signers. It is only by collecting articulatory data from a variety of signers and signed languages that we can learn what is *de facto* distinct about the structure of signed language, and not simply one possible solution among many for how to organize a language that uses the human hands as its primary articulators.

References

Arnott, Wendy L., Helen J. Chenery, Bruce E. Murdoch & Peter A. Silburn. 2005. "Morphosyntactic and Syntactic Priming: An Investigation of Underlying Processing Mechanisms and the Effects of Parkinson's Disease". *Journal of Neurolinguistics* 18:1.1–28.

Atkinson, Joanna, Ruth Campbell, Jane Marshall, Alice Thacker & Bencie Woll. 2004. "Understanding 'Not': Neuropsychological Dissociations between Hand and Head Markers of Negation in BSL". *Neuropsychologia* 42:2.214–229.

Battison, Robbin. 1978. *Lexical Borrowing in American Sign Language*. Silver Spring, Md.: Linstok.

——, Harry Markowicz & James Woodward. 1975. "A Good Rule of Thumb: Variable Phonology in American Sign Language". *Analyzing Variation in Language* ed. by Ralph W. Fasold & Roger W. Shuy, 291–302. Washington, D.C.: Linstok Press.

Bellugi, Ursula & Susan Fischer. 1972. "A Comparison of Sign Language and Spoken Language". *Cognition* 1:3.173–200.

Brentari, Diane & Howard Poizner. 1994. "A Phonological Analysis of a Deaf Parkinsonian Signer". *Language & Cognitive Processes* 9:1.69–99.

——, Howard Poizner & Judy Kegl. 1995. "Aphasic and Parkinsonian Signing: Differences in Phonological Disruption". *Brain & Language* 48:1.69–105.

Brodal, Per. 1998. *The Central Nervous System: Structure and Function.* New York: Oxford University Press.

Cheek, Adrianne, Kearsy Cormier, Ann Repp & Richard P. Meier. 2001. "Prelinguistic Gesture Predicts Mastery and Error in the Production of Early Signs". *Language* 77:2.292–323.

Collins, Steve & Karen Petronio. 1998. "What Happens in Tactile ASL?" *Pinky Extension and Eyegaze: Language in Deaf Communities* ed. by Ceil Lucas, 18–37. Washington, D.C.: Gallaudet University Press.

Cordato, Nicholas J., Andrew J. Duggins, Glenda M. Halliday, John G. L. Morris & Christos Pantelis. 2005. "Clinical Deficits Correlate with Regional Cerebral Atrophy in Progressive Supranuclear Palsy". *Brain* 128:6.1259–1266.

Corina, David P., Howard Poizner, Ursula Bellugi, Todd Feinberg & Lucinda O'Grady-Batch. 1992a. "Dissociation between Linguistic and Nonlinguistic Gestural Systems: A Case for Compositionality". *Brain & Language* 43:3.414–447.

——, Lucila San Jose-Robertson, Andre Guillemin, Julia High & Allen R. Braun. 2003. "Language Lateralization in a Bimanual Language". *Journal of Cognitive Neuroscience* 15:5.718–730.

——, Jyotsna Vaid & Ursula Bellugi. 1992b. "The Linguistic Basis of Left Hemisphere Specialization". *Science* 255:5049.1258–1260.

Dronkers, Nina. 1996. "A New Brain Region for Coordinating Speech Articulation". *Nature* 384:6605.159–161.

Fabbro, Franco, Rita Moretti & Antonio Bava. 2000. "Language Impairments in Patients with Cerebellar Lesions". *Journal of Neurolinguistics.* 13:2–3.173–188.

Fiez, Julie A., Elizabeth A. Raife, David A. Balota, Jacob P. Schwarz, Marcus E. Raichle & Steven E. Petersen. 1996. "A Positron Emission Tomography Study of the Short-Term Maintenance of Verbal Information". *Journal of Neuroscience* 16:2.808–822.

Iberall, Thea & Andrew H. Fagg. 1996. "Neural Network Models for Selecting Hand Shapes". *Hand and Brain: The Neurophysiology and Psychology of Hand Movements* ed. by Alan M. Wing, Patrick Haggard & J. Randall Flanagan, 243–264. San Diego, Calif.: Academic Press.

Jueptner, Markus, I. Harri Jenkins, David J. Brooks, Richard S. J. Frackowiak & Richard E. Passingham. 1996. "The Sensory Guidance of Movement: A Comparison of the Cerebellum and Basal Ganglia". *Experimental Brain Research* 112:3.462–474.

Kegl, Judy, Henri Cohen & Howard Poizner. 1999. "Articulatory Consequences of Parkinson's Disease: Perspectives from Two Modalities". *Brain & Cognition* 40:2.355–386.

—— & Howard Poizner. 1997. "Crosslinguistic/Crossmodal Syntactic Consequences of Left-Hemisphere Damage: Evidence from an Aphasic Signer and His Identical Twin". *Aphasiology* 11:1.1–37.

Kimura, Doreen 1981. "Neural Mechanisms in Manual Signing". *Sign Language Studies* 10:33.291–312.

Klima, Edward & Ursula Bellugi. 1979. *The Signs of Language.* Cambridge, Mass.: Harvard University Press.

Lang, Catherine E. & Amy J. Bastian. 2002. "Cerebellar Damage Impairs Automaticity of a Recently Practiced Movement". *Journal of Neurophysiology* 87:3.1336–1347.

Lieberman, Philip, Joseph Friedman & Liane S. Feldman. 1990. "Syntax Comprehension Deficits in Parkinson's Disease". *Journal of Nervous & Mental Disease* 178:6.360–365.

Loew, Ruth C., Judy A. Kegl & Howard Poizner. 1995. "Flattening of Distinctions in a Parkinsonian Signer". *Aphasiology* 9:4.381–396.

——, Judy A. Kegl & Howard Poizner. 1997. "Fractionation of the Components of Role Play in a Right-Hemispheric Lesioned Signer". *Aphasiology* 11:3.263–281.

Marien, Peter, Sebastian Engelborghs, Barbara A. Pickut & Peter P. DeDeyn. 2000. "Aphasia Following Cerebellar Damage: Fact or Fantasy?" *Journal of Neurolinguistics* 13:2–3.145–171.

Marshall, Jane, Joanna Atkinson, Elaine Smulovitch, Alice Thacker & Bencie Woll. 2004. "Aphasia in a User of British Sign Language: Dissociation between Sign and Gesture". *Cognitive Neuropsychology* 21:5.537–554.

——, Joanna R. Atkinson, Bencie Woll & Alice Thacker. 2005. "Aphasia in a Bilingual User of British Sign Language and English: Effects of Cross-Linguistic Cues". *Cognitive Neuropsychology* 22:6.719–736.

Meier, Richard P. 2002. "Why Different, Why the Same? Explaining Effects and Non-Effects of Modality Upon Linguistic Structure in Sign and Speech". *Modality and Structure in Signed and Spoken Language* ed. by Richard P. Meier, Kearsy Cormier & David Quinto-Pozos, 1–26. New York: Cambridge University Press.

Murray, Laura L. & Lisa P. Lenz. 2001. "Productive Syntax Abilities in Huntington's and Parkinson's Diseases". *Brain & Cognition* 46:1–2.213–219.

Padden, Carol A. & David M. Perlmutter. 1987. "American Sign Language and the Architecture of Phonological Theory". *Natural Language & Linguistic Theory* 5:3.335–375.

Patterson, Michael D. & Benjamin Martin Bly. 1999. "The Brain Basis of Syntactic Processes: Architecture, Ontogeny, and Phylogeny". *Cognitive Science: Handbook of Perception and Cognition* ed. by Benjamin Martin Bly & David E. Rumelhart, 255–318. San Diego, Calif.: Academic Press.

Poizner, Howard. 1990. "Language and Motor Disorders in Deaf Signers". *Cerebral Control of Speech and Limb Movements* ed. by Geoffrey R. Hammond, 303–326. North-Holland, N.Y.: Elsevier.

——, Diane Brentari, Martha E. Tyrone & Judy Kegl. 2000. "The Structure of Language as Motor Behavior: Clues from Signers with Parkinson's Disease". *The Signs of Language Revisited: An Anthology to Honor Ursula Bellugi and Edward Klima* ed. by Karen Emmorey & Harlan Lane, 509–532. Mahwah, N.J.: Lawrence Erlbaum.

—— & Judy Kegl. 1992. "Neural Basis of Language and Motor Behaviour: Perspectives from American Sign Language". *Aphasiology* 6:3.219–256.

—— & Judy Kegl. 1993. "Neural Disorders of the Linguistic Use of Space and Movement". *Annals of the New York Academy of Science, Temporal Information Processing in the Nervous System* ed. by Paula Tallal, Albert Galaburda, Rodolfo R. Llinas & Curt von Euler, 192–213. New York: New York Academy of Sciences Press.

——, Edward Klima & Ursula Bellugi. 1987. *What the Hands Reveal About the Brain.* Cambridge, Mass.: MIT Press.

Quinto-Pozos, David 2002. "Deictic Points in the Visual-Gestural and Tactile-Gestural Modalities". *Modality and Structure in Signed and Spoken Languages* ed. by Richard P. Meier, Kearsy Cormier & David Quinto-Pozos, 442–467. Cambridge: Cambridge University Press.

Schieber, Marc H. 1996. "Individuated Finger Movements: Rejecting the Labeled-Line Hypothesis". *Hand and Brain: The Neurophysiology and Psychology of Hand Movements* ed. by Alan M. Wing, Patrick Haggard & J. Randall Flanagan, 81–98. San Diego, Calif.: Academic Press.

Stokoe, William C. 1960. *Sign Language Structure: An Outline of the Visual Communication Systems of the American Deaf.* Silver Spring, Md.: Linstok Press.

Stowe, Laurie A., Marco Haverkort & Frans Zwarts. 2005. "Rethinking the Neurological Basis of Language". *Lingua* 115:7.997–1042.

Timmann, Dagmar, R. Citron, Sherry Watts & Jon Hore. 2001. "Increased Variability in Finger Position Occurs Throughout Overarm Throws Made by Cerebellar and Unskilled Subjects". *Journal of Neurophysiology* 86:6.2690–2702.

Tyrone, Martha E. 2005. *An Investigation of Sign Dysarthria*. Doctoral dissertation, City University London.

——, Judy Kegl & Howard Poizner. 1999. "Interarticulator Co-ordination in Deaf Signers with Parkinson's Disease". *Neuropsychologia* 37:11.1271–1283.

—— & Bencie Woll. in press. "Sign Phonetics and the Motor System: Implications from Parkinson's Disease". *Theoretical Issues in Sign Language Research 8* ed. by Josep Quer. Seedorf: Signum Press.

VanGemmert, Arend W. A., Hans-Leo Teulings, Jose L. Contreras-Vidal & George E. Stelmach. 1999. "Parkinson's Disease and the Control of Size and Speed in Handwriting". *Neuropsychologia* 37:6.685–694.

Wiesendanger, Mario, Oleg Kazennikov, Stephen Perrig & Pawel Kaluzny. 1996. "Two Hands- One Action: The Problem of Bimanual Coordination". *Hand and Brain: The Neurophysiology and Psychology of Hand Movements* ed. by Alan M. Wing, Patrick Haggard & J. Randall Flanagan, 283–300. San Diego: Academic Press.

Wise, Richard J. S., J. Greene, Christian Buchel & Sophie K. Scott. 1999. "Brain Regions Involved in Articulation". *Lancet* 353:9158.1057–1061.

Perspectives on linearity and simultaneity

Bencie Woll

DCAL Research Centre, University College London

1. Introduction

In the first section of this brief concluding paper, earlier approaches to the notions of simultaneity and linearity are reviewed, starting with 18th century philosophers of language and describing the views of Saussure, who founded modern linguistics at the end of the 19th century, and his successors. The second section discusses simultaneity and linearity in relation to signed languages, emphasising how much in signed language is both simultaneous and linear, and reviewing papers in this volume in relation to theoretical approaches of both linguistics and psycholinguistics. Finally, some possible directions for future research are outlined.

2. Linearity and simultaneity – an historical perspective

Throughout the 18th century, there was a lively debate among philosophers as to the correspondence between the order of words in language, and the natural order of thinking. Scaglione (1998) provides a fascinating review. Buffier (1732, cited in Scaglione) contrasted the temporal linearity of language with the simultaneity of thought. Condillac (see Aarsleff 1974) emphasised that language was the means by which simultaneous, pictorial experiences and perceptions were transformed into a sequential order. Linearity was thus perceived as an essential feature of language which enabled the chaos of thought to be analysed and converted from instantaneous and indivisible mental acts to a 'stretched-out' form for others to process. The extension of this approach was to view certain word orders as more logical than others. Beauzée (1767), for example, argued that in the most natural order for language, the subject should precede the predicate because the existence of a patient or agent precedes its predication or action. Similarly, adjectives should follow their head nouns, as qualities follow substances; prepositions should precede their objects, and dependent clauses follow the clauses they modify, since complements should logically follow what governs them. Even among European spoken languages, however, these 'natural' word orders are not always found, and concern with the simultaneous-linear distinction in terms of semantics-syntax largely disappeared until the development of cognitive linguistics at the end of the 20th century.

Writers of the 18th and 19th century who concerned themselves with signed language saw it as an intermediate form in which thoughts were represented in a more natural order, and with greater simultaneity, than in spoken languages. Tylor (1874:27) for instance, described the natural order within signed language sentences at the same time as pointing out their holistic quality:

> [he describes the natural order as] 1. object; 2. subject; 3. action; illustrating it by the gestures 'door key open' to express 'the key opens the door' [...] it must always be borne in mind that the intelligibility of a gesture-sentence depends on the whole forming a dramatic picture, while this dramatic effect is very imperfectly represented by translating signs into words and placing these one after another. Thus when Mr Hebden [the deaf consultant] expressed in gestures 'I found a pipe on the road' the order of the signs was written down as 'road pipe I-find' [...] but what the gestures actually expressed went far beyond this, for he made the spectator realize him as walking along the road and suddenly catching sight of a pipe lying on the ground.

Ferdinand de Saussure, the founder of linguistics, in his *Cours de Linguistique Generale* ("Course in General Linguistics", originally published in 1916, see also 1959) broadened the issue of linearity in language by extending it from the sphere of the relationship between semantics and syntax to all parts of language, as part of his identification of the two essential features of human language as arbitrariness and linearity. Links between the two principles of arbitrariness and linearity (and conversely, iconicity and simultaneity) are seen in many papers of the *Cours*. Signed language linguists have often grappled with both of these claims. In relation to the first, it has become increasingly agreed that the extent of arbitrariness in the symbol-referent relationship is associated with properties of language modality: all signed languages apparently make much greater use of symbols whose relationship with their referents is not arbitrary, since all signed languages extensively exploit the possibilities of iconicity, using symbols which represent some visual property associated with a referent, while spoken languages appear to have relatively few lexical items where the symbol represents some auditory property associated with a referent. It should be noted that where auditory symbolism is readily available – for example, for referents relating to sound – auditory iconicity (what Saussure called 'suggestive sounds' (des sonorités suggestives)) is the norm, and recent research on mimetics and ideophones has emphasised that iconic representations are widespread in spoken languages.

For signed language researchers, approaches to iconicity have in recent years begun to interact with approaches to simultaneity; a number of papers in this volume directly relate to this approach. Nyst's description of simultaneity in Adamorobe Sign Language (this volume) illustrates that this relationship is not simply a universal feature of signed language: Adamorobe Sign Language only has some of the types of simultaneity identified by Miller (1994) because of other restrictions in the language on the types of space used.

The principle of linearity states:

> the signifier, being auditory, is unfolded solely in time from which it gets the following characteristics: (a) it represents a span, and (b) the span is measurable in a single dimension; it is a line.   (Saussure 1959: 70)

One of the challenges of interpreting Saussure is to work out why he thought linearity so fundamentally important to language, since it is clearly a property of the auditory channel and not of the symbolic system. Although he does not elaborate on this in the *Cours*, he discusses elsewhere that linearity in the communication channel enables words to be separated from the stream of speech: "If we can separate words, it is a consequence of this [linear] principle" (CLG/E 1:157, cited by Joseph 2004). In his view, the ability to divide the communication stream into successive units is the basis for the creation of linguistic symbols. The process of making thoughts distinct by the creation of linguistic signs is, in effect, separating words. It is perhaps surprising to the modern reader that Saussure was well aware that communication in the visual modality was not linear, emphasising that visual symbols "can offer simultaneous groupings in several dimensions" (1959: 70).

Structuralist linguistics of the first half of the 20th century accepted without question the sequential concatenation of units, both at the level of articulated sounds and at the level of word combinations. Bloomfield (1933) was less sure than Saussure about whether linearity was as important as arbitrariness. The *Cours*, which underpinned structuralist linguistics, offers little if any explanation for putting linearity on a par with simultaneity. As Harris (2003) points out, there is nothing about time or sound that intrinsically imposes sequential constraints. What limits the possibilities as far as speech is concerned is the nature of the vocal apparatus. Bloomfield regarded the sequential concatenation of words as being of an entirely different status from the sequential concatenation of sounds. His position is that it would make no difference if the vocal apparatus was able to articulate two or more words simultaneously – there would still be a conceptual necessity to rank the units in some order of priority – hence the linearity of syntax. This is also taken for granted in early models of transformational grammar. Linearity at the syntactic level underpins these models: the operations invoked at that time make sense in a framework which presupposes the linearity of the linguistic sign (as surface structure) and moves elements by left-to-right rewrite rules.

It is linearity at the lexical level, which Stokoe, a structuralist linguist, identified as absent in signed languages, insisting on the simultaneity of the sub-lexical elements comprising the sign as a simultaneous "bundle" (1960). Although subsequent researchers have pointed out that signs also have linear structure, there is a general agreement that at all levels, simultaneity characterises signed languages and linearity characterises spoken languages, and that this is related to modality. In other words, the linearity of spoken language and the simultaneity of signed language are artefacts of the modalities in which they occur. An underlying assumption of Saussure, which has its roots in the 18th century debate, is that at the semantic level, or at the level at which referents and their actions are perceived, representations do not have linear elements but instead are holistic. Thus in this view, syntax exists to convert simultaneous representations to the linear ones demanded by the output system. With just one set of articulators, spoken languages have linearity; with multiple articulators (two hands, face, mouth, etc.) signed languages have simultaneity.

More recent approaches, notably that of Haiman (1985) have sought to systematically explore the notion that syntax may be non-arbitrary, returning to the issues debated in the 18th century. Diagrammatic iconicity exploits the order of elements in an utterance in a non-arbitrary way. There are numerous realisations of this: iconicity of sequence (sequence in speech is identical to sequence in actions); iconicity of adjacency (connected concepts are expressed by adjacent constituents), etc. Such approaches provide an important bridge between the concerns of linguists working on signed languages and those working on spoken languages.

3.   Contemporary approaches to simultaneity in signed languages

Linearity was viewed by Saussure as neutral in terms of production and comprehension. However, it may be more appropriate to view simultaneity and linearity as processing principles rather than linguistic principles. Linguistic symbols can be viewed as consisting of sequences and combinations of elements which take time to articulate and time to understand

A number of papers in this volume, including those of Risler; Tang, Sze & Lam; Tyrone and Perniss, explore simultaneity from a processing perspective. Risler notes that the term simultaneity does not refer to absolute time-locking of two signs, but to non-linearity, and points out that absolute simultaneity is rare. More commonly, the signer begins a sign and then begins a second sign before the completion of the first sign.

Sallandre applies Cuxac's approach, an important contribution of which is to distinguish production from perception. In most examples she and others discuss, the perception of simultaneity does not rely on seeing two moving signs; in most cases one sign is held stationary, while the other hand moves. Sallandre also makes the further observation that the non-moving hand often marks a syntactic boundary and therefore provides processing cues. Tyrone also addresses both production and perception issues. Like the other papers, she presents simultaneity as a production phenomenon, but asks how simultaneous constructions may facilitate sign perception. The possible implications of these observations for language processing models remain to be explored.

Many of the papers speculate on the possible functionality of simultaneity. If linearity serves the function that Saussure proposed, of aiding in the identification of words, then what might be the function of simultaneity? Perniss sees simultaneous constructions as a strategy for encoding locative information under the pressures of discourse constraints, while Hendriks suggests that simultaneous constructions are used to make sure that the addressee understands that both signs belong to the same syntactic constituent.

A number of earlier researchers (notably Miller (1994) and Engberg-Pedersen (1994)) have noted that one important function of simultaneity is the encoding of the distinction between foregrounded and backgrounded information. Miller observes that the dominant hand usually acts as the carrier of the foregrounded information. Engberg-Pedersen, for example, has noted that keeping one of the hands motionless results in information being backgrounded, with the foregrounded information simultaneously presented by the moving hand. Sutton-Spence (this volume) suggests that mouthings may increase the salience of, and thus aid, the foregrounding of referents, while Liddell, Vogt-Svendsen & Bergman and Vogt-Svendsen & Bergman suggest that buoys may help guide the receiver by serving as conceptual landmarks for the discourse. Leeson & Saeed posit that while the semantic roles of actor and figure are associated with the dominant hand and the roles of undergoer and ground are associated with the non-dominant hand, higher level pragmatic principles such as topic identification and maintenance may overrule the default principles.

4.   Simultaneity and linearity in grammar and semantics

Arising from the view that thought and semantics are simultaneous, grammar can be viewed as serving to convert these simultaneous structures into linear form for language output (and conversely, comprehension of linear output involves converting this back into something simultaneous). Within linguistics, linearity in syntax is frequently expressed conceptually and visually (although without ex-

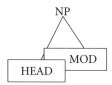

Figure 1. Outcome of partial rotation: head and modifier are simultaneous but onset of head precedes onset of modifier

plicit discussion) through 2-dimensional 'trees', in which movement is referred to as taking place on a flat plane, e.g. movement can be described as leftwards or rightwards.

An alternative, 3-dimensional type of tree, may better account for observed patterns of structure in both spoken and signed languages. Although 3-dimensional representations have been suggested in signed language phonological models, there has as yet been no systematic approach to the creation of 3-dimensional trees for syntax in signed language.

In a 3-dimensional model, elements can rotate around a node point, creating a 'hanging mobile' rather than a flat tree. For example, in a language where a modifier precedes or follows a head (i.e. where a linear output is specified), rotation results in a flat tree; where simultaneity is permitted, the modifier can rotate only partially, and be articulated simultaneously with the head (see Figure 1). Similarly, new information will be 'in front of' old information and will therefore be placed on the dominant hand. Thus, there is a direct modelling of foregrounding as represented through simultaneity.

There are a number of advantages to 3-dimensional models. Linearity and simultaneity can occur at a variety of linguistic levels and also in relation to the combination of linguistic and non-linguistic communication. Linearisation of structure is seen as occurring at a fairly late stage and as a process which reflects modality constraints rather than some underlying property of language structure. At the semantic level, examination of limitations as well as opportunities for simultaneity may return us to consideration of the notion of naturalness and non-arbitrariness in syntax.

5.   Simultaneity and linearity in discourse

Another perspective on simultaneity which has only received limited attention in sign language research is that of how two or more participants in a conversation share the floor. Early views of turn-taking in conversation as consisting of orderly one-at-a-time sequencing have been replaced by a view of conversation as occurring with greater or lesser linearity: the 'one-at-a-time' and 'collaborative' models (Edelsky 1981). Overlapping speech has a completely different meaning in the two models: in the one-at-a-time model, overlapping speech of any duration greater than a single word signals conversational malfunction, since the current speaker's right to speak is being challenged; in a collaborative model, overlapping speech is a symbol of active engagement in shared conversational space. It might be hypothesised that signed language conversation would easily tolerate overlap and collaboration, since seeing more than one person signing at the same time does not cause noise in the signal. In contrast, spoken language conversations might require overlap to be very limited for each person's message to be audible. On the other hand, because signers need to see each other to receive the linguistic message, it might be predicted that in groups of signers, only limited overlap would be possible since the participants would need to visually attend to a single person's signing. If the latter were true, reduction in simultaneity would be observed at the conversational level in signed language, in contrast to the greater potentiality for simultaneity at the lexical and grammatical levels. Most studies of interactive patterns in signed language conversation assume a one-at-a-time system (Smith & Sutton-Spence 2005; Baker & Cokely 1980). However in a study by Coates & Sutton-Spence (2001) analysis of conversations among groups of Deaf friends shows significant overlap (particularly in women's conversation). Conversational participants can attend to more than one source of talk at a time, whether in signed or spoken language and therefore regardless of modality, there is an interplay between linearity and simultaneity.

6.   Future directions in research

In the introduction to this volume, the editors refer to Engberg-Pedersen's (1994) questions about simultaneity:

> Given that signed languages have the possibility to express information consecutively or simultaneously, what sort of information is expressed simultaneously? When do simultaneous constructions have obligatory status?

The papers in this volume represent the most comprehensive collection of contributions on the subject of simultaneity in signed language. They mark an important step towards understanding the interplay between linearity and simultaneity in language – both spoken and signed. But the second question still remains to be answered, as does a third: To what extent does the simultaneity-linearity opposition arise from a linguistic base and to what extent from a psychological base? Future research will need to consider fine grained timing issues in relation to simultaneity, and the implications for linguistic and psycholinguistic theory.

References

Aarsleff, Hans. 1974. "The Tradition of Condillac: The Problem of the Origin of Language in the Eighteenth Century and the Debate in the Berlin Academy before Herder". *Studies in the History of Linguistics: Traditions and Paradigms* ed. by Dell Hymes, 93–156. Bloomington: Indiana University Press.

Baker, Charlotte & Dennis Cokely. 1980. *American Sign Language: A Teacher's Resource Text on Grammar and Culture.* Silver Spring, Md.: TJ Publishers.

Beauzée, Nicolas. 1787. *Grammaire Générale ou Exposition Raisonnée des Eléments Nécessaires du Langage, pour Servir de Fondement à l'Etude de Toutes les Langues.* Paris: Barbou.

Bloomfield, Leonard. 1933. *Language.* New York: Henry Holt and Co.

Coates, Jenny & Rachel Sutton-Spence. 2001. "Turn-taking Patterns in Deaf Conversation". *Journal of Sociolinguistics* 5:4. 507–529.

Edelsky, Carol. 1981. "Who's Got the Floor?" *Language in Society* 10. 383–342.

Engberg-Pedersen, Elisabeth. 1994. "Some Simultaneous Constructions in Danish Sign Language". *Word-order Issues in Sign Language. Working Papers* ed. by Mary Brennan & Graham H. Turner, 73–88. Durham: International Sign Linguistics Association.

Haiman, John, ed. 1985. *Iconicity in Syntax.* Amsterdam: John Benjamins.

Harris, Roy. 2003. *Saussure and his Interpreters* (2nd ed.). Edinburgh: Edinburgh University Press.

Joseph, John E. 2004. "The Linguistic Sign". *The Cambridge Companion to Saussure.* ed. by Carol Sanders, 59–75. Cambridge: Cambridge University Press.

Miller, Christopher. 1994. "Simultaneous Constructions in Quebec Sign Language". *Word-order Issues in Sign Language. Working Papers* ed. by Mary Brennan & Graham H. Turner, 89–112. Durham: International Sign Linguistics Association.

de Saussure, Ferdinand. 1959. *Course in General Linguistics* ed. by Charles Bally & Albert Sechehaye. New York: McGraw-Hill.

Scaglione, Aldo. 1998. "The 18th-Century Debate Concerning Linearity or Simultaneity in the Deep Structure of Language: From Buffier to Gottsched". *Aldo Scaglione: Essays on the Arts of Discourse: Linguistics, Rhetoric, Poetics* ed by Paolo Cherchi, Stephen Murphy, Allen Mandelbaum & Giuseppe Velli, 239–248. New York: Peter Lang.

Smith, Sandra & Rachel Sutton-Spence. 2005. "Adult-Child Interaction in a BSL Nursery – Getting Their Attention!". *Sign Language & Linguistics*, 8:1/2. 131–152

Stokoe, William C. 1960. *Sign Language Structure: An Outline of the Visual Communication System of the American Deaf. Studies in Linguistics Occasional Paper 8.* Buffalo, N.Y.: University of Buffalo.

Tylor, Edward B. 1874. *Researches into the Early History of Mankind.* London: Murray.

Name index

Language index

Subject index

CURRENT ISSUES IN LINGUISTIC THEORY

E. F. K. Koerner, Editor

Zentrum für Allgemeine Sprachwissenschaft, Typologie
und Universalienforschung, Berlin
efk.koerner@rz.hu-berlin.de

Current Issues in Linguistic Theory (CILT) is a theory-oriented series which welcomes contributions from scholars who have significant proposals to make towards the advancement of our understanding of language, its structure, functioning and development. CILT has been established in order to provide a forum for the presentation and discussion of linguistic opinions of scholars who do not necessarily accept the prevailing mode of thought in linguistic science. It offers an outlet for meaningful contributions to the current linguistic debate, and furnishes the diversity of opinion which a healthy discipline must have. A complete list of titles in this series can be found on the publishers' website, *www.benjamins.com*

261 **KAY, Christian J. and Jeremy J. SMITH (eds.):** Categorization in the History of English. 2004. viii, 268 pp.

260 **NICOLOV, Nicolas, Kalina BONTCHEVA, Galia ANGELOVA and Ruslan MITKOV (eds.):** Recent Advances in Natural Language Processing III. Selected papers from RANLP 2003. 2004. xii, 402 pp.

259 **CARR, Philip, Jacques DURAND and Colin J. EWEN (eds.):** Headhood, Elements, Specification and Contrastivity. Phonological papers in honour of John Anderson. 2005. xxviii, 405 pp.

258 **AUGER, Julie, J. Clancy CLEMENTS and Barbara VANCE (eds.):** Contemporary Approaches to Romance Linguistics. Selected Papers from the 33rd Linguistic Symposium on Romance Languages (LSRL), Bloomington, Indiana, April 2003. With the assistance of Rachel T. Anderson. 2004. viii, 404 pp.

257 **FORTESCUE, Michael, Eva Skafte JENSEN, Jens Erik MOGENSEN and Lene SCHØSLER (eds.):** Historical Linguistics 2003. Selected papers from the 16th International Conference on Historical Linguistics, Copenhagen, 11–15 August 2003. 2005. x, 312 pp.

256 **BOK-BENNEMA, Reineke, Bart HOLLEBRANDSE, Brigitte KAMPERS-MANHE and Petra SLEEMAN (eds.):** Romance Languages and Linguistic Theory 2002. Selected papers from 'Going Romance', Groningen, 28–30 November 2002. 2004. viii, 273 pp.

255 **MEULEN, Alice ter and Werner ABRAHAM (eds.):** The Composition of Meaning. From lexeme to discourse. 2004. vi, 232 pp.

254 **BALDI, Philip and Pietro U. DINI (eds.):** Studies in Baltic and Indo-European Linguistics. In honor of William R. Schmalstieg. 2004. xlvi, 302 pp.

253 **CAFFAREL, Alice, J.R. MARTIN and Christian M.I.M. MATTHIESSEN (eds.):** Language Typology. A functional perspective. 2004. xiv, 702 pp.

252 **KAY, Christian J., Carole HOUGH and Irené WOTHERSPOON (eds.):** New Perspectives on English Historical Linguistics. Selected papers from 12 ICEHL, Glasgow, 21–26 August 2002. Volume II: Lexis and Transmission. 2004. xii, 273 pp.

251 **KAY, Christian J., Simon HOROBIN and Jeremy J. SMITH (eds.):** New Perspectives on English Historical Linguistics. Selected papers from 12 ICEHL, Glasgow, 21–26 August 2002. Volume I: Syntax and Morphology. 2004. x, 264 pp.

250 **JENSEN, John T.:** Principles of Generative Phonology. An introduction. 2004. xii, 324 pp.

249 **BOWERN, Claire and Harold KOCH (eds.):** Australian Languages. Classification and the comparative method. 2004. xii, 377 pp. (incl. CD-Rom).

248 **WEIGAND, Edda (ed.):** Emotion in Dialogic Interaction. Advances in the complex. 2004. xii, 284 pp.

247 **PARKINSON, Dilworth B. and Samira FARWANEH (eds.):** Perspectives on Arabic Linguistics XV. Papers from the Fifteenth Annual Symposium on Arabic Linguistics, Salt Lake City 2001. 2003. x, 214 pp.

246 **HOLISKY, Dee Ann and Kevin TUITE (eds.):** Current Trends in Caucasian, East European and Inner Asian Linguistics. Papers in honor of Howard I. Aronson. 2003. xxviii, 426 pp.

245 **QUER, Josep, Jan SCHROTEN, Mauro SCORRETTI, Petra SLEEMAN and Els VERHEUGD (eds.):** Romance Languages and Linguistic Theory 2001. Selected papers from 'Going Romance', Amsterdam, 6–8 December 2001. 2003. viii, 355 pp.

244 **PÉREZ-LEROUX, Ana Teresa and Yves ROBERGE (eds.):** Romance Linguistics. Theory and Acquisition. Selected papers from the 32nd Linguistic Symposium on Romance Languages (LSRL), Toronto, April 2002. 2003. viii, 388 pp.

243 **CUYCKENS, Hubert, Thomas BERG, René DIRVEN and Klaus-Uwe PANTHER (eds.):** Motivation in Language. Studies in honor of Günter Radden. 2003. xxvi, 403 pp.

242 **SEUREN, Pieter A.M. and Gerard KEMPEN (eds.):** Verb Constructions in German and Dutch. 2003. vi, 316 pp.

241 **LECARME, Jacqueline (ed.):** Research in Afroasiatic Grammar II. Selected papers from the Fifth Conference on Afroasiatic Languages, Paris, 2000. 2003. viii, 550 pp.

240 **JANSE, Mark and Sijmen TOL (eds.):** Language Death and Language Maintenance. Theoretical, practical and descriptive approaches. With the assistance of Vincent Hendriks. 2003. xviii, 244 pp.

239 **ANDERSEN, Henning (ed.):** Language Contacts in Prehistory. Studies in Stratigraphy. Papers from the Workshop on Linguistic Stratigraphy and Prehistory at the Fifteenth International Conference on Historical Linguistics, Melbourne, 17 August 2001. 2003. viii, 292 pp.

238 **NÚÑEZ-CEDEÑO, Rafael, Luis LÓPEZ and Richard CAMERON (eds.):** A Romance Perspective on Language Knowledge and Use. Selected papers from the 31st Linguistic Symposium on Romance Languages (LSRL), Chicago, 19–22 April 2001. 2003. xvi, 386 pp.

237 **BLAKE, Barry J. and Kate BURRIDGE (eds.):** Historical Linguistics 2001. Selected papers from the 15th International Conference on Historical Linguistics, Melbourne, 13–17 August 2001. Editorial Assistant: Jo Taylor. 2003. x, 444 pp.

236 **SIMON-VANDENBERGEN, Anne-Marie, Miriam TAVERNIERS and Louise J. RAVELLI (eds.):** Grammatical Metaphor. Views from systemic functional linguistics. 2003. vi, 453 pp.

235 **LINN, Andrew R. and Nicola McLELLAND (eds.):** Standardization. Studies from the Germanic languages. 2002. xii, 258 pp.

234 **WEIJER, Jeroen van de, Vincent J. van HEUVEN and Harry van der HULST (eds.):** The Phonological Spectrum. Volume II: Suprasegmental structure. 2003. x, 264 pp.

233 **WEIJER, Jeroen van de, Vincent J. van HEUVEN and Harry van der HULST (eds.):** The Phonological Spectrum. Volume I: Segmental structure. 2003. x, 308 pp.

232 **BEYSSADE, Claire, Reineke BOK-BENNEMA, Frank DRIJKONINGEN and Paola MONACHESI (eds.):** Romance Languages and Linguistic Theory 2000. Selected papers from 'Going Romance' 2000, Utrecht, 30 November–2 December. 2002. viii, 354 pp.

231 **CRAVENS, Thomas D.:** Comparative Historical Dialectology. Italo-Romance clues to Ibero-Romance sound change. 2002. xii, 163 pp.

230 **PARKINSON, Dilworth B. and Elabbas BENMAMOUN (eds.):** Perspectives on Arabic Linguistics. Papers from the Annual Symposium on Arabic Linguistics. Volume XIII-XIV: Stanford, 1999 and Berkeley, California 2000. 2002. xiv, 250 pp.

229 **NEVIN, Bruce E. and Stephen B. JOHNSON (eds.):** The Legacy of Zellig Harris. Language and information into the 21st century. Volume 2: Mathematics and computability of language. 2002. xx, 312 pp.

228 **NEVIN, Bruce E. (ed.):** The Legacy of Zellig Harris. Language and information into the 21st century. Volume 1: Philosophy of science, syntax and semantics. 2002. xxxvi, 323 pp.

227 **FAVA, Elisabetta (ed.):** Clinical Linguistics. Theory and applications in speech pathology and therapy. 2002. xxiv, 353 pp.

226 **LEVIN, Saul:** Semitic and Indo-European. Volume II: Comparative morphology, syntax and phonetics. 2002. xviii, 592 pp.

225 **SHAHIN, Kimary N.:** Postvelar Harmony. 2003. viii, 344 pp.

224 **FANEGO, Teresa, Belén MÉNDEZ-NAYA and Elena SEOANE (eds.):** Sounds, Words, Texts and Change. Selected papers from 11 ICEHL, Santiago de Compostela, 7–11 September 2000. Volume 2. 2002. x, 310 pp.

223 **FANEGO, Teresa, Javier PÉREZ-GUERRA and María José LÓPEZ-COUSO (eds.):** English Historical Syntax and Morphology. Selected papers from 11 ICEHL, Santiago de Compostela, 7–11 September 2000. Volume 1. 2002. x, 306 pp.

222 **HERSCHENSOHN, Julia, Enrique MALLÉN and Karen ZAGONA (eds.):** Features and Interfaces in Romance. Essays in honor of Heles Contreras. 2001. xiv, 302 pp.

221 **D'HULST, Yves, Johan ROORYCK and Jan SCHROTEN (eds.):** Romance Languages and Linguistic Theory 1999. Selected papers from 'Going Romance' 1999, Leiden, 9–11 December 1999. 2001. viii, 406 pp.

220 **SATTERFIELD, Teresa, Christina M. TORTORA and Diana CRESTI (eds.):** Current Issues in Romance Languages. Selected papers from the 29th Linguistic Symposium on Romance Languages (LSRL), Ann Arbor, 8–11 April 1999. 2002. viii, 412 pp.

219 **ANDERSEN, Henning (ed.):** Actualization. Linguistic Change in Progress. Papers from a workshop held at the 14th International Conference on Historical Linguistics, Vancouver, B.C., 14 August 1999. 2001. vii, 250 pp.

218 **BENDJABALLAH, Sabrina, Wolfgang U. DRESSLER, Oskar E. PFEIFFER and Maria D. VOEIKOVA (eds.):** Morphology 2000. Selected papers from the 9th Morphology Meeting, Vienna, 24–28 February 2000. 2002. viii, 317 pp.

217 **WILTSHIRE, Caroline R. and Joaquim CAMPS (eds.):** Romance Phonology and Variation. Selected papers from the 30th Linguistic Symposium on Romance Languages, Gainesville, Florida, February 2000. 2002. xii, 238 pp.

216 **CAMPS, Joaquim and Caroline R. WILTSHIRE (eds.):** Romance Syntax, Semantics and L2 Acquisition. Selected papers from the 30th Linguistic Symposium on Romance Languages, Gainesville, Florida, February 2000. 2001. xii, 246 pp.

215 **BRINTON, Laurel J. (ed.):** Historical Linguistics 1999. Selected papers from the 14th International Conference on Historical Linguistics, Vancouver, 9–13 August 1999. 2001. xii, 398 pp.

214 **WEIGAND, Edda and Marcelo DASCAL (eds.):** Negotiation and Power in Dialogic Interaction. 2001. viii, 303 pp.

213 **SORNICOLA, Rosanna, Erich POPPE and Ariel SHISHA-HALEVY (eds.):** Stability, Variation and Change of Word-Order Patterns over Time. With the assistance of Paola Como. 2000. xxxii, 323 pp.

212 **REPETTI, Lori (ed.):** Phonological Theory and the Dialects of Italy. 2000. x, 301 pp.

211 **ELŠÍK, Viktor and Yaron MATRAS (eds.):** Grammatical Relations in Romani. The Noun Phrase. with a Foreword by Frans Plank (Universität Konstanz). 2000. x, 244 pp.

210 **DWORKIN, Steven N. and Dieter WANNER (eds.):** New Approaches to Old Problems. Issues in Romance historical linguistics. 2000. xiv, 235 pp.

209 **KING, Ruth:** The Lexical Basis of Grammatical Borrowing. A Prince Edward Island French case study. 2000. xvi, 241 pp.

208 **ROBINSON, Orrin W.:** Whose German? The *ach/ich* alternation and related phenomena in 'standard' and 'colloquial'. 2001. xii, 178 pp.

207 **SANZ, Montserrat:** Events and Predication. A new approach to syntactic processing in English and Spanish. 2000. xiv, 219 pp.

206 **FAWCETT, Robin P.:** A Theory of Syntax for Systemic Functional Linguistics. 2000. xxiv, 360 pp.

205 **DIRVEN, René, Roslyn M. FRANK and Cornelia ILIE (eds.):** Language and Ideology. Volume 2: descriptive cognitive approaches. 2001. vi, 264 pp.

204 **DIRVEN, René, Bruce HAWKINS and Esra SANDIKCIOGLU (eds.):** Language and Ideology. Volume 1: theoretical cognitive approaches. 2001. vi, 301 pp.

203 **NORRICK, Neal R.:** Conversational Narrative. Storytelling in everyday talk. 2000. xiv, 233 pp.

202 **LECARME, Jacqueline, Jean LOWENSTAMM and Ur SHLONSKY (eds.):** Research in Afroasiatic Grammar. Papers from the Third conference on Afroasiatic Languages, Sophia Antipolis, 1996. 2000. vi, 386 pp.

201 **DRESSLER, Wolfgang U., Oskar E. PFEIFFER, Markus A. PÖCHTRAGER and John R. RENNISON (eds.):** Morphological Analysis in Comparison. 2000. x, 261 pp.

200 **ANTTILA, Raimo:** Greek and Indo-European Etymology in Action. Proto-Indo-European *ag̑-. 2000. xii, 314 pp.

199 **PÜTZ, Martin and Marjolijn H. VERSPOOR (eds.):** Explorations in Linguistic Relativity. 2000. xvi, 369 pp.

198 **NIEMEIER, Susanne and René DIRVEN (eds.):** Evidence for Linguistic Relativity. 2000. xxii, 240 pp.

197 **COOPMANS, Peter, Martin EVERAERT and Jane GRIMSHAW (eds.):** Lexical Specification and Insertion. 2000. xviii, 476 pp.

196 **HANNAHS, S.J. and Mike DAVENPORT (eds.):** Issues in Phonological Structure. Papers from an International Workshop. 1999. xii, 268 pp.

195 **HERRING, Susan C., Pieter van REENEN and Lene SCHØSLER (eds.):** Textual Parameters in Older Languages. 2001. x, 448 pp.

194 **COLEMAN, Julie and Christian J. KAY (eds.):** Lexicology, Semantics and Lexicography. Selected papers from the Fourth G. L. Brook Symposium, Manchester, August 1998. 2000. xiv, 257 pp.

193 **KLAUSENBURGER, Jurgen:** Grammaticalization. Studies in Latin and Romance morphosyntax. 2000. xiv, 184 pp.

192 **ALEXANDROVA, Galina M. and Olga ARNAUDOVA (eds.):** The Minimalist Parameter. Selected papers from the Open Linguistics Forum, Ottawa, 21–23 March 1997. 2001. x, 360 pp.

191 **SIHLER, Andrew L.:** Language History. An introduction. 2000. xvi, 298 pp.

190 **BENMAMOUN, Elabbas (ed.):** Perspectives on Arabic Linguistics. Papers from the Annual Symposium on Arabic Linguistics. Volume XII: Urbana-Champaign, Illinois, 1998. 1999. viii, 204 pp.

189 **NICOLOV, Nicolas and Ruslan MITKOV (eds.):** Recent Advances in Natural Language Processing II. Selected papers from RANLP '97. 2000. xi, 422 pp.

188 **SIMMONS, Richard VanNess:** Chinese Dialect Classification. A comparative approach to Harngjou, Old Jintarn, and Common Northern Wu. 1999. xviii, 317 pp.

187 **FRANCO, Jon A., Alazne LANDA and Juan MARTÍN (eds.):** Grammatical Analyses in Basque and Romance Linguistics. Papers in honor of Mario Saltarelli. 1999. viii, 306 pp.

186 **MIŠESKA TOMIĆ, Olga and Milorad RADOVANOVIĆ (eds.):** History and Perspectives of Language Study. Papers in honor of Ranko Bugarski. 2000. xxii, 314 pp.

185 **AUTHIER, Jean-Marc, Barbara E. BULLOCK and Lisa A. REED (eds.):** Formal Perspectives on Romance Linguistics. Selected papers from the 28th Linguistic Symposium on Romance Languages (LSRL XXVIII), University Park, 16–19 April 1998. 1999. xii, 334 pp.

184 **SAGART, Laurent:** The Roots of Old Chinese. 1999. xii, 272 pp.

183 **CONTINI-MORAVA, Ellen and Yishai TOBIN (eds.):** Between Grammar and Lexicon. 2000. xxxii, 365 pp.

182 **KENESEI, István (ed.):** Crossing Boundaries. Advances in the theory of Central and Eastern European languages. 1999. viii, 302 pp.

181 **MOHAMMAD, Mohammad A.:** Word Order, Agreement and Pronominalization in Standard and Palestinian Arabic. 2000. xvi, 197 pp.

180 **MEREU, Lunella (ed.):** Boundaries of Morphology and Syntax. 1999. viii, 314 pp.

179 **RINI, Joel:** Exploring the Role of Morphology in the Evolution of Spanish. 1999. xvi, 187 pp.

178 **FOOLEN, Ad and Frederike van der LEEK (eds.):** Constructions in Cognitive Linguistics. Selected papers from the Fifth International Cognitive Linguistics Conference, Amsterdam, 1997. 2000. xvi, 338 pp.